Irish Bardic Poetry and Rhetorical Reality

IRISH BARDIC POETRY

and

RHETORICAL REALITY

BY

MICHELLE O RIORDAN

CORK UNIVERSITY PRESS

2007

First published in 2007 by
Cork University Press
Youngline Industrial Estate
Pouladuff Road, Togher
Cork
Ireland

ISBN 978-1-85918-414-1

Typeset by M. O Riordan

Cover: Laurentius Voltolina's (14th c.) illustration in Henricus de
Allemania *Ethics* by kind permission of bpk/Kupferstichkabinett,
SMB/Jörg P. Anders

www.corkuniversitypress.com

Contents

ABBREVIATIONS   ix

PREFACE   xiii

INTRODUCTION   xv
   Ruling the margins   xv

1 CONTINUITY OF CONTACT   1

   The Latinized vernacular   1

   Artifice   7

2 STYLE   24

   The centrality of style   24

   Ars Versificatoria   26

   Poetria Nova   39

   Parisiana Poetria   45

3 'BEIR EOLAS DÚINN . . .'   57

   Contemporaries   61

   Themes   65

   'Inventio'   67

   'Sententia'   69

   'Compassed in the mind'   72

   Overture   73

   Comparison   83

   Apologue   87

   Mac Carthaigh's journey   95

Urban Ireland   100

Name-checking   101

Eoghanacht territory   103

Timeless places   104

4 POEMS OF COMPLAINT   106

  Teacher and pupil: poet and lord   110

  Finding the theme   114

  Terms of address   115

  Fulcrum   116

  The offence   116

  Mutuality   117

  Reassessment   119

  Death-in-life   121

  Folly   124

  The two paths   126

  'Caithréim'   128

  Genealogy   132

  Love poem   133

5 BARDIC LOVE, TROUBADOUR LOVE   137

  Poet and troubadour   138

  Latin and the vernacular   144

  Studied ambiguity   146

  Appointment and disappointment   151

  Indulgence   152

  The poet as spouse   155

Reconciliation and renewal	157
6 LOVERS' QUARRELS	159
Exhaustion of topics	163
Sixteenth-century sensibilities	164
Syllabus and life	171
'A theachtaire théid ar sliabh'	172
'Cóir Dé eadram is Uilliam'	176
7 POEMS ABOUT POETRY	181
Ár n-ealaín: Our art	181
A metrical lesson	184
Teacher and student	185
The gospel of the poets	192
Enquire of the master	196
Poems about poetry	202
'Mór an feidhm deilbh an dána'	203
The 'dialogue'	204
Provocation	214
Response	217
'A fhir shealbhas duit an dán'	219
Faults and vices	228
'Créad dá sealbhuinn damh an dán'	230
Unfounded claims	233
More errors	241
Paradox	243

viii

Conclusion: the death of poetry ?   248

    The broad road   254

Notes   261

Select bibliography   395

General index   431

Index of terms   445

Index of people and places   454

Index of first lines   457

Abbreviations

See also list of additional abbreviations at the start of Notes, pp. 261–262.

AdHer: Caplan, H. 1981. transl. [Cicero] *Ad Herennium: De Ratione Dicendi*. Harvard.

*AithDD*i/ii: McKenna, L. 1939–1940. *Aithdioghluim Dána*. 2 vols. Irish Texts Society 37 and 40. Dublin.

APP: Kelly, D. 1991. *The Arts of Poetry and Prose*. [Typologie des Sources du Moyen Âge Occidental, fasc. 59]. Turnhout.

ATBT: McKenna, L. 1952. 'A Poem by Gofraidh Fionn Ó Dálaigh'. *Ériu* 16: pp. 132–139. ('*A toigh bheagh tiaghar a tteagh mór*')

AV: Parr, R. P. 1981. transl. from Latin with an Introduction, *Matthew of Vendôme: Ars Versificatoria* [Mediaeval Philosophical Texts in Translation 22]. Wisconsin.

BST: McKenna, L. [1944] 1979. ed. *Bardic Syntactical Tracts*. Dublin.

CCC: Bugge, A. 1905. ed., *Caithreim Cellachain Caisil; or The Wars between the Irishmen and the Norsemen in the Middle of the Tenth Century*. Oslo.

CHLC: Minnis, A., and I. Johnson. 2005. ed. *The Cambridge History of Literary Criticism* ii. Cambridge.

CR: Ward, J. O. 1995. *Ciceronian Rhetoric in Treatise, Scholion and Commentary* [Typologie des Sources du Moyen Âge Occidental, fasc. 58]. Turnhout.

DD: Mac Cionnaith, [McKenna] L. 1938. *Dioghluim Dána*. Dublin.

DIL: *Dictionary of the Irish Language: Based Mainly on Old and Middle Irish Materials*. 1913–1976. [1983 compact edition.] Dublin.

DOB: McErlean, J. C. 1910–1917. *Duanaire Dháibhidh Uí Bhruadair: The Poems of David Ó Bruadair*. 3 vols. [Irish Texts Society 1910 vol. 11, 1913 vol. 13, 1917 vol. 18.] London.

GFOD: McKenna, L. 1919. 'Historical Poems of Gofraidh Fionn Ó Dálaigh'. *Irish Monthly* January; successive pagings.

IBP: Bergin, O. 1970. In D. Greene and F. Kelly, eds., *Irish Bardic Poetry*. Dublin.

IGT: Bergin, O. 1916–1955. *Irish Grammatical Tracts*. Supplement to *Ériu* 8 (Introductory); *Ériu* 8–10 (Declension); *Ériu* 14 (Irregular verbs and abstract nouns); *Ériu* 17 (Metrical faults).

LAP: Faral, E. [1924] 1962. *Les Arts poétiques du xiie et du xiiie siècle*. Paris.

LMS: McKenna, L. 1947. ed. *The Book of Maguaran: Leabhar Méig Shamradháin*. Dublin.

MFBF: McKenna, L. 1947. 'A Poem by Gofraidh Fionn Ó Dálaigh'. In S. Pender, ed., *Essays and Studies Presented to Professor Tadhg Ua Donnchadha (Torna) etc.*: 66–76. Cork. (*'Madh fiafraidheach budh feasach'*).

NHIii: Cosgrove, A. 1987. ed. *A New History of Ireland, ii: Medieval Ireland 1169–1534*. Oxford.

NHIviii: Moody, T. W., F. X. Martin and F. J. Byrne. 1982. eds., *A New History of Ireland, viii: A Chronology of Irish History to 1976, a Companion to Irish History Part i*. Oxford.

PN: Geoffrey of Vinsauf's *Poetria Nova*, translated by Jane Baltzell Kopp in J. J. Murphy, *Three Medieval Rhetorical Arts*, pp. 32–108. The text is a version in English of the Latin published by E. Faral, *Les Arts poétiques du xiie et du xiiie siècle*, pp. 197–262.

PP: Lawler, T. 1974. ed., with Introduction, transl., and notes, *The Parisiana Poetria of John of Garland*. Yale.

qq.: quatrains

RMA: Murphy, J. J. 1974. *Rhetoric in the Middle Ages: A History of Rhetorical Theory from Saint Augustine to the Renaissance*. Berkeley.

RTS: Burgwinkle, W. E. 1990. *Razos and Troubadour Songs*. Garland Library of Medieval Literature 71, ser. B. New York and London.

SIB: McKenna, L. 1951. 'Some Irish Bardic Poems'. *Studies* 40: pp. 93–96; 217–222; 352–363.

SIB i: McKenna, L. 1951. 'Some Irish Bardic Poems'. *Studies* 40: pp. 93–96. (*'Mór an feidhm deilbh an dána'*.)

SIB ii: McKenna, L. 1951. 'Some Irish Bardic Poems'. *Studies* 40: pp. 217–222. (*'A fhir shealbhas duit an dán'*.)

SIB iii: McKenna, L. 1951. 'Some Irish Bardic Poems'. *Studies* 40: pp. 352–363. (*'Créad dá sealbhuinn damh an dán'*.)

TDall i/ii: Knott, E. 1922–1926. ed., *The Bardic Poems of Tadhg Dall Ó hUiginn 1550–1591* 2 vols. Irish Texts Society nos 22–23. London.

TMRA: Murphy, J. J. 1971. *Three Medieval Rhetorical Arts*. Berkeley.

Preface

This study was undertaken as part of my research commitments as an assistant professor in the School of Celtic Studies, in the Dublin Institute for Advanced Studies. I thank my friends and colleagues in that institution whose collegial qualities support and encourage research and publication. I am grateful to the Governing Board of the school and to its directors, respectively, Liam Breatnach, Fergus Kelly and Máirtín Ó Murchú, during whose terms this work was facilitated, for their support and for their positive promotion of a congenial and appropriate working environment. Among those facilities supported in the School of Celtic Studies are outstanding library services; I am grateful to Grace Toland, Cora Gunther, Niamh Walsh, Frank Brady, Charlotte Dillon and Órla Ní Chanainn for their courteous, generous and professional dealings with me and with my enquiries and requests of that library service. I thank Éibhlín Nic Dhonnchadha, administrator of the school, for making everything work.

I am indebted to those people who have listened to and read various versions of parts of this work from time to time, among them, Siobhán Ní Laoire, Aidan Doyle, Colm Breathnach, Dan McCarthy, Jenifer Ní Ghrádaigh, and the late Proinsias Mac Cana.

Special thanks are due to Paula O'Riordan and to Micheál Ó Cearúil who generously applied their high editorial standards to the rougher material which I gave them, and for their careful readings and comments. My thanks also to Tadhg Ó Dúshláine for his helpful reading and encouraging comments. I thank Louis de Paor for his sympathetic and engaged reading and comments.

I am particularly indebted to and grateful to Máirtín Ó Murchú who, with unfailing generosity, placed his time and the unparalleled depth and breadth of his expertise at my disposal.

My thanks are due to Tom Dunne of Cork University Press for his continuing support, for his encouragement with this project, and for publishing this work. I am grateful also to the staff of Cork University Press for their professional and friendly dealing with me while seeing this material through the press.

Introduction

RULING THE MARGINS

Ruling in the margins of his manuscripts, the poet-scribe marked out the area of his text. This staked the territory of the poet, the arena of his influence and the realm over which he was supreme. The fourteenth-century poet Gofraidh Fionn Ó Dálaigh (d. 1387) imagined a neatly ordered festival city for a gathering of the poets and artists of Ireland in his poem for Uilliam Ó Ceallaigh (*fl.* 1350s).[1] They would inhabit streets set one after another as lines of a text.[2]

Beautifully and artfully imagined, the 'streets' are assigned to each profession. Poets in one street, a 'separate street has been appointed . . . for the musicians' (*sráid ar leith don lucht seanma*), and similarly for chroniclers (*seanchaidhe*), 'bardic companies and jugglers' (*[ar chionn] chliar is chleasoigheadh*).[3] The entertainers are imaginatively pictured as housed in temporary accommodation for the duration of the festivities.[4] However reality might correspond to the poem, in Gofraidh Fionn Ó Dálaigh's artful depiction of the event the patron's fortress (*dún*) was the illuminated dominating capital of the page (qq. 27, 28; p. 60). The dwellings of those attending the festival were the 'characters' on the bardic page (q. 25, p. 58). How perfectly the poet captured the essence of the 'bardic' world.

The occasion presented thus in the poem encapsulates the poet's sense of the neatly bounded world created by him on the page, reflecting back on the reality of the occasion, and reflecting likewise on the origin of the race of the Gael – which, in his time, held the sovereignty of Ireland (qq. 37–41) – in a neat, poetic, synopsis of Ó Ceallaigh's historic right and genealogy. This is one of the most compelling and enduring images left to us from a certain period in the history of Ireland: the artists of Ireland converged on the dwelling of Ó Ceallaigh, entertainment and honour are satisfied at this festival, and the whole country is bereft of artists for the duration (qq. 9–10, p. 54). Such is the renown of Ó Ceallaigh that his invitation draws all seekers after rewards to his dwelling.

Gofraidh Fionn revealed in this poem the key to the craft of the 'bardic' poet, the poet of the schools. His beautiful and clever metaphor of the measured page and the presiding capital, the living lines of characters, is an image which we might well adopt in its entirety and apply to the whole of the Irish classical poets' *œuvre*: a literary world, created on the page and confined within the margins and lines of that discipline, determined much of the composition of the schools' poets.

In the twelfth and thirteenth centuries textbooks for instruction in the written arts (in Latin) were widespread in continental Europe and in England. Associating Irish classical poetry with the continental norms sketched out in these manuals provides an additional context for understanding Irish poetry.[5] The literary nature of the material assumes the foreground, and the corpus of 'bardic' poetry becomes at once more clearly a work of conscious literary endeavour and a more likely expression of Irish written culture in the high and later Middle Ages than we have heretofore understood.

The historical literary context provides an appropriate foil for the historical political context which, in the last hundred years, has been the usual context for editions of bardic poetry and for commentary on them.[6]

Identification (tentative in many instances) of those to whom poems were dedicated, locating likely battle sites, and re-establishing the political context for each poem, has been attempted in the best published editions (of bardic poetry). This information creates a framework of sorts from which to approach the poetry. The poem, then, represents 'facts' or presumed or likely circumstances in the literary artefact. The study presented below attempts to add to this fact-oriented basis by considering the literary contingencies which determined how the 'facts' are presented in the artefact – the poem.[7] In this, and in other ways, the composition assumes an independence from the 'facts' which enhances our understanding both of the cultural and of the political context of the creation of the literary artefact, which is now all that remains of many a battle, of many a devastating lordly demise, of the burnt stronghold, of destructive slaughters, of uproarious festive evenings.

Over a period of some four hundred years the best poets produced material of a sustained standard and of similar nature.[8] In many instances, compositions are hardly datable by language owing to the faithfulness to the standardized language of formal composition.

The richness of Irish literature itself provided a panoply of gods, demigods, fabulous creatures and heroes and villians to maintain a living tradition into which elements from other literatures and cultures were easily absorbed and reconstituted to fit the literary flow appropriate to the requirements of the Gaelic canon.

With the consolidation of Norse non-Christian groups in towns and ports, the rivalry between Irish and Norse languages was won by Irish. When the power of the Anglo-Normans asserted itself in Ireland, the international flavour of their connections, their links to the Levant, their attachment to foreign potentates and monarchs, their imperial pretensions, were exploited in the literary sense by poets who revelled in the expanded cast of characters. They were neither overawed nor abashed by or dismissive of them, but knit them effectively within the rubrics. With the Normans, the rival language came supported by powerful, ever-renewable resources. Their language was itself in that state of energetic development which came with their social dominance (in England in the late eleventh and twelfth centuries).[9] Along with the replenishments of men, munitions and resources, the powerful web of the Catholic Church – the intellectual headquarters of which were then in France – came rival languages, administrative structures, and new vernaculars. The Anglo-Norman Church and state structures were robust, expanding and vital at this stage. They had resources throughout Europe and contacts as far east as the Tartar kingdoms and the Islamic states of the 'Holy Land'. None of these worlds was unknown to the Irish. Nor was Ireland a remote unknown land, but another territory of Europe, a known land, now recognized as valuable territory to be fought for. It was at this stage that the styles of syllabic poetry we now call bardic praise-poetry came to the fore.

It is unlikely that such structured and admittedly stylized genres which constituted bardic praise-poetry represented a factual reality even at this early period in its datable appearance in Gaelic manuscript sources. At no point did the stylized formal praise-poem 'mirror' reality in terms of historical fact. Nor was it intended to.[10] The tradition of praise-poetry was common to Western European culture. Irish poets were particularly fortunate in the richness of their vernacular literary tradition. The 'bardic' poet drew on a literary tradition which had achieved a 'classical' status in the twelfth and thirteenth centuries.

For those who try to extract information from the poems about Irish life during the period when the poets flourished, the challenge is to bear in mind that one is depending on a body of literature produced mainly by men who were not primarily concerned with informing the future. They were concerned with practising and teaching language and literature, and in pursuit of this they perpetuated various kinds of stories of the past in order to survive the present and even thrive in the future. This is the richness of their work, its insouciance, its indifference to our needs, its decadent pursuit of its own survival. The success of their enterprise is witnessed by the several thousand lines of material in their particular formal genres still extant – a mere fraction of what must have been written through a four-hundred-year existence.

The genres among which the praise-poem is counted properly belong to the last third of the mediaeval millennium (500–1500), to the final phase of mediaeval civilization in Western Europe and in Ireland. The particular expression of the type in which this study is interested is that which came to be recognized as formal bardic praise-poetry from the twelfth century on.[11]

The praise-genres flourished in the conservative aesthetic that became the hallmark of the Irish schools from the twelfth century, at least, to the mid-seventeenth century. The poets' wholehearted commitment to the measured and predictable results is evident in the standard at which their poetry was presented over half a millennium. Their freedom was found in the central position afforded to the presentation of paradox (as will become evident below) at the heart of this strict and most unspontaneous of arts. The poet himself is a creature of paradox, whose work embraces the literary paradox.

The prose and poetry of Irish literature depict the amalgam of characteristics that have accreted to our sense of the '*bard*', the 'bardic poet', the '*file*', '*éigeas*', '*fear dána*', and involve at the same time notions of great status, wealth and power, on the one hand, and on the other, the less compelling image of ingratiation, entreaty, threat, and complaint. A range of poems associated with these identities is encountered in the poetry of the schools.

The poets' compositions merely hint at the conduct of the schools.[12] The curriculum can be inferred in part from the compositions. The learning was intensive, focused and flexible. Literacy and love of language and knowledge of its origins and grammar seem to have been the foundations of a literary mode which was remarkably long-lived.

The common discourse of letters in contemporary Europe was shared by Irish writers. One strand of the literary enterprise was the compilation of texts for students. I refer here to the great schools' manuals of writing, the *ars dictaminis*, the *ars versificatoria*, produced at ever decreasing intervals in Europe from the mid-eleventh century on. Nothing so well describes our bardic poetry as the contents of any one of these manuals – student-and-teacher handbooks on the form to be followed in all written works in Latin, from the filial letter to an anxious parent to an address to the Pope himself. While no work quite like them survives in Irish, it seems clear that a comparable instruction was adhered to in the prescribed literary conventions of Irish formal syllabic composition. In a more general sense, Irish had been open to Latin influence for previous centuries and resistance to that influence was not a feature of Hiberno-Latin literature nor of literature in the vernacular. The surviving Latin (from Norman [France] and from Anglo-Norman [England] sources) manuals, noted in the present study, are yet another guide through the labyrinth of allusion, ellusiveness, repetition, complaint, exhortion, elegy, epithalamium, and eulogy that makes up the content of the corpus of the schools' poetry that survives.

Irish bardic poets shared in a European aesthetic that was schematized and preceptive. Theories of invention and methods of formulating epideictic verse were written (based on material available since the classical era) and published from the eleventh century on. These could be regarded as manuals for writers, the recipe for a 'future poem'. They were not new in the sense of breaking new ground. They were innovative in their presentation together of grammar and modes of writing for those whose background in classical rhetoric and aesthetics was not very strong. They represented a stage in the development of literary creativity and of literary criticism. Whether Irish schools had access to versions of these textbooks is difficult to know. At the very least, it is known that the *Ars poetica* of Horace was transcribed in a continental scriptorium by an Irish scribe in the ninth century.[13]   In unbroken succession to the hybrid Irish–Latin scholarship of the earlier period, the norms of European and English education were imported into Ireland with the monastic orders which flourished from the twelfth century and with the retinue of Cambro-Norman, Anglo-Norman, English and French settlers, again from the twelfth century.

The Irish bardic poets refer continually to their art (*ealaín*). The reference is often to that which they have to offer in return for reward. They speak of selling their art. They complain about the devaluation of their art. They bemoan the death of all art as a consequence of the death of a lord. This art is the product of their learning and, at its best, displays the fruit of time and energy invested by both master and pupil in teaching and in learning the rules of the literary game in the bardic schools. This is well known and well understood.

In this study an attempt is made to add to the dimensions of the frame of reference through which the poetry of the schools is read, enjoyed and analysed. At best, it refers to directions that might lead to a more satisfactory place in our sense of historical integrity and in cultural continuity of a much loved and much misunderstood literary storehouse and historical source.

Tentative rhetorical readings are provided in this study. It is intended that these explore further avenues of analyses for bardic poetry, not *instead* of the rich analyses already in existence, but *building on* them. It is urged that the sense of a special or exotic identity for Irish poets and their literature be modified, if not abandoned. They can be afforded a full and rounded life in the polychrome world of mediaeval literature. They need not subsist as shades of an overwhelming and druidic past, or of monochrome anachronism, but can be seen and read as active elements in an evolving and organically sound literary phenomenon.

The study undertaken here discusses seven poems in some detail. These range from the fourteenth to the seventeenth centuries. Other compositions are mentioned briefly in comparison or contrast. Poems of which reliable editions have been published, translated and analysed, in various discussions of Irish syllabic poetry, have been chosen. These were selected because they have already been assigned a place in the commentary and discourse surrounding bardic poetry. It is not suggested here that the poems chosen for examination represent especially typical examples of their subgenre. They are held, merely, to be typical of their kind and, as such, useful for what must necessarily be an introductory attempt at a radical literary reading of them. They are the work of masters and of poets acknowledged in the tradition as such, and are, therefore, reasonably secure as examples of the best the schools had to offer. All the subgenres of praise are not represented here either. No elegies, for instance, are discussed. Since this study suggests that the requirements of praise and the discussion of art and its teaching underpin the poems presented here, a 'reading' of them, consciously emphasizing the literary structures arguably underlying them, is what is offered. Occasionally, other poems in which a similar form, locution or treatment is found, are noted. In general, they are ignored. The phenomenon of literary imitation is so characteristic of Irish syllabic poetry that it is taken for granted in this study, and the facile noting of them is avoided.[14]

The distinct nature of elegy,[15] or indeed of any other subcategory, would require a separate study, *after* the reading suggested here has been outlined. That is work for another day. Notably absent is any discussion of devotional poetry. The reason for this is outlined in chapters 1 and 2. It has always been accepted that devotional poetry composed by poets of the Irish schools participated in the greater arena of the literary sensibilities of Western European trends. Secular court poetry, on the other hand, has (traditionally) been disconnected from active participation in the contemporary literary trends and has had an aesthetic isolation foisted on it, with influences from outside being seen as capitulation to pressure, or exceptional borrowing.

The several collections of bardic poems edited and translated (in most cases), along with the single editions to be found in the journals, and related commentary, form the basis of all discussion of what is currently thought about Irish classical poetry in general. It is not necessary for the discussion being presented here to rehearse the consensual school of thought subsisting in all the currently available work. No attempt is made to describe any work in terms of metrical identity, fulfilment of metrical or orthographical rules and so forth, though such matters may be touched on in the explication of some passages. Nor is the textual history of any poem, its provenance and so forth, part of the discussion offered here. Nor does this study attempt to enlarge on the background of any one poet or school of poetry. Possible details, provided in E. Knott's work, of the life and times of the poet Tadhg Dall Ó hUiginn, are exceptionally discussed, in support of the suggestion that his 'biography' displays characteristics common among men of letters and popular poets.[16] The established status of the editions of the poems

noticed in this study is taken for granted. Minor emendations
in punctuation or lexicon are noted where they are made. The
poems presented here were originally published with reliable
translations. The translations provided in published editions
are normally used. In the case of editions by L. McKenna, I
retranslated for the most part, not because of any deficiency
in McKenna's work, but because of the necessity on my part to
establish an idiom which foregrounded the literary nature of the
composition.[17] There is no intention – in translation – to reach
for a seeming realistic account, description or otherwise, in any
particular quatrain or statement. The nature of the material is
necessarily repetitious; perhaps, at times, tediously so. This is
regrettable, but four hundred years of praise can lead to repeti-
tion. Failure in ingenuity to nuance and vary the presentation
is not a fault of the poetry but of the commentary.

The Latinization of Irish letters is discussed in chapter 1.
This chapter emphasizes the continuity of literary engagement
between Ireland, Britain (Wales, England and Scotland) and
the Continent from the Christianization of Western Europe to
the seventeenth century. The development of a curriculum for
the continental schools in the High Middle Ages, which resul-
ted in the dissemination of textbooks concerning composition,
and Ireland's participation in general humanities curriculum
and in the accepted norms of literary creativity, is outlined.
Chapter 2 introduces three of the most popular manuals of
the written arts in the Middle Ages. This material, neither
new, nor original, is set out here in order to emphasize those
matters that are immediately familiar to those whose interest is
in Irish poetry of the schools. Factors that will be mentioned
repeatedly in discussion of individual poems are foregrounded.
The general background is briefly sketched.

Chapter 3 looks at the poem by the fourteenth-century
poet Gofraidh Fionn Ó Dálaigh, written for Domhnall Mac

Carthaigh, lord of Desmond. The journey urged in the poem *'Beir eolas dúinn, a Dhomhnaill'* is examined as the 'found topic' (*inventio*) of the poet, and under the rubrics appropriate to such a poem found in the manuals. Chapter 4 examines poems in which the poet and lord disagree and become estranged. The early fourteenth-century poem by Ádhamh Ó Fialán, written for Tomás Mág Shamhradháin (d. 1343), lord of Tullyhaw, is chosen as an example of the type. Cattle have been stolen, offence given, and the poem steps artfully through the recriminations and reconciliations that form part of this subgenre.

Chapter 5 examines the themes of love slighted and love re-established, which form part of poems of disagreement and reconciliation. The areas in which the themes overlap with the poetry of the troubadours are noted and the nature of the love expressed in these and other examples of the genre is explored. Chapter 6 examines the survival of these tropes and themes in sixteenth-century works by the poet Tadhg Dall Ó hUiginn (*fl.* 1560–1590). His existence as a fabled literary character among later writers is noted and two of his poems, for one Uilliam Búrc, *'A theachtaire théid ar sliabh'* and *'Cóir Dé eadram is Uilliam'*, are examined in the light of the discussion presented in chapter 5.

Chapter 7 examines poems in which the poets seemingly upbraid fellow-poets for weakness in their art. The discussion is introduced in a poem by Gofraidh Fionn Ó Dálaigh, *'Madh fiafraidheach budh feasach'*, concerning the craft of poetry and correct usage. It is seen as an earlier independent literary presence in the background of the argumentative poems (from the sixteenth/seventeenth century) which follow in a suite of three poems in a seeming response sequence. These are Fear Feasa Ó'n Cháinte's *'Mór an feidhm deilbh an dána'* and *'Créad dá sealbhuinn damh an dán'*, with Gofraidh Mac an Bhaird's *'A fhir shealbhas duit an dán*' as the centrepiece. These sixteenth-/seventeenth-century poems are seen as virtuoso teachers' pieces in the tradition of the poems of contention. The emphasis is laid on the pedagogic properties of each one, and the tendency to see them as part of a genuine controversy about standards is questioned.

In chapter 8 the notion of the 'end of the tradition' is discussed with reference to Fear Flatha Ó Gnímh's poem, written [purportedly] for Fearghal Óg Mac an Bhaird, '*Cuimseach sin, a Fhearghail Óig*'. The poet accuses his fellow-poet(s) of abandoning the sober narrow ways of scholarship for the slack open highway of easy verse. This poem is read as an example of the poets' comment on the rubrics to which they adhered, which are those, it is argued, outlined in the manuals of the *ars poetriae*. Eochaidh Ó hEoghusa's '*Ionmholta malairt bhisigh*', written for Rudhraighe Ó Domhnaill, earl of Tyrconnell, brings this discussion to a close. My easy verse will make the earl laugh, he says. I dare to write it only because he is away.

1. *Continuity of contact*

The Latinized vernacular

Artifice is the hallmark of the work of the praise-poets. The devices used by the praise-poets to present their material at a uniformly high technical standard through four hundred years (1200–1600) were neither haphazardly acquired nor casually applied.[1] In fact the genre of praise, blame, exhortation, complaint, elegy and so forth in the classical syllabic metres of the *dán díreach* was built on a very firm foundation. Latin poetry in Ireland and by the Irish abroad suggests that Latin and its attendant literary culture was embraced with enthusiasm in Ireland.[2] The successful grafting of Christian Latin literary culture to a native base argues a receptivity in Irish pre-Christian culture, which found a new and natural outlet in the skills of writing, recording and composition. That this was accomplished with a sense of humour appropriate to the material, as well as with a firm grasp of the mechanics of the metrical intricacies, is well known. By the ninth century, scholars such as Sedulius Scottus (*fl.* 850–870) could produce works modelled on Virgil's *Eclogues,* adopting the pastoral note appropriate to this material.[3] His confidence also allowed broad humour.[4]

Altogether, a full enjoyment of the best that early mediaeval Latinity had to offer was enjoyed by the Irish on the Continent, and participated in, perhaps to a lesser extent, by those at home. Even by the end of the sixth century, a coalescence of Christian Latin learning and native Irish learning had taken place.[5] The Latinization of the vernacular, in the provision of grammars of the language and prosody based on available Latin patterns, took place within this period.

With this background in mind, we consider again the emergence of the distinctive syllabic praise-genre in the twelfth century, which, though building on earlier syllabic praise modes, became the vehicle of choice for all the formal poetry that survives. P. Mac Cana has outlined the prerequisites for this phenomenon and sees the baneful influence of the Norman invasion as a source of energy and disruption: ' . . . the establishment of the new poetic system of the *Dán Díreach* period presupposes not merely an evolutionary process but also an element of active planning'. How this was achieved to such a high degree of conformity and discipline 'remains a complete mystery'. It required the literati to be deprived of the 'congenial ecclesiastical environment' to give it the impetus required to establish such a secure foundation that it lasted four hundred years:

> . . . but the rapid extension of the new system throughout Ireland can hardly be explained otherwise than by assuming that there were still schools of *filidheacht* to give effect to it and that the old organization of the *filid* survived in sufficient strength to assure communication and cooperation over such a vast area (P. Mac Cana, 'The Rise of the Later Schools of *Filidheacht*', p. 139).

Mac Cana is really describing the ideal and typical conditions for the emergence of a kind of 'second rhetoric'.[6] In fact in Ireland this might even be considered a 'third rhetoric' since the vernacular had had such a head start[7] in producing the Latinized grammars of the vernacular which constituted a first step in the elevation of the vernacular to the level at which the learnèd might practise it and write it as they did Latin.[8] The primer *Auraicept na n-Éces*[9] fits well into the category thus described, and fulfils other requirements of that classification too. This indeed could be the 'second rhetoric', the *'núa-chrotha'* described by grammarians.[10] Gerard Murphy is quite clear about the connection between Irish vernacular prosody and European modes, though these were attuned to Latin.[11] *Auraicept na n-Éces* deals with the Ogham alphabet, grammar, and in some versions with poetry.[12] The matter of the grammar of the vernacular is very much – typically – influenced by the grammars of Donatus (AD 350), Priscian (AD 450), Pompeius (fifth century), and Consentius (fifth century). Even if those listed as Latin sources were not indeed used in the immediate sense, the authority of the names of the Latin grammarians was added for effect to the vernacular preceptive work. The text itself accreted commentary and glossary, interpretations and interpolations, as all such mediaeval works did.[13] J. O. Ward, while acknowledging the impossibility of defining precisely what is meant by a rhetorical treatise in the mediaeval context, attempted to summarize the nature of material produced, like the *Auraicept*, in a milieu of teaching and learning:

> There are a number of important distinctions made here; for example, between medieval glosses presented with text (*scholia*) and those presented without text (*catena* or 'chain' or continuous commentaries) or between the *summa* or independent treatise and the continuous gloss or commentary without the text but with extensive quotations from the text. The first distinction is perhaps the lesser of the two. It may reflect the difference between private study or formal curriculum study, between 'notes' of an anonymous informal sort, and an 'authored' composition; that is, it may reflect the strength of institutionalizing and validating authorities (*magistri, studia*, university, etc.) in contrast to the private scholar working on his

> own. It may thus indicate at times the importance of
> a regular curriculum subject: 'ordinary' or morning
> lectures within the later medieval universities and
> *studia* may have lead [*sic*] regularly to the composition
> of and use of *catena* glosses, whereas the extraordinary
> or afternoon or feast day lectures may have resulted
> in the compilation of more sporadic and often
> unfinished marginalia to copies of the classical texts
> (*CR*, p. 59).

We note '*tabair esemplair*' [give examples] , in G. Calder's edition of the *Auraicept* (l. 1286, p. 98), where the text explains details of difference between Latin and Ogham forms, suggesting that the material was used on one occasion, at least, as a teaching aid.

Three types of user are imagined in that work, the *Laitneoir* (l. 644, p. 48), the *fili* (l. 645, p. 48), and the *Gaedel* (l. 646, p. 48).[14] This may well cover succinctly the prospective users – the Latinist, or churchman, the vernacular poet/*fili*, and the literate Irishman *Gaedel*. Or, more likely, *Gaedel* comprises the *Laitneoir* and the *fili* and represents the student – the potential *Laitneoir* or *fili*. The primer lays the groundwork for the use of Irish after the fashion of Latin, and elevates its use in that way. The scholastic conundrums concerning genus (*cineál*) and specie (*gné*) are included in the discussion of poetic measure (ll. 752–753, p. 56). Sound and syllable count are contrasted in respect of *bairdne* (l. 778, p. 56) and *filidecht* (l. 756–757, p. 56). The great world languages are listed – Hebrew, Greek and Latin – followed by the Irish language (lit. language of Ireland *berla Eirenn*) *Gædelg/Gaidelc* (l. 1068, l. 3540) which, being the latest, is the most correct (l. 1068, p. 80).[15] Written work in a consistent metre and with suitable measure is urged, so that the 'mixed' (*cumascda*) speech of *na daerbaird* is avoided (*ar*

na rabi in indsci cumascda amal dogniat na daerbaird ll. 1687–
1691, p. 130). Notes on analysis of material according to the
meaning it denotes, according to the method it uses (*.i. imcho-
marc iar n-inni thoirni 7 imchomarc iar n-airbhirt nan-airbirenn
bith.* ll. 1894–1896, p. 144) are included and echo the classical
differentiations of the *forma tractatus / forma tractandi*.[16]

And, of course, the primer lists the faults in composition,
twelve in number, '*da locht deg na hirlabra in sin*' (l. 1943, p.
148), while there are twenty-four methods of avoiding these
errors, '*Dia nditen-sidhe cethri cenela fichet. . .*' (l. 1944, p. 148).
This material belongs to a text on poetry called *Trefhocal*,[17] and
it is given also in syllabic verse, listing the excesses, weaknesses,
and faults of poorly conceived compositions and those literary
steps that either prevent them or correct them.[18]

Referring to the *Auraicept*, R. Hofman suggests that 'In the
context of medieval Europe the *Auraicept* is unusual in that it
is classified as a medieval grammatical description of a vernacu-
lar language along with the 12th-century Icelandic *Grammatical
treatises* and the 13th-century *Donatz proensals*.'[19] The 'unusual'
element, in so far as the mediaevel European context is con-
cerned, is the early date at which the primer seems to have
achieved some core stability. Douglas Kelly's (1991) study of
vernacular arts in *The Arts of Poetry and Prose*, identifies fea-
tures common to all the primers of the vernacular arts. Among
the general characteristics he outlines are the following:

> . . . [Second], the extant treatises are quite
> elementary, even when written in Latin, being more
> nearly comparable to Latin treatises on elementary
> grammar and versification than to the twelfth-
> and thirteenth-century arts of poetry and prose
> as such. Third, besides providing the elements of
> versification together with the rudiments of vernacular
> grammar, they rely on examples drawn from earlier or

contemporary vernacular literatures. . . . Fourth and last, the vernacular treatises scarcely touch on prose writing; they are essentially arts only of poetry.

The patrons and audience were not clerical but lay. This means that the public was broader, although more often than not local; the patronage was aristocratic, bourgeois, or both. New subjects and ideals found expression, especially those suitable to a lay audience, with its particular social, moral, and religious predilections, and its own kinds of entertainment. Most vernacular treatises and manuals seek to preserve, renew, or adapt to a new language the achievements of illustrious predecessors in the vernacular. . . . The goal was more often than not public performance or competition rather than scholastic achievement or private communications. Many are linked to poetic contests wherein established rules were used to judge and reward poems written according to the rules and examples the vernacular treatises codify, outline and/or define. Many authors desire to make their vernacular a literary language worthy of its earlier achievements and equal or superior to Latin or another literary vernacular like Occitan or Italian (*APP*, pp. 146–147).

While Kelly's particular emphasis is on the vernaculars that evolved in areas that had come under direct Roman imperial influence, his comment on areas that did not is relevant for us here:[20]

Those who learned to write in medieval schools came under the influence of the dominant Latin education, even, apparently, in the Scandinavian world and in the Irish and Welsh bardic schools. This was especially true for literary composition. Even when authors trained in this tradition chose to use the vernacular, their conception of composition and the artist had been fixed by their education. Therefore, habits like those a Bernard of Chartres tried to instil in his pupils continued to determine how they wrote in the vernacular. However, no more so than with the Latin arts is it necessary to assume that the entire tradition went, lock, stock, and barrel, into the literary baggage of each author. Traditional concepts of the trivium were widespread enough to provide the framework for the training of most writers in the schools, even though that training may have been more or less thorough, depending on times and places (*APP*, p. 148).

ARTIFICE

The 'living' text of the *Auraicept* was in harmony with developments in Britain and Europe, perhaps ahead of them in the production of a vernacular prosody comprising so much of what was common currency in the curriculum of the trivium.

No great leap – cultural, academic or conceptual – was required by Irish contemporaries to find a congenial milieu for a man such as Flann Ua Gormáin (d. 1174), whose obituary in the Annals of Ulster reads as follows:

> Flann Ua Gormain, arch-lector of Ard-Macha and of all Ireland, a learnèd man, eminent in divine and human wisdom, after having been a year and twenty learning amongst the Franks and Saxons and twenty years directing the schools of Ireland, died peacefully on the 13th of the Kalends of April . . . the Wednesday before Easter, in the 70th year of his age.

> . . . *ardfherleighinn Aird-Macha agus Erenn uile, fer*
> *eolach, comarthamail i n-ecna diadha agus domunda, iar*
> *m-beith bliadhain ar fichit i Francaibh agus i Saxanaibh*
> *ic foghlaim agus fiche bliadhain ic follamhnughadh scol*
> *n-Erenn, atbath co sitheamail i tredecim Kallann Aprilis,*
> *Dia-Cetain ria Caisc, septuagesimo aetatis suae anno.*
> (W. M. Hennessy and B. MacCarthy, *Annála*
> *Uladh, s.a.* 1174).

His contemporary at Kildare, Find Úa Gormáin (sometime
pre-Cistercian abbot of Iubhar Cinn Trá [Newry]), bishop
of Kildare in 1148 (d. 1160), addressed a letter to Áed mac
Criomthainn, 'lector of the high king of Leth Moga . . .
prime historian of Leinster in wisdom and knowledge and
book lore and science and learning' (*do fir leigind ardrig*
Leithi Moga . . . do phrimsenchaid Laigen ar gaes 7 eolas 7
trebaire lebur 7 fesa 7 foglomma).[21] This letter, 'the earliest
epistolary composition, it may be remarked, in the Irish
language'[22] found on folio 206 of the Book of Leinster[23] is
described by S. Forste-Grupp as the first letter in Irish showing
familiarity with the continental rubrics of letter-writing, the
ars dictaminis.[24] One of the earliest known such handbooks
of instructions for letters, concerning the correct mode of
address, content, formulae and so forth, had been produced
by the Anonymous of Bologna in the middle of the twelfth
century.[25] Forste-Grupp claims that the letter in the Book of
Leinster, is the earliest letter, not in Latin, found in Europe
which follows the prescriptive formulae of the *ars dictaminis*.
Its existence shows a receptiveness among the educated and
literate Irish to contemporary scholarly trends, and to their
adaptation of materials referring to Latin, and in Latin, to
their own vernacular at the appropriate time.

Three Irish scribes, one Salmon (*Solamh*), a nameless
student and a man tentatively identified as Tuilecnad

(Tuileagna – a name common among the Ó Maolchonaire family of poets and teachers in later centuries), copied and annotated a manuscript in the twelfth century which drew directly on contemporary continental masters.[26] The manuscript is in four parts, containing a copy of Calcidius's Latin translation of Plato's *Timaeus*; a work on natural phenomena drawing largely on Isidore of Seville and on Bede; an epitome of John Scottus Eriugena's *Periphyseon*; and 'a single continuous extract from Book V' of the *Periphyseon*.[27] The manuscript has the characteristics of a text worked on first by the scribe Solamh, then by the student whose name does not seem to appear, and third by the *oide* Tuileagna.[28] For the purposes of this discussion, P. Ó Néill's identification of the comments that gloss the texts as coming from contemporaries Bernard of Chartres and William of Conches is significant:

> . . . the Irish glossator shows himself to be a man of his time. But the most compelling testimony to his modernity is the source that he used for most of his interpretative glosses. That source was an anonymous commentary on the *Timaeus* composed between 1100 and 1150, preserved in six manuscripts dating from the first to the final quarter of the twelfth century. The commentary has recently been attributed to Bernard of Chartres, *magister* of the school of Chartres in the first three decades of the twelfth century. . . . Evidently, Scribe 3 (and Scribe 2) had direct access to the work of the foremost neo-Platonist of his time. . . . He used another, hitherto unidentified source, a commentary on the *Timaeus* composed by William of Conches. . . . it is safe to conclude that Scribe 3 had access not only to the commentary of Bernard of Chartres but also to the ideas of William of Conches. . . . William's commentary belongs to the second

quarter of the twelfth century, a date not far removed
from that assigned to the script of Scribe 3, which
suggests that he had access to contemporary Platonic
scholarship from Chartres (P. Ó Néill, 'An Irishman at
Chartres', pp. 15–18).

The manuscript glosses are interpretative and grammatical, and
Ó Néill makes the point that a similar style of grammatical
analysis occurs in glosses in a contemporary Irish manuscript
from Armagh.[29] Etymologizing in the style favoured in the
Irish schools is also evident in the commentary, and these come
also with Irish glosses.

Most interesting from the point of view of the discussion
here, is the evidence, in the commentaries of Scribe 3
(Tuileagna), that he noted the rhetorical figures in the extracts
from the *Periphyseon* as marginal notes:

> These notes were hardly supplied by Scribe 3 for
> his own information, since their contents are quite
> elementary and some of them consist merely of terms
> without definition. Moreover, the fact that many of
> them bore no direct relationship to the main text
> suggest that their function was not to help readers
> understand the latter, but to highlight, for the teacher,
> other topics that he could discuss in the process of
> exposition (ibid., pp. 24–25).

These included *apoconu* [*sic*]:[30] '*quando unum predicatum seruit
duabas clausulis uel tribus*; *anacoliton* .i. oratio defectiua quando
praecedit "quot" et non sequitor "tot" . . .'[31] This same scribe
added a stanza in the syllabic *rannaigheacht mhór* invoking St
Martin and archangel Gabriel.[32] Ó Néill concludes:

> In a broader perspective, many of the glosses of the
> Bodleian manuscript reflect contemporary teaching

of the trivium (grammar, rhetoric and logic) and quadrivium (arithmetic, music, geometry and astronomy). The glosses of Scribe 3 . . . mainly deal with the trivium . . . In sum, the contents of the Bodleian manuscript relfect the learning of the early twelfth-century schools. . . .

. . . the evidence of his glosses and his notes suggests that Scribe 3 was an Irishman who attended school at Chartres, probably during the first half of the twelfth century and almost certainly no earlier than its second quarter . . .

. . . his choice of texts (and their accompanying glosses) bears witness to the new learning emanating from the French schools. Almost certainly he acquired this learning first-hand from a long sojourn in France, probably during the second quarter of the twelfth century. Moreover, the pedagogical bent of his glossing and his mentoring of Scribe 2 suggest that he was actively engaged in transmitting the new learning to Irish students (ibid., pp. 25, 29, 35).

The existence of this busy scholar, and his student, along with Scribe 1, is highlighted by Ó Néill's work on MS Auct. F. III.15. The careers of Find Úa Gormáin, and Flann Ua Gormáin above, are attested from two extant documents. It may not be too wide of the mark to suggest that these two were not unusual and that others like them maintained the international links that kept Irish scholarship in touch with, and in tune with, European trends.[33]

We can suggest, therefore, that readers and writers of Irish accepted standardized formulae coming from the continental schools and made appropriate use of them in their own work from the earliest availability of such materials.[34] One might say that they were abreast of the trends. It might be possible to suggest, similarly, that while continental influence was inescapable with the changes introduced by twelfth-century Church reformations, and with the arrival of the Anglo-Normans, that 'escape' was hardly what the Irish writers and educators had in mind, since, without the added immediacy of the Anglo-Norman invasion, or of the influence spread by the continental orders in Ireland, Irish people had already availed of much that continental schooling and trends had to offer and had made their own sizeable contribution in return.[35] Therefore, we can refer to shared aesthetics rather than to oblique or unwelcome or imposed influences. The evolution of literary vernaculars in Europe leaned towards the presentation of an elevated register of the spoken language in formal attire, as had been the norm in literary Latin. The explosion of handbooks to that effect bowdlerized the so-called First Rhetoric of the Ancients – the latter having lost its primary power as a praxis, 'an application of practical wisdom in public affairs' (*Rhetoric, Hermeneutics, and Translation*, p. 153) – and became an academic discipline, developing into the useful and vocational rhetoric of the graduates of the 'cathedrals, monasteries, universities, *studia*, chanceries, households and other consumption points of the middle ages' (*CR*, p. 6).[36] The results emerged in Latin and in the vernaculars in arts manuals, in a style both teachable and learnable.

In Ireland, their influence is discernible in the styles adopted for *dán díreach* compositions, in the methods taught for the *inventio* – the identification of appropriate topics for formal compositions – and in the range of literary tropes and figures appropriate for the theme chosen.[37] The fragmentation of the world of the written arts in Europe through the re-establishment of grammar, rhetoric, logic, dialectic and other sciences of language into different – sometimes opposing

– schools of thought, created a ferment of – sometimes tortuous – debate, creativity and manuscript publication.[38]

Grammar masters, the teachers in the cathedral schools, the nascent faculty masters of the emerging universities, claimed for themselves the teaching of literature and writing in the vocational sense. We recognize this development in Ireland in the emerging figures of the *ollamh* and the *file* in annal entries, whose vocation(s) seemed to include the epideictic arts, teaching, performing and other functions appropriate to the man of letters.[39]

It is clear, however, that sufficient common territory in the liberal arts, and in the shared understandings in the developing world of vernacular literature, existed between the learnèd/literate Irish and their fellows in Scotland, England and Wales and continental Europe to speak of a shared aesthetic.[40] In this uncontroversial sense of a shared aesthetic, the Anglo-Norman invasion and subsequent settlement of Ireland had perhaps its least disruptive influence upon continuity in literature and in the pursuits of literary men and women. In its negative aspect, the Anglo-Norman invasion has been, traditionally, seen as having split Ireland's literary classes asunder and to have led to a frenzied period of conservation and compilation.[41]

In that negative assessment, it would seem that only in the case of Irish literature is the urge – in the later Middle Ages – to translate and adapt seen as a major indicator of flagging energy and depleted creativity. Such activity, occurring simultaneously on the Continent, is regarded as a great flowering and sharing of culture. Even in Elizabethan England, when the vogue (in literature) was for everything Italian, while nativists cavilled at the urge to ape Italian style, the objection was never to the adaptation of tried stories and trusted formulae being given a new life in language or presentation.[42]

The great burst of creativity in Irish literature that occurred in the period after the Anglo-Norman invasion and after the ecclesiastical reforms of the twelfth century are seen – negatively by P. Mac Cana, for instance – as indicators of an etiolated and introverted aesthetic, derivative and doomed:

> . . . not so much a creative urge as a conscious effort to regroup and consolidate the resources of native learning. The foreign element is conspicuous enough in the matter of the literature – this same century saw the translation, or adaptation of *Togail Troí*, 'The Destruction of Troy', *Togail Tebe*, 'The Destruction of Thebes', *Merugud Ulix*, 'The Wandering of Ulysses', *Imthechta Aeniasa*, 'The Wandering of Aeneas', and *In Cath Catharda*, 'The Civil War of the Romans' – but this need not blind us to the fact that, spiritually and intellectually, learned Gaelic Ireland turned in upon itself in profound distrust of the unfamiliar ('The Rise of the Later Schools of *Filidheacht*', p. 141).

In a similarly negative sense of cultural opposition and resistance rather than of cultural exchange or development, B. Ó Cuív characterizes the 'consolidation' of the Irish literary language, which took place around the second half of the twelfth century – just as our continental manuals of poetic writing were becoming well known and generally used – as having value as a weapon of cultural defence in an entirely confrontational context in the aftermath of the Anglo-Norman invasion:[43]

> Nothing is known to have been recorded of how the reorganization of their craft by the professional poets of that time was carried out, but it is obvious that there was a general acceptance by them of new criteria in language as well as in metrics. The

language of the poetry of the following centuries and the detailed description of various aspects of it contained in the linguistic tracts suggest that what I have called 'a normative or prescriptive grammar' was drawn up by them. . . . The consolidation of the literary language which they achieved proved to be of immense importance in the confrontation between native and alien culture which took place after the Anglo-Norman invasion.[44]

Our discussion here, however, leads us to suggest that, intellectually and spiritually, learnèd Ireland was abreast of movements in Wales, Scotland and England, and in continental Europe. Irish involvement in ecclesiastical reform movements dated back a half a millennium to the great controversies between, for example, conservatives and 'Romani'.[45] Irish learnèd involvement in literary Europe was at one time axiomatic. The routine dissemination of learning throughout mediaeval Christendom was not at any time brought to a halt in Ireland by the reforms of the twelfth century nor by the political changes wrought by the Anglo-Normans. We might even suggest that the arrival of the Anglo-Normans and their households with their cultural biases and literary tastes introduced further layers of depth to Irish literature.[46]

This would seem to be the case in the emergence of the distinctive praise-genre, which became the normal expression of a certain literary attainment for the period 1200 to 1600. Reflecting on the impact of the Anglo-Norman invasion in the twelfth century, B. Ó Cuív makes the following point:

> The Anglo-Norman Invasion may have ended the era of the High-kings, but it did not end the individual and family ambitions for which the praise-poet and historians catered. Indeed I think that it possibly had the

effect of intensifying them. Certainly there is a vast amount of praise poetry extant from the following four centuries . . .[47]

In respect of that body of work, Ó Cuív, agreeing that the historian 'cannot afford to disregard them', allows that 'it is still difficult to assess the value of this body of material to the historian'. The difficulty arises, he suggests, in part, because 'it is clear that *owing to certain conventions* poets continued as late as the sixteenth century to allude to circumstances which could not possibly have existed after the thirteenth' ('Literary Creation', pp. 255–256 [emphasis added]). Among other things, poets conventionally 'stating that the subject of a praise-poem is fit to be or destined to be King of Ireland'. 'It is possible,' Ó Cuív states, 'that this had its origins in the twelfth century, when it must have seemed that the High-kingship could be won by a member of any sept provided he was sufficiently powerful' (ibid., p. 256).

This sense of a literal truth behind the literary reality led Ó Cuív to the following conjecture:

> Had Keating continued his *Foras Feasa ar Éirinn* beyond the twelfth century the problems which beset us in examining this later material in prose and verse, would, I suspect, have troubled him very little, for he had a capacity for ignoring, or not seeing, chronological difficulties, anachronisms, and other contradictions (ibid., p. 262).

Depending on how conversant Geoffrey Keating was with the scholarly norms of contemporary Irish literature – and, presumably, he was thoroughly familiar with the education of the bardics schools,[48]– the 'chronological difficulties, anachronisms, and other contradictions' noted by Ó Cuív would not have been 'ignored' as obstacles by Keating, but understood as appropriate *owing to certain conventions poets continued [to use] as late as the sixteenth century* (ibid., p. 255 [emphasis added]). It can be suggested that these 'conventions' which create so much difficulty for the literal interpretation of bardic praise-poetry are none other than Irish reflexes of the standard literary rhetorical conventions common in European writing during the later Middle Ages.

In his study of the 'later Irish bards', E. C. Quiggin suggests that Irish writing did not come under the benign influence of French poetry,[49] and that the 'free adaptations . . . '[50] of tales and other written works were unproductive in their influence on native literature; at the same time:

> Though the greatest poets of England and Germany in the thirteenth and fourteenth centuries were often indebted to Romance literature for their materials, yet they stamped their own impress so thoroughly on their borrowed themes that their works became truly national. Even Wales came under this influence. For it is now definitely established that Dafydd ab Gwilym owes much to Provençal poets. This is in striking contrast to what we find in Ireland . . . Ireland stood characteristically aloof from the main currents in European literature, though this does not imply that she had no connexion with the outside world ('Prolegomena', pp. 90–91).

The aloofness claimed for the profane compositions of the bardic poets is belied, by the same scholar, when he considers the devotional works of the poets:

> The more one studies the works of these bards, the more one is impressed with the range of their attainments. They were not in holy orders, yet they

must have been better versed in Latin than most of the clergy. Some of them, in all probability paid visits to Highland lords, and may have acquired English and French, though we could not assume this from merely studying the sources of their compositions. And unfortunately we have evidence of continental travel in the case of one member of the fraternity alone, viz. Murray O'Daly, who may have taken part in a Crusade. In any case, it was no mean achievement on the part of men like Tadhg O'Higgin to show such acquaintance with the voluminous Latin religious literature of the day in addition to the huge store of native learning exemplified in their other works. In addition to the compositions already mentioned, Tadhg's poems deal with Mary Magdalen, John the Baptist, St. John the Divine, St. Paul, St. Andrew, and others. He also treats the story of the Discovery of the Saviour's Cross by Helena. This is of interest as being, to my knowledge, the only poetic treatment of the subject in Irish, although a number of prose versions are known, some of which have appeared in print ('Prolegomena', pp. 124–125).

In this characterization of Irish bardic poetry, we have the insulated native profane compositions, owing nothing to the influence of the flowering French tradition. Against that, we have the devotional poetry of the same kind of poet, in the same literary metrical style, displaying every sign of being well in tune with, and effortlessly influenced by, continental European modes and matter. L. McKenna's assessment of the bardic devotional poetry[51] takes a similar line: profane poetry is self-referential and unrelieved by outside influence, while devotional poetry, by fellow-poets – and sometimes identical poets – is European in matter and tone:[52]

As models and as sources of suggestion and information, the Bards had, not merely the earlier Irish poetry, the influence of which shows clearly on their work, but the vast store of religious legends which the pious imagination of an uncritical age had produced, especially in France and Germany. There are some of these legends, such as the blindness of the Centurion who pierced Christ, the wonders of the Flight into Egypt, the Three Tears of Mary, the origin of the Holy Cross, etc., to which references are very common in all Bardic works. The number of legends to which access was possible was evidently very large, those which survive in Irish or Continental MSS being only a small proportion of the whole number. References are often found to stories of which there is no trace in the older Irish books, in the Apocrypha, or . . . in Continental literature. . . . [i]t is possible they may not imply the existence of a legend now lost, but that they are due to the poet's invention (*Dán Dé*, p. xi).

McKenna notes in particular the tendency of the bardic devotional poetry to concentrate on the Crucifixion of Christ and the events surrounding it, and the consequent scant attention paid to the parables, miracles and other incidents of the public life of Christ as depicted in the Gospels. In this context, he notes:

Christ's Redemption of the world is described almost always either as a war, or as the payment of an *éiric* or 'blood-price' to God the Father. Similar comparisons are common in all Christian writings, but their prominence in the Bards' works very likely reflects the circumstances of the Irish life of their time. A war is being waged . . . ; In this war, Christ is wounded

> defending us . . . . The other and equally common
> view of the Redemption is that Christ, by His life of
> hardships and especially by His death . . . pays the *éiric*
> or blood-price laid as a legal sanction on the human
> race . . . in Bardic poetry it is expressed in the legal
> language of the Brehon system (ibid., pp. xv–xvi).

McKenna mentions the popularity of the Day of Judgement
as a bardic devotional theme, noting that it is the commonest
theme. For our purposes here, McKenna's acknowledgement of
the shared pool of devotional themes drawn upon by the bardic
poets is noteworthy, and even more so is his observation on the
predominance of a militarizing theme in the poets' treatment of
the death of Christ. The implications of this will be discussed
below.

In a recent article on the aesthetics of bardic poetry, P. A.
Breatnach is unapologetic in indentifying European rhetorical
modes in the profane poetry as well:

> One important ingredient which should never be over-
> looked is the influence of school doctrines concerning
> the art of rhetoric, as transmitted in the medieval so-
> called *artes versificandi/artes poetriae*. . . . We should
> expect to dectect that influence in some measure in
> Irish vernacular tradition also, both in relation to the
> organization of subject matter and the use of figurative
> language ('Aesthetics', p. 53).

Breatnach's article limits the delineation of the influence to an
awareness of a general sense of the ambient discourse:

> But it is not our present purpose simply to gather evid-
> ence of the adherence to rhetorical doctrines, or indeed
> to engage in a 'figure-hunt' as though the location of
> rhetorical figures were an 'end in itself'. . . . The aim is

to observe the manner in which an awarenes of what is termed the 'environment of discourse', created by the inheritance of medieval rhetorical theory, can lead us towards a more complete and satisfying appreciation of the inherent aesthetic qualities of an early modern Irish bardic poem (ibid., pp. 53–54).

Breatnach's analysis of the seventeenth-century poem 'Fuaras iongnadh, a fhir chumainn' (by Fearghal Óg Mac an Bhaird) masterfully analyses the composition in respect of content, known and probable historical background, metre and tradition within Irish literature. And indeed, Breatnach nods to the continental schools' training, by mentioning Geoffrey of Vinsauf's strictures concerning impressive openings and by indicating where rhetorical devices enhance the effect of statements in the composition, *principium a proverbo, principium ab exemplo* (ibid., p. 60). Other techniques, such as the flourish of *conduplicatio* to cover the reiteration of the word *iongnadh* are noted (ibid., p. 63). The treatment, long or short, as dictated by the rhetorical manual, for instance of Geoffrey of Vinsauf, is discussed and it is understood that Fearghal Óg chooses the longer option incorporating an apologue (*exemplum*) (ibid.,). The modes for comparison enjoined in the formal *artes collatio aperta/collatio occulta* are also identified in the poet's use of the *exemplum*, in this case from Arthurian tradition. The composition, Breatnach notes, concludes in a virtuoso display of the device *determinatio* (ibid., p. 66). Accounting for its use by Fearghal Óg, Breatnach notes as follows:

> As the style is used very extensively in Irish poetry, it may be safely assigned in both traditions to the shared literary inheritance of the European Latin Middle Ages. Irish authors from the twelfth century to the seventeenth deploy their version of this device, consisting of

> a series of metaphorical epithets arranged paratactically
> and extending over several quatrains, usually for praise
> only . . . . A limited number of patterns for its use can
> be observed and *this suggests adherence to precepts which
> were communicated in the schools but, like all such theor-
> etical guides, have left their traces solely in the practice of
> the poets themselves* (ibid., p. 66; [emphasis added]).

This concept of the shared aesthetic, allowing for the influ-
ence of continental literary modes, and the influence of the
mediaeval schools on the work of the bards, is of immense value
in re-establishing a culturally sustainable context for the poets
and their work in mediaeval and early modern Ireland. It moves
us away from notions of cultural isolation,[53] and escapes from
the sense that a suspicious and culturally insecure Ireland aban-
doned the habit of half a millennium and suddenly cut itself
off from cultural enrichment and exchange from Britain and
Europe to embrace a twilight world of intellectual and spiritual
stagnation.[54]

Continual engagement with trends in literature from Eng-
land, Scotland, Wales and continental Europe is the cultural
norm throughout the mediaeval period and into early modern
Ireland. Work by Tadhg Ó Dúshláine on seventeenth-century
literature in Irish demonstrates how effortlessly the Irish poets
made their own of literary modes and materials of the common
contemporary European literary culture. Poets who composed
in styles other than *dán díreach* in the seventeenth century were
not catapulted from the illiterate classes or from the function-
ally lettered into a spontaneous outburst of productivity in the
rhyming metres, indicating a new strain of populist realism.
Ó Dúshláine's study shows how the influence of contemporary
continental rhetoric flourished apace in Irish literature, which
– we suggest here – it had done since the emergence of the first
written records.[55]

While maintaining a distinctly Irish complexion, those involved with literature in Irish participated in the mainstream of European literary life from the earliest times on record to the seventeenth century at least. Bearing this in mind, we can expand on aspects of the shared aesthetic, and explore some of the implications for our understanding of the poetry and its capacity to illuminate aspects of the contemporary Irish polity for us.

2. *Style*

A thousand years of thinking and writing about the nature of writing and the uses of rhetoric had already accumulated in the common learnèd culture of European civilization by the time those peoples outside the immediate influence of ancient Greece and Rome came to participate in the written culture of late antiquity.

Irish people were among those whose involvement with written Christian culture occurred when the long-established norms of classical literature were at the same time being diminished by war and destruction and enriched by the engagement of the newly Christianized peoples in the literary enterprise. The indigenous foundations onto which they grafted their new skills in literacy developed eventually into the literary vernaculars of the High Middle Ages. What concerns us here is the sense of general continuity inherent in the familiarity among the learnèd with the accumulated lore of the previous millennium. Newcomers were understandably impressed and relieved to find that the matter could be mastered with effort. Indeed, the original arts of rhetoric – those of persuasion in the political sphere – had long since evolved into the art of producing elegantly wrought verse which would in turn be a suitable vehicle for all learnèd discourse as well as for the epideictic arts.[1]

THE CENTRALITY OF STYLE

It is in this context that we approach the notion of the mediaeval 'wheel of Virgil' and its assignment of style to subject.[2] The concept was fundamental to the sense in which *inventio* was understood in the mediaeval period: the discovery of an idea or subject worthy to write about *from the traditional and already worked topics,* giving priority to the sense of recuperation involved in the concept of *translatio studii.*[3]

The late mediaeval *artes poetriae* – manuals for writers – which were a phenomenon of the High Middle Ages, appearing, for the most part, between *c.* 1175 and 1270, were:

> . . . the products of classical preceptive traditions of rhetoric, that is, the legacy of Cicero, the *Ad Herennium,* and Quintilian, along with the poetic precept of Horace's *Ars poetica.* . . . The poetics adapted established categories of topics to serve as tools for literary analysis. Matthew of Vendôme, Geoffrey of Vinsauf, and John of Garland all exploited these standardized topical systems. One historical explanation of this is that the *artes poetriae* constituted poetry as an academic discipline, and promoted its participation in the methods of logic. . . . but their preceptive techniques derive to a great extent from the tradition of the *enarratio poetarum.* They teach the art of composition through the art of formal literary analysis, and they are as much (if not more) the products of the tradition of Donatus, Priscian, and Servius as they are the product of Ciceronian rhetoric (*Rhetoric, Hermeneutics, and Translation,* pp. 160–161).

This background is identical to that of the known background of Irish writers in Latin and in Irish of the earlier period.[4] The great Irish scholar, John Scottus Eriugena (*c.* 810–*c.* 877), active in the Carolingian schools, may have influenced the developement of the status of the later rhetorical arts with his discussion of dialectic, logic and rhetoric in *Periphyseon: The Division of Nature.*[5] The Irish schools are known to have been abreast of continental and British modes and materials in the realms of devotional literature. The students and teachers of these same schools produced the epideictic praise-poetry in syllabic metres, which is referred to as bardic poetry or court poetry. Closer acquaintance with Cambro-Normans, Anglo-Normans and French Normans, as well as with the English, was unlikely to diminish the familiarity of the learnèd Irish with the literature of these peoples or with their literary fashions in the twelfth century. In fact, the reverse is more likely.

If the phenomenon of praise-poetry became identified with the period after the Anglo-Norman invasion in the twelfth century, then the nature of that praise-poetry might well have been influenced by a wider application of current scholarly and literary skills and a greater sense of participation in a wider pool of available texts, whether in translation, adaptation or in original form.[6]

In any event, the treatises of Matthew of Vendôme (c. 1175), Geoffrey of Vinsauf (c. 1210), and John of Garland (c. 1230) provide an additional and likely reference point for characteristics in Irish bardic poetry which have been thoroughly examined, annotated, and analysed from within the Irish tradition, but which have only recently begun to be situated in their wider context.[7]

ARS VERSIFICATORIA

Commenting on the phenomenon of the 'preceptive movement' in the High Middle Ages, J. J. Murphy synopsizes:

> The chronology of this preceptive movement is interesting. It begins, rather hesitantly, with Matthew of Vendôme about 1175, reaches a peak – its most 'rhetorical' stage – with Gervase of Melkley and Geoffrey of Vinsauf around 1210, begins to falter with the abortive attempt at collation by John of Garland two decades later, and sputters out almost cynically shortly after mid-century with Eberhard the German.

It was, in other words, a fairly short-lived movement with some visibly evolutionary features within it. Matthew in 1175 points to the novelty of his work, dedicated to 'the elegant joining of words, and the expression of the characteristics and the observed quality of a thing.' Eberhard eight decades or so later laments tiredly that 'when the word flowers, the mind dries up' (*RMA*, pp. 61–62).

All that is known of Matthew of Vendôme comes from information supplied in his works. Born in Vendôme (*c.* 1095),[8] from which he was named (sometimes 'Le Vendômois', *LAP*, p. 1), he studied in Tours at the time of Bernard Silvester, and at Orléans during the time of Hugh Primas. He became a grammar master there, and following what appears to have been a dispute with another master,[9] Arnulf, he went to live in Paris under the auspices of bishop Barthélemy (the second) and his brother. Sometime before 1175 is the most likely date for the composition, or at least the circulation of the *Ars Versificatoria*.[10] Other works by him are mentioned in one of his own compositions and are, for the most part, unidentifiable. The most famous surviving work, apart from the *Ars Versificatoria*, the *Tobias*, gives information about Matthew not found elsewhere. In keeping with the overwhelmingly preceptive nature of the rhetorical works we refer to here, Faral notes how the treatise itself is probably the fruit of a lesson, or lessons, in the schools in Orléans:

> *L'Art poetique*, . . . est vraisemblablement issu d'un enseignement donné par Matthieu dans les écoles d'Orléans . . . (*LAP*, p. 14).

The *Ars Versificatoria* is presented in four parts (editorial divisions by Faral), with an opening prologue. Faral breaks the text up as follows: Prologue; I Concerning Ideas; II the Form of Words; III the Quality of Expression; IV the Treatment of Material.[11]

The prologue is replete with jibes and sallies at one Arnulf (Rufinus). This may or may not be the historical character Arnulf of St Evurcius, or Arnulf of Orléans, known through his work as a glossator on classical authors, including Lucan and Ovid.[12] The seeming reality of the scholarly contretemps, well founded as it may have been, may also have had its origin (or indeed, its only reality) in the creation of a rhetorical device in the sense of *licentia* in order to give structure, or memorability, to the fairly dry contents of a scholar's manual.[13] The repeated charges of envy, promiscuity and lasciviousness levelled at this Rufinus (Arnulf?), and the use of the controversy to introduce material of a didactic nature, suggest a pedagogic foundation for the 'controversy' rather than a true state of affairs.[14] The material is rendered more memorable because of the personalization of the 'dispute' concerning matters of scholarship and method. Rhetorical tropes and figures are used throughout, even while teaching the use of those same skills. When the teacher/poet Matthew of Vendôme attempted to teach the description appropriate to a vicious character of low status to illustrate the uses of vituperation he did not choose Arnulf/Rufinus, but he chose the stock slave-character 'Davus', further strengthening the sense that the Arnulf dispute was a pedagogic device; the student should describe 'Davus' when indicating a person of low status, not 'Arnulf', execrable though he may be.[15] The Arnulf/Rufinus character belonged to the vituperation appropriate for the poet about his fellow-poet, and was not that prescribed for the description of a 'low style' character of the beggarly slave. The work of Matthew of Vendôme achieved circulation partly because of its internal coherence, and partly because of the seemingly human interest behind the dry text.

In any event, the 'Arnulf' figure affords a shape and a form to the introduction and gives the author an ostensible cause of writing. Matthew even begins with a swipe at his 'adversary': '*Spiritus invidiae cesset, non mordeat hostis / Introductivum Windocinensis opus . . .*' [Were envy to cease, the enemy of the one from Vendôme / Would not criticize an introductory work . . . (*LAP*, p. 109; *AV*, p. 17.)] This literary creation of enmity, or of a conflict between persons, becomes relevant for our discussion later (see below, chapter 7, n. 80). The formula allows Matthew to continue his introduction thus:

> . . . and in keeping with the insignificance of my feeble talent, I have wished to convert my promise into accomplishment so as to promote theory, increase learning, furnish food for envy, agony for enmity, and nourishment for slander. . . . Hence let my mutual adversary Rufinus, the disgrace of men and the outcast of the masses, set a watch on his mouth and a door to attend his lips; and let him not by kindling his envy present us with impulsive abuse of my writing without any of reason's discernment; but let him sport in his concubine's quarters and embrace red-haired Thais[16] (*AV*, p. 17).

This much alone, gilt as it is with rhetorical flourishes and bristling as it is with references to Deuteronomy, Horace, Statius, and the Psalms, ushers the reader/student into the artificial – in the sense of artifice – world of written composition in the style taught and learned in the mediaeval schools.[17]

R. P. Parr outlines the nature of the *Ars Versificatoria* as follows:

> The making of verse in the twelfth and thirteenth centuries particularly, was a process of fitting the ideal into

proper form, and the form like the matter idealized became fixed. The aim was formal perfection through the techniques of language, and the work of the versifier was judged according to the perfection of that form. Because form fell within the conscious control of the writer, the craft of medieval verse could be taught and learned (*AV*, pp. 3–4).

Matthew defines what he means by verse at the very beginning:

> A verse is metrical language moving along succinctly and clause by clause in a graceful marriage of words and depicting thoughts with the flowers of rhetoric, containing in itself nothing played down, nothing idle. A collection of utterances, measured feet, the knowledge of quantities do not constitute a verse, but the elegant joining of utterances does, the expression of distinctive features and respect for the designation of each and every thing (*AV*, p. 17 [I §i]).

He outlines the use of a succession of the most popular rhetorical figures in the schools' rhetorical canon as a method of beginning a composition: *zeugma* in the beginning, middle or end of a clause (I §5, §11, §12); *hypozeuxis* (I §14); *metonomy* (I §15); opening with a proverb or a well-known statement (I §16). The faults attending these openings are addressed (I §30–33): involving, respectively, unevenness in use of language; tending to plainness; overblown ornament – quoting Horace's famous mountain giving birth to a mouse – and overcautious, insufficiently ornamented verse. Consistency of tense, and attention to the mixing of tenses, and to the ordering of the words is urged, avoiding the fault[18] of *cacosynthesis* (I §36; I §37).[19]

Under 'description' comes discussion of attributes, characteristics and appropriateness of epithet.[20] These are matters central to our consideration of the depiction of persons or characters addressed in bardic poetry, in the genres of praise/blame. The *Ars Versificatoria* stresses, throughout, the aggregation of characteristics; it emphasizes the notion of 'appropriateness' of epithet or characterization. One might, or might not, describe the character discussed. If one does, certain rules become relevant. This regulation of the manner in which a person is presented in the metrical composition achieves the object of the writer by keeping the written matter within the bounds of acceptable literary standards and maintaining the appropriate balance between reality and its formal representation in formal composition. The matter of genre is also satisfied in this way, so that material of an unclassifiable nature, referring to real or imagined individuals, is not randomly produced.

In I §38[21] Matthew addresses the question of whether the '. . . character being treated should be described or his description omitted. Frequently the description of character is appropriate, very often, superfluous.' He notes (I §41, p. 27) those characteristics which should form part of a description, if such is required: 'For one ought to note the characteristics of rank, age, occupation, of natural sex, natural location and other attributes called by Tullius the attributes of a person.' (The reference to Cicero is typical, and is followed by another to Horace.) The language of the composition and the treatment of the topic will be influenced by these particulars in respect of the individual involved: old or young man/woman; occupational differences; racial differences. Then only adjectives and verbs suitable to these characteristics will be chosen, leading to coherence. Mismatching in these particulars brings the composition into ridicule (*AV*, p. 28).

We might take particular note of the following: 'However, everyone should be designated by that epithet which is strongest in him and for which he is best known' (*AV*, p. 28). And, therefore, Achilles should always be 'indefatigable, full of wrath, inexorable, fierce. . . . Let him . . . claim all through force of arms' (*LAP*, §44, p. 120; *AV*, p. 28). This is a rule for all descriptions: 'Therefore, a description of a church shepherd [ecclesiastic] (*ecclesiastici pastoris*) is to be made in one way, of a general another; of a girl in another, or a matron, a concubine or a waiting-woman in other ways; that of a boy or young man in one way, of an elderly woman in another . . . Horace calls these tones of the works' (*LAP*, §46, p. 120; *AV*, p. 28).

This writers' manual clearly sets out the necessity to stereotype description, with the proviso that departure from it was allowable and recommended in certain circumstances. Rules for applying epithets, likewise, has a formulaic quality, and in spite of this, has subtlety:

> For example, in an ecclesiastical pastor, firmness of faith, longing for virtue, perfect religious zeal and the charm of fidelity ought to be enlarged upon; justice, indeed, should be played down lest, because of the sterness of his justice the church pastor appear to change into a tyrant (I §65). . . . On the other hand, the stern administration of justice should be ascribed with addition to a prince or an emperor, since weakness of justice is assigned with some detriment . . . (*LAP*, §§65, 66, p. 133; *AV*, p. 41).

Matthew of Vendôme, no less than any of his contemporaries, was fully aware of the artificial nature of the skills he taught. His task was to make sure that the techniques he inherited (by being taught by masters) were passed on faithfully and with the assurance that students had a grasp of what constituted the tradition. He is unabashed in teaching the aids to composition, and in explaining their object. One of the principal concerns was to create coherence in representation; not in the sense of factual record, but in the sense of likelihood and credibilty, within the strictures of genre:

> ... my advice will be that if anything is to be described, when articulating the description let the greatest support for credibility be presented: *that the truth be said or what is probable* ... (*LAP*, I §73, p. 135; *AV*, p. 43; emphasis added).

Exterior and interior descriptions of character, physical and emotional/spiritual, are also to be considered in the general description of the addressee, in praise or in blame.[22]

In the categorization appropriate to descriptions of the person, Matthew listed eleven attributes: name (*nomen*), nature (*natura*), style of life (*convictus*), fortune (*fortuna*), quality (*habitus*), diligence (*studium*), reaction (*affectio*), deliberation (*consilium*), chance events (*casus*), deeds (*facta*), speech (*orationes*) (*LAP*, I §78, p. 136; *AV*, p. 44). The composition can be built around these eleven elements – notably, a disquisition on the force of the person's name; on a physical attribute;[23] on a personal quality; on style of life, whether of luxury or penury, and so forth.[24]

Refinements of category proliferate; for example, expanding on deeds, their quality (I §105), their timing (I §106), and capability of doing (I §104), covers all the incidentals of any deed. For instance, the subcategory concerning the timing of deeds is illustrated thus: '... As in Virgil's *Bucolics*: Now everything is in bloom; now is the most beautiful time of the year (*Omnia nunc florent, nunc formosissimus annus*)' (III, 57), (*LAP*, I §106, p. 146; *AV*, p. 54). 'Place' likewise, can be subsumed under deeds, 'when because of fitness of place it is inferred that something had been done or not done' (*AV*, p. 55).

Section II (editorial) of Matthew of Vendôme concerns itself with the forms of words. The material is introduced by a dream sequence (II §2) in which the author dreams that Philosophy, accompanied by Tragedy, Satire, Comedy and Elegy come into a springtime garden. He defines 'the three-fold elegance of skill in versifying.[25] For there are three things which are detectable in verse; polished words [*verba polita*], ornamented expression [*dicendique color*] and inner charm [*interiorque favus*]' (*LAP*, §§8–9, p. 153; *AV*, p. 63).

To this end, the forms of verbs, adverbs, adjectives, and their appropriate position and use, is outlined with copious examples for immediate use:

> Further, there are many verbs in this and in other con-jugations; because their position is ordinary and can be assigned easily and also has been assigned in the above examples, the listener[26] may change their forms accord-ing to their similarity to the preceding examples with regard to the rest of the verbs, lest he tend to rely on the verses of others; for he swims away without an area of difficulty whose head is sustained by the support of someone else (*AV*, p. 77).

The third part of this treatise sets out the stock-in-trade of mediaeval rhetorical devices in figures, tropes and rhetorical colours.[27] Figures – the categorized forms of expression, usually in a quasi-artificial construction used for effect – are dealt with first; these are followed by tropes – oblique use of a word or a phrase, lending it additional meaning not necessarily conveyed by the word or phrase in its literal sense. The terms for the figures feature very prominently in the manuals of Matthew of Vendôme, in Geoffrey of Vinsauf's *Poetria Nova*, and in the *Parisiana Poetriae* of John of Garland. These lists are characteristically repetitive and frequently contradictory. Similarly, the use of Latinized and Graecized forms interchangeably, or exclusively (inconsistently), leads to confusion. Matthew favours the Greek terms, and in his list of some fifteen figures he illustrates the use of each one with examples from the classics or those of his own composition.[28] The figures have to do with syntax, alterations in the forms of words (metaplasm), collocations, metatheses and transpositions. The tropes – 'manner of speaking' (*modus locutionis*)' – numbering thirteen (even with subsets) in Matthew's work, are for our purposes, more important. It is in the *modus locutionis* that we find the greatest resources for our reading of bardic poetry. The tropes are classed as follows: metaphor (*metaphora*) (four kinds); antithetum (four kinds); metonymy (*methonomia*) (three kinds); synecdoche (*sidonoche*) (two kinds); periphrasis (*peryfrasis*); epithetum (three kinds); metalepsis (*methalemsis/clemax*); allegory (*allegoria*); obscurity/enigma (*aenigma*). Matthew merely lists the 'rhetorical colours', the common list of ornaments attending both figures and tropes, 'for certain figures and certain tropes seem to correspond to certain rhetorical colors'.[29]

In explanation of the division of his work into the three parts which we have summarized here, Matthew synopsizes the rationale behind it. The arrangement, while pedagogically driven, serves to remind us of what Matthew – an acknowledged and popular poet and master – sought to teach, and what lay behind the ornate structures of figures and tropes presented here:

> Prior to the idea is its conception, second is the invention of the words, and there is appended, naturally, the character of the subject matter or the arrangement of the treatment (*AV*, p. 92).

Matthew's fourth section concerns the treatment of material, '*de exsecutione materiae*'.[30] The matter dealt with here is divided into the treatment of material already dealt with by other writers/poets, adaptations of others' works used as excercise material in the schools (*in scolastico versificandi exercito*); and material new to the poet/student (*materia illibata*) (*LAP*, IV §16, p. 184; *AV*, p. 97). Matthew reminds the reader, again, that the act of composition involves giving suitably wrought written form to, for instance, the attributes of a person: 'the description ought to portray such a person as is preconceived by the essence of *an imaginary description or conjecture, so that what earlier stood in one's thought may later be brought forth with the assistance of expression*' (*AV*, p. 97; emphasis added). In the case of an action: 'one will have to use conjecture and proceed according to the common thinking of all and the authority of usage' (*AV*, pp. 97–98).

We note that proceeding according to fact or actuality does not enter into the discussion. The material produced according to the rubrics of the schools did not countenance the notion of unregulated, unadorned, or spontaneous 'realistic accounts' of people or of events.

As is customary in the *artes poetriae*, faults ('vices') in composition and organization are listed and illustrated, as well as the correct modes or 'virtues'. We are very familiar with this concept in the Irish material which illustrates *cóir/'.c.'* and *lochtach/'.l.'* – correct and faulty, respectively – though, in surviving documents, with reference to grammatical usage only and metrical faults. The vices of composition are listed and are similar to those noted in the manuals.[31] Matthew suggests that matters permitted to the ancient authors – and in this instance he means the classical authors – were now forbidden by modern styles: '*Vetera enim cessavere novis supervenientibus.*' Infelicities such as tautology, redundancies of various kinds (perissologia [*parysologia*], pleonasm [*pleonasmus*], macrology [*macrologya*]), are to be avoided, as are other faults involving inappropriate linking of verbs of contrary import, and of constructions involving ambiguity (acirologia and amphibologia).[32] The notion of 'fault' in this context is itself ambiguous, and is perhaps to be understood as more of a warning to inexperienced students rather than referring to errors in those stanzas used to illustrate them: 'Anyone who would wish to be familiar with descriptions of these [and other faults] should consult the *Barbarismus*. Indeed, the instance of the above-mentioned faults should be ascribed to poet's license, not to their ignorance (*licentiae poetarum imputanda est, non ignorantiae*)' (*LAP*, IV §12, pp. 182–183; *AV*, pp. 95–96).

Returning to an earlier point, Matthew's treatise continues with the treatment of tropes: periphrasis (*peryfrasis* [§21]); change of mode from active to passive voice (§22); the use of metaphor to supplement simple statements, making them more eleborate and figurative (§23), and also, *LAP*, IV §21, pp. 185; *AV*, IV §21 p. 98.

The use of clever/punning synonyms is encouraged, with an added caution that the writer/student note the influence of connotation (*consignificatione*) and denotation (*significatione cognita*) . . . '*ex quibus duobus perpenditur vocis officium*' (*LAP*, IV §25, p. 186; *AV*, IV §25, p. 99). The list of faults include superfluity, bareness, wandering, inartistic complication, confusion, display of lack of training, indecorum (§25). The 'remedy' for these faults is given too – a commonplace of the schools' teaching and a familiar concept to those trained in the Irish schools.[33] The faults in metrics and prosody of the student is discussed metaphorically as disease (§§32–36). The ultimate remedy is daily practice, 'Hence, because he who is not fit today will be less fit tomorrow, one must insist upon daily practice without any intervals lest the insolence of ignorance create harm, lest a little spark of sickness flare up into a conflagration' (*LAP*, IV §35, p. 188; *AV*, IV §35, p. 101).

Metrical 'vices' concern the faults created in Latin verse, and in this respect, are not relevant for our purposes here. The Irish bardic poets listed metrical 'faults' and their 'remedies' in a similar way, concerning Irish prosody, but the exigencies of the different languages means that the concept is more important here than the details. Matthew concludes his treatise with a discussion, appropriately, of conclusion (*conclusio*) itself (§§49–50). Part of his conclusion involves a synopsis of the treatise – and because it outlines what Matthew understood himself to have imparted, it bears quoting here:

> Because we have spoken about the two ways of beginning material, namely through zeugma and ypozeuxis, and about proceeding with a general sententia or proverb, and about maintaining the unity of measure, the manner of writing, the attributes of action and of persons, the tripartite refinement of versifying, about figures and tropes, the handling of the material, the exchange, and correction; a discussion of conclusion follows so that the present work may happily be concluded in its conclusion. Conclusion, as is understood here, is the termination according to the rules of meter and involving uniformity of the subject-matter (*LAP*, IV §49, p. 191; *AV*, IV §49, pp. 104–105).

Matthew accepts that variety abounds in the conclusions of the 'authors'[34] (§50), and can involve an epilogue, a statement of emendation, a plea for indulgence, an expression of pride (in the work), a 'termination' involving a sense of the death of the speaker, an expression of gratitude (to the muses). Likewise, the work can end with praise of God (§51), as in the case in Matthew's work. The versified homage to the Trinity, '*Christe, tibi sit honor . . .*', concludes his treatise, and as an example of one kind of conclusion, he apostrophizes his treatise with the hypochoristic 'summula', named for its contents (*nomen ex re sortitur*) and wishes it life (*vive, precor*), though spite may decry it (*nec formida livoris hiatum*). Matthew identifies himself at the very last line – '*Explicit emeritum Vindocinensis opus*' (*LAP*, IV §51, pp. 192–193; *AV*, IV §51, pp. 105–106).

Poetria Nova

Like Matthew of Vendôme, most of what can be ascertained about Geoffrey of Vinsauf comes from his writings. From these, it is understood that he spent some time in England and travelled from there to Rome. His treatise, *Poetria Nova* – the best known of all the mediaeval *artes poeticae* – was dedicated to Pope Innocent III (r. 1198–1216).[35] Tradition has it that he was born in Normandy[36] and received his education, first at Oxford, followed by a spell in Paris, and a subsequent period in Rome. Internal evidence in the *Poetria Nova* indicates a date for its composition between 1208 and 1213.[37] As its name suggests, the *Poetria Nova* purported to be a novel approach to metrical composition. As one might expect in the tradition of mediaeval scholarship, it was nothing of the kind. Rather it re-presented traditional material – familiar in the schools and familiar in the earlier classical schools – in a pedagogic collage. The immediate reference would probably be the *Art of Poetry* by Horace.[38] Among other sources were the usual list: *Rhetorica ad Herennium*, a pseudo-Ciceronian (?Cornificius) treatise from *c.* 85 BC;[39] Cicero's *De Inventione*;[40] and, in Geoffrey's case, the works of Sidonius Apollinaris, fifth-century bishop of Auvergne.[41] While the material presented by Geoffrey was not new and, as with all manuals of that kind, merely stabilized in writing a tradition already well established, the popularity of his work above all others of the kind in the Middle Ages argues a certain element of novelty in the work, or indeed that Geoffrey's work was a more intelligible compendium than those currently available. The principal focus of the work is:

> style and structure . . . [Geoffrey being] content merely to recommend and illustrate the classical catalogue of the *colores*, or figures of speech, already familiar to his age not only from ancient treatises of grammar and rhetoric but from various contemporary manuals of *ars grammatica* as well' (*TMRA*, p. 30).[42]

Geoffrey's *Poetria Nova* is prefaced by an ornate address to Pope Innocent III.[43] The work itself is introduced with a general outline of the art of poetry. E. Faral divides the work into five sections as follows: i concerning the art in general, definitions and divisions; ii concerning arrangement; iii concerning amplification and abbreviation; iv concerning ornamentation and style; v performance (*l'action*), epilogue (*LAP*, p. 194). Subsumed under these broader categories are the intricate divisions of material, mode, diction, and ornament that made up the arts of writing.

Section i, introduction, discusses form – beginning, middle and end; the five essentials of the art – invention and arrangement; amplification and abbreviation; the practice of style; the execution of the planned work; the delivery. These are expanded upon in section ii, natural and artificial modes of beginning; eight kinds of artificial beginning; examples of natural beginnings. Each category is illustrated by an example or by illustrative description. Amplification and abbreviation, the lengthening or shortening of a composition, is covered in section iii, and is copiously illustrated with examples of each of the rhetorical devices recommended. The examples are culled from the classical authors and are also of Geoffrey's own composition.[44]

The ornaments of style and the 'ten tropes' are covered in section iv. These are the commonplaces of mediaeval style and many of the devices and tropes contain subcategories of further refinements of the same tropes. The flexibility of all these lexical, semantic, grammatical and syntactical instruments is explored with some virtuosity by Geoffrey (cf. below, p. 42). The final, fifth, section outlines the preferred methods of performance (*l'action*) (*LAP*, p. 18) and an epilogue which serves as a conclusion. The epilogue introduces ambiguity in that it clearly addresses the Pope (Innocent III), but in this instance, on behalf of someone, 'For our prince I pray (*Pro principe nostro supplico*)', and the work is then offered to one William (*Quod papae scripsi munus speciale libelli / Accipe, flos regni. Primo potiaris honore / Hujus secreti . . . Wilhelme, vir auree . . .*) (*LAP*, p. 262, ll. 2096–2101).

While Geoffrey's treatise covered ground similar to Matthew of Vendôme's *Ars Versificatoria*, his method makes his work more pleasurable to read. The 2116 lines (*LAP*, pp. 197–262) of his pedagogic poem reveal to us aspects of the mediaeval world of ordered composition and controlled creativity. Unlike Matthew, Geoffrey approaches directly the concept of invention – the creation of a topic upon which to write. The choice of topics is circumscribed by various considerations, and the scope in treatment is similarly curtailed. Within these limits, however, the range is wide and diverting. Its relation to reality is a matter that has been, and always will be, a source of dispute.[45] The focus of Geoffrey's treatise on teaching students/poets how to order material into an acceptable and 'publishable' shape leads us in the direction in which Matthew pointed his students. This path[46] led from ambient reality and from living beings and actual situations to their re-imagining and re-ordering in a structured and predictable form, creating a literary reality that conformed to conventions and standards considered appropriate by those upon whose shoulders fell the welcome burden of *translatio studii*.[47]

At the same time, Geoffrey's work allows scope for the creation or the imagining of a purely literary representation of a typical event, such as a likely hypothetical scene, or series of events. For these reasons, the matter of Geoffrey's treatise will be useful to us in the present consideration of Irish bardic poetry because the *Poetria Nova* describes how a poet made use of materials in order to create his poem. It allows us to glimpse the mechanisms by which the poet used language so that that poem became an acceptable part of the literary world to which he belonged, or sought to belong. The treatises that we have emanating from the bardic schools[48] all deal with matters of language and syntax in Irish bardic poetry, with grammar and specifically with metrics, more in the style of Matthew of Vendôme's *Ars Versificatoria* – on how to make flawless verse. Referring to material on syntax, which he edited in *Bardic Syntactical Tracts*, L. McKenna noted:

> Their whole style and matter make it clear that they were intended as hand-books to be used by the professors in the Bardic schools for the instruction of their scholars in correct Bardic language and versification (*BST*, p. vii).

Geoffrey also includes instruction on what to write and how to make the matter fit the rubrics. With Irish bardic poetry, we are missing the link which connects the language, and metrical instruction, with the matter of the poem. Editors of Irish bardic poetry have frequently taken great pains distinguishing scribal

hands, identifying authors, filling in historical detail, and flesh-
ing out known backgrounds of poems. And yet, the truism that
dogs the enterprise – that the poem of the thirteenth century
can be interchangeable with that of the sixteenth – seems to
indicate that some other factor must be accounted for in our
reading of bardic poetry.

There is no question but that Irish bardic poets studied the
Irish language formally, as noted by B. Ó Cuív :

> . . . we may be sure that there was formal study of
> the Irish language on the part of the secular poets,
> and we may suppose that from an early period this
> included grammar and related subjects, such as
> metrics ('Linguistic Training', pp. 114–115).

However, adverting directly[49] to instructions concerning use of
language, metaphors, figures and so forth – matters covered by
the treatises/tracts on the *artes poeticae* referred to above – Ó
Cuív notes that, while instructions of that nature have not sur-
vived in the Irish manuscript sources, their existence must be
taken for granted:

> In this attempt at describing some of what the poet had
> to learn and how he learned it, I have said little about
> syntax and virtually nothing about vocabulary, with
> which we might associate such important matters as the
> metaphoric use of language and figures of speech, all of
> which must have been important in the curriculum of
> the schools. It is hardly necessary to add that we can be
> reasonably sure that as well as receiving instruction on
> the various rules and usages in grammar and metrics,
> the student got valuable guidance and practice in the
> actual composition of verse.[50] And here we can ima-
> gine that the reputation of the teacher[51] would weigh

with the student in his choice of a school ('Linguistic Training', pp. 138–139).

Ó Cuív found this 'brief comment' in a fifteenth-century manuscript among a miscellany of other items:

> *An arrmainti imorro innisidh na neche do fetfaidhe do denam gen go ndernadh iat . . .*
> (*Arrmainte,*[52] moreover, relates things which could be performed even though they were not performed . . .)

The article notes that, according to the extract dealt with, Irish *scél*[53] was equated with Latin *fabula*. In the same extract *stair* was defined as follows: '*Stair*, however, is the revelation of things which in truth were performed . . .'[54] Surviving fragments of this kind suggest that commentaries, in Irish, on literary theory (as distinct from grammar) enjoyed some circulation. The evidence of the poetry suggests a substantial engagement with the main tenets of theories such as those outlined above.

This invisible layer, this step in the process, which 'must have been important in the curriculum of the schools',[55] may be supplied or at least suggested by material from outside Ireland discussed here. The intention of this study is to add a consciousness of the mediaeval sense of material, modes and creativity to our appreciation of the formal praise-poetry of the Irish syllabic poets.

To that end, in the chapters that follow, where individual poems are analysed, specific reference will be made to the manuals noted above, and so the brief outline given here is necessary. In the same spirit, a sketchy synopsis of the third and final work that will be referred to in any detail here, John of Garland's *Parisiana Poetria*, will be given.[56]

PARISIANA POETRIA

Like the works (of Matthew of Vendôme and Geoffrey of Vinsauf) already referred to above, John of Garland drew heavily on the pseudo-Ciceronian *Rhetorica ad Herennium*, on Horace's *Ars poetica*. He also used Geoffrey of Vinsauf's *Poetria Nova* and his *Documentum de Modo et de Arte Dictandi et Versificandi*.[57]

John of Garland was an Englishman who taught grammar and literature at the University of Paris during the first half of the thirteenth century. He was born *c.* 1195 and studied at Oxford, under John of London, from around 1210–1213.[58]

John went to Paris probably around 1217. His surname, reputedly, came from the district in Paris, 'clos de Garlande', where he lived. In 1229 he became Master of Grammar at the new University of Toulouse and spent three years there.[59] He returned to Paris in 1231 where he spent the remainder of his days teaching and writing, though he seems to have made some trips to England.

He lived until at least 1258 and possibly until 1278. His *œuvre* includes a typical mix of long poems, grammatical and rhetorical works, moral works, a medical work, and four works each on computus and on music and several other works attributed to him or possibly by him.[60]

Garland's authorship of *Parisiana Poetria* has never been questioned, though the date has never been fully ascertained. T. Lawler concludes that the

> . . . work was originally composed about 1220, and revised, at least to the extent of the inclusion of the letter from Archbishop Mauritius, somewhere between 1231 and 1235. No firmer date can be established (*PP*, p. xv).

Parisiana Poetria is a substantial and ambitious work with a wide scope and a coherent plan.

> It is a summary for students of contemporary thinking
> on how to learn to write, not a new departure, though
> something of a new synthesis, in literary criticism (*PP*,
> p. xvii).

John of Garland's efforts[61] meant that his almost unwieldy treatise is in a sense emblematic of the effort of the schools to co-ordinate or collate three kinds of discipline which, during the course of the High Middle Ages, had attracted discrete forms of discourse.[62] Lawler acknowledges this: '[t]o unravel all the sources of this complicated work would be to write the whole history of rhetoric and literary criticism in the Middle Ages' (*PP*, p. xv; and pp. 264–267, n. 467). The *Parisiana Poetriae* regularly slips from concentration on the subject of matter to that of form and this leads to repetition and incoherence in the treatise itself and occasionally to self-contradiction.[63]

The work was undertaken in the tradition of the University of Paris (owing much to the influence of Bernard Silvester of Chartres),[64] and regardless of whether Chartres was, or was not, a great independent school, John's work emerged from the rich tradition of the contemporary French schools.[65]

As with the works of Matthew of Vendôme and of Geoffrey of Vinsauf, John re-assembled and re-presented, he did not break new ground or re-conceptualize:

> The work offers few individual precepts that are new.
> Its originality lies rather in its totality: it is the only
> thorough attempt we have to gather three distinct
> areas of the medieval arts of discourse (*ars poetica*, *ars
> rhythmica*, and *ars dictaminis*) under a single series of
> rules. The fact is that John often fails at this attempt;
> his general rules seldom apply to more than one
> form, and most of the time he is obliged to discuss
> each form separately. Still his concept is valid, even

though he neglects to make some important general distinctions, to point out which aspects of the three forms are common, and which is peculiar to each (*PP*, p. xvi).

The *Parisiana Poetria* is more comprehensive in its scope than either Matthew of Vendôme's or Geoffrey of Vinsauf's treatises in that it takes account of all the contemporary preceptive written forms. The treatise is written in prose, illustrated generously with examples from the classics and from material of John's composition. John of Garland is quite clear about the intended scope of his work:

> Five[66] things about this short work should be examined at the start: the subject matter, the author's purpose, its usefulness for its audience, what field of knowledge it belongs to, the method. The subject matter is the art of writing letters, of quantitative verse, and of rhymed syllabic verse; but behind these three lie five others, which are: the art of invention (*ars inueniendi*), of selection ([*ars*] *eligendi*), of memory ([*ars*] *memorandi*), of arrangement ([*ars*] *ordinandi*), and of embellishment (*ars ornandi*) (*PP*, Introduction, ll. 5–6).

The book belongs to three fields of knowledge – grammar, rhetoric and ethics (*PP*, Introduction, ll. 8–10):

> The author's purpose is to publish a manual of style. Its usefulness is that it imparts a technique for treating any subject whatever in prose, quantitative verse, or rhymed syllabic verse. . . . This is the approach: the author teaches how to invent, according to the categories of invention, words, that is substantives, adjectives, and verbs used both literally and

metaphorically, in any kind of composition, whether it be a legal (*littere curiales*), or academic letter ([*littere*] *scolastice*), or an elegiac poem (*carmen elegiacum*), or a comedy (*comedia*), or a tragedy (*tragedia*), or a satire (*satyra*), or a history (*hystoria*) (*PP*, Introduction, ll. 6–7, 11–16).[67]

John, like Geoffrey of Vinsauf, is very clear about the meaning of invention:

> To invent is to come into knowledge of an unknown thing through the agency of one's own reason. Here is what Cicero says in the *Second Rhetoric*: 'Invention is thinking up things that are true or at least realistic to make your case plausible' (*PP*, I, ll. 84–85).

The matter of invention is divided into five 'species': where (*ubi*), what (*quid*), what kind (*quale*), how (*qualiter*), and why (*ad quid*).[68] The 'where' of this quinary categorization involves knowing *where* to find the sources of the invention required, and these are three: character, examples and etymologies of words related to the subject. So that if a petitioning letter is required, the invention can be that of a sick man, and the matter expanded upon through the characterizing of the sick man (the predicament of the petitioner, in this case, as most frequent, seeking appointment). The *what* pertains to the matter of the composition – war, friendship, petition and so forth. And where persons are involved in these inventions a binary system is common (or a system of contraries): a king is a good ruler or a tyrant; an ecclesiastic is an exemplary spiritual guide or a secularized scandal-giver; a merchant is a prudent businessman or a spendthrift (*PP*, I, ll. 140–146). For all of these categories, proverbs exist or can be invented to suit the *where*, and the *what* of invention. John provides very useful lists of proverbs and sample approaches for the writer seeking a suitable opening or tone for a wide variety of compositions – for instance, in the matter of students, a composition concerning students can be based on a proverb such as: 'He who desires glory and delights in many friends should fortify himself with the rules of art and the teachings of prudent men (*Qvi gloriam et amicorum delectabilem copiam desiderat, artis regulis et ratione prudencium muniatur)*' (*PP,* I, ll. 202–203). In the matter of a man who promises much and delivers little: 'Infamy is piled onto opprobrium for the man who is found to be magnificent in words and puny in deeds (*Crebrescit in eius oprobrium infamia qui magnificus in uerbis, in factis pusillanimis reperitur)*' (*PP*, I, ll. 265–267).

The *what kind* involves both honourable matter and disreputable matter. A language appropriate for both kinds must be selected – for 'honest matter', exposure in plain language; dishonest or disreputable matter called for cloaked language (*PP,* I, ll. 319–321). And the 'to what end' (*ad quid*) is always thought to be for the promotion of the right and the good, though the subject be neither of those things – 'even though he [author] intends to accuse or condemn, the purpose is still good in itself' (*PP,* I, ll. 327–330). *How* the writer achieves his literary goal involves the use of seven kinds of rhetorical figures – paronomasia (*annominatio*), transplacement (*traductio*), repetition (*repeticio*), climax (*gradatio*), synonymy (*interpretatio*), definition (*diffinicio*), and dialogue (*sermocinatio*) (*PP,* I, ll. 331–334).[69]

Under the subheading of 'the art of inventing nouns', John of Garland recommends that the nouns associated with the topic chosen for a composition be listed and included in that composition. This is what he means by '*de arte inueniendi nomina sustantiua*' (*PP,* I, ll. 381ff.), and he uses the example of the subject being a shepherd, giving a list revolving around that noun

– 'pasture, flock, sheep, ram, wolf' and so forth. If the shepherd is used metaphorically, the flexibility of the list becomes evident. Invention of adjectives is similarly categorized and is very usefully illustrated by John of Garland:

> (*De arte inueniendi adiectiua*) The next subject is the inventing of adjectives: the rule for them is different from that for nouns. Invent adjectives from the following categories: effect, outcome, dress, place, family, size, and quality. (This last is twofold: exterior and interior quality.) From effect, as 'a death-dealing spear,' 'a withering whip.' From outcome, as 'mutilated,' 'maimed,' 'clubfooted,' 'blind,' and the like. From outer dress, as 'a helmeted soldier,' 'a spear-carrying infantryman,' 'a hooded monk.' From place, as a 'Scottish hero,' 'Italian rage,' 'Italian war.' From family, as 'the Pelean virgin,' 'the Priamian hero.' From size, as 'a gigantic man,' 'a dwarf girl.' From exterior quality, as 'pale,' 'sallow,' 'black,' 'white.' From interior quality, as 'fierce,' 'benign,' 'wrathful,' 'magnanimous,' 'wanton' (*PP,* I, ll. 457–469).

John's treatise goes on to deal with the metaphorical use of verbs, transferring, for instance, those verbs appropriate in reference to the mind, metaphorically to the body, and vice versa (*PP,* I, ll. 28–29). The enduring preoccupation in all three treatises we consider here is that with lengthening and varying a composition. To that end, the treatises teach circumlocution and variety based on the change of tense in a verb and case in a noun. Examples used to illustrate these technical tricks show us clearly how some of the more – to current taste – tiresome characteristics of schools' poetry were not only taught and learned, but also, ingenuity in their application was prized. Tortuous circumlocutions and weird constructions in the passive voice,

for instance, are often displays of virtuosity in the application of
the rules of composition within the rubrics of the arts manu-
als. And so, under the category 'A way to avoid a trite and
banal mode of speech' (*argumentum vitandi usitatum loquendi
modum*), John urges:

> Again, if a phrase is overused, a verb may be turned
> into a noun, as: 'I sit' (*ego sedeo*); 'This seat receives
> me' (*me capit hec sedes*); 'Sitting, pleasing to my limbs,
> refreshes me' (*me reficit membris cessio grata meis*) (*PP*,
> I, ll. 502–504).

Similarly, one thing may be said in six ways according to the
six cases of the noun (*quod . . . materia vi modis potest dici,
secundum vi casus nominis*) (*PP*, I, ll. 505–506).

The Irish approach to the use of inflection to enlarge the
scope for variation in composition is noted by B. Ó Cuív in
his calculation in respect of the verbal systems recommended
in Irish bardic grammars:

> Taking the verbs *do-chím, a-deirim, téighim* and *do-
> ním,* we find that by drawing on both synthetic and
> analytic forms he [the poet] had a choice of seven ways
> of saying 'I shall see', twelve ways of saying 'I said'
> and 'I went', thirteen ways of saying 'I did' ('Linguistic
> Training', pp. 138–139).

John devotes chapter 2 to the idea of selection of material
and its embellishment, which in this treatise seems to be
identical with 'invention' of material and its variation.[70]
The illustrations are all those of *dictamen* or the letter style,
though the principles being taught concern all the written arts
and are directed at 'poets and writers of dictamen' (. . . *sed
poetice scribentibus et dictandibus post inuencionem utilis est ars
elegendi*)' (*PP*, II, ll. 1–5). Chapter 3 discusses the methods

of beginning – like Geoffrey of Vinsauf – involving eight varieties,[71] while chapter 4[72] seems to concentrate on the beginnings appropriate to letters (*dictamen*).[73] John's letter style included in succession 'Salutation, Supersalutation, Exordium, Narration, Request, Conclusion'.[74]

Chapter 5 of John of Garland's *Parisiana Poetria* – '*de uiciis in metro specialibus*' – deals with faults in matters of style, in the sense of 'high', 'middle' and 'low'. Propriety in matching style with subject and content is an important part of John's treatise. The sense of propriety and appropriateness governs the depiction of characters, activities and things, as well as nouns chosen for the composition. Reference to matters, people or activities outside the rubrics of the 'style' have to be couched in terms that raise or lower the register suitable to the basic style: '. . . if you must put a "high" detail in a low poem, put it in low terms, and vice versa' (*PP*, p. 251, nn. 51–60).

Virgil is the chosen example for John's illustration of the styles. In chapter 2, the manuscript copies of *Parisiana Poetria* have two diagrams, one a diagram of the *area disponere*, that secluded spot to which the poet/student retreats to gather his mind.[75] It is a tricolumnar construct, to be imagined as separated into three main sections and columns. The first section or column is subdivided into three parts[76] – the first for the distinctions of style; the second for the matter taught and learned, from teachers or books; the third column for categories for language and register:

> This vacant spot is to be imagined as separated into three main sections and columns. The first section or column is subdivided into three parts, for courtiers (*curiales*), city dwellers (*ciuiles*), and peasants (*rurales*), with their arms and their respective implements, their concerns and their duties . . . The second part or column should be imagined as containing, in separate

compartments, examples and sayings and facts from
the authors, and the teachers from whom we hear
them, and the books in which we have read them. . . .
In the third column let us imagine to be written all
kinds of languages, sounds, and voices of the various
living creatures, etymologies, explanations of words,
distinctions between words, all in alphabetical order;
and with a ready mind let each consider what word
fits his own language. But since we do not know
every language, nor have heard every word, we resort
to those which we have heard; and when the teacher
makes a philological or etymological explanation of
any word, let us gather it into that third column, along
with some natural phenomenon that may symbolize
the word in question; and by means of its symbol we
shall be able to memorize it and later select it for our
own use (*PP,* II, ll. 92–115).

The treatise also has a diagram of 'Virgil's wheel' (*rota
Virgilii*), which

> . . . also contains an arrangement of three columns;
> here the three styles are arranged inside a circle along a
> series of concentric circumferences. The first column
> contains comparisons, similitudes and names of things
> appropriate to the low style (*comparationes,* . . . *simil-
> itudines . . . nomina rerum ad humilem stilum* . . .); the
> second to the middle (*ad mediocrem*); the third to the
> high (*ad grauem*). To express in one style a sentiment
> which is only to be found in the next is clearly a depar-
> ture from the proper style; we should select for any
> given style only words invented in that style (*PP,* II,
> ll. 116–123).

The high style in this very simple diagrammatic present-
ation contains a soldier (*miles*), a governor (*dominans*),
persons/characters such as Hector, Ajax; animals suitable for
use in that style, such as a horse (*equus*), and instruments
pertaining to the high style such as a sword (*gladius*). It
is seemly in this scheme to mention city (*urbs*) and camp
(*castrum*); suitable natural objects are likewise categorized so
that the trees laurel (*laurus*) and cedar (*cedrus*) are allowable
in this style. The middle style refers to matters such as
the farmer (*agricola*); personifications like Triptolemus and
Ceres (*Tritolomus, Ceres*), animals such as the cow (*bos*),
the appropriate instruments/implements might include the
plough (*aratrum*), and the place might be a field (*ager*). The
appropriate trees here include the apple-tree (*pomus*) and the
pear-tree (*pirus*). For the low style, the leisurely shepherd is
chosen, with all his characterizations and accoutrements –
the sheep (*ouis*); the implement might be the shepherd's staff
(*baculus*); the place would be the pasture (*pascua*); and the tree
the beech (*fagus*).[77] The three kinds of style were outlined in
the pseudo-Ciceronian *Ad Herennium IV*. The author makes it
clear that the 'types' (*genera*) (*AdHer*, p. 253) involved the use
of words of different register, or diction, and would involve
topics appropriately assigned to those.

In chapter 5, John offers outline definitions of the various
categories of writing, none of which is original, nor entirely
exclusive of several differing interpretations. He deals with
'*dictamen*', 'kinds of narration' (*de speciebus narrationum*),
'fable' (*de fabulo*), 'history' (*de hystoria*), 'realistic fiction' (*de
argumento: argumentum est res ficta que tamen fieri potuit*);[78]
subdivisions (of historical narrative) including epithalamium
(*epytalamicum*), epicedium (*epichedion*), georgic, bucolic, lyric,
invective (*inuectiuum*), reprimand (*reprehensio*), satire (*satyra*)
(*PP*, V, ll. 303–372). 'Historical', according to this schema,

also included fictions that were naturalistic, as opposed to our sense of fabulous. The concepts of 'could have happened' and 'happened' are very close in the treatises on composition. The *fieri potuit* could cover the historicity required by the historical genre, especially if it also included naturalistic treatment.

In chapter 5, also, the vices of composition are outlined. Predictably, these are illustrated by examples. Each style (high, middle and low) carries with it faults peculiar to itself. And so, the high style is prey to inflation and bombast (*turgidem et inflatum*); the middle style is prone to 'fluctuation of words or diction' (*fluctuans ex parte uerbi uel uocis*) and to 'looseness of ideas' (*dissolutum ex parte sentenciarum*). 'Aridity' and 'bloodlessness' attach themselves to the low style: 'aridity refers to ideas that are not juicy and tasty; bloodlessness refers to words whose surface is not purpled' (*arridum quantum ad sentencias que non sunt succose et sapide, exsangue quantum ad uoces quarum superficies non est purpurata*) (*PP,* V, ll. 61–62; ll. 66–67, ll. 80–83).

The elevation of any subject into the high style can be achieved by using language appropriate to the high style, and this usually involves militarization of the subject:

> High matter can be lowered (*potest grauis materia humiliari*), in imitation of Virgil, who calls Caesar – or himself – Tityrus and Rome a beech; and low matter can be exalted (*potest et humilis materia exaltari*), as when in a treatment of a high subject women's distaffs are called 'the spears of peace' (*inbelles haste*) (*PP,* V, ll. 51–54).

Chapter 7 presents examples suitable to various styles and genres. An example of a tragedy, written in the high style (*graui stilo describitur*) is given.[79]

John uses a version of a well-known tale about washerwomen in a soldiers' barracks to illustrate the 'high' style in a tragedy. What concerns us here, is that the low matter of washerwomen and the comi-tragic events of the story itself are all elevated by diction into the high style. This is achieved principally by militarizing the language and the story. Lawler's comment explains the mechanism:

> If it seems curious that the story of two washerwomen can exemplify the high style, it should be noted in the first place that, though the chief characters are washerwomen, a military action is the scene, and soldiers appear . . . (*PP,* p. 263, n. 24).

The schematization of composition at this level makes it very clear indeed that the enterprise of composition was not left to chance or to nature, but carefully managed, controlled and categorized. Our sense of Irish bardic poetry fits very well into this greater context of composition and its rules, of memory and its mnemonics, of language and its organization.

3. 'Beir eolas dúinn . . .'

The poet Gofraidh Fionn Ó Dálaigh (d. 1387) was a member of a Cork branch of the famous Uí Dhálaigh family of poets. It is to be understood from a poem by Maolmhuire Mac Craith that he was educated at a school kept by the Mac Craith family.[1] Compositions attributed to him, mostly from the second half of the fourteenth century, are to members, variously, of the Mac Carthaighs (different branches), FitzGeralds of Desmond, members of the Ó Briain, Ó Madagáin, Ó Conchobhair and Ó Ceallaigh families, not including quatrains in poems to these, possibly principal patrons, dedicated to others such as Ó Súilleabháin, Ó Donnchadha, Ó Caoimh.[2] Elegies and religious compositions are numbered among the works attributed to this poet, conventionally one of the most highly regarded by other Irish poets.[3]

The intention here is to show how a poem by Gofraidh Fionn Ó Dálaigh, '*Beir eolas dúinn, a Dhomhnuill,*'[4] can be read as example of the Irish contribution to and participation in the wider world of European schools' compositions.[5] It involves, briefly, an invitation by the poet to Domhnall Mac Carthaigh, future king, *rí-dhamhna,* of Desmond (heir apparent to his father Cormac), to return at the head of his people to the original seat of his ancestral power-base, Cashel.[6] Domhnall Mac Carthaigh is to exchange the wild lands of his present patrimony ('the western third of the present county [Cork]'[7] along with the adjoining south western portion of modern Co. Kerry) in south-west Munster, for the pleasant rich lands of his mythological ancestors, and of which Cashel is the centre. This journey is compared to that taken by Moses leading his people from the tyranny of the Egyptians to the Promised Land.

Mac Carthaigh is a beautiful, fair-skinned, grey/blue-eyed, dark-haired man, generous with his wealth and humane in his dealings. This Domhnall (d. 1392) was the son of Cormac son of Domhnall Rua son of Cormac Fionn son of Domhnall Mór son of Diarmuid of Cill Báidhne son of Cormac of Magh Tamhnach son of Muireadhach son of Carthach. He was, therefore, eighth in direct line from the Carthach from whom the family took what became its surname.[8] The progress in power and stability of this family of Mac Carthaigh coincided with the expansion and consolidation of the Desmond family which achieved suzerainty of the liberty of Desmond under Maurice first earl of Desmond in 1329.

Domhnall, king of Desmond, 'continued his father's policy of seeking favours from the administration; in 1365 as "captain of the Irish of Desmond" he obtained from the lord lieutenant, the Duke of Clarence, confirmation of a formal entail which he had made of the lands – an extraordinary adoption of English legal practice by an Irish "king"'.[9] However 'extraordinary' this very practical and useful stratagem was for an 'Irish king', it served the Mac Carthaigh family well – after Domhnall's death in 1392 the succession of the Mac Carthaigh Mór passed from father to son for four generations until the death of Domhnall (mac Taidhg) in 1508.

Conditions were not ideal in the fourteenth century for Domhnall Mac Carthaigh's return to Cashel, leading seventeen companies of his followers. Cashel, a regional ecclesiastical capital, was also well inside the boundaries of what the Butler family, under Thomas, would consider its territory. He, the latter, would have been supported, in this sense of his hegemony, by the Crown authorities and by surrounding lords who might not have welcomed any further extension of the already substantial Mac Carthaigh claims throughout south and west Munster.

Cashel was granted to the Church by Muircheartach Ó Briain in 1101.[10] It was originally the seat of the Eoghanacht kings of Munster and was known variously in literature as 'Caiseal Mumhan', 'Caiseal Coirc', etc.[11] Notably, a market-place occupied a site in the town in the twelfth century, reference to which is found in an entry under 1134 in the Annals of Tigernach. The entry notes unusually large hailstones, which, when they melted, caused horses to resort to swimming in the market-place.[12] The mediaeval town covered roughly twenty-eight acres south of the outstanding feature associated with it, the ecclesiastical buildings on the Rock of Cashel. It incorporated several of the features needed to qualify as a 'mediaeval town', including, at least, town walls, a cathedral, established houses of religious orders, a hospital (and possibly a leperhouse) and suburbs.[13] The town wall, punctuated by at least five gates, was maintained with the help of murage grants at least during 1303–1307 and 1319–1324. In 1228 the town was granted an annual fair; and the constableship of Cashel castle was maintained – from 1348 to 1355, for instance, by one Adam White (Whyt, Whyte, Wyte) who was paid fees as constable of the castle and for his expenses, variously £3 6s. 8d., £5, £6 13s. 4d., £13 6s. 8d.[14] Among the ecclesiastical centres in and about Cashel were a Dominican friary, established by the archbishop in 1243, a Franciscan friary *c.* 1265, Hore Abbey Cistercian house founded by the archbishop in 1272, replacing an earlier Benedictine establishment. The Hospital of St Nicholas (est. 1224–1237) became amalgamated with Hore Abbey. The archbishop of Cashel founded the town, and the archbishopric defended the rights associated with this throughout 1218 to 1228 when the justiciar of Ireland took the town from the Church. It was given back to Maurianus O'Brien in 1228.[15]

Cashel was a key archbishopric in the mediaeval Church and a vital mediaeval administrative centre for the earl of Ormond.

Cashel's identity in the fourteenth century was built on the significant role of Cashel in the Irish pre-Norman Church, which was given the historic site by the king of Munster. Altogether, Cashel in the fourteenth century was a vigorous participant in the well-ordered Butler lordship (liberty of Tipperary 1329) under the direct control of the earl of Ormond.[16]

The 'official' situation (in south Munster) at the beginning of the fourteenth century is synopsized by K. W. Nicholls:

> . . . if we turn back to the year 1300 we find that, while the western third of the present county [Cork] was left to the rule of various MacCarthy princes and their clients, the remainder was under the control of an efficient county administration, conforming to the normal practice of England itself and responsible to the administration in Dublin and in the last resort to the king of England himself, even if the social and political realities, not only the incessant frontier pressure from the increasingly aggressive Gaelic Irish, but, more seriously, the multiplication of the lordly lineages and the social instablility to which they gave rise, were increasingly transforming it into an empty shell. And this administration was a royal one, depending on the king's officials and not on local lords. While the latter enjoyed massive resources in land and retainers, and in the ever-multiplying members of their lineages, their political and judicial authority was, in strict legal theory, minimal if not non-existent (K. W. Nicholls, 'The Development of Lordship in County Cork, 1300–1600', pp. 158–159).

Nicholls likewise points out that 'in general we know little or nothing of the internal arrangements in the Gaelic regions'.[17]

These regions are those over which Domhnall of our poem presided. The poem addressed to him here adds nothing to our knowledge of the 'internal arrangements' in the immediately obvious sense. In another context, however, it provides evidence of a rich and confident contemporary literary culture, expressive of a vital and open education system which throve on secure patronage.

CONTEMPORARIES

The contemporary history of the Mac Carthaigh lords, their overlords and their dependants is well documented, and so is the history of their contemporary Anglo-Norman (fifth-generation) neighbours, the earls of Desmond. Nothing in the political behaviour of Cormac Mac Carthaigh, king of Desmond until 1359, nor in that of his son, Domhnall of the poem, indicates that either of them might have entertained realistic expectations of marching on Cashel to reclaim their Eoghanacht ancestral territory. At the same time, no Irish lord, in any part of Ireland, nor indeed, no Scottish Gaelic lord was confined to realistic political goals or aspirations in the bardic poems that praised them.

The bardic poem generally transcends the immediate political circumstances. The context is normally that of the bardic polity, the conceptual world of poet and patron, which was predicated on a literary continuum and sustained by a nuanced and flexible knowledge and presentation of a written and known historical and pseudo-historical narrative. There is no deception or misinformation in Ó Dálaigh's poem. Nor is Domhnall Mac Carthaigh misrepresented to us.

The same poet, Gofraidh Fionn Ó Dálaigh, composed poems for Domhnall's immediate contemporary, the Anglo-Norman third earl of Desmond, the legendary Gearóid Iarla (d. 1399).[18] It was to this interesting historical character that the poem – which is subsequently often cited as the paramount example of bardic cynicism or self-interest – '*A Ghearóid déana mo dháil*' was written.[19] The poem, written to the future third earl of Desmond, purports to be an approach through a minor (Gearóid) to his father, Maurice, the first earl of Desmond (d. 1356). The conceit is that of the estrangement of poet and patron, a genre that will be looked at later below. For the purposes of this discussion, it is interesting to note that the first earl of Desmond, and, subsequently, the third, maintained a series of fortified houses or castles along the Maigue river, and that a principal seat of the third earl was at Lough Gur.[20]

Essentially, two patrons of the poet Gofraidh Fionn Ó Dálaigh were neighbours whose local wars and local and distant military alliances put themselves and their followers and families in competition with each other. Marriage alliances, in a similar spirit, joined and divided families and loyalties (Gearóid Iarla's daughter married Domhnall Óg's son Tadhg Mainistreach [d. 1428]). West and north central Munster were the immediate settings for their exploits. Superimposed upon the vicissitudes of the day was the complex of competing networks, cultural, political and social, created by the Anglo-Norman origins of the one and the Gaelic origins of the other. The considerable international connections of both through feudal links with superior lords, magnates in Wales, England, Normandy, Anjou, Outremer and so forth, and with the elaborate structures of the mediaeval Church[21] linking the remotest territories of Christendom with Rome and with Avignon, created a shared culture of considerable vitality and strength.[22]

The historian Norman Davies summarized international ties, which the expansion of the Normans into England,

Wales, Scotland and Ireland created or strengthened in each country respectively:

> England, though geographically distant from the Latin states of Outremer, was in no sense distant from its political, social, and cultural affairs. For the Anglo-Norman ruling class, which had annexed England after 1066 and which was now advancing rapidly into the other kingdoms of the Isles, was an offshoot of that wider French-dominated feudal community of which Outremer was the furthest limb. England's French elite not only shared that inimitable concoction of feudalism and militant Catholicism which constituted the ethos of the 'Age of Crusade', they were also intimately related to the leading personalities among the crusaders. They were kith and kin of Outremer's own elite. . . . But the feudal nobles, whose lifeblood ran through this maze of kinship, would have known it all by heart (N. Davies, *The Isles: A History* (London, 2000), pp. 267–268).

Ireland's élites were likewise enmeshed in this robust network, and the political protagonists exploited the connections to advance themselves in any way they thought feasible. None of the Irish kings was excluded from the benefits and debits of the Norman cultural and physical expansion from the eleventh century until the end of the Crusades.[23] Indeed, Irish poets were connected with Plantagenet lords and their satellites through their own patrons, through the vicissitudes of political links and in the incidental brushes with authorities, ecclesiastical and secular, which attended all kinds of travel. The Plantagenet connections linked Irish poets, culturally, with other poets who wrote in the vernacular for their overlords – the troubadours who followed their patrons in their ever-changing allegiances in twelfth- and thirteenth-century Aquitaine.

Three quatrains of Gofraidh Fionn's poem for the young Gearóid[24] have been quoted time and again to illustrate a political point every time the work of Ó Dálaigh has been discussed, and every time the politics of the bardic poet has been addressed. It is appropriate to quote them again here, and to note in them a certain kind of admission that is to be kept in mind:

> *Flaitheas nach gabhaid Gaoidhil*
> *geallmaoid dóibh i nduanlaoidhibh;*
> *a ráthughadh dhúibh níor dhluigh,*
> *gnáthughadh dhúinn a dhéanaimh.*
>
> *Dá chineadh[25] dá gcumthar dán*
> *i gcrích Éireann na n-uarán*
> *na Gaoidhil-se ag boing re bladh*
> *is Goill bhraoininse Breatan.*
>
> *I ndán na nGall gealltar linn*
> *Gaoidhil d'ionnarba a hÉirinn;*
> *Goill do shraoineadh tar sál sair*
> *i ndán na nGaoidheal gealltair.*
> (*DD*, pp. 201–206, qq. 44–46)

[In lyric quatrains we promise to the Irish a sovereignty which they do not possess; you ought not heed them, it is our custom to do so.

In Ireland of the wells, there are two races for whom poetry is composed – these glory-seeking Gael and the Gall of the dewy isle of Britain.

In poetry for the Gall we promise the banishment of the Gael from Ireland; to hurl the Gall eastward across the sea is what is promised in poetry for the Gael.]

This is not a large admission by Gofraidh Fionn; it is, in the greater context of the poem in which it occurs, part of his appeal to the young Gearóid to intercede with his father on the poet's behalf. It suffices here to note that the poet who urges Domhnall Mac Carthaigh to retake Cashel on behalf of the Eoghanacht ('*Beir eolas dúinn, a Dhomnuill*') is the poet who seems to make explicit, in the quatrains above, the nature of such exhortations. In the analysis which will be urged here, the characterization of the poet as self-server or cynic is not recognized. The poet as ruler of the realm of poetry is emphasized. The territories comprising this literary commonwealth, the lords, kings, enemies and challenges entertained in the domain of the poem are seen as the building materials of a composition — such as that for Domhnall — which can extend for some seventy-three quatrains. There is no difficulty here in identifying the rubrics laid down by the teachers of grammar and poetry in the mediaeval treatises. They will be briefly considered here.

THEMES

There are at least three themes in (seventy-three quatrains in L. McKenna's edition) '*Beir eolas dúinn, a Dhomhnuill*', by Gofraidh Fionn Ó Dálaigh for Domhnall Mac Carthaigh. The theme introduced in the opening quatrain is that Domhnall Mac Carthaigh is urged to teach his people the paths through Banba (Ireland). This theme is carried on in a conceit from the historical mythology of the family from which the Mac Carthaigh originated — the theme of the discovery of Cashel and the journey made by the ancestor Conall Corc; Domhnall is to lead his people *home* to Cashel (q. 8).[26] A subtheme appended to this involves the comparison of territories, the rugged land of coastal south-west Munster being compared, unfavourably here, with the fat lands surrounding Cashel (qq. 12, 13, 14). Domhnall is to take his commanders and his vassal lords (*do thúisigh uile is t'uirrígh*) and seventeen *taoisigh* each commanding a hundred men (qq. 16, 17) across the country in a north-easterly direction towards Cashel, and to vanquish the 'foreigners' in their way.[27] Ceallachán of the saga, for instance, spent a year and a half travelling and searching through Munster learning about it: '. . . *do bhi bliadhain co leith ag iaraidh na Muman idir choill & chnoc & caeim-ghlenn. Idir linn & loch & lan-abhuinn idir chuan & chaemh-thraigh & caladphort. idir lis & laech-dhun & lethan-tuaith . . . innus gu m-beith eolus a h-iath & a h-es & a h-ur-choilltedh aigi . . .*' (*CCC*, §4). This is like the journey undertaken by Domhnall. And he is urged by the poet to share that '*eolas*' to lead his people back to Cashel. The number seventeen here is picked up later in quatrain fifty-seven when these companies are to be set over seventeen appropriate *tuaithe* or lordships around Cashel.[28]

A second theme is contained in the apologue, the story which provides an allegorical exemplar for the poem. It is the tale of the biblical character Moses, suitably surnamed with a Gaelicized patronymic (Maoise mac Amhra, qq. 24–33), leading the Hebrews out of exile and captivity in Egypt.[29] The identification of Domhnall mac Cormaic (Mac Carthaigh) with Maoise mac Amhra is explicit in quatrains thirty-four and thirty-five: the Hebrews had Moses to rescue them, the Eoghanacht have Domhnall – Domhnall is Moses.

A third theme is the journey itself, that taken by Domhnall leading his people from near modern Waterville (from Íochtar Cua) in south-west Kerry to Cashel in Tipperary (q. 40). The trip is made in twenty quatrains.

The poet then praises the physical perfection of Domhnall, his generosity, his hospitality and his humanity (qq. 62–65). Some half-a-dozen further quatrains praise other local dignitaries, contemporaries of Domhnall, both men and women. The poem ends with an appeal to Michael the Archangel to lead the poet to heaven.[30] This envoy is a personal note of the poet, and similar appeals are appended to several other works attributed to him.

This is the skeletal outline of the enchanting poem composed for Domhnall Mac Carthaigh, possibly before he became king of Desmond – that is, before 1359, when his father, Cormac, died.

'INVENTIO'

It is useful to begin, where the mediaeval teachers of poetry began, with the concept of *inventio*, the discovery of an idea or subject to write about. In the tradition of panegyric (or any of the epideictic arts)[31] the subject could always be found in the person and exploits of the lord. Invention involved deliberation on a subject, not the conjuring of a topic from nowhere, nor, necessarily, the contemplation of contemporary fact. Crucially, '*inventio* can often assume the existence of a textual legacy, an inherited tradition of written authority which will provide a topical reserve'.[32] The bardic poet, literate at least in Irish and more than likely in Latin – the latter, the universal written language of Christendom – had two substantial sources for the creation of his own contribution to the living written tradition.

An elegant collection of rhetorical utterances, linked together by the judicial marriage of theme and language, topic and expression, is the goal of the writer that Matthew of Vendôme sought to teach (*AV*, §1, p. 17). Each of the quatrains in most bardic poems is complete of itself and can be said to constitute a rhetorical poetic utterence.

Matthew of Vendôme urges that the conception of the subject precede any attempt to write:

> Prior to the idea is its conception, second is the invention of the words, and there is appended, naturally, the

> character of the subject matter or the arrangement of
> the treatment (*LAP*, III §52, p. 180; *AV*, p. 92).

The poet has conceived of a regal journey to Cashel led by Domhnall. The 'written authority' and 'topical reserve' were brimming with possibilities. The Mac Carthaigh family, prominent in active politics from the twelfth century in west Munster, had an earlier ancestral existence as kings of Cashel, as did many of the prominent families of Loch Léin and others throughout Munster. In historical times, in the fifth century, the Eoghanacht group of political families had dominated the kingship of Munster centred on Cashel.[33] Just before that time (sixty years before St Patrick baptized Aonghus at Cashel, according to one version of the tale), Corc mac Lughaidh,[34] a member of the Eoghanacht of Loch Léin in Killarney – part of the patrimony of Domhnall Mac Carthaigh – had through various serendipitous and semi-magical circumstances discovered Cashel itself and became king there. His story, variously titled, but generally known as '*Loingeas Chonaill Choirc*',[35] forms part of the 'topical reserve'[36] on which the poet would naturally draw.

Gofraidh Fionn Ó Dálaigh may well have drawn on *Caithréim Chellacháin Chaisil* for *materia* to support his particular *inventio*. By modern standards, he is therefore at a further remove again from drawing on 'historical' material.[37] According to the rubrics of his time, however, the saga was a text, worthy of reference and exploited in the way it is suggested that Gofraidh Fionn has done. It makes perfect sense for Gofraidh to have used it, as it can be suggested he did, to create his literary historicized regal tour for Domhnall Óg. The ekphrastic style lying behind the *inventio* of the journey accounts for the description of the journey, realistically presented, embellished with wonderfully inconsequential detail such as that of Domhnall's chess-set being brought along. The journey takes in the important sites of Eoghanacht identity, it incorporates *stodh* sites, and it generally avoids mentioning towns, and other 'transient' elements in the landscape.[38]

Ó Dálaigh's poem for Domhnall Mac Carthaigh introduces the name and quality of the lord Domhnall in the first quatrain, '*Beir eolas dúinn, a Dhomhnuill . . . a ríodhamhna*' (*DD*, p. 228, q. 1ad): 'Lead us Domhnall, . . . heir apparent'. A refinement of the 'quality' (*habitus* in Matthew of Vendôme [*LAP*, I §78, p. 136]) is the reference to Domhnall, the heir apparent, as one who settles every great difficulty (*réidhigheas gach rodhoghruing* [*DD*, p. 228, q. 1b]). The characterization of Domhnall as a knowledgeable one, skilled in resolving difficulties, qualifies him to take the role assigned in the poet's *inventio* that Domhnall lead his people in this project that the poet has literally *invented* for him: *seol romhuinn, a ríodhamhna* [advance before us, heir apparent (*DD*, p. 228, q. 1d)].

'SENTENTIA'

This brief petition to Domhnall serves as the poem's opening *sententia*; that is to say, 'sense, meaning, signification, idea, notion, proverb' (*TMRA*, p. 35, n. 12). The thematic structure of the poem is predicated on the *sententia* invoking Domhnall's qualities to lead his people. Geoffrey of Vinsauf describes the function of the well-placed *sententia*:

> . . . let a well-chosen *sententia* incline in no respect to the particular, but rather rise its head higher, to something universal. . . . Let the *sententia* stand above the given theme, but glance straight at it; let it say nothing outright, but develop its thought therefrom.
>
> This kind of beginning is threefold, rising from three shoots. The shoots are the first, second and third parts within the material (*PN*, pp. 37–38).

Beginning with an *exemplum* is also encouraged in Geoffrey's treatise, the two kinds of beginning (*sententia, exemplum*) being the most beautiful, dignified and authoritative (*PN*, p. 38). The naming and qualification of Domhnall, along with refinement of the name or the qualification, was enough in itself to carry a creditable poem. Matthew of Vendôme listed eleven elements upon which an entire poem could be built, and these involved the simple expedients of name, quality, character, deeds and so on (*LAP*, I §§77, 78, p. 136; *AV*, §§77, p. 44, and see above, p. 33).

The description of Domhnall's person, coming as it does towards the end of the composition, is almost as an afterthought. The lack of prominence given to the physical description of the 'hero' of the poem in this instance is in accord with the flexibility permitted the poet. The schooled composition can promote or demote elements in the composition to suit the poet himself or to influence the overall tone of the poem (*LAP*, I §38, p. 118; *AV*, p. 27). Gofraidh Fionn's fertile imagination already had enough material with the conception of Conall Corc's journey to Cashel, the analogy (or *uirsgéal*) of the Mosaic journey; and the new 'old' journey of Domhnall's return to Cashel. The standard glowing description of Domhnall – dark hair, fair skin, grey-blue eyes, red cheeks (*DD*, p. 234, qq. 62, 63), merely concludes the picture created by the apostrophization of Domhnall under various titles, including his given name throughout the poem.

The epithetized addresses to Domhnall throughout the poem serve, among other purposes, in place of a greater number of quatrains describing his beauty. Out of the seventy-three quatrains he is named in twenty-four of them, allowing that he is present by analogy in the twelve quatrains (*DD*, pp. 230–231, qq. 20–32) depicting the exemplary journey of Moses, and in the four quatrains (*DD*, pp. 232–233, qq.

39–42) in which he is addressed directly – *bhur* (your) and *tú* (you) and *duit* (to you). The epithetic use of Domhnall's name carries the charge laid on the poet to apply appropriate characteristics to the subject of the poem. These were not limited, but their use was strictly confined in categories. Indeed, Matthew of Vendôme went so far as to state that 'the main exercise of poetic talent consists of descriptive skill . . .' (*LAP*, §73, p. 135; *AV*, p. 42). This skill was carefully cultivated among bardic poets, as we shall see. Matthew's emphasis was on the aggregation of characteristics to create the character in the mind of the reader. Central to the entire project was the sense of appropriateness:

> For one ought to note the characteristics of rank, age, occupation, of natural sex, natural location and other attributes called by Tullius the attributes of a person (*LAP*, I §45, p. 120; *AV*, p. 28).

Heroism and regality are the attributes of Domhnall – all the words and epithets applied to him support this image. Similarly, the consignment of notable territories to him, or their epithetic use in the poem, perform the same role: '*A Dhomhnaill*' (1a); '*a ríoghdhamhna*' [Domhnall, heir apparent] (1d); '*a eomhaighre Easa Ruaidh*' [salmon of Eas Ruadh] (2c);[39] '*a Dhomhnaill mheic Mhéig Charthaigh*' [Domhnall, son of Mac Carthaigh] (3b); '*a mheic Mhéig Carthaigh*' [son of Mac Carthaigh] (34a); '*A mheic Cormuic an chnis ghil*' [son of Cormac of the fair skin] (4a); '*oidhre Cuirc Chaisil*' [heir to Corc of Cashel] (6a); '*a Dhomhnaill*' (8a, 9b, 16a, 33c, 35d; '*a Dhomhnoill*' (37b); *a Dhomhnaill*, 38a, 63b *a Dhomhnuill*, 65b; '*a Dhomhnaill Óig, a ucht bog*' [Domhnall, generous heart] (13a); '*a bharrchais bhaisghéagdha*' [curled head, shapely limbed] (15b);[40] '*a ghnúis naoidheannta*' [youthful face] (18b); '*a thuir Éirne*' [tower of Éirne] (19d); '*a rí finnEithne*' [king of fair Eithne] (38c); '*a Dhomhnaill Óig airmghéir*' [keen-armoured Domhnall Óg] (43b); '*a Dhomhnaill Dúin Inbhir*' [Domhnall of Dún Innbhir] (47a); '*a chraobh Ealla*' [prince (distinctive tree) of Ealla] (56a); '*a mheic Mhóire ó mhúr Chruachan*' [Móire's son from the rampart of Cruachain] (61b); '*a chinn Bhreagh*' [chief of Breagha] (64a); '*a Dhomhnaill mheic mheic Dhomhnuill*' [Domhnall grandson of Domhnall] (66b).

A range of metonymic and metaphoric rhetorical flourishes is displayed in this deceptively simple use of Domhnall's name. The attributions concerning place associate Domhnall with royal and mythological places throughout Ireland, establishing his entitlement to be named along with ancient royal centres such as Cruachain (*DD*, p. 234, q. 61b) which have nothing to do with his supposed or possible hegemonic reach or ambition.[41]

Deeds, likewise, are conceived of as having a preconceived form either in literature or in lore. Matthew of Vendôme's *Ars Versificatoria* instructs thus in the case of an action: 'one will have to use conjecture and proceed according to the common thinking of all and the authority of usage' (*LAP*, IV §19, p. 184; *AV*, pp. 97–98).

'COMPASSED IN THE MIND'

Geoffrey of Vinsauf's *Poetria Nova*, the most compelling of the three treatises outlined in chapter 2, demands that the poet desist from writing until the matter is entirely planned in his head:

Let the mind's inner compass circumscribe the whole area of the subject matter in advance. Let a definite plan predetermine the area in which the pen will make its way or where it will fix its Gibraltar. Ever circumspect, assemble the whole work in the stronghold of your mind, and let it be first in the mind before it is in words. When a plan has sorted out the subject in the secret places of your mind, then let Poetry come to clothe your material with words . . . (*PN*, pp. 34–35).

The journey urged on Domhnall, the retaking of Cashel, is the *inventio* by which the poet 'come[s] into knowledge of an unknown thing through the agency of one's own reason . . . "thinking up things that are true or at least realistic to make your case plausible"' (*PP*, I, ll. 84–85). According to this schema, Domhnall, his attributes, both as *ríodhamhna* and as compassionate, knowledgeable leader, his personal physical beauty (qq. 61–63), and the attendant incidentals of the journey envisaged by the poet, complete a cycle of invention (*inventio*).

It is probable that this is the matter that the poet was urged to arrange mentally before committing himself to the expense of writing – a method of composition taught in the schools.[42] The sense of this practice seems to have become transformed over time and misinformation, or misunderstanding, into a notion that the poet created an entire poem before writing it. Such methods are claimed by some to be characteristic of the Irish bardic poets.[43] The basis of the poem can even be as simple as that outlined by Matthew of Vendôme (*LAP*, I §78, p. 136; *AV*, p. 44) and applied to this project of Gofraidh Fionn: *who is Domhnall and what did/would he do?* Domhnall Mac Carthaigh presented here, is son of Cormac (q. 4), heir of Conall Corc (q. 6), a second Moses (qq. 20, 33, 34). He would/could lead his people back to Cashel in the manner of Corc of Cashel and of Moses leading his people out of Egypt.

Overture

Skilful and entirely appropriate metaplasm characterizes the opening quatrain:

> *Beir eolas dúinn, a Dhomhnaill*
> *réidhigheas gach rodhoghruing;*
> *is ceisd oruinn eol Banbha;*
> *seol romhuinn, a ríodhamhna.*
> (*DD*, p. 228, q. 1)

[Guide us, Domhnall, who settles every great difficulty; we are anxious concerning knowledge of Banbha (Ireland), advance before us, heir apparent.]

The skilful use of the metaplasmic pair, *eol* and *seol*, their overlapping and yet distinct semantic range, their physical similarity, and their near homophony signal the school character of the composition. The innate suitability of both words in respect of the main conceit of the composition – which is that of a journey to be taken under the direction of a knowledgeable leader – marks the composition as the work of a master in the rhetorical methods favoured in Gofraidh Fionn's day.[44]

The metaplasmic pair *eol* and *seol* dominate the theme concerned with the re-enactment of the mythical journey of Corc to Cashel. The apologue – the *exemplum* – is a re-enactment of another mythological journey, that of Moses leading his people back to the Promised Land, and the adventures incidental to that journey. The poem concludes with some quatrains in praise of other lords and notables, significant locally; Gofraidh Fionn's final quatrains include a prayer to the Archangel Michael (q. 73; see chapter 3, n. 30). The quatrain forms a coda to the main theme, in that the Archangel Michael is asked to guide the poet on his journey to the heavenly city:

> *Beir eolas díreach damh-sa,*
> *a naoimhMhíchíl neamhfhallsa*
> *don chathraigh óghaigh aingligh*

shlóghaigh rathmhair ríoghshaidhbhir.
(*DD*, p. 235, q. 73)

[Guide me directly, reliable St Michael, to the pure,
angelic, thronged, prosperous, royal-rich city.]

The single *damh-sa* contrasts, likewise, with the *dúinn* of q. 1a.
The poet directs the attention towards himself, Domhnall is to
guide 'us' (though the first person plural is often used to indicate
the singular); Michael is to guide 'me'.

Matthew of Vendôme noted that the classical authors
concluded their works in various ways, and all of these were
acceptable, including a concluding quatrain in praise of God
(see above, p. 39). Irish practice often involved the regular
dúnadh, which required that the final quatrain ended on the
word, or phrase, that began the composition or, at least, on a
word or syllable that was formally similar. In this instance, the
-bhir of the final word *saidhbhir* is evocative of the opening
beir.

An entire section is devoted by Geoffrey of Vinsauf in *Poetria
Nova* to the matter of length. A substantial piece of writing
is nearly always to be preferred over brief statement. Length
displays learning, and its ornamentation exhibits cultivation of
letters (*LAP*, p. 194). His instructions as to how to extend a
simple matter are very clear:

> . . . let one and the same thing be disguised in multiple
> form; be various and yet the same. . . .
>
> In order that the work may be longer, do not put
> down the simple nouns for things: set down other par-
> ticulars; neither plainly lay bare, but rather intimate a
> thing through little clues; do not let your expression
> march squarely through the subject, but, circumscrib-
> ing it with long roundabout routes, circle what was on
> the point of being said abruptly, and retard your tempo,

> so giving increase of words. And a little forethought
> may spin out the various ways of expressing a thing,
> when abrupt statements [*sic*] abdicates in order that a
> long passage may be its heir (*PN*, p. 42).

Comparison, apostrophe, prosopopoeia and description are all
called upon as devices of 'delay' (*PN*, pp. 42–52, 43). Quite
succinctly, Geoffrey of Vinsauf disposes of the modes of
abbreviation, indeed, in an abbreviated manner:

> If you wish to be brief, first cut out all the aforemen-
> tioned devices, which make for conspicuousness; and
> let there be compressed into a modest circumference a
> little summary of the material . . . (*PN*, p. 58).

This style depended on understatment (*litotes*), cryptic and
oblique style and a very sparing use of verbs (*PN*, pp. 58–59).

Brevity, clearly, is not the object of Gofraidh Fionn's com-
position for Domhnall Mac Carthaigh. His choice is the ample
and extended composition – in this case of seventy-three quat-
rains on a narrative confection that conforms in all points to
a well-wrought mediaeval composition in a style favoured by
the masters of the schools in Ireland and in Europe. Geoffrey
of Vinsauf insisted that the composition be 'coloured', whether
brief or expansive (*PN*, p. 60).

The fecund *sententia* – '*Beir eolas dúinn, a Dhomhnuill*' –
with which Gofraidh Fionn wisely began his composition,
yielded the fruits of composition promised in Geoffrey of
Vinsauf's manual (*PN*, pp. 37–38). 'Guide us', 'lead us,
Domhnall' is the poet's opening plea. 'We are anxious
concerning knowledge of Banbha [Ireland].' The knowledge
here – *eol* (q. 1c) – echoes the *eolas* of the opening line.
All of the mediaeval manuals of instruction (considered in
chapter 2), and those which resembled them, accepted as
axiomatic the central role played by grammar and the variety

of grammatical forms, including all the apparatus linked to essential grammar. Matters of syntax, semantics, inflection and so forth were considered intrinsic to the project of producing literary compositions of a required and predictable standard. Departure from the standards was tolerated provided that the digression could be defended, and the result pleasing. The norm, however, was a close adherence to the formulae, which were seriously prescriptive but ingeniously porous. And while the manuals described composition in the Latin tongue, and the Irish poets wrote in their vernacular, the spirit of pleasure in the word and in all its possibilities – oral, aural, visual and semantic – was not diminished in their compositions.

Geoffrey of Vinsauf described ways of deriving nouns from verbs, verbs from nouns, adjectives from both, and various other 'transsumptions' (*PN*, pp. 89–99) all tending to the adornment of the written word. The grammatical structure of Latin facilitated the use of the rhetorical devices connected with the inflectional use of forms, alterations of tense, mood and case. Irish poets, too, could flex the joints and sinews of Irish to create the complex compositions of which Gofraidh Fionn's poem is a good example.[45]

And so Gofraidh Fionn's second quatrain introduces the verb *seol*, semantically contiguous to *eol/eolus* (especially in the phrase '*beir eolas do*') and very similar in form. This creates the pleasing homophony and, in certain collocations, homonymical ambiguity.[46] (It furnishes the figure *adnominatio/paronomasia*). It also adds to the sense of a journey to be undertaken. And developing in a most natural fashion from the notion of the journey – a creation of the poet – is the literary lingering or the poetic dallying with another source of rhetorical amplification: the cardinal points. In quatrain two, the poet lists the names of four points (though not as four cardinal points) in pursuit of the main theme.

Domhnall is to lead in a north-easterly direction, not west or south.

Gofraidh Fionn's second quatrain exploits the opening *sententia* to amplify the material. The terms for the cardinal points are introduced here (though only three cardinal points are indicated – west, south, and east): '*Na beir siar*' [westward], '*ná seol bu dheas*' [southward] (q. 2a); '*neasa ar seolaidh-ne soir-thuaidh*' [north-eastward] (q. 2d); '*seol inn ar ar n-aghaidh soir*' [eastward] (q. 3a). In this clearly rhetorical repetition of the compass points, the poet lists those to be excluded as well as those to be followed. Domhnall is to take a north-easterly direction from south-west Kerry to Cashel, north-east of it. The repetition (*exargasia/commoratio*) of the same idea through these quatrains is a feature of Geoffrey of Vinsauf's recommendation to 'dwell' on the topic in order to add ornament and length to a composition:

> Either I come down on one same point, and dwell there over and over, or else, when I compare two things, the propositions clash head-on; frequently, I derive an analogy from something quite dissimilar; or I supply an exemplum . . . (*PN*, pp. 78, 79).

The language of the quatrain exploits semantic and lexical links with the *sententia* and the reiteration of the verb *beir* in a slightly different way creates an example of the figure:

> *Ná beir siar ná seol bu dheas . . . neasa ar seolaidh-ne soir-thuaidh.*
> (*DD*, p. 228, q. 2ad)
>
> [Do not take a westward route, do not head southward . . . to direct us north-eastward is more fitting.]

For the purposes of amplification, encouraged in all the prescriptive treatises noted above, the poet can now labour the points East and North, serving at once to keep the poem marching in tandem with Domhnall and the hosts, and also to transform the progress of the journey – the material of the poem – into a bardic itinerary. For there is no doubt that the country through which Domhnall is to travel is the imagined territory of the poet – mapped on the physical territory of the district. As such, it is not, nor is it intended to be, the journey likely to be taken by an individual, let alone seventeen military companies, in mid-fourteenth-century Ireland. As a realistic itinerary, it might have been, and probably frequently was, taken by individuals – though not by individuals bent on challenging existing territorial controls.

For the poet, on the other hand, the itinerary is entirely correct, and realistic within the poets' world and within the realms over which they claimed, and enjoyed, hegemony. The control they exercise is over the presentation of the subject. Gofraidh Fionn is exhorting Domhnall to march on Cashel and to 're'-take it in the name of the Eoghanacht dynasty from which he is descended and which at one point, hundreds of years earlier, enjoyed the kingship of Cashel. This is the truth of the poem, it is the *inventio* of Gofraidh Fionn, rooted in a well-known source within the contemporary learnèd tradition. The landscape, while it has physical characteristics, is not entirely a physical environment, nor altogether a 'realist' geographical territory; that is to say, although the journey can be traced in realistic geographical terms, it is primarily a metaphysical journey. Gofraidh Fionn's poem plots a journey for Domhnall that traverses a temporal and literary landscape. Temporally, the journey takes place on three levels. On the analogical level, Moses' journey from Egypt to the Promised Land gives the poem a timeless basis and a creditable base for the rhetorical device of apologue and comparison. The mythological odyssey of Conall Corc and the finding of Cashel roots the poem in the Irish tradition and creates a template for the physical features of the journey; it also brings the temporal framework of the poem within the millennium of Gofraidh Fionn's newly imagined journey. On the physical/realistic level, the proposed itinerary for Domhnall is skilfully conceived of as a repeat of these two journeys. The realistic prospect of such an undertaking, in real time, across a vigorously contested landscape did not concern Gofraidh Fionn. The exigencies of Domhnall's political strategems belonged to a plane of reality that had less influence on Gofraidh Fionn's *inventio* than the demands of his own craft, because the writerly profession to which he belonged was forged and practised in the greater culture of mediaeval Europe in all the ways outlined above, and it was not essentially responsive to the vagaries of the ambitions, successes or failures of any one nobleman.

Therefore, it is without responsibility to any other than his professional peers, his students and his patron, that Gofraidh Fionn can call on Domhnall Mac Carthaigh to lead 'us' to the east. Repeating *seol* and the direction *soir* [east], the poet carries the poem into its third quatrain, having advanced from calling on Domhnall to lead his people in a generalized open *sententia*, to specific directions in the second quatrain, suggesting a roughly north-easterly direction, to a sidelong reference to *dún Choirc* in the third quatrain (q. 3c).

Oblique references and tantalizing hints are sprinkled through quatrains four and five – Domhnall is to lead the Eoghanacht of Cashel *back* to their forebears' lands – '*sín soir is an seandúthaigh*' [extend eastward to the old country] (q. 4d); to the place of *Pobal Phádraig* (q. 5b). The rhetorical forestalling of the mini-climax (a kind of *gradatio*) in quatrain eight, where Gofraidh Fionn finally announces the destination of Domhnall and his people, is a masterpiece of the mediaeval rhetorical arts of professional poetry:

This is the method of the man of skill – to compass in half a speech all the force of a whole speech. The thought that has arrived at elegant 'colour' by such means does not come so as to be clearly detected, but instead reveals itself through signs. It sheds light from off to one side; it does not care to proceed directly into the light. There are five varieties, but it is all one and the same colour (*PN*, pp. 88–89).

The castle in Cashel must be fought for (q. 5) – the presence of foreign dwellings in *Pobal Phádraig* (a figure of *denominatio* denoting Cashel) are simple challenges to be overcome by Domhnall (q. 5ab). His entitlement is vested in the donation by Domhnall's ancestors of that site to St Patrick (a donation, in fact, made by a member of a rival dynasty – Muircheartach Ó Briain of Dál gCais). This variety of 'colour', the vindication of the claim, comes straight from the eristic origins of the uses of rhetoric, when legal debate was the object of persuasive oratory (judicial, deliberative and epideictic oratory). The culture of legal debate underlying all the rhetorical devices evolved into the very wide remit accorded poetry in the mediaeval period. Poetic claims were considered well upheld if the poet could cite materials from the ancient authors, or any authoritative force, including passable forgeries. Gofraidh Fionn has not even begun to stretch his resources in this proof of Domhnall's right to reclaim Cashel. It is merely the second salvo from his armoury of literature and history (the first, his insistence that Domhnall's 'people' are the Eoghanacht of Cashel). The third 'proof' is that Domhnall is the heir of Corc of Cashel – '*Is tú oidhre Cuirc Chaisil*' (q. 6a). The seventh quatrain, the penultimate quatrain before the mini-climax of quatrain eight, poses the hypophoraic question (or the *interrogatio*, the 'rhetorical question'): '*Créad nach leanfaithea lorg Cuirc?*' [Why would you not follow Corc's path?] (q. 7a).

Closing in on the iconic name of Cashel, Gofraidh Fionn notes that Corc held the castle there, 'a place after which Cashel Corc was called/named': (*port ór canadh CaisealChorc*, q. 7d). The seven quatrains lead to the eighth bardic assertion, delivered with the full authority that attends the poetic pronouncements of the best poets, assuring Domhnall that he *shall* hold Cashel:

> *Agaibh fa dheoidh, a Dhomhnaill*
> *bhias Caiseal . . .*
> (*DD*, p. 229, q. 8ab).
>
> [You, Domhnall, shall finally have Cashel . . .]

This conclusion of the first part of the poem also performs the function called *transitio/metabasis*, which summarizes what has gone before and introduces what is to follow.

This is the overture to the entire poem, the burden of which the ingenuity of Gofraidh Fionn manages to tease out over more than fifty following quatrains. A change in tone is to be noticed after the climactic eighth quatrain: the forward movement urging the journey in the first eight quatrains, the verbs of leading and directing, the nouns of direction and destination, are slackened. The poet now dwells (*commoratio/epimone*) further on the proofs of Domhnall's entitlements. The saints have prophesied that he, who had come from the east (*anoir*), would yet find his home in the east (*thoir*, q. 9acd). The metaplasmic *soir/anoir* satisfied the verbal ornamentation required in the creation of interesting poetry, apart altogether from the metrical and rhyming requirements of which the poet was an acknowledged master (which are not part of the discussion presented here). The Psalter of Cashel[47] foretold the journey to be made by Domhnall (q. 10ab); he would 'behold' (*d'fhéachain*, q. 10c) his ancestral stronghold. The understatement (*litotes/meiosis/emphasis*) in this introduces a measure of humour, the wry self-referential humour that is such a feature of the poetry (and so often overlooked in the frantic search for historical 'relevance'). The levity is balanced by the declaratory '*IonChuirc do chuairt go Caiseal*' [Your journey to Cashel is worthy of Corc] (q. 10d).

COMPARISON

The next six quatrains (qq. 9–14) depend on a form of comparison and are expressed under the cover of a variety of *licentia*, meaning that the poet is taking a certain liberty with the tone in order gently (or not so gently) to point out some fault.

The rhetorical background of legal debate is involved, too, in the rallying of reasons for Domhnall's journey north-east to Cashel: the written authorities witness the return (prophesied in the Psalter, q. 9) of the Eoghanacht to Cashel (q. 10a) – in *Saltair Chaisil* the poet has read that Domhnall (or perhaps just a member of that family, dynasty) would return to Cashel. This prophesied person was, in this poem, Domhnall Mac Carthaigh (q. 9). Again, the poet makes use of 'east', *thoir* [in the east], balanced in the next line with '*a-noir*' [from the east] (q. 9cd), to create internal rhyme and also to exploit the elements of initial (or final) inflexions that changed meaning, so treasured in the writing manuals. This emphasis on the cardinal points echoes the opening quatrains where north[ward], south[ward], east[ward] and west[ward] are used to create a central point of reference for the location of the poem in a notional place.

Equally persuasive rhetorically is that Domhnall, in going to Cashel, will exchange wild mountainous regions for fertile plains. This second cause creates the basis for comparison between the two territories, and also for the use of the figures of reproval. The use of terms of abuse, or reproval, or remonstration, fell well within the most exploited devices of mediaeval rhetoric. And their use, too, has given rise to some of the most pervasive misunderstandings concerning the tone of certain compositions. In this poem, Gofraidh Fionn chooses to urge Domhnall on this journey by suggesting that the lord of Loch Léin has been bewitched into forgetting the beauties of his former homeland (q. 11) – the territory and kingship bestowed through miraculous means on his ancestor Conall Corc.[48] Comparison between the two territories favours the area around Cashel. Comparison itself (a figure of thought), and the rhetorical device of exchanging x for y, are employed by Gofraidh Fionn to give 'colour' to his *inventio* that Domhnall march on Cashel. He gives Cashel a fully allusive title, '*Caiseal Cuirc mhóir mheic Luighdheach*' (q. 11a), giving a hint as to the direction of the poem. The character named fully here, Corc mac Luighdheach, is the eponymous and mythic founder of Cashel and of the Eoghanacht hegemony there. The full mention in quatrain eleven is, however, only a tantalizing hint of where the poet will take the composition, and a suitably subtle device of delay.

The comparison between the wild south Kerry and mild fertile Cashel has echoes of one of the most famous poems in the tradition, that of the *Cailleach Bhéarra*. F. J. Byrne's suggestion that the poem exploits the comparison of two territories in a metaphorical representation of the comparison of two kinds of life is suited to the echo that Gofraidh Fionn may be waking from that poem in his own composition.[49] The note of reproval[50] offered to Domhnall is tempered by the suggestion that he drank a magic drink causing him to forget his true homeland:

> *Caiseal Cuirc mhóir mheic Luighdheach*
> *tángabhair – toisg mhearchuimhneach –*
> *ón ráith ghil bhiliodhain bhuig*
> *dar ibhiobhair digh ndearmaid.*
> (*DD*, p. 229, q. 11)

[You came from that bright, pure-wooded, generous fort – Cashel of great Corc (son of Lughaidh) – an ill-considered undertaking, as a consequence of which you drank a potion of forgetfulness.]

The apposition here is between the bright fort and Cashel itself. The quatrain following amplifies the point, reminding the forgetful Domhnall that it is the lands around Cashel that his people abandoned, though quatrain eleven accuses Domhnall (or apostrophizing his ancestors with the plural 'you', a nice ambiguity) of having drunk a magic potion. This excuse for Domhnall's tarrying in inhospitable south Kerry performs the function frequently used to temper any kind of remonstrance in the poetry. The poet may accuse the lord, but the accusation is presented with its amelioration or with a qualifying element that makes the accusation either a kind of praise or a harmless mention of a trivial and now satisfied source of discontent. (This quality is more pronounced in poems of blame, which are considered below.)

To favour the wild glens (*fiadh-ghleannta* q. 12c) over the territories around Cashel (q. 12b) is as one who exchanged wine for small beer (dregs):⁵¹ '*fion ar iairleanntaibh*' (12d) (a pun on *iar* 'remote', 'west', 'western', may well have been intended here). Further to the arguments in support of Domhnall's journey are the two causes stated by the poet:

A Dhomhnaill Óig, a ucht bog,
dá chúis athroighthe agad:
fearr suth na talmhan tréigthir
's is guth adhradh d'fhuairshléibhtibh.
(*DD*, p. 229, q. 13)

[Domhnall Óg, generous heart, you have two causes to change: better the fruits of the land which is abandoned, and it is a reproach to adhere to cold mountains.]

Gofraidh Fionn repeats, in apposition, the same reproof and the same comparison, drawing his composition out in repetition and delay, saying the same thing a little differently each time, following exactly the instructions found explicit in Geoffrey of Vinsauf's *Poetria Nova*.[52]

In quatrain fourteen, the poet anticipates the details of the project of retaking Cashel, which he is urging on the lord of Desmond. Wonderment is felt at the original abandonment of such fine territories as those seventeen *tuatha* comprising the homeland that the poet is suggesting Domhnall retake:

> . . . *na seacht dtuatha déag do dhol*
> *ar séad uatha do b'iongnadh.*
> (*DD*, p. 229, q. 14cd)
>
> [. . . that the seventeen *tuatha* should ever have
> abandoned them is a matter of wonderment.]

In a recitative, quatrain fifteen repeats the pleas of quatrains one, two and three, using the verb *seol*, carrying with it this time the meanings of 'direct' and 'lead':

> *Seol is in slighidh chéadna*
> *sinn, a bharrchais bhaisghéagdha,*
> *mór an brad a seachna sain,*
> *lór fad ar ndeabhtha ór ndúthaigh.*
> (*DD*, p. 229, q. 15)
>
> [Direct us on the same path, curly-haired one, shapely
> limbed; avoiding it is a great loss, our separation from
> our proper land has lasted long enough.]

This recitative is a compositional pause giving an opportunity to absorb the import of the previous quatrains, and rallying imaginative energy for the four quatrains that usher in the lengthy apologue using the story of Moses leading the Israelites through the Red Sea. Domhnall's people are the seventeen martial groups of one hundred, which he must marshal for the journey (qq. 16, 17).

APOLOGUE

The Mosaic apologue extending from quatrain twenty to thirty-five conforms in all respects to the requirements of the manuals in the use of exemplary tales to illustrate an aspect of the argument being put forward in the composition.[53]

The pseudo-Ciceronian *Rhetorica ad Herennium* defines the *exemplum* and its uses, as follows:

> *Exemplum*: (*paradigma*), 'exemplification is the citing of something done or said in the past, along with the definite naming of the doer or author. . . . It renders a thought more brilliant when used for no other purpose than beauty; clearer, when throwing more light upon what was somewhat obscure; more plausible, when giving the thought greater verisimilitude; more vivid when, expressing everything so lucidly that the matter can, I may almost say, be touched by the hand' (*AdHer*, §59, pp. 382–384).

Demonstrating the use of *exempla* in his treatise, Geoffrey of Vinsauf noted how the comparison encouraged by the *exemplum*, apologue or tale incorporated into the composition need not be spelt out (*PN*, pp. 88–89). Sometimes the apologue follows a statement of analogy, and the tale expands on the hint given there.[54]

Geoffrey states clearly that the matter need not be laboured for sense, though that alternative is also acceptable:

> The speaker wished his point to be compared to the exemplum. And since he cleverly gave only part of his meaning to the ear, he saved part for the mind. This

is the method of a man of skill – to compass in half a
speech all the force of a whole speech (*PN*, p. 88).

Characters, animals and chattels are assembled in quatrains
sixteen to eighteen: *taoisigh* (captains), *uirríthe* (vassal
lords/underkings), *groigh* ([stud of] horses), *buar* . . .
mbrughadh (hospitallers' cattle). These, led by Domhnall
Mac Carthaigh, are the players in this particular composition.
They stand, as it were, on the brink of a stormy sea in need
of leadership to steer them through the maelstrom to their
destination, Cashel. This is the burden of quatrain nineteen,
an anticipatory quatrain, introducing the Mosaic apologue,
which invites comparison and encourages emulation:

> *Ní fhuil as so go Sliabh gCrot*
> *– Dia [dá] réidhioghadh romhat! –*
> *achd muir ar n-éirghe anfaidh,*
> *a thuir Éirne, d'Allmhurcaibh.*
> (*DD*, p. 230, q. 19)

[Tower of Erne, all there is from here to Sliabh gCrot –
as far as foreigners are concerned – is a sea after a storm
has arisen, may God calm it before you.]

The sea, Domhnall's Red Sea, is a metaphorical sea of strangers,
or foreigners.[55] He must lead his people through them like
Moses led the Israelites. Quatrain twenty makes the apologue
and the comparison explicit:

> *Imirce Mhaoise tar muir*
> *gá tabhairt 'na tír dhúthaigh*
> *dar thráigh an Mhoir Ruadh rompa*
> *re shluagh soin ba samhalta.*
> (*DD*, p. 230, q. 20)

[Moses' migrating company, crossing the sea being
taken to its (their) native territory, when the Red Sea

ebbed before them, with his host comparison should
be made.][56]

The apologue could quite legitimately have ended here. The
comparison is well made – Domhnall's journey through a sea of
foreigners is to be compared with Moses' journey through the
Red Sea. The brief mention would immediately evoke the well-
known tale of the parting of the waters, the comparison would
be satisfactory and complete. In the interests of amplification
and delay, two devices encouraged in the effort to lengthen a
composition – the apologue is drawn out, and used to embellish
the work – exercise the poet's literary skill, and enhance the
praise offered to the lord.

The Mosaic rod is a leitmotif in the apologue. The *slat* 'rod'
could also serve to symbolize the investiture of the lord, part
of a ceremony frequently associated with his appointment in
the capacity of ruler. As part of a play on words, the same
expression *slat* also served in the sense of 'scion' in a genea-
logical context. The single word was capable of the kind of
literary exploitation that was the essence of Gofraidh Fionn's
craft. And so, addressing Domhnall as '*a shlat Bhanbha*' (q.
21c), while referring to Moses as '*Maoise mac Amhra*' (q. 21a)
and as '*mac Amhra*' (q. 21d), introduces the double use of the
word *slat* – in this instance epithetically of Domhnall, later as
an instrument of God's power in Moses' hand. This apologue
will portray Domhnall *slat Bhanbha* likewise as an instrument
in God's hand too. The comparison is urged directly – using
the word *samhalta* – in quatrain 20d: '. . . *re shluagh soin ba
samhalta*' [with his host comparison should be made].

Moses together with his people are identified as '*Oireacht
Mhaoise mheic Amhra*' (q. 21a); this familiarizes the name of
Moses, giving his paternal relation in the Irish form, and apply-
ing a technical Irish term to his following, *oireacht* (assembly
of nobles), which had the necessary social connotation. The

elevation of Moses' companions into an *oireacht* in this sense maintains the tone of the style, which, as is frequent in the syllabic praise-poems, refers only to noblemen and their pursuits in each narrative, to achieve the high or the middle style.[57]
Domhnall has been asked (q. 16ab) to help his people in their affliction (. . . *d'fhóirithin ar n-anfhorlainn*) – their being so far from their homeland, Cashel; Moses' people (*oireacht Mhaoise*) were likewise in banishment and exile from their patrimony (*i n-éagmhais a n-athardha*, q. 21b) until delivered by *mac Amhra* (q. 21d). The 'patrimony' here is unidentified, a tantalizing and utterly satisfying rhetorical reticence. The unfolding of the tale develops in quatrain twenty-two when the same information is given again, with a little more detail:

> *Clann Israhél re headh gcian*
> *i gcrích Éighipte ar ainrian;*
> *go ceann a mbróin 's a mbroide*
> *níor ghearr dhóibh a ndochruide.*
> (*DD*, p. 230, q. 22)

> [The Children of Israel were for a long time astray in the land of Egypt, their suffering was long felt by them until the end of their sorrow and oppression.]

Moses, through God's help, brought his hosting out of exile, a fortunate outcome, not seen by any other *oireacht*. Gofraidh Fionn uses a language applicable to military companies, '*sluagh*'. The expression '*oireacht*' (q. 23bc) sustains the sense of a noble company, not any kind of rabble.

Quatrains twenty-four to twenty-seven synopsize the reason for Moses' journey with his people: the burden placed on the Israelites by the idolatrous Pharaoh (*Forann*) who prevented them from worshipping the true God. It was owing to this that Moses led his distinguished company (*a dhíorma deaghshluaigh*, q. 27d) towards the royal Red Sea (*an raMhuir ríoghdha Ruaidh*, q. 27c).

This cryptic treatment of the theme leads Gofraidh Fionn to the matter of the crossing of the Red Sea, which is the point he wishes to labour. Moses possesses a rod (*slat*), which has special attributes (*slat bhuadha*, q. 28b). The ingenious couplet concluding this quatrain makes the defining statement of this apologue:

> . . . *maith an bhuaidh do bhí ar an tslait;*
> *na sluaigh is í do anaic.*
> (*DD*, p. 231, q. 28cd)
> [. . . the rod had a good attribute,
> it (was it which) protected the hosts.]

Colours from the spectrum give metaphorical 'colour' to the quatrain following:

> *An mhuir shriobhuaine shrothach*
> *do thráigh mar mhuigh míonsgothach*
> *mar fhuair ó ghlaic bhairrghil béim*
> *do shlait aingligh an fhiréin.*
> (*DD*, p. 231, q. 29)
> [The green-streamed flowing sea ebbed to become like
> a gentle-flowered plain, when it received a blow of the
> angelic rod from the fair hand of the faithful man.]

The foolish and dangerous pursuit by Pharaoh and his hosts resulted in their drowning. Only the faithful were covered by the enchantment of that miraculous rod (qq. 30–31). Echoing the main theme of the poem – Domhnall's leading his people on a march to Cashel – with a subtle variation to account for the fabulous nature of the path that Moses' rod created, and its marine character, Gofraidh Fionn notes the path/road/track of the journey taken here by Moses:

> *Ó 'dchonncadar an ród réidh*
> *tré iomdhomhain an aigéin*

gabhaid rian Mhaoise san mhuir;
do budh triall baoise is baoghail.
(*DD*, p. 231, q. 31)
[When they saw the level road through the depths of
the ocean, they followed Moses' track in the sea – it was
a foolish and dangerous undertaking.]

Not only is Domhnall Moses, but wonderfully, and –
possible only in the language in which the poem was written
– Domhnall can also be the miracle-working rod/*slat*. The
immediate comparison is between Moses' rod (*slat*) and
Domhnall's warrior lance/blue sword (*gormlonn*, q. 33d).
Gofraidh Fionn spells it out in quatrain thirty-three, taking the
opportunity, parenthetically, to echo the third quatrain with
a variation on (including both the entreaty and the direction)
'*Seol inn ar ar n-aghaidh soir*' (q. 3a) – '*sdiuir, a Dhomhnaill,
na sluaigh soir*' (q. 33c):

> *Mar do bhuail Maoise an Muir Ruaidh*
> *don tslait le rug gach robhuaidh*
> *sdiuir, a Dhomhnaill, na sluaigh soir*
> *buail do ghormloinn ar Ghallaibh.*
> (*DD*, p. 231, q. 33)
> [As Moses struck the Red Sea with the rod by which he
> achieved every great victory, Domhnall, direct the hosts
> east, wield your blue sword against the foreigners.]

The following two quatrains confirm the message of
the apologue: Eoghan's race (the dynasty from which the
Mac Carthaigh and most of the Munster princes and kings
descended) are the Children of Israel, oppressed by the power
of foreigners; Domhnall is their Moses (q. 34) –

> *rug Maoise a mhaicne tar muir,*
> *a-taoi-se ag aicme Eoghain.*
> (*DD*, p. 231, q. 34cd)

[Moses brought his people over the sea, Eoghan's people have you.]

There is no need to point out the satisfying alliterations achieved in this couplet, nor the skilful *maicne, aicme* rhyme. The abilities of Gofraidh Fionn to fulfil the well-known rules of bardic metrics and rhyme is not at issue here. It is important, however, to see this achievement in the wider context of the European literary world, and to allow Irish poets to participate as willing members of a self-conscious and dignified literary stratum within Europe. This is distinct from the more familiar sense of the Irish bardic poet as a liminal character uncomfortably trapped in a Christianized bourgeois world, which restrained his wayward, heroic and largely pagan character, articulated through arcane, unusual and recondite quatrains, which mirrored a similar character in the person of the lord or prince who patronized him.

The tone adopted in quatrains thirty-six, thirty-seven and thirty-eight becomes one of gentle admonishment and exhortation: Domhnall is – unselfishly – to leave the remote fastness of his south Kerry territory and advance into the richer lands of Cashel, the headquarters of the Eoghanacht kingship and Domhnall's rightful destination. Munster, the Eoghanacht province, is represented as being under the sway of people who have no right to her while Domhnall keeps himself remote in Kerry:

. . . *Mumha ag dreim nachar dhúla*
's bhar gcura i n-eirr iargcúla.
(*DD*, p. 232, q. 36cd)

[. . . Munster held by an unwarranted crowd, while you are settled in a remote foreland.]

This remonstration extends to suggesting that Domhnall's people have fled in fear of foreigners to Kerry. Gofraidh Fionn, taking Domhnall's victory in any encounter with the sea for granted, declares that none of his people would feel compelled to flee for fear of oppression from these again (q. 37). The notion that Domhnall's territory of south-west Kerry is remote from his ancestral headquarters, and that his remaining there can be misinterpreted as pusillanimity, is merely a pretext for the extravagant journey that Gofraidh has conceived of for this poem. The plausibility of the pretext is covered with the Gael/Gall conflict. This is an assured ground for any praise-poem, which required an apparatus of militarism, a ready cause, a hero, a location and a precedent. In other words, it fulfilled the requirement that the poet present a *historia*, a *narratio*, a *scéal* – realistic and true, in the sense that the rhetoricians intended. A poetic exposition on a likely theme that used scenaria[58] from life or from literature to present material that could be true, and was true, perforce, within the confines of the literature, resulted in this poem, which Gofraidh Fionn composed for Domhnall Mac Carthaigh.

And so, Domhnall Mac Carthaigh, a Moses to his people, is to advance from south-west Kerry and reclaim his ancestral patrimony in Cashel, vanquishing the foreigners who try to thwart his destiny. This is the premise from which Gofraidh Fionn embarks on the itinerary that his composition lays out for Domhnall. It takes Domhnall from his homeland in Kerry to the remotely related headquarters of the Eoghanacht in Cashel. It takes the reader/audience on an enchanting trip through the salient places in the sagas and genealogies concerning Eoghanacht histories. And it carries the poet through his richly stocked coffers of toponymic literature, genealogies, sagas, myths and sundry histories and the works of other poets. It does not, however, bring to the modern reader a chronicle of a historical attempt by Domhnall to 'retake' Cashel, nor does it encourage the notion that the poet had a function of political exhortation in that respect and that this is an example of his efforts.

MAC CARTHAIGH'S JOURNEY

At this point, it is possible to return to quatrain fifteen to where Gofraidh Fionn entreats:

> *Seol is an slighidh chéadna*
> *sinn, a bharrchais bhaisghéagdha,*
> *mór an brad a seachna sain,*
> *lór fad ar ndeabhtha ór ndúthaigh.*
> (*DD*, p. 229, q. 15)

[Direct us on the same path, curly-haired one, shapely limbed; avoiding it is a great loss, our separation from our proper land has lasted long enough.]

Had Gofraidh Fionn decided against the Mosaic apologue and its attendant introductory and concluding quatrains, he might well have proceeded from quatrain fifteen to quatrain thirty-nine. It is entirely consistent with the aesthetics of the bardic poem that such a leap might logically be made. Each quatrain normally constituted a mini-poem and a discrete metrical statement within itself, frequently interchangeable. It has been shown how the apologue constitutes an aesthetic unit within this composition; its extraction leaves the composition intact logically. As though picking up the thread of the poet's original *inventio*, embellished with the by-story concerning Moses and the establishment of Domhnall as the Moses of the Eoghanacht, quatrain thirty-nine makes a full revolution, returning to Domhnall's current home. Dramatically the poet goes to the furthest extreme of Domhnall's lands, Dairbhre (*Oileán Dairbhre*, Valentia Island). He names three places or regions which represent the direction from which Domhnall Mac Carthaigh would proceed: '*caladh Dairbhre*' (q. 39a);[59] '. . . *cuan Béirre*' (q.

39b);[60] and 'Corca Dhuibhne' (q. 39c), an archaism, reflecting the earlier extent of the territory so named; as an afterthought he mentions 'porta Uidhne' (q. 39d). From quatrain thirty-nine to quatrain fifty-seven, Gofraidh Fionn makes a selection of destinations for Domhnall's trip. The conceit of the journey includes the naming of places and of peoples in a teasingly inclusive yet hugely allusive way.

A cursory reading of these quatrains would suggest that Gofraidh Fionn is outlining the itinerary of a probable or realistic programme for the recovery of Cashel from the earl of Ormond and the incidental defeat of the forces of the earl of Desmond on the way to the greater goal. That is what would have been necessary for the conversion of Gofraidh Fionn's *inventio* into a realizable political goal for Domhnall Mac Carthaigh. Except, of course, that this was not the object of Gofraidh's composition. If contemplation of its contents had the effect of arousing a sense of grievance or of military expansionism in Domhnall Mac Carthaigh, then perhaps the poem would have had an unforeseen, or at least an unfortunate or serendipitous effect. Historical record seems to suggest that the poem, however it was received by Domhnall Mac Carthaigh, did not lead him to undertake any part of this particular journey; his political activities did not include a Risorgimento-style advance on Cashel. There is no known record of a lord's direct appreciation of any individual poetic offering (as distinct from payment in general); there are records of a lord's displeasure – but not in respect of a particular poem.

Gofraidh Fionn's proposed itinerary follows a credible and reasonably direct route from Íochtar Cua (q. 40b) to Cashel. Moving around the west and north of Loch Luighdheach (q. 40d), he travels north-westwards parallel to the River Inny, (*re porta Uidhne*, q. 39d), then northwards on the west side of Lough Caragh (*tar Carrthaigh*, q. 49a), reaching the coast at Glenbeigh (*tar cuan mBeithbhe*, q. 49a); he then travels north-eastwards (along the route followed by the modern N70), passing by Lough Leane (*tar Loch Léin*, q. 49c) to the east and the Laune estuary (*tar cuan Leamhna*, q. 49c) to the west, until he reaches the southern borders (= the River Maine, q. 50a) of Ciarraighe; he then turns eastwards through the northern limits of *Magh gCoinchinn* (q. 50b), following something like the route of the modern R561; then from the Farranfore area, in a slightly more north-easterly direction, he travels to the east of Castleisland; his itinerary from there to *Uí Chonaill Ghabhra* (q. 51a) and *Claonghlais* (east of Abbeyfeale in *Uí Chonaill Ghabhra*, q. 51c) would probably have continued in the same north-easterly direction (e.g. towards Brosna and through the Mullaghareirk mountains, rather than along the route of the modern N21) from Castleisland to Abbeyfeale; continuing the same north-easterly direction from *Claonghlais*, he crosses the Deel (*tar Daoil*, q. 51d) between Killeedy and Kilmeedy (near Shanrath), thus travelling directly eastwards (his route coincides with the line of the modern R518 east of Castletown), and this brings him to Bruree (*Dún Eochair Máighe*, q. 52a). From Bruree, Gofraidh Fionn envisages a more north-easterly route (than that of the modern R518 to Kilmallock), e.g. through Dromin towards Knockainy; moving eastwards from Knockainy (q. 53), he passes to the north of Emly (but his intinerary must soon coincide with the route of the modern R515) and thence, with *Cliú* (q. 54) to the north and the Galtees to the south, he travels through *Magh Feimhin* (q. 55) (the final stage being along the line of the modern N74) to Cashel (q. 56). As he approaches his destination, *Cnoc Grafann*, site of an Anglo-Norman stronghold, lies to the south in the direction of Cahir.[61] In terms of the stages of the trip, this is a realistic journey that can be traced almost in its entirety along mostly minor roads on a modern map.

In keeping with the high style of the poem, which presents a noble assemblage, and a military expedition in which all matters pertain to warriors and their equipment, to enemies, valour and battle, no particulars are given that introduce matters in conflict with that style.[62] Though a considerable maritime lord in his own right, any expedition Domhnall Mac Carthaigh might have undertaken using a fleet would have had to use either Limerick or Lismore (or both) and continue on foot, in any case, to Cashel. Gofraidh Fionn does not regard these (Limerick and Lismore) as relevant to his imagined itinerary; nor has he any reference to Tralee, Dingle, and Killorglin, which were wellknown trading ports; and his references to 'cuan Béirre' and 'caladh Dairbhre', also significant ports, were simply to define Domhnall Óg's point of departure.[63] The studding of the natural boundaries of the Maigue river and the Eas, the Feale and others with Anglo-Norman and Irish fortresses are alluded to in the most general way, accounted for in the sense that Domhnall must overcome foreigners – though it would be but like contending with heavy seas (to one of his naval expertise, q. 19; and see above, p. 88) – to reach Cashel.[64] The maritime theme of Moses and the Red Sea is underpinned by the sense that Domhnall Mac Carthaigh is a lord familiar with the sea, as with conflict on land and on sea.

As early as 1198, annal entries in Mac Carthaigh's Book (S. Ó hInnse, *Miscellaneous Irish Annals*, p. 79) record that a castle was built by foreigners at Askeaton, Co. Limerick (*Caisleán le Gallaibh in Eas Geibhtine*). The same source synopsizes a spate of encastellation in Desmond, *s.a.* 1214:

> A castle was built by Mac Cuidithe in Muinntear Bháire, and one at Dún na mBárc by Carew, and another at Ard Tuilithe. Another castle [was built]

by the son of Thomas [FitzGerald] at Dún Lóich,
and one at Killorglin. A castle [was built] by Roche
at Oirbhealach. A castle by the son of Maurice
[FitzGerald] at Magh Uí Fhlaithimh. A castle by
FitzStephen in Corca Laighdhe. A castle by Barrett in
the village [*sráidbhaile*] above Cuan Dor. A castle by
Nicholas Buidhe [de Barry] at Teach Mo-Laige. And
it was during the war of Diarmaid Dúna Droighneáin
and Cormac Liathánach [Mac Carthaigh] that the
Galls overran the whole of Munster in every direction
from the Shannon to the sea (ibid., p. 91).

Note also that some of these castles had a short life – an entry
for 1262 records how the castles of Dún Mic Thoghmainn
(demolished again in 1310 [ibid., p. 107]), Dún Uisni,
Macroom, Magh Oiligh, Dún Lóich, Killorglin, and many of
the castles of Uí Chonaill, were demolished and burned by
Fínghin Reanna Róin and (the people of) Desmond (ibid., p.
105).

To complete his journey, Domhnall would also have had to
overcome other Mac Carthaigh lords,[65] along with the lords
of peoples and territories whose ambitions would include the
reclaiming of territories once ascribed to their peoples in rival
readings of the Eoghanacht histories.

The landscape facing Domhnall Óg on his march north-
eastward presented something of the picture outlined by R. E.
Glasscock:

In the landscape of 1300 almost all the large castles
stood occupied, essential and 'living' elements within
the country in contrast to their ruined and often
desolate appearance today. By 1300 those castles built
a century before must already have been thought
of as old; others were newly built, their stone still

unweathered and fresh with the marks of the masons'
chisels (R. E. Glasscock, 'Land and People, *c.* 1300', p.
220).[66]

URBAN IRELAND

The question of urban centres in the High Middle Ages in
Ireland is not one to be addressed here, but it is well to bear
in mind that Irish centres of commercial enterprise and trade,
craft and population were established in what must have been
a normal ratio to the population.[67] While the particular style
of urban settlement spread throughout the Frankish/Norman
world, or that evolved from earlier Roman sites in continental
Europe, may not have been the characteristic style in Ireland,
the uncontroversial existence of trading ports and towns and
consequent necessary network of fords and roads must be taken
for granted.[68] Irish literature takes for granted the existence of
a network of roads, possibly fictionalized to some degree, but
by all means feasible.[69]

K. Nicholls identifies ecclesiastical sites as centres of popu-
lation and craft.[70] Mining for minerals, precious stones and
other elements led to the development of manufacturing settle-
ments of some importance – otherwise the provision of raw
materials for the processing of colours for the decoration of
churches and manuscripts could not have taken place.[71] Men-
dicant friars, such as those Dominicans and Franciscans who
had settled in south-west Kerry early in the thirteenth century,
normally chose areas that were more densely populated than
could be the case where no urban centres of any substance exis-
ted. Their mission was to townspeople, and the rhythm of
their daily life was tuned to the life of the settled urban centre
from the smaller size, perhaps, in Ireland to the largest Italian
city-states. The style cultivated by Gofraidh Fionn does not
accommodate the sense of the urban nobility in the manner

cultivated in contemporary Italian poetry, for example. The high style for the poet, in this instance, focused on the unchanging physical territories, the deathless mythical stories, and the prophesied re-establishment of the Eoghanacht (personified in the 'warrior' Domhnall Mac Carthaigh) in Cashel.

NAME-CHECKING

In Gofraidh Fionn's poem, '*Beir eolas dúinn, a Dhomhnuill*', in over twenty topographical references in the intinerary, almost all are to physical features of the landscape or to ancient territorial divisions (see above, p. 96). The poet gives little recognition to places of contemporary communal or political significance; in the case of two such places, Bruree and Knockainy, there is a preference for ancient, semi-mythical, designations – respectively, Dún Eochair Máighe, and Sídhe Eoghabhail.[72] Indeed, in keeping with the high style of the poem, there is a degree of tautology in the allusive and literary reference to a few central points in the itinerary: Dún Eochair Máighe ∼ Máigh an Iobhair and Loch Goir; Sídh Eoghabhail ∼ (Cnoc) Áine.[73] The ecclesiastical centre at Cill Orglan, from which the modern town takes its name, was flourishing during the lifetime of Domhnall Mac Carthaigh; there is no mention of the foundation here, nor of the church nor the churchmen who played such a role in the ruling families of Munster, and which were readily and even greedily patronized by them. Noting Loch Léin (q. 49c), Gofraidh Fionn knew well that like Cill Orglan, Cill Áirne boasted an ecclesiastical establishment in the fourteenth century. Gofraidh Fionn's composition, tracing its itinerary primarily with reference to physical and territorial features, ignores this characteristic of the place, excluding any hint at the name, or the naming element *cill*. The place is the *loch*, Loch Léin, carrying with it all the weight of the literary heritage, but ignoring, tacitly, the very rich ecclesiastical heritage in the island monastery of Inis Faithleann (a monastery promoted by the Mac Carthaigh and familiar to the learnèd family of Uí Dhálaigh in their turn). Maolsuthain Ó Cearbhaill in Inis Faithleann, a member of the community on the island, is remembered in the annals (AFM, *s.a.* 1009) as '*príomhshaoi iarthair domhain ina aimsir, agus tighearna Eoghanachta Locha Léin*'.[74]

Apart from the places that lie between Domhnall's headquarters in Íochtar Cua and the destination, Cashel, which are listed by Gofraidh Fionn, another layer of place-names occurs epithetically. These are the places ascribed to Domhnall in respect of his relation to the personality Banbha, namely Ireland. Places resounding with dignity, sovereignty and mythological weight are attached to Domhnall's name as a commonplace of the praise-genre. These places are not confined to the lord's immediate sphere of influence, nor even to his most outrageous ambitions.[75] Gofraidh apostrophizes Domhnall in the quatrains covering the itinerary, and throughout the poem: '*Domhnall Dúin Innbhir*' (q. 47a) [Domhnall of Dún Innbhir]; '*a sgoth Eamhna*' (q. 49d) [flower of Eamhain]; '*a chraobh Ealla*' (q. 56a) [branch of Ealla]; '*a mheic Mhóire ó mhúr Cruachan*' (q. 61b) [son of Mór from the fortress of Cruachain]; '*a sgath Moighe Modhuirne*' (q. 63d) [choice of Mourne]; '*a chinn Bhreagh*' (q. 64a) [prince of Breagha]; '*a mheic na ríoghna ó Ráth Chuinn*' (q. 66a) [son of the queen from Ráth Chuinn].

These places belong to the poet, rather than to the lord. They have their true existence in other poems, and in other literary sources. They pertain to the realms ruled by the poet and bestowed by him on rulers as he sees fit. This is one of the functions claimed by the poets, the making and unmaking of kings and lords, not in the political sense, but in the poetic sense. Most of them are kennings, meaning Ireland in general.

Domhnall Mac Carthaigh's journey takes him from Íochtar Cua to Cashel. The journey is made with his warriors (the seventeen companies of quatrain fourteen), 'sochraide throm thionóile' (q. 42b) [it is a sturdy host that you assemble]. Along with this troop, Gofraidh Fionn advises that Domhnall not forget horns, games-pieces (chessmen):

> Bhar gcuirn bhláithe is bhar mbrannaimh
> cuimhnighthior do chéadarraibh;
> ní ba socht dáibh i ndún Chuirc
> sa mhúr mar tháir a dtabhairt.
>
> (DD, p. 233, q. 48)

[Remember your fine goblets and your chessmen, as a first priority; they shall not be idle in Corc's fort (Cashel), when you succeed in bringing them to the fortress.]

Gofraidh Fionn juxtaposes the weighty assemblage of warriors and troops with the instruments of lordly pleasure and feudal leisure, the horns/goblets and the chessmen. Within the walls of Cashel, it is understood, the pursuits of the lord in a period of peace are to be provided for.

EOGHANACHT TERRITORY

The listing of territories resonant with the earlier sagas of Eoghanacht[76] hegemony gave great pleasure to the poet who fulfilled the task of his profession in decking his invention with plausible and likely clothing at the appropriate level of style. Gofraidh Fionn exploits toponymy (the exceedingly well-supplied sources of dinnsheanchas), historical sources (including pseudo-historical sources) of the Eoghanacht peoples, and syntheses such as An Leabhar Gabhála, the sagas concerning the origin-legends of Cashel in the tales about Conall Corc, chronicles and annals, individual tales such as that of *Caithréim Ceallacháin Chaisil* and all the resources of extant literature available to him, and familiar to him from the well-stocked schools of the Uí Dhálaigh poets.

It is probable that Gofraidh Fionn's main concerns, when *creating his composition*, did not include the immediate or long- -term political goals of Domhnall Mac Carthaigh. Domhnall Mac Carthaigh's political success or defeat concerned Gofraidh Fionn, as did the fortunes of his patrons, the earls of Des- mond, and those of other lords in Munster. It is impossible to determine the part played by Gofraidh Fionn in local polit- ics. It may be as well to understand his role as being similar to that of any prominent professional person in an Irish or Anglo- Norman lordship. Much of his influence or vulnerability would depend on the allegiances and dues owed to him and by him as a member of an important family. The image of him sit- ting at the right elbow of his lord chivvying him into political action against the 'foreigner' is a debased version of the image which the poet wished to create, and a burlesque of the elegant metaphorical relationship outlined countless times in poems of praise and blame in Irish syllabic poetry.

TIMELESS PLACES

It is not as an expert in military logistics, however, that Gofraidh Fionn is proposing this feasible but fabulous journey – rather he is following a timeless track, a literary map, a never-changing landscape of natural features and non-attributable placenames, no *Cill-* or *Baile-* besmirches his itinerary. He compliments the earls of Desmond, or teases them, as he guides Domhnall. He lists lakes, rivers, and *stodh* sites, mountains and places that are not immediately amenable to change in name or function, nor can their identity in the tradition be affected by the temporary hegemony exercised by a neverceasing succession of lords. The literary identity conferred on the places named by Gofraidh Fionn in this composition is the one to which he is referring. Changes wrought by temporary political, economic or social circumstances do not affect the journey outlined in his poem. The modern traveller can take the route suggested in the poem, and enjoy the contrasting landscapes and the natural beauties listed in the fourteenth-century poem.[77] Had Gofraidh Fionn outlined the likely journey of an army on the march to Cashel on contemporary roads, paths, tracks; over fords, bridges, passes; through towns, hamlets, villages; overrunning tolls, guards, sentries, and so forth; let alone the overnight stops, the provisioning and so on, the composition would be immensely interesting as a record of conditions in fourteenth-century Munster. The marvel would be at how things have changed. As it is, the record stands for all time, the lakes, plains, hills and territories traversed in Gofraidh Fionn's *inventio* are the same as those encountered by a modern traveller taking the route he suggests. The territories named by Gofraidh Fionn on this trip of Domhnall's are sacred to the Eoghanacht and mythologically significant in their links with the *stodh*.

This is the poet's triumph. The claim to preserve the history of the lord's family, to ensure immortality in the literary tradition is achieved in the precise generalities to which the formality of the composition gives shape. Underpinning the durability of this method is the pseudo-history of origin-tale, mythological saga and toponymic literature. The enduring truth of the journey outlined above is achieved by its basis in the physical landscape, the textual legacy upon which it is built, and the certainty of its never having been invalidated by a failure in its execution.

4. Poems of complaint

Prominent among the works of the poets, forming a variety of the praise-genre, are the poems of complaint, reconciliation, and petition.[1]

The nuances of dispraise that characterize poems in these categories make them, in many ways, more interesting than eulogies of unstinting commendation and laudation. They have always added a spice to the corpus of bardic praise-poetry in seeming to address the reverse of the coin of praise and compliment, with blame and recrimination. Elements of the three categories often overlap. Poems in which the poet upbraids a lord can base their recrimination on a number of causes, which can include the failure of the lord to reconcile with the poet after a quarrel, or the poet's sense of neglect from want of patronage, or from stingy rewards. The individual addressed in such pieces is sometimes named (and indentifiable), sometimes not.[2]

In compositions involving an accusation made by the poet concerning the lord's material neglect of him, the case is often presented as though the poet has been overlooked; the poet, who – the poet insists – was once, and whose predecessors were, cherished by the lord's seniors and his ancestors. Sometimes the lord is accused of raiding the privileged property of the poet, of taking cattle or other valuables during the course of a raid, when tradition and law dictated that the poet be free of the effects of warfare in this, and other, respects. A lord may also be reprimanded with reference to his political actions or respecting his neglect of war or peace.[3] There may be a sense of accusation implied in some poems that urge action and normally are considered a separate variety of exhortative composition.

These poems can be read literally as literary expressions of the political role assigned to the poet. The social, political, and cultural status of the poet would, for instance, be understood to be challenged when a raiding lord overlooked a poet's immunity and invaded his land, driving off his cattle and seizing other goods.[4] Likewise, the status of the poet and that of his brethren in the arts was at risk if and when any individual poet was overlooked or neglected. Such is the import of the literal reading of this subgenre of complaint. Similarly with poems of petition or reconciliation.

The events outlined in the poems can be read as representing factual, if stylized, circumstances, which would occur in the normal social and economic interchange between lord and poet. And indeed, poems in the categories outlined here have frequently been described, and commented upon, and interpreted as glimpses beyond the confection of the composition into the vicissitudes of life in court circles, or into the quotidian vexations of the poet–patron relationship.

Underlying the petition, the quarrel, the reconciliation, the exhortation, or the reprimand, is a seam of complaint that is transumed – in the most literary way – into conceits of love, obligation, devotion, praise and so forth.[5]

The function of this literary 'complaint' is now unknowable for a number of reasons. There may even be grounds for suggesting that it had no function beyond that of providing a foil for praise. In Irish schools' poetry, complaint is not the 'opposite' of, nor the negation of, praise.[6] It does not list attributes that can be seen as contrary to the virtues which are the commonplaces of praise. Complaint has its own measure of derogation from virtue. As a simple instance, a poem of complaint does not normally present a reverse picture of that prevailing under the conditions of *fíor flatha*. The flourishing fertile land, rivers full of life, poets well treated, which are standard signals in the poetry of the reign of a rightful/righteous king, are the obverse of that which is often presented (in the period considered in this study) not in satire, but in elegy. It is on the death of a lord that the land shrivels, the rivers dry up and poets are neglected.[7] Indeed, in the classic Irish complaint room is always provided for praise.[8]

In the spirit fostered by consciousness of the literary environment that surrounded (literary) composition in the vernacular and in Latin in the High Middle Ages – some treatises of which have been examined above – it is worthwhile looking at some Irish schools' examples of the use of some of the most common rhetorical devices employed in complaint/blame.

Poems of blame, complaint, reconciliation, and even petition, use the figure of *licentia* to identify the source of their discontent, sense of betrayal or impatience and disappointment. *Licentia* in the pseudo-Ciceronian *Rhetorica ad Herennium* outlines the nature of the figure:

> . . . Frankness of Speech when, talking before those to whom we owe reverence or fear, we yet exercise our right to speak out, because we seem justified in reprehending them, or persons dear to them, for some fault (*AdHer*, §36, pp. 348–353).

The amelioration of the 'frankness' is comprehended within the use of this figure. It can be palliated with flattering statements – 'as a result, the praise frees the hearer from wrath and annoyance' (*AdHer*, §36, p. 351). In short, the flexibility of the device of Frankness of Speech (*licentia*) is assured by the latitude allowed in its use:

> This figure, called Frankness of Speech will, as I have shown, be handled in two ways: with pungency, which, if too severe, will be mitigated by praise; and with pretence, . . . which does not require mitigation, because it assumes the guise of Frank Speech and is

itself agreeable to the hearer's frame of mind (*AdHer*, §36, p. 355).

In *On Style* the description by the author 'Demetrius' (*fl.* first century AD) *On Style*[9] is even more explicit as to the effect sought by poets using these features from the rhetorical menu:

§291 People often use words with an equivocal meaning. If you wanted to be like them and use invective which does not seem invective, there is an example in Aeschines' passage about Telauges. Almost the whole account . . . will leave you puzzled whether it is meant as admiration or mockery. This ambiguous way of speaking, although not irony, yet has a suggestion of irony.

§292 Innuendo may be used in yet another way, as in this case: since powerful men and women dislike hearing their own faults mentioned, we will not speak openly, if we are advising them against a fault, but we will either blame others who have acted in a similar way, . . . or we will praise people who have acted in the opposite way . . .

§294 . . . Flattery is shameful, open criticsm is dangerous, and the best course lies in the middle, namely innuendo (D. Innes, *Demetrius, On Style*, pp. 515–519).

An early fourteenth-century Ulster lord, Tomás Mág Shamhradháin (*c.* 1303–1343) is, presumably, the patron of one of the earliest extant collections of bardic poetry dedicated to members of one family – the earliest extant *duanaire*.[10] The collection contains poems to Brian Mág Shamhradháin who died in 1298, to Maghnus Mág Shamhradháin (d. 1303), to Tomás Mág Shamhradháin (1303–1343), to Niall Mág Shamhradháin (d. 1363) and to Fearghal Mág Shamhradháin (d. 1393); to Gormlaidh, daughter of Brian (wife of Matha Ó

Raghallaigh [*LMS*, p. 409]), and to Sadhbh Ní Chonchubhair (d. 1373) wife of Niall. Three generations of a branch of the Í Bhriuin Bréifne who became surnamed Mág Shamhradháin some time after the eponymous Samhradhán (*fl. c.* 1100) are celebrated in the *duanaire*. The family, noted in annal entries for four hundred years from the early thirteenth century, were based in modern Co. Cavan with headquarters in the barony of Tullyhaw (Teallach n-Eachach, named for the eighth-century ancestor, Eochaidh). The family were allied personally and politically to the neighbouring lords Ó Ruairc, Ó Raghallaigh, Mac Tighearnáin, and Ó Conchubhair (*LMS*, pp. viii–ix). *Leabhar Mhéig Shamhradháin* provides a very satisfactory sample of the work of a number of poets for one family in the High Middle Ages.

TEACHER AND PUPIL: POET AND LORD

In a poem, '*Geabh do mhúnadh, a mheic bhaoith*', dedicated to Tomás by Ádhamh Ó Fialán,[11] we find that the poet has been despoiled of cattle. L. McKenna's terse note reads, 'Poet seeks restitution of cattle' (*LMS*, p. 420). The poem reads exactly as though that were indeed the case. In a classic *sententia* opening, the poet urges that the '*mac baoth*' [foolish youth] listen to the old adage with which the poem is begun:[12]

> '*Geabh do mhúnudh, a mheic bhaoith*'
> *seanfhocul glan glóir bhionnghaoith*
> *sdiuraidh fear láimh re lochtaibh;*
> *cáir seadh is na seanfhoclaibh.*
> (*LMS*, p. 153, q. 1)

> ['Accept instruction, foolish youth', the precisely stated, sweetly wise, proverb guides a man safely past faults; attention to the proverbs is proper.]

Such a classic beginning prepares one for the schooled nature of what may follow. The introductory proverb signals a composition that intends to follow form in its subject and in its presentation. The poet urges conformity, he himself conforms to the norms of composition and he uses the proverb to direct the didactic tone of what follows: instruction is now to be given. The poet purports to instruct Tomás Mág Shamhradháin, lord of Tullyhaw. In the background to this style of opening is the possibility that the poet, as a teacher in a grammar school patronized by the Mág Shamhradháin family and other prominent members of the local community, may well be the local *ollamh*/master/precentor of grammar, composition and whatever else was taught in the bardic schools. At all events, the poet, Ó Fialán, trusting to the jaded truth of the proverb – whatever its origin (*gidh créad an chúis bhar*[13] *canadh*, q. 2b) – indicates that his composition will be guided by proverbs.

Some seven hundred years of time, and changes in cultural taste among other things, make it difficult now to measure the intentions of compositions such as this by Ó Fialán for Tomás Mág Shamhradháin. However, laying aside the need to equate the poems with actual events liberates the modern reader to detect and to appreciate an engaging irony in this poem. This, it is suggested here, is the intended tone of the composition: the precise timbre for which the poet reached. The balance of allusion, illusion, urbane wit, literary virtuosity and praise tempered with satire, or more correctly – praise in the satirical mode – which signals a mastery of the skills that the training of the poet inculcated, and which the educated listener/reader could thoroughly appreciate.

Understanding the necessity to which poets were put to renew and to recharge the interest of the patron in new works which, convention-bound as they were, were limited as to the scope for novelty in treatment, allows one to appreciate the artifice of the variety of praise offered in a poem such as Ó Fialán's poem for Tomás Mág Shamhradháin. The proverbial qualities in all the formal poems, the qualities of triteness and cliché which they share with the proverbs and adages with which one might legitimately launch a poem, at the same time legitimize a further composition by any poet in that same vein, and accommodate permitted changes which a skilful poet might ring on such familiar material. Occasion and motivation for compositions that are patently stereotypical, and only very vaguely credible as any kind of record of fact, are thus provided and rationalized within the literary enterprise which resulted in the poems which survive to the present.

Having launched his poem with a proverb, and having spoken as old to young, teacher to pupil, philospher to scholar, poet to lord, Ó Fialán continues – almost in a tone of insolence – in the same vein. Quatrains three, four, five, six and seven present proverbs in the nature of the *speculum principis*. These urge the lord to adhere to good seemly conduct, generosity with worldly wealth, gentleness with poets, loyalty to one's lord, avoidance of tilting at untrimmed hedges, care with sharp weapons, prudence in combat, avoidance of the serpent's bite, the dangerous lion, the bear, unjustified aggression, and fighting with dragons, whose breath can kill from afar. This cryptic and clichéd list brings with it the air of the schoolroom, the scholar's primer of listed proverbs, the riddling adages of the teacher. These proverbs are as valid as that with which the poet began the poem, and which are defended by the poet in the second quatrain. They are dedicated to Tomás in quatrain three:

> Ag so treas múinte as mhaith duid,
> a mheic bhaoith as bhorb gcomhraig,
> ná tréig maith ar olc gan ádh,

ná caith go docht an domhnán.
(*LMS*, p. 153, q. 3)

[Herewith, a course of instruction for your good, foolish youth, rough in combat; do not exchange good for luckless evil, do not be niggardly in your dealings with the transitory world.]

The address '*a mheic bhaoith*' echoes that in the opening quatrain, indicating that the adages are directed at the same character and in the same spirit. They are part of the poem's introduction, and set a tone of tradition in precept and usage. In addition to the import of the improving proverbs themselves, the poet presents himself as instructor of a lord, as a master to a pupil. Quatrain eight makes this explicit:

Déana orum, adhair dhi,
ná troid ris an tuinn mbáidhte;
ní fhoghain duid arm re hucht,
tuig, tuig, is garbh an guasacht.
(*LMS*, p. 155, q. 8)

[Obey me, yield to it (instruction): do not struggle with the inundating wave, it does not serve you to confront it with arms; understand, understand, the peril is harsh.]

This quatrain is a warning of a truth to be revealed – some circumstance which threatens the lord. This feature of *transitio* with overtones of *cataplexis* anticipates what follows and creates a sense of expectation and of menace. It adds an interest to a composition which up to now has presented a succession of proverbs. The explication of these *sententia* is given in quatrain nine following. The ten quatrains form a complete unit of anticipation and explication (*prolepsis*):

Tusa an mac baothsa, a bhéal dearg,
a mheic Bhriain nach baoth Gaoidhealg,

tre thocht, a fhir Ché, bham chrodh
olc do dhligh mé do mhúnodh.
(*LMS*, p. 155, q. 9)

[You, red mouth, are this foolish youth, son of Brian
whose language is not foolish; regrettably I was entitled
to instruct you, lord of Cé, because of your coming
after my wealth/cattle.]

Tomás Mág Shamhradháin is addressed here as '*a mheic Bhri-
ain*', a rhetorical feature that allows for postponement of the
form of direct address, lending that – '*a Thomás*' (in q. 20d)
– and that in the form of the title, '*Mág Shamhradháin*' (in q.
25d), an additional emotive force.

FINDING THE THEME

The *inventio* of this poem is a notional theft of cattle. The poet
claims that the lord, Tomás, has stolen what he had already
granted. The fecundity of this *inventio* is exceptionally satis-
factory. The grounds – theft of cattle – allow for the use of the
three styles, high, middle and low, since discussion of attend-
ant circumstances can involve farce (which can be expressed in
the low style) and the highest style, calling on the language of
warfare, valour and the discussion of the honour of the poet
himself. Ó Fialán encapsulates the matter to be explored in his
'found' topic in quatrain ten:

> *Maith dlighim gé a-dubhart sin*
> *do mhúnudhsa, a laoich Luimnigh;*
> *mé do theann, do chlú, a chleath Chláir,*
> *tú leath rob fhearr dom éadáil.*
> (*LMS*, p. 155, q. 10)
>
> [I am fully entitled, as I have said, to teach you, warrior
> of Luimneach; I am your strength, your renown, rod
> of Clár, you are the better half of my wealth.[14]]

TERMS OF ADDRESS

Addressing Tomás here as warrior of Luimneach and support of Clár, the poet alludes to a conventional sense of the scope of Mág Shamhradháin's sway. Although the Clár mentioned here may well have been local, Tomás Mág Shamhradháin was far from being in a position to exercise power over Luimneach or any territory outside of his own lordship in north Connacht, but in the vicissitudes of marriage, of war and of floating alliances, he *could* or *might* be. Similarly, some ancestor of his *could* or *might* have dominated this area at some distant point.

The synecdochical use of '*a bhéal dearg*' (q. 9a) to address Tomás by a part of his body is a commonplace, so frequent in the poetry that its rhetorical impact can often go unremarked. Its skilful use allows for continual reference to the subject of the poem without overuse of the forename or the title. A fortunate consequence of this is the additional impact achieved by the naming of the subject at crucial points in the composition. Frequently the use of the subject's name elevates a banal quatrain to a higher level of interest simply because of the employment of the name or title. The poem can be punctuated by the use of the title or forename, and the cruciality of the quatrain is created simply by the use of the direct formal address in that quatrain.

Quatrains nine and ten together advance the intention of the preceding list of proverbs and declare the type of composition that is intended: Brian's son, Tomás, is the foolish youth of the opening quatrains – the red lip whose language is not foolish. He has abused the poet, interfering with his cattle; the poet is given an entitlement to counsel him. And he shall do so, for as he declares, '*mé do theann, do chlú*' (q. 10c) [I am your strength and your reknown]; Tomás, in this reciprocal relation is the (provider of) the greater portion of the poet's wealth – '*tú leath rob fhearr dom éadáil*' (q. 10d).

FULCRUM

This is a rhetorical fulcrum, understood, whether stated or not, in all the formal poetry of the Irish school poets. The balance to be achieved on either side of this is the stuff of all praise-poetry. The poet uses a version of the reciprocal relation in this poem. The variety is the complaint – the balance is out of kilter, the poet is fulfilling his side of the bargain, the lord is neglectful of, or in violation of, his. The scope offered to poets in this variety of praise ensured its popularity. Ó Fialán's treatment of this hackneyed theme in this poem is masterful.

THE OFFENCE

The sixteen quatrains following (to quatrain twenty-six) outline various ways in which the lord has offended the poet, all concerning property – including the poet's intellectual property of poetry, and that of his honour – and due rewards. In the low style[15] appropriate to the market-place chosen in quatrain eleven, the poet indicates the kind of payment he has already received from Tomás:

> Trí mairg déag do dháilis damh
> re taobh t'éadaigh is t'arradh
> i n-iongnais bhó is [eich][16] is óir,
> mó ná an [bhreith] ionnmhais m'onóir.
> (LMS, p. 155, q. 11)

[Thirteen marks, you gave me, along with your clothes and your equipage, besides cows, horses and gold; greater than the securing of wealth is my honour.]

Thirteen marks, a gift of the lord's clothes and equipage, cows, horses and gold, which the poet has received from the lord, are to be weighed against the value of the poet's honour. He finds himself more concerned for honour than for wealth: 'mó ná an [bhreith] ionmhais m'onóir' (q. 11d). Focusing here on his honour, the poet steers the composition in the direction of umbrage, an affront to his honour that cannot be assuaged by material wealth, such as the undoubted riches outlined in quatrain eleven. It is not a simple matter therefore of restitution of goods by the lord to the poet, though this might well have formed the basis of the poem. Ó Fialán's composition is more ambitious in its approach. The option to amplify the composition, which we have seen as the popular option in the poems that have survived, is seized upon by Ó Fialán on this occasion, creating a poem of some fifty-seven quatrains. Ó Fialán was, on the evidence of this poem alone, trained in the skills required to keep such a composition airborne. The necessity to adorn, embellish and bedeck a poem of this length called on quite a number of the features taught in the schools. Those which we know were taught in the manuals of composition serve as signposts for a journey through Ó Fialán's extravagant address to Tomás Mág Shamhradháin.

MUTUALITY

Quatrain twelve, therefore, reiterates the grounds on which the poet stands – the premises of the argument[17] which governs the poet/lord relationship:

Ionbhaidh duid, a dhearc mhallsa,
teacht ar ceann cruidh chugamsa;
gnáth leam gan rian sguir bham[18] sgoil
triall ar ceann cruidh dod chathroigh.
(*LMS*, p. 155, q. 12)
[Slow eye, it is timely for you to come to fetch wealth from me; I am accustomed – without interrupting my school – to travel to fetch wealth from your city/court.]

This ingenious quatrain indicates the headquarters of both parties: the *cathair* (city, citadel) of the lord; and the *sgoil*, headquarters of the poet. They each have a stronghold from which they act in the reciprocal arrangement that characterizes their relationship. The quatrain attempts to redistribute the weights on either side of the fulcrum to restore the 'imbalance', which is the driving force of this composition. The poet has received gifts and payment at the lord's citadel (q. 11); the lord must now – in this engaging plot – attend at the poet's sphere of activity, the *sgoil*. Though, crucially, the poet does not abandon his school when he visits the lord. The school – here meaning the building, the collected masters and scholars, or the poet's identity as master of the school – keeps the nature of the poem in focus. The address here is that of a poet to a lord, *in the manner of the schools*. What follows is a virtuoso display of that manner.

The cause of complaint in respect of the stolen cattle is made more forcefully in the four quatrains following (quatrains thirteen to sixteen). Tomás Mág Shamhradháin is addressed in these quatrains as '*a chleath ghormAichle; a bharr cró*' (q. 13bd) [support of rich green Achall;[19] leader of the battle group[20]], '*a fhir Challmhoighe*' (q. 14b) [lord of Callmhagh], '*A bharr Cliach*' (q. 15b) [prince of Cliu], '*a chleath Chuilt*' (q. 16c) [rod of Colt]. The epithets of place here, all in the vocative case, attribute qualities to and assign territories to Tomás Mág Shamhradháin. These areas are not necessarily (in each of these cases, perhaps not at all) to be counted among the territories over which Mág Shamhradháin had, or aspired to have, any influence. They perform the function (along with the very important one of adornment and styling) of ameliorating, and at the same time, amplifying the scolding tone of the quatrains. Addressing Tomás as prince in so many ways is a flattery; juxtaposing that with his unspecified interference with the poet's property (q. 9), makes that transgression all the more petty and execrable.

Ó Fialán is careful here to follow the rules of *licentia* – keeping the censorious tone well within the bounds of flattery. It is suggested in this discussion that the censure in this, and in other poems like it, is a use of *inventio* catering to the ever-present necessity to 'find' a variation on a theme of praise that will divert, amuse, remind and flatter. The reminding function is more useful, and more likely, than any notion that the poet might indeed censure a lord. It were easy, the poet suggests, for the lord Tomás to have recognized the poet's animals, since they once were his before becoming part of an exchange (*coimhcheannach*, q. 13d) – poems for cattle.

Saying the same thing only slightly differently (as recommended in Geoffrey of Vinsauf's *Poetria Nova*),[21] quatrain fourteen reiterates the deal: a poem, not gold or other valuables, was exchanged for those cattle. However, it seems that this arrangement has been imperilled (q. 9), and that a reassessment must take place.

REASSESSMENT

Quatrain fifteen ushers in the point at which the poem liberates itself to exploit the freedom offered by the tentative tone indicated by the challenging and exploratory '*Más aithiomlaoid as áil lat*' (q. 15 a) [If your desire is to reassess (with a view to changing the relationship involving a mutual return of our contributions to one another)] :

> *Más aithiomlaoid as áil lat,*
> *a bharr Cliach, mar ad-chonnac*
> *do-bhéar slán choidhche do chradh*
> *'s toirche rem dhán do dhiultadh.*
> (*LMS*, p. 157, q. 16)
> [Prince of Cliu, if your desire is to reassess – as I perceived – I will bid farewell to cattle for ever, and you proceed to refuse my poem.]

This quatrain is a hypothetical readjustment of the relationship, actually cancelling the usual understandings. Use of the provisional '*más*' establishes the conditional or provisional tone of the state of affairs. The seeming narrative truth of this poem, given in the first person by the poet, conforms to the conventions of 'narrative' and 'historia',[22] requiring the recounting of a plausibly possible event that *fieri potuit*, 'could have happened'.[23]

Moving from the hypothetical case indicated by '*más*', the poet advances safely into the territory of blame and threat, after all the crucial 'if it be' has established the rules for this excursus on how matters *might* stand were both poet and lord to abandon their established relationship in the matter of poems and payment.

Quatrain sixteen more or less reiterates the matter of quatrain fifteen. This repetition with slight variation is a common method of achieving length in a composition. An alternative method would be the introduction, perhaps at this point, of a lengthy apologue illustrating some aspect of the dilemma in which the poet and the lord supposedly find themselves. At all events, quatrain sixteen enhances the sense of impending mischief: the poet has heretofore maintained silence on his wrongs, but though the lord has been spared thereby, this will change if the offence go unavenged:

> *Riot im thosd gé tú go se*
> *tríd an aithiomlaoid n-éigne,*
> *gé taoise slán, a chleath Chuilt,*
> *is ágh dá ndeach gan díoghuilt.*
> (*LMS*, p. 157, q. 16)

[Though I have been silent towards you, until now, because of the forced reassessment; though you are safe, rod of Colt, it is war if it go unavenged.]

No harm has been done until now – there is a threat of mischief, and the threat is conditional: '*dá ndeach gan dtoghuilt*' [*if* it go unavenged]. What follows is therefore a projection of a possible reality, featuring real people in a situation that 'might/could' have happened. This satisfies the requirement that satirical writing remain within the realms of reality and contain its salve within its bite. This was important in the context of Irish bardic poetry, the remit of which was overwhelmingly that of eulogy and elegy, and the literary background of which had a very strong sense of satire. Over and above the ability of satire to heal itself is the opportunity afforded by the combination of complaint and reconciliation – common in the body of Irish bardic poetry – for the continual *renewal* of the poet/lord relationship. A predictable re-establishment of terms and a pseudo-negotiation of conditions takes place in poems of complaint/reconciliation. It is mirrored in many ways by the tropes of loss, aridity, sterility and abandonment, which are articulated in elegies.[24]

Elegies almost invariably announce the death of hospitality, art, cultural pursuits, sporting activities, the sovereignty of Banba/Éire/Fódla, and the shrivelling and death of the whole of Nature on the occasion of the death of a lord. The emphasis laid on the departure of all life and art with the demise of the lord is counterpointed by the rebirth and re-establishment of art, the fecundity of Nature, and the sovereignty of Ireland, with the establishment of a new lord.[25]

DEATH-IN-LIFE

Poems of complaint/blame and reconciliation exploit the themes of elegy. They dally with temporary and recoverable deaths: the death of mutual understanding, the death of the contract, the death of love. They create the circumstances in which a living lord can be praised anew, as though returned from the kind of death-in-life which is that suffered by both lord and poet when their relationship breaks down: the poet is no longer supported materially, the lord is dead to history, unsung and anonymous. Ádhamh Ó Fialán's poem for Tomás Mág Shamhradháin is not recounting an episode of depredation by the lord on the poet, nor is it an illustration of the power of the poet to threaten even a great lord with more or less impunity. It is the work of a master-poet applying the skills acquired by study in language and in literature to eulogize his lord with a diverting and virtuoso flourish of his art, employing rhetorical devices guaranteed to produce the desired effect.

At quatrain seventeen, Ó Fialán introduces parallelism: quatrains seventeen to twenty-one parallel the earlier quatrains three to nine. This carefully crafted arabesque finally launches Ó Fialán's poem into the rough waters of threat and entreaty that he needs to take his poem through to the next level. From the list of the proverbs tritely trotted out in the first eight quatrains, the poet has fashioned a very effective weapon: the lesson in each proverb, generalized in the earlier quatrains, is particularized in the parallel quatrains now, and directed at Tomás Mág Shamhradháin. Ó Fialán quite literally flags the literary strategem – '*Ó chianaibh do chan mé sain*' (q. 17a) [Just now I recited this] – and continues to personalize the import of each of the proverbs in a most colourful and bewitching way; the effect is that of incantation:

> *Ó chianaibh do chan mé sain*
> *mise an tonn bháidhte bhunaidh;*
> *dírghidh sé seoladh mo rann,*
> *is mé an leomhan 's an losgann.*[26]
> (*LMS*, p. 157, q. 17)

[Just now I recited this – it guides the direction of my quatrain – I am the earlier inundating wave (q. 8b), I am the lion (q. 6b) and the dragon/lizard (q. 7a).]

Ó Fialán identifies himself in all the warning proverbial statements: he is the bear (q. 18a and q. 6c), the poisonous dragon (q. 17d, 18b and q. 7a), the untrimmed hedge fence (q. 20b and q. 4d).

The impact of Ó Fialán's explication of the proverbs – a technique often applied when an apologue has been used – is enhanced by the series of direct addresses to Tomás in quatrains thirteen to sixteen (see above, p. 118). Tomás's identity is presented in placenames and in synecdoche. The poet is concealed in proverbs, he releases the meaning of both, and climaxes in quatrain twenty using the lord's forename, Tomás, and in associating the lord and poet – 'as you are, I am':

> *Is mé an gríos dearg, a dhaighfir,*
> *mé an fál sgiach nach sgothfaidhir;*
> *is baois rod laoi ar lár na sás*
> *mar a-taoi a-tám, a Thomás.*
> (*LMS*, p. 157, q. 20)

[I am the red ember, good man; I am the untrimmed hedge fence, foolishness brought you to the midst of traps (ensnared), as you are, am I, Tomás.]

In a triumphant flourish this quatrain expresses – in anticipation – the dilemma (*ar lár na sás*) in which the poet and the lord find themselves (*mar a-taoi a-tám*). They are equally affected by a dilemma that has yet to be made clear.

Accompanying this parallel and explicatory treatment of the proverbs, another fugue-like feature adds texture to the composition, and brings it into conformity with the poets' tendency to identify themselves within the poem, whether in support of an argument concerning status or as part of a petitionary appeal. The pattern is normally: You are lord of x, prince of y, pillar of z: *I* am your poet; or *I* am x, and so forth. This device enhances the sense of balance in the petitionary composition, where the poet needs to emphasize the complementarity of the lord/poet relationship.

FOLLY

Meantime, teasing out the implications of the lord's folly (addressed '*a Thomáis mheic Bhriain bhratduinn*' [q. 21b]), the poet makes clear that departure from the lord '*is mó an toghaois do thréagun*' (q. 21d) [the greater deceit would be to desert you] would aggravate the already foolish situation: this threat of departure will put an end to the relationship that generates the poems that give deathless profile to the lord.

The dilemma – its expression here must have given great pleasure and amusement at its boldness and ingeniousness – is the overweening love both lord and poet have for cattle (q. 22). The play on language here is centred on the metaplasmic '*baois*' [folly] (q. 20c; q. 21a); '*robhaois*' [excessive folly] (q. 21c); '*toghaois*' [deceit] (q. 21d; q. 22a). They have the same problem (excessive folly versus greater impropriety), yet the obvious solution that they depart from each other – '*tréigin a chéile*' (q. 22c) – would be a greater betrayal than the original foolishness concerning their dispute about the cattle. Perfect balance is achieved in the language, in the presentation and in the resolution of the dilemma:

> *Gidh baois duid a ndearnois ruinn,*
> *a Thomáis mheic Bhriain bhratduinn,*
> *rem robhaois nocho ró cur;*
> *is mó an toghaois do thréagun.*
> (*LMS*, p. 159, q. 21)

[Though you behaved foolishly towards me, Tomás son
of Brian of the brown cloaks, there will be no increase
in my foolishness: it is a greater deceit to leave you.]

Less than halfway through the poem, the crux of the matter
is faced: the poet has been violated in his property; he was
awarded this property in exchange for poetry; the lord has paid
him otherwise too but his honour has been violated and a re-
establishment of the relationship must take place. The only
solution appears to be mutual separation since both covet cattle,
but that itself would betray both of them and must not be
considered:

> Toghaois mhór dhuid is damhsa
> ar ghrádh bhó, a bharr Ceanannsa,
> tréigin a chéile, a chraobh Mhis,
> 's ar bhféile ar-aon gá haithris.
> (LMS, p. 159, q. 22)

[Lord of Ceanannas, it would be a great deceit for
you and for me, for the sake of cows, to abandon one
another, and our mutual generosity similarly, tree of
Mis.]

Bridging the chasm between the intention to separate and the
impossibility of that happening (else the poem and the poet are
redundant), quatrain twenty-three refocuses the poem.[27] The
poet, suggesting that his nobility is not equal to that of his lord,
indicates that he can forgive the loss of his cattle for better cattle.
This quatrain is neatly completed with another proverb: 'ní dú
an dá chruaidh go coimhtheann' (q. 23d) [it is not fitting that
two solid objects are equally rigid]; the poet is the irresistible
force, the lord the immovable object.

THE TWO PATHS

Quatrain twenty-four changes the tone of the poem into that of exasperated love. The gender ambiguity in Ó Fialán's appeal to Mág Shamhradháin is a noted feature of Irish bardic poetry.[28] It is not a characteristic restricted to Irish poetry, however, and the flexibility of gender identity – as distinct from sexual identity – in the poetry of the schools in general can sometimes confuse and lead to absurd claims about lord/poet relationships.

At all events, Ó Fialán is seduced by his love of Tomás Mág Shamhradháin and this defeats his sense of wrong. It were falsehood for the prince of Almha to change *his* feelings towards the poet:[29]

> *An grádh mór is mealladh damh*
> *tugas duid, a fhir Almhan;*
> *dod dhreich amlaigh*[30] *rob fhallsa*
> *gan bheith amhlaidh umamsa.*
> (*LMS*, p. 159, q. 24)
>
> [The great love that I gave you seduces me, prince of Almha; it were false for your fair face not to be the same towards me.]

A paronomastic play on *Almha, amhlaigh* and *amhlaidh* is just one of the ornaments of rhetorical colour on display here.

The hypothesis of the lord's falsehood becomes the certainty permitting the following quatrain; what has been a suggested separation in the preceding quatrains, and what has been eschewed in view of their mutual love, is presented as the case in fact in quatrain twenty-five: the separation has taken place in revenge for the lord's faithlessness:

> *'Mat fhallsacht aiseag d'fhagháil*
> *[rod] thréag mé, a Mhéig Shamhradháin;*
> *suil tréiginn tú, a ghruadh mar ghlain,*

truagh nach gan bhú do bhámair.
(*LMS*, p. 159: q. 25³¹)

[Seeking restitution in your duplicity, lord Mág Shamhradháin, I have abandoned, before I would abandon you, glass-like cheek; a pity it is that we had any cows at all.]

The poet regrets that either of them had any cattle, since it has led to the separation.³²

This faithlessness, the despoliation of the poet's property hinted at in quatrain nine, must be such a tiny matter for the lord *'Créad acht [beag] agad uile . . . mo chrodhsa'* (q. 26ab), the resigned poet declares that he will no longer scold about it since the lord understands exactly what he is saying: *'tuige go léir a labhroim'* (q. 26d).

The stalemate is resolved in the invocation of that most mischievous event, the hasty word spoken against the lord. Ó Fialán denies that he ever uttered the unmeasured word against Mág Shamhradháin. Addressing his lord as *'a ghríobh Orc'* (q. 27c) [griffin of Orkney] he declares that neither in earnest, nor in jest, had he expressed himself against Mág Shamhradháin. The poem has, with this quatrain, been turned around from the threat of the poet's wrath, expressed in the explication of the proverbs; to the threatened separation, which then became a reality that must be resolved; to the declaration, now by the poet, that, far from having spoken against the lord, his love for him prevented him from doing so (q. 27):

. . . is mór an grádh, a ghríobh Orc,
gan a rádh d'fhíor nó d'ábhocht.
(*LMS*, p. 159, q. 27cd).

[Griffin of Orkney great love it is not to say it (*aonghuth* 'a single word') in earnest nor in jest.]

Great as that love is, however, it is not love that prevented the poet from the rough word, but the fact that – in spite of himself – he could find no fault with Mág Shamhradháin.

> *Ní hé an grádh ro anaic orm*
> *do ghnúis gcorcra, a chleath Mhughdhorn,*
> *gidh ionmhain t'fholt craobhnocht cam*
> *acht gan aonlocht ort agam.*
> (*LMS*, p. 159, q. 28)

[Not love protected your noble purple cheek from me, rod of Mughdhorn – though your curled ungarlanded hair is beloved – but that I find no fault with you.]

A scenario of disappointed/slighted but righteous love is created by Ó Fialán's declaration that his love was sincere (*neamhfhallsa*, q. 29a) and of serious consequence (*díochra a iarmuirt*, q. 29b). 'Others' warned him that his behaviour would mean a devaluation of his poem – '*ger iomdha neach gá rádh ruinn / gor mheath dom dhán a ndéanuinn*' (q. 29cd).

'CAITHRÉIM'

This 'wronged love' theme is parlayed into a list (qq. 31–39) of Mág Shamhradháin's victories in battle, a *caithréim* that ascribes to him the ravaging and subduing of territories within and beyond his realistic sphere of influence. The introduction to the *caithréim*, presented in accordance with the conventions of the rhetorical *occultatio/paralipsis* (of emphasis by declaring what will *not* be said), is the poet's admission of equal fear and love of Mág Shamhradháin:

> *Dá chúis b[h]ar dhéachussa dhuid*
> *gan t'aoradh trá is tú id charuid*
> *– d'fhios do fhreagra a-tám ag triall –*
> *do ghrádh is t'eagla ar éinrian.*
> (*LMS*, p. 161, q. 30)

[Two reasons why I looked to you without satirizing
you however, since you are my friend: love for you
and fear of you at the same time – I am seeking your
answer.³³]

This is a thematically zeugmatic quatrain: the poet's fear and
love of Mág Shamhradháin is on a single track split into two
paths. Fear is the emotion calling forth the *caithréim*:

> *Cá hiath nach badh eagail leam*
> *t'oirbheart fada ar fud Éireann?*
> . . .
> *is tearc críoch nachar chreachois.*
> (*LMS*, p. 161, q. 31abd)

[In what land need I not fear your extensive exploits
throughout Ireland? . . . there is scarely a territory you
have not despoiled.]

Using the synonomous verbs *creach* (plunder, despoil)
and *airg* (harass, spoil) to build an image of splendid
military chaos through eight quatrains, the poet eulogizes
Mág Shamhradháin's effectiveness as military lord. This is
true panegyric to a lord addressed successively as '*a dhreach
amhlach*' [handsome face, q. 32b], '*a ghríobh fhaltbhuidhe*'
[yellow-haired griffin (hero), q. 32d], '*a chleath Mhis*' [rod of
Mis, q. 33c], '*a bharr cleath*' [topmost of supports, q. 34d],
'*a airgnigh Gailian*' [harasser of Leinster, q. 35b], '*a fhir
Chualann*' (q. 37b).³⁴

The figure of *traductio* is used to exploit the expression *creach*
as noun and verb, q. 33 cd; q. 34a. A nice variety of this is
involved in q. 34c where the verb *airg* and the noun *creach*
are combined – '*do airg bhar gcreach . . .*' (q. 34c). Master-
fully, Ó Fialán combines the verb '*do airgis tar Sionainn siar*'
(q. 35a) with the agent noun in the vocative '*a airgnigh Gailian*'
(q. 35ab). The continual use of *creach* and *airg* create an effect

of relentlessness, fully intended by the poet in his employment of *conduplicatio* and of *interpretatio*, using successive words of equivalent meaning and repeating them: '. . . *nachar chreachois*' (q. 31d); '*do chreachais . . . chrích nDartraighe . . .*' (q. 32ab); '*do airgis . . . maicne . . . Pheodachán*' (q. 33ab); '*do chreach sibh síos go Soilchis*' (q. 33d); '*do chreachais . . . sluagh . . . clann Raghoilligh*' (q. 34ab); '*do airg bhar gcreach clann F.*' (q. 34c); '*do airgis tar Sionainn siar*' (q. 35a); *do airgis . . . Thír n-Oilealla*' (q. 36ab); '*Breifne . . . d'airgis*' (q. 37ab), '*a agra ort*' in line c is intended to echo *airg*. The litany of destruction is concluded with a derivative of *creach*: '*Is tú creachaire i gcrích Thé . . .*' (q. 38a). Whatever the impact this multi-textured list had on the lord to whom it was addressed, the poet's peers, those trained in the schools with him, would have revelled in the stunning employment of the range of ornaments noted here.[35]

At quatrain thirty-nine, having followed the lord Mág Shamhradháin's victories through eight quatrains, the poet declares, using the standard figure *occultatio/paralipsis*, that as revenge for the loss of his cattle, he will mention no more of Mág Shamhradháin's victories, regretting even those he has mentioned:

> *Ní áireomh th'ágh seacha soin*
> *i n-íoc mo bhó, a bharr Beannchoir;*
> *díoghailt chruaidh ghrod do-ghéanom,*
> *buaidh do throd ní thuiréamhom.*
> (*LMS*, p. 163, q. 39)
>
> [I shall mention no more of your valour beyond that,
> in recompense for my cows, lord of Beannchor; I shall
> exact a hard, prompt revenge: I shall not recite your
> battle victories.]

This future tense, the poet's intention to avoid all further mention of Mág Shamhradháin's victories, has the force of a threat after the fact. The victories have already been celebrated, and the poet's threat is calibrated to ensure that the praise overwhelms the implied censure.

Never loath to repeat a variation of the same point in another quatrain, Ó Fialán, in quatrain forty, regrets that little he has expressed already: this form of *litotes*, or understatement, serves to highlight the figure governing this *caithréim*, a combination of *conduplicatio*, of *repetitio* and of *gradatio*.

Quatrains forty and forty-one hammer home the point that the poet has mentioned only a handful of the lord's victorious raids and wars:

> *Gidh beag do áirmhius dot ágh*
> *dearmad tug orm a iomrádh,*
> *a chúl fionn na bhfaichleath gcas,*
> *is aithreach liom ar labhras.*
> (*LMS*, p. 163, q. 40)

[Though I have mentioned but little of your valour, forgetfulness caused me to note it; fair-haired one of the curled ringlets; I regret what I have spoken.]

This regret is that of a lover who has misread his love's interest, and exposed his own excessive love.

The love-theme is supported throughout by the synecdochical references to, and addresses to, Mág Shamhradháin in respect of his person – and particularly of his hair – before Ó Fialán makes the love-theme explicit from quatrain forty-nine: '*a bhéal dearg*' (q. 9a); '*a dhearc mhallsa*' (q. 12a); '*. . . red chéibh gcoim*' (q. 26c); '*. . . red ndreich n-amhlaigh*' (q. 27b; q. 32b); '*do ghnúis gcorcra*' (q. 28b); ' *[gidh] ionmhain t'fholt craobhnocht cam*' (q. 28c); '*a ghríobh fhaltbhuidhe*' (q. 32d); *a chúl fionn na bhfaichleath gcas*' (q. 40 c); '*. . . fat fholt chas*' (q. 44b); '*. . . dod ghnúis mhínréidh*' (q. 47b); '*a fholt mar órshnáth*' (q. 48b); '*a fholt fháinneach*' (q. 49b).

GENEALOGY

But before Ó Fialán picks up the thread of the second '*cúis*' of quatrain thirty (*Dá chúis bar dhéachussa dhuid . . . . do g*h*rádh is t'*eagla *ar éinrian* [*LMS*, p. 161, q. 30ad, emphasis added], following the second of the two paths, fear and love), quatrains forty-one and forty-two actually introduce the word '*aor*' (q. 41d; q. 42b), employed in both cases to emphasize why the poet could *not* satirize the lord. This sense is separate to that of the figure used earlier, in that it is more directly a figure of eulogy: it is because of his great vigour and long campaigning that Ó Fialán feared to satirize Mág Shamhradháin. This fear/awe serves to introduce another measure of praise – the poet's respect for Mág Shamhradháin's ancestors and family connections. As an elaboration of the 'fear' path mentioned in quatrain thirty, it allows the poet to present the genealogical material in a very pleasant and varied way. Instead of listing those nobles to whom the lord is related, he links the 'list' to his [the poet's] fear of satirizing Mág Shamhradháin because of his extensive links with the most formidable families in Ireland. The nature of this fear enhances the reputation and status of poet and lord. The 'warrior of Bóroimhe' (*a fhir Bhóroimhe*, q. 42b), the 'captain' (*taoiseach*, q. 42d) is related to all the heroes of Ireland. No province in Ireland is without noble families who would not permit that Mág Shamhradháin be satirized (q. 45b, q. 46b, q. 47c, q. 48b). The Munstermen would not tolerate any satirizing of Mág Shamhradháin (q. 45), nor would the men of Connacht (q. 46), nor those of Leinster (q. 46).

The esteem in which Mág Shamhradháin is generally held, along with his ferocity and awe-inspiring valour, prevents Ó Fialán from satirizing him. The two fears are paths to eulogy and, along with the earlier use of the figures of repetition and creation of a sense of climax (*conduplicatio* and *gradatio*) (see above, p. 131), Ó Fialán has exploited the technique comprehensively. The digression into the *caithréim* and the genealogical material, which, in themselves, are unambiguously eulogistic, is concluded in quatrains forty-seven and forty-eight. Quatrain forty-seven reminds the lord that his close kinship with the Ulster dynasties of Eoghan and Conall forbids all satire of him:

> *Conall is síol Eoghain fhéil*
> *mór a ngaol dod ghnúis mhínréidh;*
> *ní léig th'aoir ngrinn do ghabháil,*
> *a Mhéig bhinn shaoir Shamhradháin.*[36]
> (*LMS*, p. 165, q. 47)

[Conall and the descendants of liberal Eoghan, great is their kinship with your smooth gentle face; it does not allow sharp satire of you, noble sweet Mág Shamhradháin.]

LOVE-POEM

Mág Shamhradháin is addressed as having a 'gentle sweet face' (*gnúis mhínréidh*, q. 47 b), and in a eulogistic flourish: '*a Mhéig bhinn shaoir Shamhradháin*' (q. 47 d) [Sweet noble Mág Shamhradháin]. These are terms of unmixed endearment and praise.[37] In quatrain forty-eight the threat is abandoned, at once finishing the theme of menace in the poem, summing up the argument against satire, and emphasizing Mág Shamhradháin's reputation and influence throughout Ireland:

> *Aonrann dá gcuirinn fa cháidh*
> *dot aoir, a fholt mar órshnáth,*
> *ro badh cian ó siobhal sinn*
> *ní bhiadh m'ionudh i n-Éirinn.*
> (*LMS*, p. 165, q. 48)

[Were I to broadcast a single quatrain satirizing you, hair like gold thread; I would be far from travelling it, (i.e. being free to travel round it) – there would be no place for me in Ireland.]

Again, the lord is addressed in respect of his beautiful hair, in this instance in the lover-like terms: '*a fholt mar órshnáth*'. With this quatrain, Ó Fialán returns to the second strand of the two causes of quatrain thirty: '*Dá chúis bhar dhéachussa dhuid. . . / do ghrádh is t'eagla ar éinrian*' (q. 30ad).[38] The theme of fear has been dealt with, now for that of love. It is as a lover that Ó Fialán addresses Mág Shamhradháin. He summarizes the events, invoking Christ's blessing on them both: an unlikely/improbable anger befell the poet. In other words, a mutual misunderstanding has taken place. It is now time to overcome this:

> *Crois Chríosd tarainn leath ar leath;*
> *do chosg m'fheirge, a fholt fáinneach,*
> *fearg éadáigh a-dréacht damhsa,*
> *sléacht an chéadáir chugamsa.*
> (*LMS*, p. 165, q. 50)

[Christ's cross over us both; to check my anger, curled-haired one, an improbable anger arose in me (befell me), incline at once toward me.]

The 'curled-haired one' (Mág Shamhradháin) is requested to incline now to the poet. The request, such as only a lover could make, is amplified into an order in quatrains fifty, fifty-one and fifty-two. '*Sléacht an chéadáir chugamsa*' is the basic order, 'Incline at once toward me'. This audacious demand is repeated in the two quatrains following, with elaboration:[39]

> *Sléacht chugam ó chionn go cois,*
> *sir loghudh, a laoich Bhearnais,*
> *sléacht an malaigh ndrumchaoil nduibh,*

's an aghaidh subhchaoimh sochruidh.
(*LMS*, p. 165, q. 50)

[Incline to me from head to toe, seek forgiveness, hero
of Bearnas, incline the dark, narrow-topped brow, and
the handsome face, sweet as berries.]

Sléacht an t-abhra craobhach corr,
sin [sin] an béal corcra chugom,
tabhair phóig go díochra dhamh,
dar móid fhíochdha budh athchar.
(*LMS*, p. 165, q. 51)

[Incline the flowing curled eyelash, extend the purple
mouth to me, give me a fervent kiss, by my oath for
my (lit. 'our') ferocious resolve it would be banishment
(i.e. it would dispel my furious mood).]

These demands come also with a demand that the lord seek
forgiveness, '*sir loghudh*' (q. 50b). This is in the context of
his rights as a lover, forgiveness is the gift of the hurt one –
the powerful lord can afford to indulge the importunate poet.
The plea for the renewal of affectionate terms in quatrain fifty-
two is exactly that of pride and imploring. This is achieved by
exchanging the abandoner for the abandoned. Ó Fialán intro-
duced the threat of abandoning Mág Shamhradháin, now it is
the lord who abandons the poet:

Athchrom ar n-éissíoth uainn as
– gom thréagon ó taoi deanas –
fa ghnaoi nochon éadubh ás
gom thréagun ó taoi, a Thomás.
(*LMS*, p. 165, q. 52)

[Let us put aside our strife as a result of it (following the
sléachtadh) – since you have abandoned me for a while
(lit. 'the space of a day') – I cannot grow in repute,
Tomás, since you are abandoning me.]

This theme is concluded at quatrain fifty-three when Ó Fialán, addressing the lord with the full title '*A Thomás mhac Briain Bhearbha, Mhéig Shamhradháin shaoirfheardha*' (q. 53ab) [noble manly, Tomás Mág Shamhradháin, son of Brian of Bearbha], pleads for 'cows' without deceit. The poet is entitled to ask for this without arousing the ire of his lord, '*cuid d'fhalaidh ní dú dham dhe, / tabhair bhú gan chradh ceilge*' (q. 53cd). The poem has successfully mingled the gifts of cattle and poems with those of love and intimacy, so that this final quatrain is pleading for both, gifts without complications and love without deception.

The final four quatrains are envoy quatrains to Mág Shamhradháin's wife, Nualaidh, daughter of Mág Uidhir and Éadaoin (Ní Cheallaigh), a woman whose generosity and nobility shield her from the fumes of his language '*saor thú ar ghal mo Ghaoidheilge*' (q. 55d) (a poet's displeasure expressed in satire); to Lasair Fhíona (daughter of Tomás and Nualaidh[?]); and Athracht, a saint to whom the poet offers this quatrain (q. 57), is addressed similarly, with different import: '*saor thú ón chrábhudh cheilge*' (q. 57d) [you are free of deceitful piety].

5. Bardic love, troubadour love

The nature of the 'love' expressed in the literary genres associated with *amour courtois* has long been understood to have influenced Irish literature.[1] Seán Ó Tuama traces a background in *amour courtois* for many of the traditional songs known to the Irish oral tradition.[2] The love-poetry in the learnèd tradition (and that of the so-called nobleman amateur),[3] which emerged from the fourteenth century on and seemed to find its culmen in Irish syllabic love-poems of the sixteenth century, is another branch of the same phenomenon.[4] Its debt to French and English contemporary literature has been examined by M. Mac Craith.[5] The particular kind of love, poet for lord, as expressed throughout the schools' poetry, and characteristic of the eulogy, elegy, complaint and petition, has much in common with both types.

The metaphors and tropes of 'love', as expressed in the Irish schools' poetry, as that pertaining to the lord and poet, are ubiquitous. But the function of the 'love' expressed in such poems as that of Ádhamh Ó Fialán for Tomás Mág Shamhradháin, or that later expressed by Tadhg Óg Ó hUiginn, for instance, for Uilliam Búrc (see below, p. 171), and so forth, was quite different to that expressed in love-poetry *per se*.[6] The language of physical beauty and attempted seduction (including success and failure) used in the schools' formal praise/blame poetry, though it shares many features of male/female love-poetry, was put to different use. The use of the language 'love'-poems by poets for lords extended the life of composition and allowed the utilization, by the poet, of the rich literary heritage of love-genres. The richness of the literary hinterland of the tropes and techniques used in the 'love'-themes of the schools' poetry allows a connection to be made (in this study) between the works of the Irish bardic poets and those of the archetypal love-poets, the troubadours.

POET AND TROUBADOUR

Many of the areas of unclarity that surround the cultural identity and compositions of Irish bardic poets are similar to those that puzzle those who study the works of the troubadours. The similarities are evident at many levels. For instance, the characteristics of the troubadour language, the courtly range of their topics, and their expressed unease about their social and literary status, are features shared with Irish bardic poets. The decline in the production of troubadour lyrics is generally attributed the expansion of the French monarchy, to the ravages of the Albigensian Crusade, and to political changes in the area of their enterprise. The tendency to attribute the demise of a literary genre to political causes is mirrored in the case of Irish bardic poetry. The expansion of Tudor dynastic rule and its effects in Ireland in the sixteenth century is generally credited with the decline in the production of the classical syllabic praise-poems.[7] In both cases, that of the troubadour lyrics and of the Irish syllabic praise-genres, all the causes of diminishment and evaporation referred to above can be seen as remarkably coincidental, and not entirely improbable.

Such conclusions are, however, also determinedly predicated on a more or less literal, or, at least, selectively literal, reading of both literatures. Nevertheless, while troubadour lyrics and Irish syllabic poetry seem to overlap in topics, themes and treatments, it seems illogical in cause, in effect, and in sequence, to suggest that the Anglo-Norman military invasion of Ireland led to the flourishing of Irish syllabic poetry in the courtly praise genres – with their similarities to the troubadour lyric – while the expansion of Norman courtly culture, and those same conditions, into Provence, and other troubadour territories should be seen as the cause of the latter's demise.[8]

It is likewise somewhat contradictory that in the case of Irish literature the development of the syllabic verse composed between 1200 and 1650 is seen as a derogation of the high standard of Irish literary creativity that existed before the Anglo-Norman military intervention in the twelfth century, while its demise in the seventeenth century is viewed as a catastrophic effect of Tudor expansion. A less dramatically literal presentation of the material itself, and an enhanced sense of its belonging to a literary continuum, reduces the need for identifying peaks of achievement and troughs of decline, especially when the apogee and corresponding nadir are made to coincide with interpretations of political developments that are understandably subject to the vagaries of historiographical trends.[9]

Troubadours – from what W. E. Burgwinkle describes as the 'Hispano-Catalan-Italiano-Provençal region'[10] – shared a common literary language. And in sharing a language (Provençal [Occitan]), which was used for their lyrics,[11] they shared in a literary world as well:

> [troubadours] . . . actually expressed themselves
> . . . not in the common *romana lingua*, but in
> clearly distinct linguistic systems as well as in the
> supranational Occitan literary *koiné*. . . . Common
> literary language meant also common themes: courtly
> lover, political and religious debate, and laments for
> the dead.[12]

There is, of course, some similarity between the use of Provençal across a dialectally diverse region and the use of the bardic norm throughout Gaelic Scotland and Ireland: both forms were used by poets and writers whose colloquial forms may have differed significantly. There is, however, a noteworthy difference of status: Provençal was a regional form thought appropriate to a particular literary function; the bardic norm was a non-regional standard.[13] The register of the language used in Irish schools' poetry was common to Ireland and to Scotland.[14]   Themes and treatments were similarly shared in Ireland and Gaelic Scotland.   Irish place-lore, legends and mythologies and genealogies were sewn into Scottish compositions and woven into the fabric of their works.   Prominent families on both sides of the Sea of Moyle (Sruth na Maoile) shared genealogical roots and resources and aspired to positions of consequence in each generation. Poets perpetuated these links and celebrated them generation after generation in formal compositions.[15]   The common literary product was the fruit of an identical education. Poets travelled, interchangeably, from Ireland to Scotland in pursuit of training in poetry.

The reflex of the distinctions involved in the grades of Irish poets originally centred on a notional legal status, and a careful calibration in respect of ecclesiastical grades. These devolved eventually to the distinctions between *file*, *draoi* and *bard*.[16] Writing on grades in Irish poetry and the status of the poets of the varying grades occupied commentators in the Middle Ages. L. Breatnach, editor of the principal text on poetic grades, *Uraicecht na Ríar*, presents in tabular form the grades of poet, the attainments in composition, the legal compensation due to and from, the permitted number in retinue of each grade. Technical terms for the grades themselves and other details changed from text to text. Whatever the original validity of the matter, by the twelfth century the distinctions between grades were part of the rhetorical armoury of the poet in petitions, in comparisons with other poets, in challenges to patrons, and in the humorous exchanges probably intended for fellow-poets.

Many of the definitions surrounding the appropriate levels of composition involved under the different titles – apart from those which indicate a realistic stage in professional attainment – suggest an effort to attribute a creating personality to the compositions rather than to rank the composer. Reference to attainment of the highest rank and the steps required to reach it created an endless source of material for exploitation. The sense of categorization and ranking is analogous to the division of diction and theme in the theories of style. The moral status and social behaviour of the varying grades (of poet) suggest the permitted 'voices' for certain kinds of composition. This seems a very likely background for the kind of hair-splitting distinctions that seem to attend the following rankings in Provençal literature:

> Like the *trovador*, the *segrel* composes his own poems; this is an inherent part of his profession and not a merely accidental occurrence as is the case with the *jogral*. He differs from the *trovador* in that his public performances also include the works of other poets, and above all, in that he expects to be paid for his songs while the *trovador* is an independent *fidalgo*. . . . At the social level, the *segrel* is a nobleman of the lowest rank, a poor *escudeiro* who has to earn a living through his poetry, but some scholars, reluctant to grant noble rank to the *segreis*, view them rather as forming 'una burguesía literaria entre la nobleza trovadoresca y los juglares villanos'. Although the *segrel* believes in his own professional dignity, his life-style is that of a *jogral*; he is a heavy drinker, he frequents women of ill repute, and he is deep into quarrels and gambling (F. Jensen, *The Earliest Portuguese Lyrics*, pp. 29–30).

Efforts to distinguish between the different levels and status of Irish poets, and between self-identifications of *bard* and *file*, involve similar categorizations. The relative inferiority of the *bard* in contrast to the elevated status of the *file*, and to the unquestioned primacy of the *ollamh*, have all revolved around questions of honour, status, and practice.[17]

The seeming obsession of Irish poets and continental poets[18] with degrees of status likewise evolved into what amounted to a literary theme with endless elaborations on what was involved with the varying titles attributed to poets and to their compositions. A species of 'defence of poets/poetry' literature became a commonplace among the literati, as outlined here by E. Schulze-Busacker:

> Guiraut Riquier's famous defense of the troubadours addressed to Alfonso X of Castile, and the king's answer, explain the different designations given to the Occitan poets in an analytic way and with certainly two things in mind: the real cultural decline of Occitan culture and the new linguistic situation under Northern French power, about to impose French as the official language, even in the Midi. Alfonso states in 1285 that *joglar* has been the current Occitan name for the *ioculator*, the public entertainer. With the decline of Occitan, it is now extended to the troubadours, who are called by the same terms as the *joglars: remendadors, segriers, cazuros* in Spain, *bufos* in Lombardy. The king wants them to be distinguished once more as *trobador* – or even for the best of them, *doctor de trobar*. This document confirms what is obvious in the didactic works of the same period, that Castilian and Lombard . . . are considered different idioms

by Occitan-writing poets in the second half of the
13th century, as were French, Galician-Portuguese,
Gascon, and Sicilian by the first theorists of Occitan
literature, Jofre de Foixà, Raimon Vidal, and Guilhem
Molinier . . . [19]

The rhetoric of the troubadours indicated a dislike, a distrust and a rejection of the literary culture of Northern France,
though the reality of this is belied in the familiarity among
the more well-known troubadours with the literary works of
the North, and the survival of contemporary lists of works to
be learned (by them) included standard texts of the northern
literary canon:

> The three authors, a Catalan and two Occitans,
> knew the same epic material as the Northern poets,
> for they mention the 'matière de Bretagne', . . the
> romances of Chrétien de Troyes, the Tristan legend,
> and even the four romances, *Thebes*, *Troie*, *Eneas*,
> and *Alexandre*. This proves that Guiraut de Cabrera,
> Guiraut de Calanson, and Bertrand de Paris were able
> to understand French. The same is probably true
> for the unknown author of *Flamenca*, who provides
> an analogous list of Northern works presented at
> the heroine's marriage, and for a great number of
> troubadours quoting French literature (ibid., p. 34).

Likewise the expansion of Plantagenet dynastic rule from the
south of France to the south of Scotland made the works of
various troubadours attached to noblemen and courtiers, and
of course to the king, known throughout their territories.[20]
Twelfth-century Ireland was part of this world.[21]

LATIN AND THE VERNACULAR

Churchmen exchanged poetry and literary materials and indulged in literary games with known troubadours.[22] Both churchmen and troubadours were educated in the basics of Latin literature – literacy, for the most part, meant basic literacy in Latin.[23] The Irish poets who, being literate in Irish and in Latin, participated wholly in the grammar school ethos of the Latin schools, advanced into their own literary domain when they adapted their learning and applied it to the creation and pursuit of vernacular poetry, but they kept abreast of literary trends in general in so doing.[24] There was no audience or readership for what modern sensibilities would understand as 'original' or eccentrically personal presentations of material.[25]

A predictable and diverting variation on the expected was the goal of any creative writer. Among the literate, composition in the vernacular and in Latin was a matter of choice, of style and of occasion. C. H. Haskins notes the porosity of the two systems in the career of the poet and scholar Piero della Vigne (d. 1249):

> . . . Piero della Vigne was one trained in Bologna who practised both Latin and vernacular verse. . . . Piero della Vigne is himself said to have studied at Bologna, with whose masters he was in correspondence; and Terrisio writes a letter of condolence on the death of the Bolognese professor Bene, who may have been his own teacher. . . . Piero della Vigna . . . also has his traditional place in the Sicilian school of vernacular poets, though . . . the parallelism of theme in Latin is rather to be sought in certain of the imaginative debates in prose . . . . In this fluid period both themes and forms pass readily back and forth between Latin and vernacular and from one vernacular to another.[26]

According to biographical (possibly autobiographical) information on the well-known troubadour Uc de Saint Circ (*c*. 1217–*c*. 1253), 'he was sent to school at Montpellier to become a cleric but while his family thought he was studying "letras", i.e. biblical and rhetorical studies in Latin, he was in fact, learning "... love songs, verses, sirventes, tensos, couplets, and the facts and deeds of the valiant men and ladies who were then, or had ever been, in the world: and with this knowledge he became a joglar . . ."' (cited in *RTS*, p. xxiii). It is not clear whether the two disciplines could be pursued in the same institution, and, at any rate, the conceit of diverting from respectable learning to follow the life of the vernacular poet or vagabond singer (in Latin or in the vernacular) became, in itself, a commonplace of poetic biography. The reverse was also true; scholars like Peter Abelard 'regretted' – in verse – the idle folly of their youth spent in writing profane verse. Irish poets commonly 'apologized' for the secularity of their compositions in well-known expressions of regret, and by attaching envoys to the poems dedicated to the deity, or some particular saint.

The biography of Uc de Saint Circ notes, significantly, that he did not write many love-songs, because he had never been in love, 'but that with his fine rhetorical skills he was quite capable of feigning love' (cited in *RTS*, p. xxiii). The artifice of the profession, including the endless declarations of love and devotion that characterized the troubadour lyric, was recognized by those who later prefaced them with vidas (biographical sketches) and razos (introductory/context-ualizing tales), perhaps to give a 'realistic' context to the lyrics.[27] Grading the different compositions, likewise occupied troubadours, who were at great pains to emphasize the difficulty and scholarship involved in their profession, though it was practised in the vernacular.[28]

STUDIED AMBIGUITY

Describing the profession of the troubadour, even in the most general way, as in the following by K. W. Klein (in *The Partisan Voice*, pp. 44–45), recalls, in its roughest outlines, traditional descriptions of the Irish school poet:[29]

> The relationship of the poet to the patron was quite simply a business arrangement. The poet wrote for the patron, to flatter and to amuse him, and was rewarded by the patron or patroness for his services by gifts of money, clothes, a horse, or infrequently, an improvement in his social position. As in other official relationships of the early and High Middle Ages, the dominant note was contractual, with obligations on both sides. . . . The poet wrote for a patron, to praise him, to publicize him, to counsel him, and, if angered, to criticize or shame him publicly. He wrote to promote and propagandize his patron's cause and, in some cases, it was the cause he himself espoused; to denigrate or defy his patron's enemies; to rally his patron's allies or to scold them for not coming to his assistance. . . . Richard the Lionheart and Frederick II, especially, became hero-figures and attracted to themselves certain actions and characteristics which became conventional in the songs which praised or supported them. Conversely, Philip Augustus was almost universally condemned by poets who had no connection with him and who wrote against him because he was the enemy of their hero. In the same way that actions and attributes were conventionally used in connection with the hero-figures, certain insults and detractions

became conventional in the poems in which Philip was mentioned.

In a manner that recalls descriptions of Irish bardic poetry, Klein refers specifically to the obscure and allusive style practised by the most well-known troubadours. Reasoning from a standpoint that gives some prominence to the political nature of the troubadours' works, Klein explains as follows:

> Medieval political lyrics, then, are partisan and pragmatic; their contents deal with specific persons and events. As such, one might suppose them to be clear and direct, but paradoxically, they are arcane: these poems are full of allusions. This is partially due to the manner of presenting an event, for these poets generally dealt with events by alluding to them rather than detailing or describing them. . . . Some of the allusions are deliberately obscure; these represent that technique known as the 'closed style', *trobar clus*. . . . There are several possible reasons for the deliberate obscurantism. It could be . . . the consequence of the artificial nature of the poetry in this period. In certain cases, the poet may wish to protect himself from possible reprisals. . . . but it is most likely that these political poems were written for a small 'in-group' audience at the courts. The allusions were part of the game played by the poet and his audience: he teased them with difficult references at which they could amuse themselves by guessing; or, if they immediately recognized the references, they could flatter themselves that they were 'in the know',

and admire the poet's skill (Klein, *The Partisan Voice*, pp. 52–53).

Furthermore, accounting for the the style of the *trobar clus*, which seemed to require the 'deliberate obscurantism' (noted above),[30] Klein notes the allusive nature of the troubadour compositions which creates a sense of difficulty in the language which is created merely by circumlocution and obliqueness of reference:

> ... the political lyrics are filled with allusions; this technique, rather than imagery or metaphor, characterizes their poetic texture. . . . Many are relatively easy: a simple circumlocution . . . [often describing] a person with a formula of possession rather than directly naming him. . . . Moderately difficult allusions are those in which the person is not named nor are there any direct allusions to deeds done by the person, only clues. . . . Deliberate obscurantism is practised by the poets who wrote *trobar clus*, the 'closed style'.

The description (above, by Klein) could broadly be applied to the work of both Gofraidh Fionn Ó Dálaigh (above, pp. 57ff) and Ádhamh Ó Fialáin (above, pp. 110ff.). And yet 'deliberate obscurantism' does not accurately describe the multi-textured and disciplined application of the rules of composition, which was the guiding principle of both the work of the Irish poets and of the troubadours. As for the Irish poets, the most common form of formal poetry practised in Ireland for four hundred years was the *dán díreach*. The rhetoric of the poets involved descriptions of their 'art', and this art was celebrated as difficult, dark and obscure – effectively, a form of the 'closed style'.[31]

K. W. Klein's description of the aesthetics of the *trobar clus* seems to indicate that the vernacular poets of Southern

France and their fellows in Northern Italy, Northern Spain and in Northern Portugal were consciously adapting the norms of Latin composition,[32] such as are outlined in the manuals mentioned above (pp. 25ff. and passim), to their vernacular compositions. Instructions such as those given by Geoffrey of Vinsauf have clearly had their influence on works described by Klein, though these predate in some cases the formulations of Geoffrey of Vinsauf, but do not predate the matter of the works, since all are working from the shared notions of composition and presentation, which were merely assembled and presented afresh by masters such as Geoffrey. And perhaps because Klein (like S. Ó Tuama, for instance, in the case of Irish bardic poetry) is looking for a modern political sensibility in this material, he recognizes neither 'progressive' development of a theme, nor a 'logic' in the works he describes:

> The structure of the Provençal political songs is some-what similar to that of the *canso*; rather than evince a progressive or logical development of thought, the poems circle round a theme, or one or two themes. Some of the strophes have no direct relation to the one preceding or the one following and could be placed anywhere in the poem. In other cases, however, the strophes connect consecutively; the message of the first is picked up and developed in the second (*The Partisan Voice*, pp. 78–79).

It is worth bearing in mind, too, that troubadours, like Irish poets, have classically been assigned a role akin to that of the modern quality journalist, or even 'public relations' officer. J. O'Donovan's and O. Bergin's universally accepted description of the poet as 'discharging the functions of a modern journalist'

(*IBP*, p. 4) is echoed in the disputed similar description of the troubadour:

> In an attempt to bring present-day readers closer to this poetry, to make it familiar, and therefore comfortably acceptable, many eminent critics have compared these political poems to our contemporary newspapers. Considering the arcane nature of this poetry and the frequent use of obscure allusions, we find it difficult to see how this idea has received such widespread currency. Jeanroy calls the political *sirventes* a 'campagne de presse' . . .; de Boysson claims 'les sirventes des troubadours constituaient, au XIIe-siècle, de véritables gazettes . . .' . . . Isabel Alpin says, 'Reading them, one can fancy one is reading medieval newspaper leaders'; and Martin de Riquier states '. . . la poésie des troubadours est réellement une sorte de précédent de la presse de nos jours . . .' . . . Such comparisons are objectionable because of the distortion of certain characteristics of the poems. True, the poets do publicize the figures and events of which they write, but not for a 'newspaper' kind of audience. The medieval political lyric is not popular poetry. . . . The purpose of these poems is not, as a newspaper's is, to reach as wide a public as possible. Further, the opinions expressed in newspapers are ephemeral; the opinions of these poets are transmuted into partisan feelings which have vitality centuries later. Finally, and foremost, these are poems written by poets, not articles written by journalists . . . (Klein, *The Partisan Voice*, pp. 53–54).

Klein, while favouring the politically partisan voice over the journalistic voice, notes the importance of the literary nature of the troubadour songs. It is this emphasis on the literary voice that is supported by the study of bardic poetry presented here. The notion of the poet being involved in the presentation of a 'politically partisan' voice, or of current affairs in any of the senses that would suggest specific political engagement or journalism, is not supported in the analyses of the literary background to their compositions, nor of the ethos that informed their work.[33]

APPOINTMENT AND DISAPPOINTMENT

The *Bittspruch*, the petitioning poem, common among the Irish poets – and certainly a feature of most poems, even if the focus of the composition is on battle, or death, or complaint, or panegyric – was also a standard composition among the troubadours:

> There is a group of poems which praise a public figure, which are not political: these are the *Bittspruch* or request poems. In these, the poet extravagantly praises the ruler, or his noble patron, and then reminds him of his duty to reward the poet, or directly asks for payment. Such poems have no political significance; they are personal poems reflecting the poet's sitiuation in the patronage relationship (Klein, *The Partisan Voice*, p. 86).

In the case of the troubadour lyrics, and especially in the case of Irish syllabic poetry in the praise-genres, there is almost no poem that is not also essentially a *Bittspruch*. There is no case to be made for isolating the petitioning element in Irish poems from the vehicle that carried it, or in which it was carried – even elegy was used to make a claim on the successors of the deceased. 'Indulgence and appointment'[34] are the two demands of the poet, whether writing in Latin, in Provençal[35] or in Irish.

This is the very quality noted by P. A. Breatnach in respect of the importunate poets' demands:

> The phrase [*anáir ealadhna*] alludes to the 'indulgence' the generality of poets expected to be shown as of right by society. It is a commonplace of medieval Irish verse that such indulgence should extend to manifestations of poetic unruliness (*aindligheadh*), arrogance (*uabhar*) and exorbitant demands of all kinds (*ainbhreath*). . . . So, arrogance is regularly represented as being essential to the poetic ethos. Chiefs are urged to come to terms with it and to show forbearance (*umhla*) towards poets ('The Chief's Poet', p. 39).

INDULGENCE

'Indulgence' is probably too understated an expression to account for the spirit in which the lords to whose courts troubadours were attached were expected to tolerate the flagrant wooing of their ladies by troubadours. The conceit of the troubadour and his lady is recognized for the elaborate literary and courtly confection that it is. The gender ambiguity in the use of code names (*senhal*), and in the creation of webs of sexual intrigue and opportunity, in the compositions of the best-known troubadours, flag their works as belonging to a learnèd and sophisticated tradition.[36]

Commentators have noted the political and social interpretations applicable to such material. Irish poetry has likewise attracted similar attention and commentators have, similarly, extrapolated social and political and even economic circumstances from the tantalizing and allusive syllabic praise-poetry.[37] The specialized vocabulary employed by Irish poets has been studied for what it signifies of poet/lord relations. P. A. Breatnach notes, especially, the vocabulary concerned with status (*ollamh, ollamh flatha*), the espousal of the poet with the lord (*céile, leannán*), intimacy and confidences (*guala, cogar, rún*), special favour (*muirn, díoghrais*), and contractual service (*connradh*).[38] A similar vocabulary of intimacy and entreaty, claim and threat, is characteristic of the troubadour poems to the 'ladies' of their compositions.[39] Breatnach conceptualized the 'chief's poet' as a particularly coveted appointment, not depending necessarily on poetic attainment ('The Chief's Poet', p. 39), and frequently hereditary. The work of P. A. Breatnach and of K. Simms presents the image of an integral and cogent world conveyed through the, admittedly, artificial medium of the formal poems of the school poetry.

The image of Irish life and culture in the later Middle Ages has been coloured and enhanced by such work. It is very satisfying to track the careers of poets from apprenticeship, to professorship, to appointment at a great lord's house. The language of the poetry supports readings of this kind. The urgent request by poets to be considered for 'appointment' as *ollamh*, citations of other lords who appointed their ancestors, suggestions as to where and how they might be materially supported, all indicate that what Breatnach describes as 'appointments, tenure, rivalry' are factually, if artistically, represented in the poetry. And yet there are more exceptions to the expected lord/poet link than there are attestations of longstanding or similar relationships. Indeed, striving for appointment, expressing disappointment, hoping for better, challenging for improvement, begging for special consideration, and so forth, appear to form the bulk of the compositions that were the basis of the poet's career suggested in Breatnach.

There is also the phenomenon of the poet who is materially independent, such as the late sixteenth-century Eochaidh

Ó hEoghusa, and his relationship with the Maguire lords.[40] His works are as importunate and persistent as those of supposedly totally dependent poets on their lord's patronage. The same is the case for poets of the earlier period whose material circumstances are unknowable now, but who came from established landed families and families connected with ecclesiastical centres for many successive generations and whose 'free' lands were probably those granted for the purpose of providing for schools and masters.[41]

These vernacular writers were keeping pace in tone and in topic with those whose Latin verse has survived. The element of petition in the compositions of the clerks of mediaeval Europe is axiomatic. The manuals of style taught the formulae in which requests for support, for benefices, and for appointments might be couched. Examples of personal letters even to family members exhibit the influence of the schools' training in modes of address, terms of flattery, measures of threat and the extent of entreaty.[42]

Those examples of the extant vernacular composition in Provençal – the troubadour lyrics which because of their widespread nature, and because of the enthusiasm with which they were collected into songbooks by later patrons, survived – are those which overwhelmingly exhibit the conceits of love and seduction.[43] The ancillary prose matter that accreted to these lyrics, the razos and vidas that explained and contextualized the lyrics for later ages, appeared to rationalize and factualize the literary excesses that characterized them. The attachment of explications in prose to Irish poems[44] seems not to have been the norm, though some examples of the work of the sixteenth-century poet Tadhg Dall Ó hUiginn seem to have been the subject of razo- and vida-style additions over time.[45] Nevertheless, modern commentators, linking poems with events that are noted in annals, and so forth, identifying poets and patrons, and providing cogent social, political and economic contexts to hold the poems, perform a similar task.

THE POET AS SPOUSE

Accepting the validity of literal or near literal readings of Irish praise poetry does not rule out the exploration of other interpretations. Perhaps it is the vexing longevity of the themes and tropes of Irish schools' poetry that creates dissatisfaction with the association of certain of the tropes with life outside the poem. The nature of the love expressed by the poet for the patron, and the demands made on the grounds of that love, has been linked with the poet's claims to be an *ollamh flatha* and this in turn has been associated by commentators with an official appointment carrying with it duties and privileges. This may be the case in any particular instance. The approaches made by the poet, on the other hand, require that the discourse involve a 'gender confluence' or a measure of gender ambiguity. These are exigencies linked to the composition, and are not necessary to validate a *Bittspruch*, an elegy, or any other kind of compliment or complaint. The use of the 'love' discourse made each of these genre compositions at once more interesting, more lasting, richer in allusion and possibility, and easier to compose.

The following description of the progress of a troubadour in Spain-Portugal, as described by Jensen, gives an idea of the the conceit when directed by a troubadour towards the lady or queen:[46]

> The concept of amorous vassalage is a troubadour invention, carrying the stamp of the feudal structure of the society in which it evolved. This concept, in itself a condensed expression of the spirit and the customs of the period, is indicative of a ritual which the troubadours refer to as *domnei*: the poet courts a

lady of high rank to whom he pledges his steadfast
loyalty as a humble vassal. His submission to the lady
is total, for in her role as *suzerain* she is free to treat
her vassal as she sees fit. Within this socio-poetic
convention, the poet-vassal's inspiration gravitates
toward two motifs: the sublimation of the lady whose
qualities receive incessant praise, and the unhappiness
or *coita* born of his unrequited love for a lady of
superior rank and usually of a cruel indifference.

Dominated by a spirit of *cortesia*, the Galician- Por-
tuguese *trovadores,* though fully cognizant of the rules
of the amorous vassalage game, appear less earthy than
the troubadours; content with achieving the status of
entendedores 'declared wooers', they shun the complic-
ated set of rules devised by the Provençal poet-lovers
as a means to gradually gain access to the lady's favor
(Jensen, *The Earliest Portuguese Lyrics*, pp. 42–43).

The paradigm here keeps pace with the attainment of the prized
status *ollamh flatha* persuasively outlined by Breatnach:

There is another theme found in the verse which is
of key importance not only for the understanding of
poetic patronage in general, but also for the assessment
of the favour shown chiefs' poets in particular. It is
the theme of the poet as lover or spouse of his pat-
ron, . . . In its most striking expression this represents
the relationship between poet and patron as a marriage,
the two parties sharing the same bed. A poet can tell
his patron that it is no act of adultery against his wife
to 'lie with me and my kind', while another who has
fallen out of favour can seek reconciliation by saying:
*Ná bíom ní as fhaide a fholt fionn/ gan luighe ar aon ar
éinphioll* . . . [Let us not refrain any longer from lying

together on one couch, O fair one ('The Chief's Poet',
p. 40)].

Some of the complementary conceits of the features indicat-
ing intimacy which are characteristic of Irish school poetry are
noted by Breatnach:

> One of the most recurring terms in the poets'
> vocabulary of affection is *muirn*. Regularly it denotes
> the special 'favour' or 'esteem' due to an ollamh from
> his chief. . . . Another word used often in the same
> specialized sense is *díoghrais*, to be translated 'love,
> zeal, fervour'. . . . The poets regularly invoke two
> gestures, of a more or less symbolic nature, which the
> chief may make in order to signal bestowal of especial
> favour. These are: to allow a poet to sit at his elbow
> (*uille*) or shoulder (*guala*) at drinking time, and to
> share his secret (*rún*) or whisper (*cogar*) (ibid., pp.
> 44–45).

The lover/beloved image is indisputable. The fluency of the
gender identity allows the poet to take a female role, and allows,
confusingly perhaps, that the lord also be described in terms
more usually associated with a female lover.[47]

RECONCILIATION AND RENEWAL

'Recognize me as your official lover, and allow no others to pay
court' is the demand of the troubadour; 'recognize me as your
official *ollamh*, and accept the overtures of no other' seems to
be that of the Irish school poet. The appeals are very often
part of a composition that seeks reconciliation – a trope of
renewal; or a trope of seeking patronage, a theme underlying
the poetry considered here. The rubrics allowed both themes
to be addressed as part of a complaint leading to praise. The dis-
play of allegiance on both sides to a society where the 'standards'

– supposedly perpetuated through the poet/patron relationship – suited the taste of the time is, at any rate, a formal production from schools supported by local lords.[48]

6. Lovers' quarrels

Three poems, one by Tadhg Óg Ó hUiginn (d. 1448) ('*Fada an ráitheise romham*'), and two by Tadhg Dall Ó hUiginn (d. c. 1590) ('*A theachtaire théid ar sliabh*' and '*Cóir Dé eadram is Uilliam*') will be considered here as examples of praise using *licential permissio*. The quality of the complaint, entreaty and love expressed in them is to be noted in respect of that which has been noted of the troubadour style of 'love' poem. The poem '*Fada an ráitheise romham*' [This is a long season before me] by Tadhg Óg Ó hUiginn, addressed to Uilleog Búrc Mac Uilliam Uachtair (lord of Clanrickard 1424–1485), is an interesting example of the Irish expression of the European literary phenomenon of the complaint/petition predicated on a falling out. Uilleog Búrc was a grandson of Muircheartach Ó Ceallaigh – his mother was Beanmhumhan Ní Cheallaigh – and he was married to Mór Ní Chonchubhair Fáilghe (d. 1452) (*AithDD* i, p. 163). L. McKenna dates the poem between 1424 and 1448. In any event, it appears to belong to the first half of the fifteenth century. The poem begins as a seeming classic disagreement between the poet and the lord. An unwise word spoken in drink is reputed to be the source of disagreement. The poet is confined to the de Búrca household throughout the three winter months and wishes he had departed on the immediate occasion of the quarrel rather than be held as he is until the weather becomes more suitable for travel.

This is the *inventio* of the poem strung out to forty-four quatrains in McKenna's edition. The *inventio* – disagreement – is teased out sinuously through the first ten quatrains. The 'cause' given is the indiscreet drunken word.[1] This is a classic complaint, and the mischief it has caused is a classic pretext for the poem. Held prisoner by Uilleog Búrc, Tadhg Óg is unable to express his anger, he must suppress it since he is still in the lord's house. The imprisonment is therefore twofold: physically he is unfree; metaphorically his tongue/pen is restrained.[2]

He, the poet, ought to have heeded the warnings commonly heard (proverbial), that those who consorted with the Gall risked greater danger than those who undertook travel in winter. The two parts to this proverb are exploited for the poem's structure, the menace of de Búrca's house (de Búrca of Norman background [Gall]) for the poet; the hostility of the season. Now he is skulking[3] from house to house, and his forced silence is like a death to him.

By quatrain ten, the discord between the poet and his lord is being attributed to those who sowed it among them with rumour and innuendo. These 'others' are servants of the figure of *licentia*, which allows for the allocation of blame close to the source, without implicating the source directly.[4] These two elements, ingeniously – and in keeping with the best practice of the treatises – provide the matter of the poem also.

An olive branch is offered, however: if Uilleog Búrc take the poet's hand in friendship, their old relationship will be renewed. This allows for the rhetorical breath to be drawn here, a pause in the composition leading to another virtuoso twist in the creation of this convoluted literary item of praise/blame. The plea for reconciliation is also the function of the poem. The effort is that of renewal, a re-establishment of intimacy and respectful familiarity.

Quatrain eleven constitutes the poet's threat. Let them – members of de Búrca's household, not Uilleog himself – not unlock his (the poet's) tongue for fear of what might be expressed.[5] Let the de Búrca household not further enrage him to give vent to his anger. These are disloyal followers coming between Uilleog and Tadhg Óg.[6]

The reason for the lack of peace (*eisídh*, q. 13b) is the '*guth meisge*' [the drunken word/the unguarded tongue], which led to unguarded words. This leads to a personification of the accuser and the accused: the plaintiff and the defendant; the poet and the covert enemy, among de Búrca's entourage.[7] Now must the lord, Uilleog Óg, judge between them.[8] The poem, which could have taken this prompt to adopt a legalistic tone, and to use the terminology of the courts,[9] instead, at this point, takes a transsumptive detour into a love-poem, where relations are referred to specifically, and the appeal is made to be accepted once again, face to face with the (beloved) lord: '*aigthe a chéile do-chífeam*' (q. 16d).

At quatrain sixteen, the poet has delivered the essence of the poem. Indeed, he could finish here with the direct – emotional – address to Uilleog Búrc, the appeal for reconciliation, with the prior acknowledgement of Uilleog's entitlement to judge between the poet and his detractors. This is the feature used to secure a strategic advantage, that of *permissio* by which the matter in contention is submitted to the will of another, its effect is to simulate an objectivity, while the exploitation of the device is utterly subjective. Here is the mini-climax,[10] which completes the original *inventio*, and which can be considered as closed, or used as the basis of a longer – in some cases much longer – poem. The poet, it can be suggested, is opting for the amplified expression of the *inventio* rather than the brief treatment which he might well have chosen.

And so, in keeping with the 'lover' tone into which the tone of 'wrong' has been metamorphosed, the poet declares that his affection and loyalty is more cheaply bought than that of others – stranger-poets – by whom the lord might be approached (q. 17).[11] Tadhg Óg has, successfully at this point, moved his composition from complaint, to accusation, to threat, to entreaty, and at the eighteenth quatrain will employ a form of *paromologia*[12] to enter into the self-accusation, and the atonement that will turn the poem into a praise-poem. He, the poet, is entirely to blame for the misunderstanding; he should take example from the unchanging Uilleog and he himself be unchanging, thereby sealing their mutual friendship, which were it to remain unchanged, would be perfect as before (q. 18).[13] Tadhg Óg must atone for his infringement of their understanding; what can he offer but a poem?

The poem is an earnest of his devotion, and an atonement for his transgression.[14] But it must be accepted as such by the lord, and the episode of disharmony must be closed by the lord's acceptance of an example of the poet's art '*ball éigin dem ealadhain*' (q. 21b). The key to the figure of *licentia* is in this quatrain (q. 21): the tense is subjunctive,[15] *if I were to, were it to be so* and so forth. *Were* the poet unthinkingly *to make* an unwise statement in reference to his lord, the atonement for that *would be* an example of his art. The offer is now a love-token, a '*séad suirghe*' (q. 22c). The lord can have his choice from the store, the tavern of his art, the lord's favourite from among his store (*freagair tús an tábhairne*, q. 23d).

We arrive then at the crux of the composition, and the flourish that demonstrates the poet's artistry: if the lord does not accept the poem as restitution for the wrong, then the poet will maintain his unwilling silence, originally (self-)imposed on him by the disfavour shown him at de Búrca's house. The great deeds of de Búrca will be as hostages in the poet's keep until the lord accepts his terms of reconciliation (q. 25). No mention will be made by him of de Búrca's great victories, deeds, and so forth. The figure of emphasis by claim not to mention (*occupacio/praeteritio* [*PN*, p. 125]) is the engine that drives what is essentially a *caithréim*, which follows from quatrain twenty-five to forty-four.

The popularity of every conceit used in this poem, the complex of tropes and rhetorical devices that presents itself as a realistic episode in the life of a typical poet, of a typical lord, are part of the intrinsic interest of this poem, and of this *kind* of poem. Artfully combining the topoi of recrimination, contrition, petition, eulogy, threat and entreaty, the poet fulfils the requirements of his craft. Any one of the topoi is sufficient for a genre poem.

EXHAUSTION OF TOPICS

Occasions for praise and dispraise within the confines of literary expression were limited – birth, marriage, death, victory, defeat, generosity, nobility, frugality, ignobility. The possibilities presented by the positive among these topics could be exhausted within a year's work of a prolific poet. The negative versions could be used only sparingly, perhaps even only once, if at all. The challenge, for which the education of the poet equipped him, was to combine, with style and cunning, themes, topics and treatments. Ó hUiginn's triumph in this poem for Uilleog Búrc is to present a narrative that is seemingly factual,[16] permitting it the status of *historia* – allowing us to read it as factually based; varying its interest with titillating 'menace'; beguiling with contrition and love-bargaining. The assured tone in his composition, and in the complacent mastery of the poet over his prescribed palette, is immensely satisfying.

There is no way to prove whether or not any of the events suggested in the poem took place in the way they are presented here. It is impossible to determine the tenor of the relationship between the poet and the lord, in this specific case or in general.[17] Court life in the High Middle Ages and in the later Middle Ages presented features alike in the most structured secular and ecclesiastical courts, of which miniature versions existed in the courts of lords, barons and lesser nobility of varying degrees of wealth. The pretensions of Irish kings and lords were not inferior to those of any other country or state in contemporary Christendom. Their courts and principal houses shared the preoccupations of power, its maintenance and the expansion of the realm, in the same way as did those of any part of Europe. Irish ruling families warred and dissented no more frequently or bloodily than did their English, Welsh, Scottish and European counterparts. Anglo- and Cambro-Norman lords who conquered land by war or by marriage in Ireland were immediately at home in the continual strife demanded in their efforts to keep a grip on their possessions, and to expand their power and influence.[18]

SIXTEENTH-CENTURY SENSIBILITIES

E. Knott's monograph study of Tadhg Dall Ó hUiginn and his works presented a patchy, but interesting, outline of the life and career of a man whose poetry was chosen by Knott herself as 'typical' of the compositions of the Irish bardic poets in their heyday. In so far as Knott's scholarly assessment of Tadhg Dall's work would regard it as characteristic or typical, it may be tentatively suggested that the man, his career and what we know of his life was also, perhaps, uncontroversially 'typical'.[19] Most of the works attributed to the poet Tadhg Dall come from manuscripts later than 1650, the poems themselves are addressed 'to individuals who flourished during the period 1560–1590' (*TDall* i, p. xiv). Exchequer Inquisitions from Sligo during 1584, and again at Sligo in 1590, list a juror named 'Tege Dall O Higgen *generosus*'. Knott identifies this individual as the poet. The latter inquisition notes that the man 'Teg dall O Higyn' was forty years old in 1585.[20] This means that we would seem to have a little more information about Tadhg Dall than we have for most of the bardic poets, especially for those from earlier centuries. An Inquisition taken in Sligo in 1593 notes the death of

'Thadeus, alias Teage Dall O Higgen' on 31 March 1591 (*TDall* i, pp. xiv–xv). At another taken at Sligo in 1617, the jurors (one of whom – Teige Oge O Higgen – possibly a son of Tadhg Dall) heard it attested that Tadhg Dall, his wife and his son had been murdered some time at the turn of the century by members of the O'Hara family. Knott is at pains – assuming that this 'Tadhg Dall' is indeed the poet Tadhg Dall – in her assessment of the surviving documentation to show that it is far from clear how Tadhg Dall died, and whether the imputation of the murder to the O'Haras was not an additional accusation in an effort to secure their (the O'Haras) dispossession.[21] At all events, by around 1714, a poem by Muiris Ó Nuabha bore the heading '*Ag so in aoir do-rinnigh Tadhg Dall Ó Huiggin dona daoinibh da Mhuintir Eadhra fár bhaineadar a theangaigh as et cetera*' [This is the satire which Tadhg Dall Ó Huiginn composed on the people of the O'Hara family, for which they cut out his tongue etc.] (*TDall* i, p. xvi).

Several elements in the saga of Tadhg Dall, the O'Haras' cutting out his tongue, and the manner of his death, present elements that confirm the gentleman (*generosus*) Tadhg Dall as a 'poet'-character, apart altogether from the surviving works ascribed to him. The razo-like preface in a poem by another poet referring back to a personage 'Tadhg Dall' – as in this example of Muiris Ó Nuabha – flags Tadhg Dall as one who has become a character in literature, to whom writings and characteristics might be attributed. In the character of the sharp-tongued or pointy-penned poet (or satirist) – as is suggested in the Ó Nuabha preface, '*in aoir do-rinnigh Tadhg Dall...*' – Ó hUiginn is awarded a traditional come-uppance: his tongue is cut out by the O'Haras (this would have added the second cognomen *balbh* to his name). His supposed murder, also attributed to the O'Haras, may have played a part in this tale too. Interestingly both fates are assigned

respectively to three well-known troubadours – Marcabru
(*fl.* 1129–1150); Guillem de Berguedà (*fl.* 1170–1195); Peire Vidal
(*fl.* 1175–1205) – in posthumous vidas, and are cited by C.
Léglu in her study of defamation, satire and legislation:

> The twelfth-century troubadour Marcabru is
> described in one of the fourteenth-century *vidas*
> composed about him as a slanderer: . . . This
> definition is made clearer by the fate assigned the poet
> in the other *vida*: . . . 'and he was much cried out
> [reputed?] and listened to throughout the world,
> and feared for his tongue: for he was so slanderous
> that, in the end, the castellans of Guyenne, whom
> he had slandered very badly, killed him'. The precise
> definition of this *maldir* is left to the songs attributed
> to Marcabru in the manuscripts. The eventual murder
> may be a fictional device, similar to Peire Vidal having
> his tongue cut out by a knight, for claiming to be his
> wife's lover, or the death of Guillem de Berguedà at
> the hands of a footsoldier after a career of mayhem
> but these violent punishments may be related to
> contemporary ideas about slander in poetry.[22]

Tadhg Dall's name survives likewise in the remnants of a
poetic debate from the end of the seventeenth century preserved
in the Book of Clanranald, in which he is quoted as an author-
ity on the provenance of the *Lámh Dhearg* (*TDall* i, p. xvii).[23]
It is of greater interest to the discussion here that the composer
of the works referred to in early eighteenth century debate was
an even earlier Ó hUiginn poet than Tadhg Dall – one Maol
Seachlainn na nUirsgéal Ó hUiginn (*fl.* late fourteenth, early
fifteenth century) (*TDall* i, pp. xvii–xix). The consistency of
standard, topic and treatment in Irish bardic poetry make such

anachronistic attributions neither damaging to the debate in hand, nor internally contradictory.

In her discussion of the construction of the Ó hUiginn pedigrees, Knott, quoting a written communication from Eóin Mac Néill, makes a sidelong reference to a twelfth-century Ó hUiginn which reflects obliquely on some of the matter under discussion in this study:

> The second Uiginn '*ó táit Uí Uiginn*' [*sic*] should have flourished *c.* 1100, which is within the period of Ó surnames. It is rather remarkable that his son is named Robert, no doubt after Robert of Normandy,[24] the crusader (*TDall* i, pp. xxi).

No doubt, indeed, that an Irish family in the midlands (Co. Offaly)[25] – possibly professionally involved in education and letters – should name a son after an eminent Norman crusader. Cultural interchange and the extent of the fame of a man such as Robert of Normandy and his exploits meant that a family, with a possible Viking background (*TDall* i, p. xxi), would find it attractive to adopt his forename into their family.[26] A learnèd family such as the Uí Uiginn would have been equally receptive of other cultural influences from similar sources.[27] The Connacht branch of the family to which Tadhg Óg Ó hUiginn, Maol Seachlainn na nUirsgéal Ó hUiginn and Tadhg Dall Ó hUiginn belonged emerged as a family prominent in teaching and in poetry from the fourteenth century.[28]

One of earliest extant poems attributed to Tadhg Dall is addressed to Shane O'Neill.[29] In the case that he did address this poem at seventeen years of age to an important lord like Shane O'Neill, and that the poem survives, suggests that a student in his later teens could have achieved the proficiency in his education that would allow him to offer juvenile work to a lord. This may be at variance with the sense of the years of young adulthood spent by the poet in apprenticeship indicated by the imperishable account by Thomas O'Sullevane prefacing the *Memoirs of the Marquis of Clanricard*.[30] Alternatively, the address may be posthumous, which would highlight the literary, rather than the documentary, nature of the exercise. At all events, it is as well to bear in mind that the education that Tadhg Dall received presumably at the/an Ó hUiginn school in Connacht, or in Donegal, where he may have been in fosterage (*TDall* i, pp. xxii–xxv),[31] and which equipped him to take the role of *generosus*, juror, and prominent Irish poet and professor of poetry, was also the schooling probably given his brother, Maol Muire Ó hUiginn (d. *c.* 1590 in Antwerp), who became archbishop of Tuam in a period when standards of education, civility and conformity were high in the post-Reformation Roman Church.

The agreement known as the Composition of Connacht, which was agreed with various Irish lords in 1585, involved the surrender of lands to the Crown and their return with full patents for a named annual sum and military services. The arrangement was intended to dissipate the military power of Irish lords, whose vassals seemed (to the Crown) to owe unlimited military and other services, which provided the backbone of the lords' military boldness and flexibility. Several of Tadhg Dall's patrons availed themselves of this new agreement. The state of affairs seems to Knott to be reflected in some of Tadhg Dall's poems, especially in that addressed to Cormac Ó hEadhra, '*Ag so an chomairce a Chormaic*' (*TDall* i, p. xxix); her comment is relevant here:

> The condition of 'the meaner sort of freeholders',
> amongst whom Tadhg Dall would perhaps have been
> reckoned by the English officials, does not appear to
> have been materially altered, either in intention or in

fact by the new arrangement. . . . [T]he poet refers
to the enforcement of new regulations by the English
in Ireland; the inhabitants of each territory are to be
summoned; the name of each one is to be recorded on
a parchment roll, and every man is to acknowledge
as his lord some chief who will take responsibility
for him. Those without a chief to protect them
are to be put to death summarily. The date of this
poem is 1584 or 1585. Tadhg selects Cormac as his
guarantor, ostensibly for that nobleman's goodness
and generosity, and acceptability to the authorities on
both sides, but it is not clear that anyone but the chief
of Leyney, where his lands were situated, could have
been of any help to him. As to his tenure under the
Composition the inquisitions give it as one of military
service. In that case he held direct from O'Conor
Sligo, as did the ordinary freeholders of the county.[32]

The failure here of the likely reality to tally with the account
that can be gleaned from Tadhg Dall's poems of praise, entreaty
and so forth, seems to indicate that while ambient 'reality' could
provide matter for the school poet, the method and the manner
followed a pattern that transcended the individual factuality of
any particular composition.[33]

Considering the course of study to be undertaken to qual-
ify as a poet and its overwhelmingly literary nature, requiring a
variety of skills of literacy, it is unlikely the the *Dall* (blind)
of Tadhg's name indicated a blind man.[34] Other details of
Tadhg Dall's life are conjectured by Knott from references in
the poetry. Most of these details concern misunderstandings
between the poet and the lord, and involve appeals by the poet
to the lord's wife:

From a few vague references in his own poems we learn
that he was, . . . fostered in Tirconnel; that in 1572,

or thereabouts, he quarrelled with Hugh O'Donnell
on account of the latter's refusal to safeguard the
poet's friends and kinsfolk during one of his punitive
expeditions into north Connacht.[35] . . . Nor have I
found any addressed by him to Donnell [O'Connor
Sligo] himself; but from the curious appeal to Mór,
Donnell's wife . . . [w]e learn that the chieftain took
offence at a poem which Tadhg had addressed to
O'Donnell (Hugh son of Manus), and that deprived
of his powerful patronage, the poet had lived in great
misery for over a year. The patron with whom he had
most intimacy was *an unidentifiable William Burke*.
With this chief his relation was not only that of a
follower, they were united by the bond of art. Each
taught the other what he himself had learned; music,
history and poetry; all the delights afforded by such
books as they had, brought these two together, and
united them in an apparently indissoluble friendship.
However, in after years *it befell the chief, whether
by accident or design is unknown, to spoil the poet of
his cattle on a reaving expedition. Tadhg expresses his
feelings . . . a piece which was obviously composed more
in sorrow than in anger.* The imperious note of his
remonstrance with O'Donnell . . . is completely
lacking here (*TDall* i, pp. xxv–xxvi; emphasis added).

This, of course, is an image of Tadhg Dall's life through the
compositions of praise/blame, especially those seeking restitu-
tion and reconciliation. Indeed, a similar outline biography
in respect of lords, patronage and estrangements could be cre-
ated for any of the poets for whom a sizeable body of attributed
works survives.

SYLLABUS AND LIFE

The syllabus of composition allowed for, and may even have required, a virtuoso display in this genre. Aspects of the two poems ('*A theachtaire théid ar sliabh*' and '*Cóir Dé eadram is Uilliam*')[36] addressed to an unidentified William Burke are noted by E. Knott as puzzling or remarkable. In the first place, Knott suggests that the same Uilliam Búrc is addressed in both poems. She conjectures that he is a son of a Seán Búrc to whom Tadhg Dall addressed another poem.[37]

It is, perhaps, particularly significant that this lord, with whom Tadhg Dall was on specially intimate terms ('[t]he patron with whom he had most intimacy' [*TDall* ii, xxv]), is the '*unidentifiable* William Burke'. The terms of their sometime friendship provided all the required features of a poem of reconciliation (in '*Cóir Dé eadram is Uilliam*'). They had enjoyed friendship, companionship, collegiality as fellow-students. The despoiling of the poet's property ruptured the intimacy and easy freedom of their friendship.[38] Reproach, in both poems, is protected by the usual carapace of praise. They may, indeed, have been offered to a historical person. But the anonymity – for us – of this William Burke, for whom no status as lord can be divined from the poem, and for whom no identifying ancestors or other relations are provided in the poems, could mean that the works may have been pieces awaiting a patron, they may have been trial pieces of genre-writing, or pedagogic pieces for students.

In any event, they display all the classic features of the complaint poem, the abandoned love, the puzzlement of betrayal and the earnest wish for reconciliation and, in their vagueness, they are perfect examples of the universal application of the features of the genre to any lord at any time between 1200 and 1650.

'A THEACHTAIRE THÉID AR SLIABH'

E. Knott's note to the poem 'A theachtaire théid ar sliabh' refers directly to the matters of meaning, diction and rhetorics being discussed here:

> The meaning of this piece depends on the proper connotation here of the illusive legal terms *fiach* and *geall*, and without a precise knowledge of the circumstances referred to, this remains in doubt. Something due, a debt, a rent payment, a tax or fine can all be denoted by *fiach*. The person liable is usually indicated by the prep. *ar*. The word *geall* 'pledge' is generally used in the 15th–16th century land deeds somewhat in the sense of chattel-mortgage, e.g. it is used of a number of cows given for piece of land, the latter being redeemable on the payment of cows equal in number and value on the date specified in the agreement; it is also used of land mortgaged (*TDall* ii, p. 262).

All the denotative and connotative meanings that can be applied to the technical terms noted here by Knott are intended in the composition. The flexibility of the terms *geall* and *fiach*, and the unclarity [39] concerning to whom and from whom the debt, pledge, and so forth, are due, enhance their value for the poet. On the other hand, the 'meaning' of the poem does not, perhaps, depend at all on the precise legal meanings of these words in the context understood by Knott. [40]

The clever, and somewhat tortuous, description of the vexations visited upon the poet as a consequence of his being without a powerful protector, like any ordinary man (qq. 17, 18, p. 158), is interesting in itself, and represents a certain kind of reality. This 'reality' is to be compared with the pseudo-court proceedings in the *jeux d'esprits* and tongue-in-cheek compositions using the 'warrant' formula, popular in the eighteenth century.[41]

In '*A theachtaire théid ar sliabh*' [Messenger departing for the mountain] Tadhg Dall, sends a messenger to Uilliam Búrc[42] to let him know (q. 1c) – discreetly (*fá rún*, q. 2a) – how matters now stand with him. There follows a very brisk description of Tadhg Dall's experience with the payment of some fines (q. 3ab). He is made destitute by repeated unwarranted demands and pledges, which are redeemed at up to six times their value in his efforts to clear a series of fines that were levied on him. In spite of loss of goods and the intractability of his dealings with the court (qq. 4cd, 5a), his ineffectual patent (q. 7a), the unhelpful sheriff (q. 9ab), and his visit to the president (q. 14ab), it is only the return of Uilliam Búrc that will guarantee his satisfaction (q. 19cd). Rumours abound that he has returned (q. 20), but the poet will rely on the report of his own messenger[43] (q. 21) to let him know that his deliverance is at hand with the return of Uilliam (q. 23).

This relatively short composition finishes with a proper *dúnadh* and fulfils many other requirements of the complaint poem besides. The poet has grounds for complaint, a troublesome fine. The story allows for the use of court terminology and for persons of rank to be mentioned, upper and lower; Tadhg Dall lists his household servants too.[44] The traditional opening of the messenger is well established. The *inventio* of the complaint implies censure of a lord who has left his loyal poet at the mercy of rapacious officials for three years. The censure is implied, the compliment is explicit, when Uilliam – '*Cuiléan leóghan Locha Con, / maighre Sionna na sruth ngeal, / éanchú inbhir Easa Ruaidh*' (*TDall* i, p. 159, q. 22abc) [Lion cub of Locha Con, salmon of the bright streamed Sionann; principal hound of the estuary of Eas Ruadh] – returns, the poet can hope for respite and restitution.

The 'low style' is practised here. Matters concerning everyday life, tedious proceedings at court, redemption of pledges, harassment by officials are properly dealt with in the low style.[45] Tadhg Dall's mastery of the low style articulates perfectly the mock-heroic trials he has undergone following petty demands from post to pillar. The other characters in this drama – apart from Uilliam – are the persons who properly belong to the low style:[46]

> Giolla an eich, buachoill na mbó,
> caile na brón, bean na gcíor –
> téid uile i n-aoineacht uaim
> lé cois tsaighdiúir, truagh an gníomh.
> (TDall i, p. 158, q. 17)

[The horseboy, the cowherd, the quern-woman, the comb-woman, they all go, as one from me, along with a soldier, a pitiable deed.]

> Sé adeir buachoill mo bhó féin
> tar gach duine dá dtéid uaim,
> ag cur na teineadh ann m'ucht –
> 'créad do-bheir ort gan drud suas?'
> (TDall i, p. 158, q. 18)

[And my own cowherd himself – above all who have left me – indicating the fire there to me, says, 'why don't you move up?']

This hardship is caused by the three-year absence of Uilliam Búrc – 'Atámaoid, . . . le trí bliadhnoibh fan mbreith truim . . .' (TDall i, p. 158, q. 19ab). The social and financial death of the poet is a result of Uilliam Búrc's being away. This is a form of the death that follows the departure of the lord for any reason – the death of their mutual love/friendship; the death of poetry; the death of the land; the death of honour and so forth. The messenger is to find out if he (Uilliam) has returned, because 'lucht na mbréag', those anonymous 'others'

who try to cause ill-feeling between the poet and his lord, are
suggesting maliciously that indeed Uilliam has returned and
the poet is the last to know:[47]

> Mallacht Dé do lucht na mbréag,
> nách gcuirionn a sgéal go bun:
> adeirid cách liom tré rún
> go bhfuil Uilliam Búrc i bhus.
> (*TDall* i, p. 158, q. 20)

[God's curse on the liars, who leave their message
incomplete; everyone tells me in secret that Uilliam
Búrc is here.]

The absurdity of the messenger going to Uilliam Búrc to speak
to him and *to find out if he had yet returned* is in keeping with
the frothy nature of this witty poem:

> A theachtaire théid 'na cheann,
> ná bíoth th'aire ar ghreann nó ar spóirt:
> labhair rém chompánach féin,
> 's féacha a dtáinig sé fós.
> (*TDall* i, p. 159, q. 21)

[Messenger who goes to meet him, take no heed of fun
or sport, speak to my own companion, and see if he
has come yet.]

A desultory epithetical address closes this relatively short
(22 qq.) poem, which is formally closed in the manner of the
schools:[48]

> Cuiléan leóghan Locha Con,
> maighre Sionna na sruth ngeal,
> éanchú inbhir Easa Ruaidh –
> is mór atá uaim ar a theacht.
> (*TDall* i, 159, q. 22)

[Lion cub of Locha Con, salmon of the bright streamed
Sionann; principal hound of the estuary of Eas Ruadh,
I want much on his coming.]

This formal poem in the low style, addressed to a now unidentifiable, and possibly to an intentionally vaguely indicated, personage, plays lightly with the complaint genre, and stays well within the bounds of rebuke tempered with praise, using the device *if my lord were here, I should not be dealt with thus*. All the echoes of the special love between the poet and the lord are understood to lie behind the hurt caused by the 'others' taunting the poet that Uilliam is returned unknown to him. The 'messenger' is the traditional go-between from lover to beloved.[49]

'CÓIR DÉ EADRAM IS UILLIAM'

E. Knott suggests that the same Uilliam Búrc, whoever he may be, is the person addressed in '*Cóir Dé eadram is Uilliam*' [God's justice between myself and William] (*TDall* i, p. 169).

Beginning with a declaration of proverbial import '*Cóir Dé eadram is Uilliam*' (*sententia*), the poem flags its intention to adhere to the rubrics. Again, ruination of the poet by some action or inaction (as in the former poem '*A theachtaire théid ar sliabh*') on the part of his lord, Uilliam Búrc, is the *inventio* offered in this poem: Uilliam (Búrc) has, seemingly, sought or connived at the ruination of the poet. This is all the more difficult to understand because he (Uilliam) – as would befit a powerful man/lord – has plenty of legitimate objects of plunder and sources of spoil (q. 2bc). It is hurtful because of the relationship of long standing between Uilliam and the poet: Tadhg Dall was his *ollamh* and a member of his household (*fear leanamhna*, qq. 5c; 11b). On two counts were they linked: by the poet being his follower and by their joint pursuit of the arts ('*s bágh na healadhna eadruinn*, qq. 5; 11cd). This relationship in scholarship is spelled out: Tadhg Dall was both teacher and pupil (q. 10a) of Uilliam – what one read the other heard (qq. 7, 8). They had a mutual relationship in teaching and learning

(q. 6). He was master and pupil to him: '*Mé a mhaighstir, mé a dhalta, / mé a chompán 'sa chomhalta*' (q. 10ab), 'companion to him and comrade' (*TDall* i, p. 170).[50] He, Tadhg Dall, was also a follower of his[51] and Uilliam should have borne this in mind before the plundering:

> *Olc nár smuain re hucht m'faghla*
> *mé aige im' fíor leanamhna,*
> *'s a bheith ar éinleabhar riom riamh*
> *don mhéirleabhar fíonn, d'Uilliam.*[52]
> (*TDall* i, p. 170, q. 11)

[It was wrong of him not to think before plundering me that I was a client of his – and that the fair nimble fingers, Uilliam, always shared a book with me.]

The emotive force of naming Uilliam in the final line of quatrain eleven, above, is strengthened by the common use of the predicative '*don mhéirleabhair fíonn*', and by the balancing identification of the poet coming before it: '*mé aige im' fíor leanamhna*' in the pattern of I: he, or I: you.[53]

Quatrain twelve states how the case may have changed: if it were that he (Tadhg Dall) were not as he had been, though he still is:

> *Im' dhalta dá mbeth nách beinn,*
> *aige fós mar go bhfuilim –*
> *níor ghníomh cóir dá chéibh . . .*
> *béin a hóir don ealadhain.*
> (*TDall* i, p. 170, q. 12)

[If it were that I had not been a pupil of his, though I am – it were not a just act for his (. . .) hair, to subtract from the gold assigned to art.]

The hypothetical change, indicated by the supposed alteration in their circumstances, is made into reality in quatrain fifteen.[54]

Now all that has been changed by the plundering of Tadhg Dall by Uilliam. Uilliam is now an enemy (*gidh námha*, q. 15c) and source of Tadhg's destruction ([*d'fhior*] *dhéinmhe mo dhtoghbhála*, q. 15d). The restraint of the poet – an unusual characteristic – was presumed upon by Uilliam, he knew that their former friendship would prevent the poet from allowing himself the full expression of his anger and, indeed, it did:

> . . . *go raibhe a fíos ag Uilliam*
> *nách díghéalainn m'fhíoch nó m'olc* . . .
> (*TDall* i, p. 171, q. 16bc)
> [. . . that Uilliam knew that I would not avenge my fury or my spite . . .]

> *Do bhí a fíos aigesion féin*
> *nách gríosfainn a ghruaidh soilléir –*
> (*TDall* i, p. 171, q. 17ab)
> [He himself knew that I would not cause his bright face to burn –]

The poet suggests that Uilliam understands that because of the great bond between them, the poet would not satirize him, in spite of his wrongdoing (q. 17). This allows the poet to praise Uilliam without cause, and to link him to illustrious ancestors, while having little enough to say. The addressee is not a person of great rank, the poet cannot refer to him as lord of any territory, nor does he specify exactly who he might be by referring to parents or grandparents. He might be any Uilliam Búrc; it may be a piece written for no one in particular, and a trial of the type (see above, p. 171). And though it is normally unwise to rely on the poems for biographical information of a factual nature, it could be that the pair were fellow-students and that these pieces represent compositions that Tadhg Dall fashioned to suit his 'companion' and colleague, Uilliam Búrc, in a variety of praise/blame poems. The quatrains of praise are introduced with '*Ní aorfuinn*' [I would not satirize] (qq. 18a, 19a, 20a); '*Ní cháinfinn*' [I would not . . . dispraise] (*TDall* i, p. 171). This epanaphoraic (*repetitio*) list, combined with the disavowing feature of *paralipsis* (*occulatio*), produces a very effective litany of praise. The measures of praise are allusive and fulsome, but of vague genealogical import: '*déar aille*ss *d'fhuil na n-iarladh, / planda do phór chéibhfionn Chuinn*' [pure object of praise of the blood of the earls / a plant from the seed of the bright-haired Conn] (q. 18bc); '*gríobh do chloinn Chonaill Ghulban / . . . dreagan do saorchlainn Séarlais*' [a griffin of the race of Conall Gulban / dragon of the noble race of Charlemagne] (q. 19cd); '. . . *neimh naithreach / d'fuil Bhriain . . / an ghnúis ríleoghain ngéir ngloin / d'fírfeólfuil Í Néill náraigh*' [venomous serpent of the blood of Brian / the kingly, leonine, sharp, clear, countenance of the true blood of modest Niall] (q. 20); '*an bheithir mbuirb mbéimeannaigh / d'iarsma síl chrannghailte Chuirc / 'sdo chlannmhaicne Ír oirdhuirc*' [the fierce, violent bear of the inheritance of spear-fierce descendants of Corc, and of the sons of renowned Ír] (q. 21bcd); '*barr truimfiar na ngéigfeadh nglan . . .*' [curled-headed one of the fresh branches . . . (or) heavily bending top of the pure branching woods] (q. 23c).

No term in this list is typical of the kind of epithet or attribute that would characterize the *aor* which the poet cannot find it in him to write about the erring Uilliam. The poem may be unfinished, since it has no clear formal *dúnadh*.

Tadhg Dall was not a mediaeval poet, and he did not live in a mediaeval world. His familiarity with the legal system, possibly displayed in the poem, '*A theachtaire théid ar shliabh*', was from the level of privilege that qualified him to act as a juror. A son of Tadhg Dall (Tadhg Óg Ó hUiginn) became sheriff of Sligo.[56] The two Tadhg Dall compositions discussed here are from early modern Ireland. Their similarity to the mediaeval poems of earlier school poets is a literary phenomenon. The world in which such compositions were made and copied were fixed only by educational norms and formulae. The administrative systems in Ireland, both of the Irish and of the English, belonged, in the sixteenth century, to early modern Europe and displayed all the features of the development of centralized authority. The Europe-wide opposition to the centralizing power of the state and its effect on personalized and smaller lordships was the background against which Irish lords interacted with the Tudor monarchy. The struggle to maintain sovereign power over tiny lordships, baronies, city-states, and so forth, was the problem for sovereign lords throughout Europe. The Roman Church, re-establishing its diminished authority after the ravages of the several reformations of the sixteenth century, was likewise bound on a centralizing course.[57] Tadhg Dall's brother, Maol Muire, the archbishop of Tuam, was involved personally and professionally with one of the most dynamic and 'modern' institutions, the Roman Church.[58]

When the poets abandoned the style that had sustained the mediaeval feeling in their poetry, they were not abandoning a mediaeval life. Their lives, apart from their compositions, bore as little resemblance to that of their professional forebears as did that of any member of society to their ancestors some two or three hundred years before.

7. Poems about poetry

Generations of poets self-consciously provided examples of the written arts for their sponsoring lords. As teachers, the poets taught their arts to pupils in schools. As critics, they perpetuated a style and a standard adhered to by some four centuries of poets.[1] At the same time the practice of letters took many other forms: poets whose formal compositions conformed to the rhetorical confections of praise and elegy practised other styles of literature for other purposes.[2]

In any event, apart from any consideration of the representation of Irish life in elegies, eulogies and other bardic poems, poets often wrote poems that are clearly simply about the craft of writing and of poetry. The purely literary preoccupations of a poem such as that of Gofraidh Fionn Ó Dálaigh's '*Madh fiafraidheach budh feasach*'[3] present the poet/teacher as a man of letters providing material for students or peers about their shared profession. There may even be an element of self-advertisement in such poems, which always promote or aggrandize the poet's abilty and reputation.

ÁR N-EALAÍN: OUR ART

Throughout the four-hundred-year life of the classical style in Irish poetry, poets referred continually to their 'art', their efforts, their training and their rewards. The end of the *dán díreach* style came as a natural, and perhaps long-awaited, demise of a certain kind of schooling and a certain kind of literary taste.

The scholar and archbishop Flaithrí Ó Maolchonaire (*c.* 1560–1629) quoted St Augustine many times in his various works, and it was said of him, with pride, that he had read Augustine's works through, the proverbial seven times.[4] Ó Maolchonaire's use of Augustine's image of the golden key and the wooden key[5] was echoed through the seventeenth century in the formulaic apologies that writers of prose in the vernacular made for their infelicity in the Irish language and their boldness in attempting a work in a language in which they were but faltering scholars.[6] This formula complemented the boasting and pride in their style of the syllabic poets. Both claims were formulae practised only by those who had received a literary education.

The golden key and the wooden key may have had a special resonance for the school poets. Their polished and honed style, fruit of rigorous training, was indeed a golden key, giving access over the centuries to the particular idiom of the classical poem. The wooden key, far from being the faulty and uncouth instrument pretended by those who wielded it, represented a different register of the literary language, was no less a tool of access, and was the most obvious indicator of the expansion of Irish letters.[7] The fillip given to Irish education that was made possible by the availability of further education to hundreds of Irish students in the continental colleges is often seen in its negative aspects only. The many students who left Ireland, the majority to become priests, others who became soldiers, or began as soldiers and became students, were merely going further afield than the English universities to which their forebears had gone, and there were many more of them doing so. The students of whom we have information who went to Salamanca were already well educated in Ireland. The same, or similar, may be said about others who joined their cohorts in other colleges, and who attended the universities to which the colleges were affiliated. The future of bardic schools, on the other hand, may have been at risk because of this alternative. The promotion of the 'wooden key', the less ornate, less allusive – but no less literary – register of Irish practised by important, and classically trained, Irish scholars abroad, created a vogue for, or at least seemed to coincide with, a trend that commented upon the devaluation of the bardic training at home.

Quatrains about the collapse of cultural values in Ireland were produced at the death of any lord lamented by any poet. Poetry died with the lord, it was restored miraculously by the lord's successor. This timeless trope was employed at the end of the sixteenth century just as it was in the fourteenth century.[8] Themes concerning the exaltation of uneducated men, the rewarding of inferior verse, the promotion of clowns and buffoons over the learnèd occurred in every generation of poets from the thirteenth century onwards.[9]

Prose, for example, represented a separate continuum from which those who apologized for their literary inadequacies were scarcely making a radical departure. In verse, on the other hand, there may have been a more radical change of vogue, but the innovators appear to have been unapologetic. All of the authors mentioned below were practitioners of strict *dán díreach* but played with the conceit of unconventionality.

Apparent discussion of this change appears in the witty exchanges between poets, as poets and as teachers. Arch references to the methods of study, the code of mnemonics, the grammatical drills, which were part of the shared cultural training of the poets, are to be understood in poems attributed to Fear Feasa Ó'n Cháinte, in poems by by Eochaidh Ó hEoghusa, by Fear Flatha Ó Gnímh, by Fearghal Óg Mac an Bhaird and others.[10] Among the more amusing are poems that appear to address changes in literary style, like that (early seventeenth-century poem) addressed to Fearghal Óg Mac an Bhaird by Fear Flatha Ó Gnímh, '*Cuimseach sin, a Fhearghail Óig*'.[11]

A METRICAL LESSON

A trio of poems from the final decades of the sixteenth century or the early seventeenth century, published by L. McKenna[12] – '*Mór an feidhm deilbh an dána*' [Shaping a poem is a great undertaking], by Fear Feasa Ó'n Cháinte; '*A fhir shealbhas duit an dán*' [Man who would possess the (art of the) poem (or 'of poetry')], by Gofraidh Mac an Bhaird; '*Créad dá sealbhuinn damh an dán*' [What if I were to (claim to) possess the (art of the) poem (or 'of poetry')], by Fear Feasa Ó'n Cháinte[13] – reads like a didactic exercise cast in the mould of a dialogue between a teacher and an opinionated student, and/or between wrangling peers.

The ocean of learning and the forges of perfection, the finish of the schools and the long apprenticeship are outlined in Fear Feasa's '*Mór an feidhm deilbh an dána*' (late sixteenth/early seventeenth century). The whole account of the poet's learning in this composition is a matter of general knowledge to Fear Feasa's fellow-poets. The details are hardly a matter of interest to the unlettered. The poem is unlikely to have been an appeal to those who did not appreciate school poetry, it is not addressed to any particular lord or patron. In the context of the two other poems edited by McKenna with it, it has the characteristics of a teaching poem that survived from some school collection.

Gofraidh Mac an Bhaird's '*A fhir shealbhas duit an dán*' attacks the hauteur of a fellow-poet's effort and, in a manner recalling the school teaching aids, lists the 'faults' (*lochtanna*) in a clearly didactic manner, again listing the requirements of the true poem and the behaviour expected of a true poet.

A 'low' style is adopted, enhancing the complaints made by the poet, Mac an Bhaird, at the arrogance of Ó'n Cháinte. The 'ignoble' crafts of weaving, tucking and so forth are the metaphorical webs upon which the poet hangs his lesson.

Ó'n Cháinte's 'response', '*Créad dá sealbhuinn damh an dán*', defends his arrogance and excoriates his 'critic'.

TEACHER AND STUDENT

Gofraidh Fionn Ó Dálaigh's fourteenth-century composition '*Madh fiafraidheach budh feasach*' [If one be questioning one becomes knowledgeable][14] is a fifty-four-quatrain metrical lesson about the skills and knowledge required by a scholar to produce such a poem. It represents much of the instruction given in the *Trefhocal*.[15] Undergoing the syllabic treatment by Gofraidh Fionn, it makes a worthy poem in itself. A poet frequently quoted in the manuals of grammar and syntax,[16] Gofraidh Fionn was a recognized master. Though not a composition about poetry in the same sense as that of the three poems following (by Fear Feasa Ó'n Cháinte and Gofraidh Mac an Bhaird, respectively), his poem is a ghostly presence informing the exchanges between the later poets, Fear Feasa Ó'n Cháinte and Gofraidh Mac an Bhaird (see above, p. 184). Gofraidh Fionn's poem refers to the instructions that equip one to compose in accordance with *sgiaimhdhénmha na sgol* [. . . the polished composition of the schools] (q. 5c), which surely indicates the formal polished syllabic poem.

Beginning in the time-honoured way with a *sententia* – '*madh fiafraidheach budh feasach*'[17] — Gofraidh Fionn exalts the trait of intellectual curiosity or inquisitiveness to set the tone for a poem that will bear the scholastic characteristics of question and answer:

> *Madh fiafraidheach budh feasach;*
> *glic an éicsi ilcheasach;*
> *solas na ceasa ad-chluine,*
> *doras feasa fiafruighe.*
> (*MFBF*, q. 1)

[If one is questioning one will be knowledgeable; the
art of poetry with its many challenges is clever (subtle);
enquiry is the door of knowledge, the clarity of the
problem you hear.]

The opening adage sanctions the schoolroom litany of *cá
méad* [how many], with which quatrains four to eight begin.
This use of *repetitio* (*epanaphora*) strengthens another rhetorical
device, that of *conduplicatio*, which is a feature of amplification.
This draws attention to the ritual of question–answer, which is
a characteristic appropriate to the *inventio* of this poem. The
answers are not explicit, for the most part.[18] The questions
imply answers that are to be found with the teacher. The build-
ing of a sense of authority to question, created by the continued
repetition of *cá méad*, involves the use of *gradatio*, a device
that evokes a sense of climax. The 'climax' here is in quatrain
nine – Gofraidh Fionn, the poet, the professor, will provide the
answers. The use of *divisio*, the posing of a question which is
then addressed as though a series of questions had been pos-
ited, enhances the pedagogic style in the poem and also enables
elaboration, essential to the whole poetic enterprise.

The *sententia* that opens the quatrain is balanced in the final
line by another concluding one, '*doras feasa fiafruighe*' (q. 1d).
This makes an entire, even logical, unit of this quatrain, which
completes a stanzaic cycle in itself. It is well ornamented in
the style recommended by the best practice of the *ars poet-
ica*: the poet echoes the *ilcheasach* [many difficulties] of line
b with the inflected *ceasa* of line c. Indeed, within this line
itself there is the synaesthetic association of *solas* and *ad-chluine*,
which skirted on the faults of poetry (mismatched verb and
object: in this case to hear light [clarity can of course be audit-
ory and this is the principle meaning here; the play is on *solus* as
clarity and lucidity in the intellectual sense, and light and light-
giving]),[19] while – to the satisfaction of master-poet – being

entirely correct when *solas* means lucidity in interpretation or speech.

Quatrain two introduces the second character in the interlocutary pair suggested by the opening *sententia* of question and answer. This is ubiquitous *fear*, always in the vocative *a fhir* of the poetry: claims are understood to have been made by this 'man' to some knowledge of the arts of poetry. This is the *inventio* of the teaching poem, which may (also) have been a composition to secure graduation or regrading of some kind.[20]

> *A fhir a-deir inntleacht and,*
> *freagra bheag dhúinn,*[21] *go ndearbham*
> *fréamha cneasda na ceirde,*
> *ceasda géara Gaoidheilge.*
> (*MFBF*, q. 2).

[Man who asserts discernment in the matter, let us have a brief answer so that we may determine the graceful roots of the art, keen questions about Irish.]

Gofraidh Fionn employs the Latinate term *inntleacht* here, evoking the learning of Latin, over a choice of a variety of other terms that many later poets used to enhance the mystery of their skills and to evoke the sense of magic surrounding the creative processes.[22]

The question and answer sequence begins immediately in quatrain three. *Cá méad* is the formula and it opens each of the following five quatrains. The questions themselves deal with the grammatical minutiae of correct inflection and declension in the manner of the schools: '. . . *do réir sgiaimhdhénmha na sgol*' [in accordance with the polished composition of the schools] (q. 5c).[23] Supporting the questions presented in each quatrain is a comment on the significance of the knowledge, and of the importance of those who possess it: '*breitheamh an tí le ttuigthir*' [he is a judge by whom it is understood] (q. 3d)

– referring to the understanding of *'réim focail'* [the inflection of a word] (q. 3a).[24]

The rules are difficult, this must be emphasized in order to enhance the status of those who master them, and perhaps to encourage students, who, when they have learnt the rules can feel a justified pride. Quatrain four concludes:

> . . . *an tomhasso a-tá n-a ghlas,*
> *ní horasa thrá a thomhas.*
> (*MFBF*, q. 4cd)
> [. . . this riddle which is impenetrable, it is not easy, indeed, to guess at it.][25]

The play on *tomhas* – 'riddle, guess' and 'measure of poetry' – which is used here as noun and verb, shows very well, even perhaps to those whom Gofraidh Fionn sought to teach, or impress, how closely he followed the rules of ornamentation and rhetorical colouring recommended for literary composition. The phatic *'freagair mhé'* [answer me] of quatrain 6a maintains the 'reality' of the interlocution:

> *Cá mhéad focal – freagair mhé –*
> *as dual do dhéanamh réime?*
> (*MFBF*, q. 6ab)
>
> [How many words – answer me – naturally cause inflection?]

The reinforcing coda to this quatrain assures the knowledgeable that it is information worth having:

> *tuar teasda dá tteagmha ag dreim*
> *freagra na ceasda chuirim.*
> (*MFBF*, q. 6cd)
>
> [it is a sign of merit if some happen to have the answer to the questions I put.]

An image of the person who is master of these rules is created by the description of him as a *'breitheamh'* [judge] (q. 3d); and his reputation is made by his ability to answer the question put in quatrain six (*tuar teasda*). The man who can resolve the significant problem of how many *iairmbéarla* [unstressed particles of speech] formed from words cause inflection is the best man – *'fear a réidhighthe as é 's fhearr'* (q. 7c), and in contrast, he who cannot answer or resolve this question is to be impugned: *'éilighthe an té nach tuigeann'* (q. 7d). The image of the schoolroom is maintained in quatrain eight when the poet seeks the answer from the 'student', who must, if he cannot answer, *'léig don té (dan) tualuing'* [leave it to someone capable of it] (q. 8d). The *inventio* of master and student is sustained without a break to this point. At quatrain nine, the basis of the *inventio* is reiterated, if the 'student' cannot come up with the answers, then the 'teacher' will find them for him. This device of *transitio* creates a pause in the compostion, a repetition that creates a break, after which the poem may advance in a different direction. Quatrain nine also introduces a form of contract, *'muna fhagha . . . cúis gach réime as réim d'fhocal dhamh . . . eolas a ngéag do-ghébh dheid . . .'* [If you do not find the cause of inflection . . . for me, . . . I shall give you information concerning their roots . . . .] (q. 9). If the student cannot answer, the master shall inform him. The roles are redefined to create a new start in quatrain ten.

The first nine quatrains introduce the characters involved in the dialogue and their business: teacher, student; one to teach, the other to learn. Supporting the description of the knowledge that must be mastered by the aspiring scholar (or poet) is the implied image of the master: one who has this knowledge is a judge, is well thought of and so forth.

From quatrain ten, therefore, the poet undertakes the imparting of the information in earnest – numbers of forms, lists of inflectional situations, exceptions, technical terms. This material is the matter of the schools, probably available in many forms in each school throughout the country. Gofraidh Fionn's effort here stabilizes a version of the important questions in a manner which, at the same time, demonstrates the use of the skills being taught. This is the case with each of the manuals referred to earlier. The authors, Matthew of Vendôme, Geoffrey of Vinsauf, and John of Garland, demonstrate with their own pedagogic compositions, the very tenets they seek to instil in, or explain to, the reader, pupil.

Each detail is backed by asides concerning the authority of the poet himself, the relative difficulty of the material, and the corresponding status of those who can learn it. The thirty-one subjects that cause inflection: 'rádh nach derméd' [a statement I shall not forget . . .] (q. 10b); the thirty-one 'tochluighthe', which the poet will illuminate, '. . . soillseochad duid' (q. 11a). The poet, as teacher, imparts true learning 'as léigheann fíor a bhfuighlim' [what I state is true learning] (q. 12d). An imaginary controversy or debate about the facts which the poet is imparting is sustained with challenges to 'others' to disagree in a hypophoraic or rhetorical question.[26] Following on quatrain twelve's statement about 'léigheann fíor', comes the challenge in quatrain thirteen to those who might disagree – 'cia nach aointeogha a n-abram?' [who would not agree with what I say?] (q. 13d). These rhetorical questions serve at least four purposes: they maintain the momentum of the inventio's teacher–student relationship; they create a picture of the authoritative teacher; they re-create the schools' atmosphere of statement and challenge, and they have the mnemonic function of creating a plausible narrative structure for the rules.[27] Quatrain fourteen's covert challenge, again after a description of a further aspect of inflection, is worded:

'*mar só nach dóigh a dhiultadh*' [for it will turn out that it is not likely to be denied] (q. 14d).

Quatrain fifteen, dealing with a list of items numbering eight, attaches a mnemonic concerning the eight words of the philosphers to fix the memory on the number: '. . . the number of words which naturally create inflection is eight': '. . . *dream ochtair nach olc an sdair, / i n-a n-ocht bhfoclaibh feallsaimh*' [a group of eight of no bad account, are the eight words of the philospher].[28] And so the poem continues, each rule enumerated and ballasted with some extraneous comment about its difficulty, or the merits of mastering it. Encouragement to master the recondite knowledge of a further two forms is the bribe in quatrain seventeen: '*fios an dá fhocal eile* . . . / *– uathadh líon danadh léir soin –*' [knowledge of the two other words, . . . this is clear to few people –] (q. 17ac). The exclusive few to whom this knowledge is clear, includes the poet/teacher – a group the successful student will join. Further exceptional words inflect in other ways, this too is knowledge for the select group which hears the rules from the master, such as the poet: '*– as mór sgol ara snaidhm soin*' [many are the schools for which this is a problem] (q. 18c) – knowledge unobtainable for those unfortunate others who have not the best teacher is the implication of this line.

In keeping with the Latinate/Christian '*inntleacht*' (q. 2a), '*sgoil*' (q. 5c), '*léigheann*' (q. 12d), and '*feallsamh*' (q. 15d), quatrain nineteen refers to the rules of metrical composition, which this poem teaches, as '*soisgéal: atá só n-ar soisgéalaibh*' [. . . this is in our gospels] (q. 19d) – the gospel of the grammatical rules taught to a disciple.

To whom are the difficult matters of the diphthongs not difficult? Quatrain twenty's factual declaration, anticipatory (*prolepsis*) of the matter of quatrains twenty-one and twenty-two, creates a compositional pause. Here, the poet, returning to the lists of numbers, recalls wandering attention with the order or suggestion '*éisdidh féin foghluim ronua*' [listen yourselves to this very new lesson] (q. 21b). Concerning the diphthongs (*iu* and *ea*), though they occur infrequently, discarding the correct usage is a violation of the canon: '*dáibh do-bhéarthar cor don chóir, / do-ghéabhthar col don chanóin*' [in them the norm will be deviated from, the canon will be violated] (q. 22cd). The term '*canóin*' [canon] here sustains the sense of a system described in terms analogous to the scriptures, or of a dogma compatible with, or parallel to, scriptural instruction. At all events, it speaks of an approach to the teaching of the syllabic rules that would resonate with students already familiar with or becoming familiar with education in the scriptures at whatever level. Gofraidh Fionn's poem does not suggest that those who specialized in poetry were involved in an exclusive system referring only to its own rubrics. It also suggests that a grounding in the grammatical rules were taught to those whose future careers would not necessarily involve them in the profession of poetry.[29]

THE GOSPEL OF THE POETS

The knowledge that leads to familiarity with the rules is to be found with the poet: '*do-gheabhthar a n-iul aguind*' [knowledge of them is found with us] (q. 23d) and in re-enforcement of that statement, quatrain twenty-four begins '*As maith ar n-aithne orra / a-déar uile a n-anmanna*' [We know them well, I shall give them all their names] (q. 24ab).[30] Quatrain twenty-five summarizes the teaching of the preceding fourteen quatrains (from quatrain eleven):

> *Gurab iad sin – suairc an ríomh –*
> *ó ollamhnaibh na n-airdríogh*

fios gan trothlughadh re throid –
an tochlughadh ar thríochaid.
(*MFBF*, q. 25)

[That these are the thirty-one *tochlughadh* [accusative plurals] – pleasant the count – a knowledge from the professors of the high-kings, uncorrupted with contention.]

This use of *transitio* looks back at what has been said and looks forward to future references to the professors, with whom knowledge of the science of grammar and composition resides.

Just as quatrain nine completed the first part of the poem, quatrains eleven to twenty-five complete the second element, a cycle beginning with the thirty-one *tochluighthe*, in quatrain eleven, and finishing with them in quatrain twenty-five. The man who declared that he would furnish the necessary information in quatrain nine, '*eolas a ngéag do-ghébh dheid*' (q. 9c), has indeed done that in the ensuing fifteen quatrains, and has also let one know that he is among the professors, *ollaimh*, associated with the high-kings, *airdríghthe*. Only those of that status are masters of the knowledge imparted, and hinted at, in those quatrains.

Quatrains twenty-six and twenty-seven make observations about inflections in the masculine and the feminine, which affect all those words mentioned before, and the poet effectively closes that session with quatrain twenty-eight. Having finished the synopsis of the rules, the poet returns to the opening verse, and his ruling *sententia* – with a creative twist – re-establishing the tone and reiterating the *inventio* that gave his poem structure from the beginning. This recapitulation effectively ushers in a further list of rules, couched again in a question and reply formula:

Leigfeat go fóill sin mar sin,
fiafróchad foghluim thuillimh;

> *bheith ris is eadh nach aithreach,*
> *madh fear fis badh fiafraightheach.*
> (*MFBF*, q. 28)
>
> [I shall leave that as it is for a while, I shall question learning further, attending to it is not a matter of regret: if he be a man of wisdom he will be inquisitive.]

This poem might well have concluded here, the echo of the opening quatrain in quatrain twenty-eight would constitute a slightly faulty closure (*dúnadh*), but would provide a perfect conclusion in recapitulating the opening *sententia* with slight variation.

Quatrain thirty introduces a note of levity. The bombardment of information contained in the preceding quatrains is likened to an assault from which the 'student' may be thought to need time to 'recover'. The term *rúaig* can also mean a course or career and, in this case, maximum effect is achieved by allowing the former to carry the humour and the latter to carry the sense.[31]

> *Ón ruaigsin má taoi ar ttéarnamh*
> *féch leat cá líon iairmbéarladh*
> *– as é soin snaidhm na haithne –*
> *ag a bhfuil ainm illraighthe.*
> (*MFBF*, q. 29)
>
> [If you have recovered from that ordeal, consider how many *iairmbéarladh* there are – this is the difficulty of the precept – which are termed plural.]

Once again, the range of meanings covered by *aithne* includes that of the scriptural Commandments. In keeping with earlier quasi-scriptural references in this poem, the semantic breadth covering *aithne* could well be exploited here to correspond with, for instance, *soisgéal* in quatrain 19d and *canóin* of quatrain 22d.

In any event, the 'student' is addressed, with a certain amount of levity, as though he had been through an ordeal/vigorous course – of learning – from which he may well need recovery time. This creates the pause, like that after quatrain nine, and after quatrain twenty-seven, which allows for a new direction in the composition. In this case the poet replaces the teacher–student relationship, temporarily, with an apostrophic[32] appeal to the practitioners of the science of poetry itself – *aos ceirde* – and to the professors of poetry:[33]

> *Cia an dá innsgne abuir ruinn*
> *as eochracha don fhoghluim,*
> *sí uatha ar-aon gá heagar?*
> *ní gaol fuatha an foirceadal.*
> (*MFBF*, q. 30)

> *Cia na sé fréamha ghá bhfuil*
> *tighearnas ar gach teangaidh*
> *innisidh, a aos ceirde,*[34]
> *d'innisin ghaos nGaoidheilge?*
> (*MFBF*, q. 31)

[Tell me, what are the two genders that are the keys to learning, by both of which learning is organized; this instruction is not odious.

What are the six roots that have mastery over every language, tell, speak, persons of skill, to recount the wisdoms of Irish.]

The key (*eochair*) here to learning is knowledge of the *inscne* of words. The key to the composition of this and the following quatrain is the term *inis* (*indisid*), and its verbal noun *insint* (*indisin*). In a virtuoso display of the skills of the *aos ceirde*, of whom the poet Gofraidh Fionn was a pre-eminent member, the verb and verbal noun are exploited in the lines *c* and *d* of quatrain thirty-one: '*innisidh, a aos ceirde, / d'innisin ghaos nGaoidheilge?*'; and in the lines *b c* and *d* of quatrain thirty-two:

Dénasa a ndiaigh an tseisir
a n-imdheachta d'innisin;
ar n-indisin a n-imtheacht
innisidh a n-edircheart.
(*MFBF*, q. 32)

[After this six (the six roots of quatrain thirty-one), recount their processes; after telling of their processes, discuss their interpretation.]

The shades of meaning involved in this wordplay on the terms *inis* (*indisid*), and its verbal noun *insint* (*indisin*), employ a variety of *adnominatio* often used to create puns.

ENQUIRE OF THE MASTER
Quatrain thirty-two builds on the use of *inis* in quatrain thirty-one, and uses *gradatio* to build up a sense of development in the poem and in the information, repeating the forms of *inis*, and keeping the term '*imtheacht*' [exploit/proceeding/process] as a device to carry the request: first tell about x and after x tell about y, in the pretence of a 'causal chain'.[35] Quatrain thirty-three returns the authoritative voice to the poet; he answers on behalf of the *aos ceirde*/(*aos dána*) to whom he appealed in quatrains thirty-one and thirty-two. This quatrain also finishes the immediate sequence of which *inis* is the key term:

Indistear leam gan leisge,
ó nach éasgaidh n-indisde,
na briathra a-déar 's a-dobhart,
sgéal as iarrtha d'iarmhoracht.
(*MFBF*, q. 33)

[Let the words which I shall speak and have spoken be related without reluctance by me, since they are not easy to relate; (it is) a matter that must be sought as a sequel.]

This quatrain gives to understand that the *aos dánal (aos ceirde)* – those 'experts' to whom Gofraidh Fionn had recourse – included, pre-eminently, himself. It also ushers in a sequence of informing quatrains containing the grammatical terms concerning masculine and feminine forms, the two most noble genders: *'an dá innsgne is uaisle ann'* (q. 35a). Knowing these is the 'door to knowledge' (*doras foghlama an fissin*) (q. 35c).[36] While these are 'two correctly equivalent roots' (*dhá fhréimh chearta chomhthruma*) (q. 36d), the *deimhinnsgne* [neuter gender] is the third 'branch' of Irish – *'an treas gobhlán don Ghaoidheilg'* (q. 37d). In this instance, 'branch' is listed as the third of a trio, of which the earlier two examples are described as 'roots'.

Mastery of the categorizations and classifications necessary to create syllabic compositions in the approved styles is the object of the lessons hinted at and the information imparted in this poem. Needless to say, the composition of grammatical prose is also imparted in the lessons outlined here. Nevertheless, it is in syllabic verse that the display of learning normally took place. These are terms to be used when discussing the art (of skilled composition): *'as í sin . . . gidh chuin bheas comhrádh ar cheird . . .'* (q. 37bc). And so the poem progresses with the investigation of the number, quality and terms appropriate for the genders, vowels, consonants and so forth. At quatrain forty-one the poet, once again, turns to the experts, as he had done in quatrains thirty-one and thirty-two (*innisidh, a aos ceirde*). This is, in effect, another pause in the composition, and these pauses punctuate every ten or so quatrains: *'ceist agam ar na h-eolchaibh /fagham uathaibh a n-aithne'* [my question to the experts – let us get the precept from them] (q. 41bc).

The poem poses questions intended to prompt replies.[37] The questions direct attention to the matters that must be mastered by the aspiring scholar/poet. L. McKenna associates them with the rules known from the grammatical tracts. Learning such a poem by heart and committing the answers to memory would certainly equip the student with some of the basic rules concerning verbal inflection, declension, and so forth.

Ornamention apart from the metrical, such as *litotes* – which even lends humour to the dry descriptions of vowels and consonants – recalls the humour sprinkled through Matthew of Vendôme's manual for his scholars. Understatement in the following quatrain makes the precept and the quatrain itself unforgettable:

> *Do-ghéabhthaoi guthaidhe lom*
> *gan chonsuine n-a chonclann;*
> *gan ghuthaidhe n-a ghoire*
> *ní cruthaighe connsuine.*
> (*MFBF*, q. 45)

> [A solitary vowel is to be found without the accompaniment of a consonant; a consonant is not the more shapely for having no vowel near it.]

Attributes of brightness and shapeliness, sweetness and clarity, are distributed on the masculine and feminine forms: '*bainninsgne bhinn*' [(the) sweet feminine] (q. 39a); '*dream is cruthaighe ad-chluine*' [the most shapely group which you shall hear] (q. 39c); '*guthaidhe ghreadhnacha*' [sparkling vowels] (q. 40b); '*an bhainindsgne bhionnorlamh*' [the sweet-ready feminine] (q. 43 b); '*guthaidhe ghlóirbheachta*' [clear-sounding vowels] (q. 44b). References to groups of vowels and consonants by the collectives *drong* and *dream*, associated mainly with groups of people, animals or living things, lend an animation and a personality to the groups of words and forms with which the poet is dealing. This use of personification (*conformatio*) enlivens the dry matter under discussion and encourages interest in the grammatical fate or evolution of the words. This information, the poet recalls, puzzles many, but is known to the poets:

> *Cá consaine is lia re luagh,*
> *nó cá guthaidhe glanfhuar?*
> *a-tá céad ara snaidhm sin;*
> *créd a n-ainm ag na héigsibh?*
> (*MFBF*, q. 46)

[What is the consonant that is most numerous to mention, or what pure clear vowel? – a hundred men find that a problem – what names have the poets for them?]

The poets, it is implied here, have long had the power of naming in the matter of grammar and poetic diction.[38] Being one of those poets, Gofraidh Fionn, giving the answer to the question posed above, allows that he, indeed, is better able to answer: '– *fearr do-chiu ná do-chí sibh* – ' [– I can see (this) better than you do –] (q. 47c). Likewise, he has a further store of information concerning these matters: '*Do-ghéabhthar leam gan lochta / neithe oile as ionmholta*' [Other praiseworthy matters will be found without fault in my possession] (q. 48ab). The pedagogic style included mention of wrong usage too, and in only one quatrain of this poem does Gofraidh Fionn allow mention of an incorrect usage concerning diphthongs, 'a good professor takes it to be a transgression [of the rules]' (*n-a chol dóibh ag deaghollamh*) (q. 49d).

To achieve mastery in the matter of composition in the approved style to the required standard, Gofraidh Fionn's example should be followed:

> *Ar na ceasdaibh ad-chluine*
> *dá n-urmaise énduine*
> *– an aithnesi ní haisgidh –*
> *ar mh'aithrisi urmaisdir.*
> (*MFBF*, q. 50)

[If anyone should attempt the questions which you
hear, let the attempt follow my example – this precept
is not a gift.[39]]

Gofraidh Fionn is the 'first' (*is gan iad dá rádh romhuinn*) *ollamh*
to deliver this knowledge to students, though the poets know
it all along, since they have spent their lives with poetry. This
suggestion that the material is being made available for the first
time is equivalent to the *nova* of Geoffrey of Vinsauf's *Poetria
Nova*.[40] The latest of any redaction is 'new' in the terms under-
stood by the writers, though the content is always based on
ancient authority:

> *In fhoghluimsi an iongnadh libh*
> *dá mbeith a haithne ag éigsibh,*
> *'s iad leisin ndán druim ar druim,*
> *is gan iad dá rádh romhuinn.*
> (*MFBF*, q. 51)

[(As for) this learning, are you surprised that poets
should follow its teaching given that they are
continuously involved with poetry, though before me
they did not express it.]

Situating himself well within the world of learning and disputa-
tion, Gofraidh Fionn anticipates objections to his work at some
future date. This anticipation, a form of self-praise, conceals
itself with mild dispraise:

> *Meinic shaoilim ó so suas*
> *– ní hionann do chách coguas –*
> *ó nach fuighe uirre eol*
> *duine uime dom áithcheodh.*
> (*MFBF*, q. 52)

[I anticipate that, frequently, from now on, someone
who acquires no knowledge of it will contradict me as
a consequence – all consciences are not alike.]

In response to the second person singular/plural in use throughout the poem – in the sense of the addressee in the teacher–student(s) dialogue – the poet finally names himself, the *sinn* [I/we] corresponding to the *sibh* [you/ye] (and the final line of this quatrain includes a loose *dúnadh*, which could have been used to conclude a shorter version of this composition):

Is mé Gofraidh mac meic Thaidhg
a-ndeas ón Mhumhan mhíonaird;
tearc trá ón lios i luighim
gá dtá fios a bhfiafruighim.
(*MFBF*, q. 53)

[I am Gofraidh grandson of Tadhg, from Munster of the gentle heights in the south; few have the knowledge about which I enquire, beyond the house in which I dwell.]

The final quatrain takes the form of two *sententiae*, both commenting on the difficulty of mastering the learning required for composing poetry:

Tacmhang na héigse uile
conntabhairt é ag énduine;
tearc as ionchomhráidh orra
friothghobhláin na foghloma.
(*MFBF*, q. 54)

[Mastery of all literary scholarship, it is doubtful if anyone possess it; few are capable of dicussing them, (all) the divergent branches of learning.[41]]

This quatrain, along with furnishing an acceptable bardic *dúnadh*, provides an even more satisfactory *conclusio*, summing up, as it does, the import of what the poet had to say throughout about the difficulty in acquiring the skills needed to compose work to the required standard.

The imagery of *doras* [door] and *eochair* [key] occurs in Gofraidh Fionn Ó Dálaigh's '*Madh fiafraidheach budh feasach*', but is not central to its *inventio*, which is that of master–student. The casual use of these two images, nevertheless, has significance for all the poems concerning the poets' art, its rules and obtaining access to them by learning and by imitation. This knowledge is not an *aisce* (*MFBF*, q. 50c), a free gift. It is a hard-won expertise, acquired properly only from the teaching of experts and the emulation of them or through instruction by them. *Aithris* can also mean to 'rehearse', 'repeat' and 'relate', all of which will have been intended by the poet in the employment of this expression (*MFBF*, q. 50d). The poets contested in verse with each other, a circumstance anticipated by Gofraidh Fionn in quatrain fifty-two. Worthy poets in times to come *ought* to contend with his interpretation of the rules.

POEMS ABOUT POETRY

The genre of poems about composition and poetry – of which the fourteenth-century '*Madh fiafraidheach badh feasach*' is one of the best known in the tradition – is the category to which three poems of the sixteenth/seventeenth century belong: Fear Feasa Ó'n Cháinte's '*Mór an feidhm deilbh an dána*'; '*Créad dá sealbhuinn damh an dán*'; and Gofraidh Mac an Bhaird's '*A fhir shealbhas duit an dán*'.[42]

The poem attributed to Fear Flatha Ó Gnímh, '*Cuimseach sin, a Fhearghail Óig*',[43] in which the poet seems to upbraid fellow-poet Fearghal Óg Mac an Bhaird for lack of discipline in his approach to composition, has achieved an iconic status as a poem that registers the changes for the worse, which overwhelmed the poets in that period in the seventeenth-century.

Of a piece with this, sharing the same sly humour, is another by the same poet: '*Mairg do-chuaidh re ceird ndúthchais*'.[44] In a different vein, on a similar theme, Eochaidh Ó hEoghusa's '*Ionmholta malairt bhisigh*' suggests that it may well be time for him to imitate the philosophers of the fable and go into the rain with the deluded majority.[45] The poems by Ó hEoghusa, and Ó Gnímh will be briefly examined later in the context of their self-referential and literary qualities, and in the light of the suit of the three debating poems by Fear Feasa Ó'n Cháinte and Gofraidh Mac an Bhaird, looked at below.

'MÓR AN FEIDHM DEILBH AN DÁNA'

Bearing in mind Gofraidh Fionn's poem, '*Madh fiafraidheach budh feasach*', a composition probably known by heart by the poet Fear Feasa Ó'n Cháinte (and possibly by all the poets whose work is considered here), an overwhelming sense of the genre nature of such poems is felt. The two centuries and some years that separate both poems may account for the absolute assurance evident in the second, later poem that the poet addresses a readership/audience which is aware of the tradition in which he sets his composition, especially of the tradition of other such poems. The pedagogical imperative is comparatively faint in the content, yet the production is full of examples of usage. The course to be followed by the poet is emphasized, as is the identity of the teacher to whom one might have recourse – the poet himself, Fear Feasa Ó'n Cháinte. The poem makes no overt reference to the probable origin of the poet's particular surname – Ó'n Cháinte – in the pursuit by at least one of his remote ancestors of one branch of poetry, that of satire.[46]

THE 'DIALOGUE'

The poem, '*Mór an feidhm deilbh an dána*', too, like Gofraidh Fionn's '*Madh fiafraidheach budh feasach*', is a form of dialogue. Its *inventio* is the reprimanding, and the impugning of the faulty, slipshod work of the careless, or ignorant, or unqualified poet. This group can include lazy students, and half-skilled or infelicitous graduates. The dialogue involves an implied inferior poet, and after that, whomever might respond to the provocation of the poem. The implied participation of 'others' is part of the dynamic of the poem. It is part of the schools' tradition that the gauntlet thrown down by a poet/poem in this manner will be used as material for another poem in a similar way. Gofraidh Fionn invites response in his '*Madh fiafraidheach budh feasach*': '*Meinic shaoilim ó so suas . . . duine uime dom áithcheodh*' (*MFBF*, q. 52ad; and see above, p. 200).

The poem is formed of three strands woven to create its fabric. The image of weaving is also present in the poem and, as in the web of fabric, the three strands cross and recross each other to form quite a dense composition. Teasing them apart, though unnecessary to the sense of the poem – and contrary to its (inferred) intention in some measure – reveals three poems within the whole: the poem about poetry itself, the quatrains concerning Fear Feasa's expertise, and the quatrains devoted to denigration of inferior work and ill-educated poets. Each strand, as in a woven fabric, takes strength from the other, so that the pre-eminence of Fear Feasa is highlighted by the inability of the detractors; the rigour of the course properly followed by a poet is in contrast to the lax approach of the pretenders. Identifying the strands does not mean that any of the three would stand alone as a poem about excellence, training or shoddy work. Fear Feasa's 'discovery' of topic, his *inventio*, is the combination of the three to create a poem recognizable in the genre, which will be a participant in other poems like it, even as his work is supported by his knowledge of, and our awareness of, a work like the Gofraidh Fionn poem '*Madh fiafraidheach budh feasach*'. Ó'n Cháinte's contention is that there is no easy way to poetry. Its undertaking is onerous. Those who are not fit for it are foolish to concern themselves with his craft. The first couplet introduces two of the elements of the *inventio*: the skill needed to create a poem of quality, and the foolhardiness of attempting it without the necessary skill or training. The second couplet introduces the poet as one with the training and the skill to claim the status of *ollamh* for himself. The first quatrain, therefore, lays out the matter of the poem; the following twenty quatrains weave it into the composition that gives Fear Feasa (and his professional peers) so much satisfaction. It may have had the desired effect too of engendering the poem identified as a response poem by L. McKenna – Gofraidh Mac an Bhaird's '*A fhir shealbhas duit an dán*'.[47]

The opening adage has all the ponderousness of an established *sententia*. Indeed, the poet's use of it here makes it so:

> *Mór an feidhm deilbh an dána*
> *baoth don dreim nach diongmhála*
> *car re céadfaidh mo cheirde,*
> *téachtmhuir*[48] *ghlan na Gaoidheilge.*
> (*SIB* i, q. 1)

[Making poetry is an onerous task, it is foolish for that group who are not capable to struggle with the principles (tenets of my craft); the clear viscous sea of Irish.]

The *inventio* of the poem conceives of the fully qualified poet as having braved the ocean of learning and tamed it to the point of perfection in the award of professorship. '*An t-aos dána*' [those skilled in the arts] (q. 5) are contrasted with '*aos an ainbhis*' [the ignorant (unskilled poets)] and with '*drong anbháil don aos dána*' [an excessive group among the poets] (q. 3):

> *An t-oigéan dorcha domhuin,*
> *an sruth aidhbhseach éagsom[h]ail*
> *ní [fios][49] acht baos righe ris,*
> *ní slighe[50] d'aos an ainbhis.*
> (*SIB* i, q. 2)

[The dark deep ocean, the vast and various stream, it is not wisdom but folly to contend with it; it is not a path for the ignorant.]

This description of learning as a vast expanse navigable only by the skilled is in anticipation (*prolepsis*) of an outline of the steps required to become qualified. Fear Feasa claims ownership of the skills as a personal matter: '*céadfaidh mo cheirde*' [. . . the skill of my craft] (q. 1c). His successful pursuit of that path through the ocean of knowledge has gained him honour in the grades of poetry:

> *[An t-aos dána] ceann a gceann*
> *tearc gá bhfuil a gcoing[h]eall*
> *slighe ána ónab uaisle mé,*
> *grádha uaisle na héigse.*
> (*SIB* i, q. 5)

[(Of) those skilled in the arts, taken together, few are they who have (fulfilled) their conditions, (the conditions of) the noble grades of poetic learning, splendid the paths which have brought me advancement.]

This profound art is known only to the intiates. The poet has been through all the stages of learning and has triumphed. Like Gofraidh Fionn (*MFBF*, q. 53), Fear Feasa's poem reads as an advertisement for himself as qualified professor/teacher:

Do [shnámhas]⁵¹iad tar a n-ais
srotha ionnalta an iomhais,
do ghlé mé m'oige eisdibh,
oide mé 's as maighisdir.
(*SIB* i, q. 20)

[I swam them repeatedly – the cleansing streams of
inspiration, I purified my text (web of cloth) in them;
I am a teacher and a master.]

Fear Feasa Ó'n Cháinte's education has followed the familiar
seven stages from new scholar to fully-fledged professor.⁵² The
poet, in quatrain nine, gives the full list of grades by which one
qualifies as an *ollamh*.

Do bhreith na suadh iar sodhain
na hoide na hollamhain,
fagháil anma ní dleacht dáibh
gan seacht ngarma do ghabháil.
(*SIB* i, q. 8)

Fochlag, Mac Fuirmidh feasach,
Dos, Clí na gceard neimhcheasach,
fiu an [daghbhoth],⁵³ a chara, a ccradh
Cana, Ánshruth is Ollamh.
(*SIB* i, q. 9)

[In the opinion of the men of learning, then, the
teachers, the professors acquiring title is not permitted
to them, without having taken the seven professions
(callings).

A *Fochlog*, a knowledgeable *Mac Fuirmidh*, a *Dos*, a *Clí*
of easy skills, a *Cana*, an *Ánshruth* and an *Ollamh*, their
reward is worthy of the good hut, my friend.]

There is nothing wanting in Fear Feasa's education or training,
he is not to be tripped up by anyone in respect of his profession:

Ar ngabháil na ngrádh suthain
ní thabhraim troigh[54] mhearuchaidh
'n-a rianaibh doilghe budh deacht,
ní diamhair oirne a n-imtheacht.
(*SIB* i, q. 11)

[After attaining the immortal grades, I make no step
in error (I make no erroneous syllabic count); in its
difficult paths (it) (I) would be exact,[55] their processes
are not mysterious to me.]

There are other degrees of poetry. These are indicated obliq-
uely by Gofraidh Fionn in '*Madh fiafraidheach budh feasach*' in
quatrain forty-nine (d) when he refers to the preference among
deaghollaimh for the realization of diphthongs in a certain way.
The implication is that there are 'other' *ollaimh* poets/teachers
who might favour the freer development of the realization of
the particular diphthongs as *oi*, and one might surmise that
these poets/teachers may be among those who would contra-
dict Gofraidh Fionn eventually. These 'others' – in this case of
inferior skill or knowledge – exist in Fear Feasa Ó'n Cháinte's
scheme of things also:

Gé táid foghráidh 'n-a bhfochair
bhíos anbhfann a n-ealothain,
a ngrádha foirfe as siad sin
doirche iad acht ar oidibh.
(*SIB* i, q. 10)

[Though there are inferior grades besides them,[56]
who are weak in art; they (aforementioned) are the
accomplished grades, they are opaque (to all) except
to teachers.]

This web of composition is a fabric, the nature of which is not
understood by those who have not had the same education as
the poet. Ó'n Cháinte, having swum through the deep oceans

of learning, is not to be commented upon by those who have stood on its brink:

> *Córuide gan righe riom*
> *don lucht anas 'n-a himioll;*
> *ní fhuil troigh nar thomhais mé*
> *do mhoir fhorais na héigse.*
> (*SIB* i, q. 19)

[It were better for those who dally on the verge (of the sea of learning) not to contend with me; there is not a foot of the deep sea of poetry that I have not measured.]

Ó'n Cháinte's employment of *troigh* [foot] and *tomhas* [measure] is further assurance of his absolute mastery of his skill; the two terms exploit their sense in the schools: 'foot' meaning 'measure of poetry', and 'measure' meaning 'foot of poetry'. This is a poem for students and poets who can enjoy these flourishes and learn from them by emulation. The pedagogic element is here, too, in that such a quatrain reinforces the meaning of those terms and provides a suitable example of them *in situ*, which was the practice of all the best manuals and teaching aids.[57] In contrast to those of superficial familiarity with learning, those who have been through the approved routes to poetry, the smithies of purification, recognize immediately the genuinely skilled production:

> *Ní léir (leo) lés 'n-a fighe,*
> *aos aitheanta ar cceirdne;*
> *gach oige dar innigh mé[58]*
> *a hinnibh oide is éigse.*
> (*SIB* i, q. 17)

[Those who know our craft can find no mistake in its weave – every web which I weft from the wealth of teachers and poets.]

While weaving is not among the crafts associated with the 'high' or 'middle' style in the normal manner, its connection with composition, and the overwhelming use of images derived from that craft in the description of metrical styles, and kinds of prosody makes it – when associated with composition – very acceptable for poems of the 'middle' style, which is probably where these poems about poetry are best situated.

Associated with this craft of weaving, is the craft of the smith: the forges of creativity and purging. These two crafts are the metaphorical equivalents in the poetry for the creation of poetry and the purification of style. The term *ceard* synonymously covers both the generalized 'craft' and the particular craft of the smith, particularly gold- and silver-smithery. The craft of the smith enjoyed a high status and position of privilege in Irish legal sources and traditionally.[59] The highest style could have included imagery of smithery as well, concentrating mainly on a military application of the craft, the forging of spears, the reddening of weapons, the tempering of the hero in battle and so forth. The use of such imagery elevates the style in poems about poetry; the forging of strophes and forms in the smithies of the school.[60]

It is in the forge of difficult questions that the poet formed his particular mastery:

> *A gceardcha na cceasd ndorcha*
> *do sgiamhas sgath m'ealathna;*
> *a hucht a ttroide as teann sinn*
> *na hoide dob fhearr d'Éirinn.*
> (*SIB* i, q. 15)

[I embellished the flower of my art in the forge of diffi-cult questions; I/we am/are confident as a consequence of their disputation, the teachers who were the best in Ireland.]

Indeed, since he first attempted the difficult course that eventually qualified him as he is now, the poet has been equipped to defend his art:

Deacroide teagmháil rem throid
ó do ghabhas grádh Focloig;
i mbéilshlighe na mbalg bhfis
ní thard éinfhile m'éislis.
(*SIB* i, q. 18)

[Since I attained the grade of *Fochlog*, it was the more difficult to engage me in a dispute; (even) on the threshold of poetic power no poet disdained me.]

The poet praises his teachers, '*na hoide dob fhearr d'Éirinn*' (q. 15d), and proclaims himself a teacher and master, '*oide mé 's as maighisdir*' (q. 20d). Being taught by him, even as he learned with his masters, even from the earliest stage (that of *fochlog*), allows one to become familiar with the teaching of the schools, and prepares one for the exalted status of master in turn.

The strands of the poem are intertwined at the points where the proof of Fear Feasa's ability are contrasted with the inferior efforts of those less well skilled. Their lack of training or education, the outlines of which form another strand in the poem, creates the theme, ridicules the untrained, the half-trained and the presumptious. The contrast is between the confidence of the true graduate of the schools in his skill and the presumptious attacks and unwise attacks of the more feebly equipped. Those who are truly skilled enjoy debate; the unskilled blunder about with blunted instruments:

An tan thagraid rer oile
ní cás don aos eagnoidhe
dul ó dhiomdhaidh na ttuagh ttais
tre lionnmhuir uar an iomhais.
(*SIB* i, q. 7)

[When they dispute with one another, the learnèd have no difficulty in escaping the vexation of the feeble axes through the cool limpid sea of knowledge.]

These vexatious feeble axes are the attacks by the unskilled. Such detractors attack the poet's style and his writings without having understood his art:

Le neart ainbhis dá n-aslach
labhruid – lór do dhíomussruth,
gé thig sár a n-iomráidh as –
glár nach ionráidh dá n-eolas.
(*SIB* i, q. 4)

[Goaded on by force of their ignorance, they speak – full of vainglory, though it causes the destruction of their reputation – a sound that does not speak for their knowledge.]

Far from understanding the subtleties of the art, these unabashed poets – and Ó'n Cháinte refers to them as such, '*drong anbháil don aos dána*' – seek plaudits through the employment of a miscellany of indifferent effects, and alliterative rhapsodies of inspiration. They are included, all the same, among *aos dána*, and are, possibly, those who are not counted *deaghollaimh,* in Gofraidh Fionn's configuration (*MFBF*, q. 49d, and see above, p. 199):

Drong anbháil don aos dána
gabhaid d'iarraidh anára
ilchearda uara re a n-ais,
rithlearga uama an iomhais.
(*SIB* i, q. 3)

[An unabashed group among the poets in seeking honour adopt many untried techniques, the alliterative rhapsodies of inspiration.]

They are similar to those castigated by Matthew of Vendôme, who also uses the metaphors of fabric – 'patchwork' in this case – to describe the perversion of true composition:

> Moreover, here are certain braggarts and triflers, who have an urge to awkward presumption and presume to caw and abuse the meaning of words in this fashion . . . (*AV*, §42, p. 77).

And

> . . . I have chosen for myself a personal and familiar path . . . . Further, stitchers of patches should be excluded from examining this work. When many are the versifiers called but few the chosen, some rely on the title[61] alone and pant[62] according to the meter of the verses rather than the beauty of what is in the meter. Some merely rearrange the patchwork line which throws the shadow of a trunk, not of foliage, and strive to pound into a unit an aggregate of triffles [*sic*], which because of their own deformity . . . seem to take turns among themselves in shouting[63] (*AV*, §§6–7, p. 18).

Being able to defend himself against the best teachers in Ireland (*SIB* i, q. 18) leaves the poet contemptuous of attacks from the unqualified. The device *descriptio* outlines the action taken: a good education – the consequence is the poet's ability to face any challenge to his learning. The repetition of this series of circumstances, which is a feature of the poem – and is essential to the development of the *inventio* – employs the feature *commoratio*, a device that is a characteristic of the whole poem (and of most Irish classical poems), involving a continual return to the main theme: the poet's education, his detractors' lack of it.

His education has taken place in the 'three houses', or realms,[64] 'in which Irish resides':

Do iarras go foirfe ar gceird
na trí tighe a-tá a nGaoidheilg;
mairg dan dualas déagsoin ruinn
ní ar éansgoil fhuaras m'fhoghluim.
(*SIB* i, q. 16)

[I diligently sought out our craft – the three houses in which Irish resides; unlucky the one whose task it is to compete with me (us), I got my education in more than one school.]

PROVOCATION

With such an apprenticeship supporting him, Ó'n Cháinte may attack the weak scholars, or the pretentious, with impunity. The poem, intertwining quatrains concerning Ó'n Cháinte's ability, and the poor work of others, creates an internal dialogue, as though objections were being made 'off-stage' to his claims. This technique, likewise, sustains the sense of dialogue that is a feature of the *inventio* of the composition, and is anticipatory, and even provocative of, response *outside* the poem. This common feature in such poems reminds one again of the eristic origins of the theories of composition that were popularized in innumerable manuals of writing from classical times. *Rhetorica ad Herennium*, the ghostly presence behind most of the mediaeval *artes poetriae*, notes that the use of features of 'refining' (*expolitio*) is 'not isolated from the whole cause like some limb, but like blood, it is spread through the whole body of the discourse' (*AdHer*, §XLIV.58, p. 375). In the course of describing the use of features that 'spread through the body of the discourse', the author urged the invention of causes, and the creation of occasions in which the devices might be used in the service of embellishment:

> It will be advantageous therefore to practise the principles of Refining in exercises divorced from a real

cause, and in actual pleading to them to use in the Embellishment of an argument . . . (ibid.).

The situating of a pedagogical poem, or a poem of self-advertisment, or an example of right usage – all of which descriptions might fit this poem of Fear Feasa's – within the fictive dialogue, or the feigned defence, can be seen as an exemplar-in-practice of a style of composition taught in the Irish schools. The trope of defence against named or unnamed 'others' is common in mediaeval Latin compositions, and is very familiar from the poems of complaint in Ireland, and in troubadour compositions in Europe.[65]

Fear Feasa's poem addresses the phenomenon of the derelict poets directly:

> *Dá n-abradh daoi [dod] dhaoidhibh*
> *tre mheisge[66] dtruim dtathaoirigh*
> *ní riomsa nach do réir ghráidh*
> *[dom] chéill dob ionnsa an admháil.*
> (*SIB* i, q. 12)

[If one of your ignoramuses, through ponderous censorious inebriety, were to say something not in accordance with (my) qualifications against me, in my view the claim would be difficult.]

The measured tone of this quatrain, the poet allowing the imprudence of the ignorant to be equivalent to an intoxication, functions here as a quiet preface to the fury that could be unleashed. It is a form of antiphrasis, and allows the development of irony. The feeble attempts to attack his work or standards are no threat to him (see q. 7 above). It is another thing entirely to goad him into retaliation. Two quatrains of rhetorical hyperbole indicate just how foolish it would be to challenge him:

Teagmháil riom tar éis m'ionnlaigh
do badh ceann i gcaithiorghail,[67]
nó cosg muire i dtrágh do theacht
nó snámh tuile dá treiseacht.

Nó déanamh brogha as a bharr
nó bas do [bhearnadh bearann]
nó cor eich tre fháinne slán
nó breith ar sgáile a sgáthán.

(*SIB* i, qq. 13, 14)

[To encounter me, after reviling me, were to put one's head into a battle fray, or to halt the incoming tide, or to swim the strongest flood.

Or to build a house from the top down, or to set one's palm to break through spears, or to put a horse through a closed hoop, or to seize a reflection from a looking-glass.]

This sequence could, indeed, be counted among the rhapsodies earlier condemned by Ó'n Cháinte (q. 3d). It serves as a form of mock-apologue. The anaphoric repetition of *nó* in six successive phrases is a self-conscious exercise in bathos, using the false sense of climax created by the list (a function of *gradatio*) of nonsensical events, which have no real culmination but which succeed in expressing ignorance and foolhardiness. The irony hinted at in quatrain twelve is compounded in this list of foolish things. Matthew of Vendôme employs the same device to describe how the 'frivolous collections of trifles' of inferior composition compare to the well-wrought, and serious, works of poets who follow the precepts he has gathered in his work:

. . . let verses lacking content and sweet-sounding trifles be excluded from this presentation, namely, frivolous collections of trifles, which like jesters or mimers play to the ears with the sole appeal of consonance, which can imitate a lifeless cadaver, a storeroom without wine, a sheaf without grain, rations without seasoning. They can be compared to a distended bladder which has expanded with a noisy windiness[68] and lacking beauty dribbling the sound, drawing its beauty from only the windiness of its own swelling . . . (*AV,* II §43, p. 78).

After that description of futile effort, the poet returns to his own grades and qualifications. In the final quatrain, the matter is summed up once again – quatrains eleven, twelve, thirteen, fifteen, and sixteen could equally have concluded the matter, from the point of sense, though not carrying the technical *dúnadh* – the poet giving both a warning and a reiteration of his own qualities:

> *Gomadh aithreach leo a labhra*
> *lucht ainbhis na healadhna*
> *mo sproigeacht riu dá ronnar*
> *as fiu an oideacht fhuaromar.*
> (*SIB* i, q. 21)

> [That they should regret their comment, that group ignorant of the arts, if I direct my rebuke against them the education I got is worthwhile.[69]]

RESPONSE

Ó'n Cháinte's contribution to the pool of poems about poetry may have had the desired effect of provoking another poet into composition.[70] Gofraidh Mac an Bhaird's poem '*A fhir shealbhas duit an dán*' is considered[71] to be a response to Fear Feasa Ó'n Cháinte's '*Mór an feidhm deilbh an dána*' (see below, chapter 7, nn. 12, 13). The poem itself refers in a general way to the bombast and self-praise evident in what survives of Fear Feasa's poem. Other details concerning the content of the poem/poet to which Mac an Bhaird is 'responding' are not in the poem attributed to Fear Feasa. In so far as Fear Feasa seemingly addressed detractors – the ignorant, the ill-judged, to whom he boasted of his qualifications – in the same fashion, Gofraidh Mac an Bhaird addresses an 'other' like Fear Feasa. The poem falls into the category noted above, of compositions about composing. The didactic element is never far away, the matter of the poem teaches some branch of the curriculum. In Gofraidh Fionn Ó Dálaigh's case (*'Madh fiafraidheach budh feasach'*, above, pp. 185ff.), the poem outlined the matters over which the aspiring poet needed to acquire mastery. In Fear Feasa's case, the stages of poetry were emphasized, and the many ways in which the body of Irish literary learning could be described. The *inventio* that creates a structure for Gofraidh Mac an Bhaird's '*A fhir shealbhas duit an dán*' is the attack on a fellow-poet who demonstrates many of the faults that Mac an Bhaird wishes to describe. It is hardly likely that the classic production by Ó'n Cháinte is seriously attacked in this poem. The man of straw necessary to the *inventio* may, or may not, be Fear Feasa's '*Mór an feidhm deilbh an dána*'. The 'truth'[72] of the case is not to be decided here. For the purposes of composition and teaching and the production of interesting and informative poems, which demonstrated the precepts that they sought to teach, and in the spirit of the debate genre, the Ó'n Cháinte poem, or the character of Ó'n Cháinte in the poem, performs the same antonomastic role as Rufinus in Matthew of Vendôme's *Ars Versificatoria*; objective correlative to the task of composition.[73]

At all events, the Mac an Bhaird poem echoes[74] the Ó'n Cháinte poem, even to the extent of including the opening *sententia* – '*mór an feidhm dealbh an dána*' (q. 29c) – as an adage against this 'other' faulty poet, who has brought poetry into disrepute with his empty boasting.[75] The *inventio* of the boastful and erroneous poet allows for an artful disquisition on the 'faults' of poetry. These 'faults' were discussed in every manual of the *artes* as they were in the Irish preceptive treatises.[76] The teachers/poets took a wide view of faulty usages in practice, accepting the concept of 'poetic licence' from the outset, though theory stressed the rule and infringements always attracted extreme vituperation. The energy of Mac an Bhaird's poem of castigation here, is fuelled by his exuberant listing of faults in the composition of the 'other'. This dispraise is in the same relation to 'reality' as the measures of praise are in eulogy. They serve the requirements of the *inventio*. In this case, the poem, in a mixture of the 'middle' and 'low' styles, outlines the faults of poetry, with the fiction that examples are to hand. The examples are not found in this poem, nor in the poem, above, of Fear Feasa, but in a poem that *might/could* have been written by a bombastic half-poet, whose training went astray.

'A FHIR SHEALBHAS DUIT AN DÁN'

Fear Feasa'a '*Mór an feidhm deilbh an dána*' survives as a twenty-three quatrain composition. '*A fhir shealbhas duit an dán*', is a longer composition of thirty quatrains. The *inventio* embraces the dialogue formula from its beginning in the apostrophic '*A fhir shealbhas duit an dán*' [Man who arrogates to yourself the art of poetry] (q. 1a). Two familiar characters take part in this dialogue: the interlocutors are, respectively, the presumptuous 'man' who has claimed for himself expertise in the the arts of poetry, and the professor, who must disabuse him and the reader/audience of his notions.

The premise of the poem, the *inventio*, 'finds' a wrong to be corrected. The poet to whom the poem is addressed (*a fhir*) has claimed to be a poet qualified in the learning of the schools.[77] This could be a direct reference to the poem '*Mór an feidhm*

deilbh an dána' by Fear Feasa Ó'n Cháinte, but not necess-
arily so. The *inventio* provides for the existence of such a poem
against which to rail. The formula of poems about poetry in
this vein require the true poet and the false poet. Gofraidh Mac
an Bhaird, the poet making use of this ground for his poem, is at
once the accuser – in this, his poem – and notionally performs
the role of the 'other' in, for instance, Fear Feasa's poem.[78] The
poems are participants in a continuing debate about composi-
tion, teaching, and learning. Gofraidh Fionn's poem, '*Madh
fiafraidheach budh feasach*', anticipates contradiction, '*meinic
shaoilim ó so suas . . .*' etc. (*MFBF*, q. 52), and, in the terms
of his profession, welcomes the addition of poems such as his
to the works to which he has made his contribution. There is
no sense of achieving a definitive statement on the material or
its worth.

Fear Feasa – for the purposes of his *inventio*, taking
contradiction as an indication of lack of knowledge – took
detractors and ignoramuses into account in his poem. His
remarks were addressed to them, whether they recognized
themselves or not. Gofraidh Mac an Bhaird's poem addresses
a poem and a poet, seeming to refer to quatrains in a known
poem. The duelling pairs of writers are essential to this genre,
whether the participants[79] be actual poets/scholars or not.
Matthew of Vendôme attacked Rufinus at every opportunity,
using him and characteristics of his person and writing to
illustrate pedagogical points throughout his treatise, and
perhaps to create amusement among a literary clique. The
poets Henry of Avranches (*fl.* 1214–1260) and Michael of
Cornwall (*fl.* 1250), for example, conducted a heated 'dialogue'
of vituperation in the thirteenth century.[80]

Gofraidh Mac an Bhaird's poem '*A fhir shealbhas duit an dán*'
attacks the work of a boastful bluffer (*SIB* ii, q. 12), and using
the imagery of weaving and tucking or fulling, suggests that

the poetry resulting from his efforts is inferior. While Matthew of Vendôme (see above, p. 213), identified 'patchwork' as the characteristic of the bad poet, Gofraidh Mac an Bhaird condemns the inexpert badly textured work of the ill-educated, self-praising poet (*SIB* ii, q. 15). The poem comprises three 'movements': quatrains one to fourteen, sprinkled with proverbial sayings, denigrates the learning of the 'other' poet. Since learning has gone into decline, there is no one to refute his claims. But, wait! there is, Gofraidh Mac an Bhaird is familiar with true standards and he will unpick the rude fabric of the botchy work of the 'other'.

The second 'movement' (quatrains fifteen to twenty-three) unravels the faulty fabric. These nine quatrains rehearse the 'faults' of poetry, known to Irish poets at the very least from the *Trefhocal*, and known in general from the lists in Donatus.[81] All the mediaeval treatises spent considerable energy in describing and illustrating the 'faults'.[82] This is the pedagogic heart of the poem, just as the outlining of the parts of speech was in Gofraidh Fionn's '*Madh fiafraidheach budh feasach*', and as the outlining of the course of studies and the language of learning was to Fear Feasa's '*Mór an feidhm deilbh an dána*'. Gofraidh Mac an Bhaird's poem teaches the 'faults' of poetry and is an excellent example of the kind of scolding vituperation characteristic of poems that instil knowledge of the faults. The 'faults', it must be stressed, are also part of the knowledge of composition. Proper use of the faults was the hallmark of a very skilled poet.[83] Knowledge of them allowed for their judicious employment. Compositions finding faults in the writings of 'others' rehearsed the information. The style appropriate to such poems was a kind of pedagogical harassment. Gofraidh Mac an Bhaird's poem is a very skilled example.

The third 'movement' indulges in the permitted vituperation and personal invective familiar from Rufinus, and from Michael of Cornwall, and Henry of Avranches. This third part is studded with possible references to Fear Feasa's poem, and quotations of his lines, his claim to familiarity with the streams of inspiration, and his castigation of 'bad' poets:[84]

Adhbhar sbéise do sbroigeacht,
cúis aithis bhar n-ardoideacht,[85]
gidh (do) bhéilshlighe bhalg bhfís
is dréimire ard anbhfís.
(*SIB* ii, q. 26)

[Your provocation is a matter of interest, your great teaching is a cause of opprobrium, though it is your threshold of inspiration, it is a high ladder to ignorance.]

Gofraidh Mac an Bhaird notes the 'other' poet's (Fear Feasa's?) reference to the world of learning as the ocean of knowledge, his familiarity with the navigation of that sea:[86]

Gidh glórach ghabhthaoi ret ais
asgnamh[87] *na n-aigéan n-iomhais*
[iul eisde] go bhfaghadh sibh
meisde gan anadh idir.
(*SIB* ii, q. 27)

[Though noisily you set about voyaging the oceans of inspiration – so that you might get knowledge from it – it is the worse for (your) persevering at all.]

Most tellingly, Fear Feasa's opening *sententia* (*SIB* i, 1a) is repeated, and, cunningly, Gofraidh's opening '*A fhir shealbhas duit an dán*' is echoed here too, both of them cleverly woven into this concluding quatrain, which mirrors itself in sense and in language:

Gidh diongmhála, a-deir tusa,
a sealbhadh [d'] fhior eolasa

mór an feidhm dealbh an dána
do dhealbh ní deilbh dhiongmhála.
(*SIB* ii, q. 29)

[Though, you say, a knowledgeable man is entitled to possess it, the fashioning of the poem that he fashioned[88] is a great task, your composition is not a worthy creation.]

There is no doubting the pleasure the poet took in this word-play on *dealbh/deilbh*. The use of the device of *traductio,* which rings the changes on each form of *dealbh*, as verb, as noun, inflected, uninflected, is at the heart of the instruction given to Irish poets, as it was given to continental poets. Gofraidh Mac an Bhaird demonstrates in this quatrain how it is best done.

A final reference to Fear Feasa's woven fabric concludes the unpicking of that 'other' poem/poet (*SIB* i, q. 17):

Ar dhlúth ar inneach t'oige
tarla tacha banchoige;
a deilbh gan déanamh go se
meirbh le a féaghadh a fighe.
(*SIB* ii, q. 30)

[The lack of a female cook is (evident) on the warp, on the woof of your web; its shaping, undone until now, its weave is flimsy to behold.]

Fear Feasa's quatrain seven had stated:

An tan thagraid rer oile
ní cás don aos eagnoidhe
dul ó dhiomhdhaidh na ttuagh ttais
tre lionnmhuir uar an iomhais.
(*SIB* i, q. 7)

[When they dispute with one another, the learnèd have no difficulty in escaping the vexation of the feeble axes through the cool limpid sea of knowledge.]

Engaging with this work – or some poem very like it – Gofraidh Mac an Bhaird proves the truth of this quatrain. His refutation of the claims of the 'other' poet is a masterpiece of the contention between poets.

Quatrain twenty-nine, '*Gid diongbhála, a-deir tusa . . .*' (see above, p. 223), could hardly be more skilful. Nor could it fail to give utmost satisfaction to the poet to whom it is obliquely addressed, or to those poets into whose literary pool it fell. More than any other feature, perhaps, this poem is characterized by its wonderful weaving of Fear Feasa's expressions and images into its own fabric. The tangling of these poets, these representatives of the *aos eagnoidhe* (*SIB* i, q. 7b), is indeed of a very high order.

Gofraidh Mac an Bhaird's poem makes much of the self-praise of the 'other' poet. His first seven quatrains dwell on this point. The opening quatrain addresses the proverbial 'man' '*a fhir*'. This 'man' is the 'other' poet. In this case, one who represents himself as a truly qualified and skilled poet. Gofraidh suggests that, on the contrary, the claims that the poet makes cannot withstand his scrutiny. The poem itself is a kind of scrutiny of the work of the 'other' poet. It contributes to the discussion of poetry by poets. It aggrandizes the claims of Gofraidh to mastery by presenting him as a reasonable and thorough judge of poetry, it teaches the list of the 'faults', and it sustains both poems in the tradition. Gofraidh's poem is another version of Fear Feasa's poem, presented as such with quotations of lines and expressions reinforcing the sense of textual interdependency:

A fhir shealbhas duit an dán,
coimseach re cách do bhélrádh;
a dhuine maith, mas maith sibh
do mhaith ní maith gan mhaoidhimh.
(*SIB* ii, q. 1)

[Man who arrogates to yourself the art of poetry, your language is fitting for everyone; [my] good man – if good you are – your goodness is no good without boasting.]

The feature of *traductio*, which makes quadruple use of '*maith*', exploiting its abstract, substantive and qualitative and expletive varieties, demonstrates the poet's skill in verbal weaving.[89] His poem does not shy away from the images introduced in Fear Feasa's poem. His poem is woven from the materials provided in the former.

The second quatrain advises that the poet take heed of the proverb '*neach féin go mór dá mholadh / céim is lór dá lochtoghadh*' [one who praises himself excessively – a step sufficient to fault him] (*SIB* ii, q. 2cd).

Quatrains three to six summarize the 'other' poet's estimation of himself, a measure that creates ground for the current poet's refutation of it. This debating trick, known to the manuals as *interrogatio*, in this instance also brings to life the interlocutor in the dialogue, so that the poem, which castigates his works/claims, can be built in reference to them. The summary of Fear Feasa's case provides the material for Gofraidh Mac an Bhaird's poem. The clearly literary nature of the relationship between the two poems suggests that the poets/poems are complementary to rather than contradictory of each other. The pedagogic value of Gofraidh's poem is similarly built on the material in Fear Feasa's poem. Fear Feasa's collection of monstrous words (*d'fhoclaibh arrachta*, *SIB* ii, q. 3b) as a laudatory testament (*teasd molta*, *SIB* ii, q. 3a) would be a source of reproach if applied to himself:[90] he has declared himself to be an exacting (possibly 'professional') judge[91] (*ad breitheamh bhalach*, q. 4a), successful chronicler (*croinicidh comhramhach*, q. 4b), and a 'threshold' of *dán díreach* (q. 4d).[92] These claims are not all specifically made in the poem '*Mór an feidhm deilbh an dána* (as edited by L. McKenna), but are implied in the stand taken by the author of the poem.

There is a version of *permissio*, when Gofraidh suggests that the more one knows of Fear Feasa, the less one thinks of his poetry, i.e. others will affirm his weakness. *Definitio* is used in quatrain eight, when Gofraidh states plainly that Fear Feasa is wrong about *Cath Muighe Tuireadh*. A kind of 'proof' of the poet's ignorance breaks the flow of reprimand at quatrain eight, which questions the 'other' poet's knowledge of the story of a great battle (*Cath Maighe Tuireadh*),[93] which in turn casts doubt on his having gone through the seven degrees of qualification for professorship (*SIB* i, qq. 8 and 9):

> *Aduimh marbhtha míle fear,*
> *lá an mhórchatha [ar Mhuigh] Thuireadh,*
> *mar admhus sibhse seacht ngráidh;*
> *do cheart irse an dá admháil.*
> (*SIB* ii, q. 8)

[Declare a thousand men killed on the day of the great battle on Magh Tuireadh; just as you proclaim seven degrees; both claims pertain (equally) to professional recognition/status.[94]]

Standards have fallen all round, and this is what allows the inferior work of the slipshod poet to be seen or heard at all. Quatrain nine declares that the schools are scattered, art sterile, at a low ebb, and that the infelicities of bad work are overlooked:

> *Do-chuaidh sgaoileadh*[95] *fa sgolaibh*
> *díosg ar ndul fan ealodhain,*
> *a-tá do theannfhacal libh,*
> *neambacadh trá ar do thuislibh.*
> (*SIB* ii, q. 9)

[The schools are dispersed, art has become barren; your arrogant word has succeeded, therefore, (there is) no hindrance to your stumbling.][96]

It is as though a flood of abusive behaviour had overcome everyone, with unfounded authorities (*freagra arsaidh gan ughdar*, *SIB* ii, q. 10d) being cited in defiance of true learning. The poet warns that unstoppable outpouring of boastful nonsense which pleases the layman will never make a learnèd man of the one who behaves thus (*SIB* ii, q. 11).

The motif of the game, very popular a century later,[97] appears in this poem as a metaphor for the conduct of the boastful poet of quatrains ten and eleven:[98]

> *Bíd daoine ag na bíd bearta*
> *chanfas caint na himearta;*
> *ná [brath] ar a mbéalaibh sain*
> *féagaidh le [cath] an chearrbhaigh.*
> (*SIB* ii, q. 12)

> [There are those who have no moves (to make), who will speak the language of the play; do not rely on their mouths (words), observe the gambler's game.]

This quatrain refers retrospectively to the previous description of the fluent nonsense coming from the inferior poet, and prospectively to the next two quatrains, which describe the kind of literary bluffing in which he indulges. The attention he, the inferior poet, attracts by his antics increases his vulnerability to being judged, and, in this case, judged harshly:

> *Na daoine ar ndul at aithne*
> *liaide lucht do bhreathnaighthe;*
> *fear slimbearta dá rádh ruibh*
> *glár na [himearta] aguibh.*
> (*SIB* ii, q. 13)

> [After people have come to know you, the greater is the number of those judging you; you are spoken of as a man of deceitful action, (though) your speech is of (fair) play (lit. you have the speech of play).]

The kind of play outlined in quatrain twelve – the bluffing game of a card-sharp – is applied to the inferior poet's efforts to present himself as a poet:

> *Do thaidhbhse dána dalbhuigh,*
> *t'iarraidh anma a n-ealadhnuibh,*
> *súr ceana is meisde do mhodh,*
> *meisge fa-deara a dhéanamh.*
> (*SIB* ii, q. 14)

[Your display of presumptious poetry, your effort to gain repute in the arts, your methods are the worse in (your) seeking esteem; inebriety is the cause of your so doing.]

Intoxicated by his own ignorance, the inferior poet flaunts his inability, regardless of the opprobrium he incurs. The reference to inebriety here, echoes Fear Feasa Ó'n Cháinte's taunt – '*tre mheisge dtruim dtathaoraigh*' (*SIB* i, q. 12b).

Quatrains fifteen to twenty-four of this poem, by Gofraidh Mac an Bhaird, address the faults of poetry. The general lists of faults is particularized on the work of the putative inferior poet. The poem of Fear Feasa Ó'n Cháinte, which may be the poem in question, is not an inferior poem in any respect. It is the work of a master-poet, as is the work in question here. Neither poet is to be faulted in the matters attacked in their poetic exchange. The sham battle fought in their poems is enlightening for students and pleasurable for the poets and for other informed readers/hearers.

FAULTS AND VICES

In a sequence of ten quatrains, the poet outlines the vices, or faults in composition, that characterize the shoddy poetry of his interlocutor. He adopts the weaving metaphor from the earlier poem (*SIB* i, qq. 3, 17) and turns it to the disadvantage of the 'other' poet, disputing that the inferior weaving of the 'poet' had ever been through the seven grades:

Ní d'abhras saor na seacht ngrádh
snáth t'oige ar aba iomrádh;
a shnas ar a shníomh ní fhuil,
gach gníomh dar chas fad chrobhuibh.

(*SIB* ii, q. 15)

[Not of the noble stuff of the seven grades is the thread of your cloth (pattern of your poem) for the sake of fame; it has not been wrought to perfection, each product which was turned out by your hands (lit. its finish is not as its formation, every action which twisted under your hands).]

This quatrain is rich in the semantic play on verbs and nouns indicating twisting, weaving and turning (*sním, cas*), and of the application of those words to composition. The imagery is sustained in quatrain sixteen and is exploited to introduce a list of faults/vices. The faults (see above, p. 5) include the standard list, familiar to Irish schools at least since the introduction of the grammatical works of the fourth-century Donatus (see above, p. 3). The poets' primers reiterated these and knowledge of them was reinforced by rote over the centuries. The manuals of the arts of writing (noted above, pp. 25ff.) continually repeated the lists of faults and demonstrated them with examples, as did the Irish textbooks (*IGT* and *BST* as they subsisted in their various original forms). A sense of flexibility about these faults was part of the training, and skilful poets were permitted artfully to bend the rules; leniency was, similarly, shown to students who transgressed without being artful. Manuals concerning the rules, and poems illustrating their use, and poems in the genre under consideration here, were vehement in their condemnation of any infractions, though the works that did so frequently exhibited the faults decried.[99]

'CRÉAD DÁ SEALBHUINN DAMH AN DÁN'

At all events, a student who sucessfully committed to memory this poem by Gofraidh Mac an Bhaird would learn the list and remember it because of its vituperative tone, and the sense that it addressed a living, boastful, slipshod, fraudulent poetaster.[100] The technical terms with which the next eight quatrains bristle build on the material already available in Gofraidh Fionn Ó Dálaigh's poem *'Madh fiafraidheach budh feasach'*; on that of the degrees in Fear Feasa Ó'n Cháinte's *'Mór an feidhm déanamh an dána'*; and anticipates the detailed response in Fear Feasa's echoing *'Créad dá sealbhuinn damh an dán'*.[101]

Errors include infelicitous arrangement of adjectives and verbs (q. 16), showing evidence of having learnt from a poor master. This reference to the inferiority of the master is significant: Fear Feasa Ó'n Cháinte's 'response' to this poem *'Créad dá sealbhuinn damh an dán'*, suggest that *he*, Ó'n Cháinte, was once the teacher of the author of *'A fhir shealbhas duit an dán'*:

> *Fuair tú tuisleadh fad ghrádhaibh*
> *ar gcaill ar do chéaddálaibh;*
> *bíodh gur chná hoige m'anaimse*
> *do bhá am oide aguibhse.*
> (*SIB* iii, q. 45)

[You took a stumble with regard to your degrees, after failing in your first dissertations (group sessions); though your text tormented my soul, I used to be your teacher.]

The crux of the matter – were either poet dealing with a genuine case of mutual disparagement – would be that Gofraidh Mac an Bhaird had been taught by an ill-educated teacher; and that Fear Feasa Ó'n Cháinte had taught a buffoon. Neither case is true, manifestly, even from the evidence of the three compositions at issue here.[102] Fear Feasa's Ó'n Cháinte's *Créad dá sealbhuinn damh an dán* is a lengthy composition of some sixty-eight quatrains. Such a long poem needs both structure and momentum to keep the composition intact. Ó'n Cháinte's mastery of the currently accepted rules of composition – apart altogether from his ability in the complexities of grammar, syntax and metrics[103] – create a poem of sustained interest and flexible structure. The dialectic element, which is an essential feature of the disputatious style, is presented immediately in the opening quatrain, which is itself both an enquiry and a rhetorical question. The composition contains within itself the answer to the question with which the poem opens, and the query that serves also to create the imaginary interlocuter within the poem, in that the 'other' – who raised the doubt – is addressed. 'Outside' the poem are the (two) poems that led to this one, and those other poems in the tradition. They, in turn, echo and re-echo the pedagogical, grammatical and other texts in the tradition that inform this whole literary exercise.

Pinning down his share in this rich literary world, Fear Feasa makes the challenge:

> *Créad dá sealbhuinn damh an dán,*
> *a fhir do thairg mo thochrádh?*
> *cuma dhuitse cia dan ceart*
> *go ria do thuigse a ttreiseacht.*
> (*SIB* iii, q. 1)

[What if I were to appropriate to myself the (art of the) poem (or 'of poetry'), man who attempts to annoy me? little does it matter to you who is right, until your understanding becomes more powerful.]

This is in contrast to the statement, sixty-one quatrains later, which concludes that while he (Fear Feasa) is assured of his place

and his share of learning, he is equally certain that the 'other'
poet's 'share' in a scholarly dispute is moderate:

> *Tuigse 'n-a tuigse ghloine*
> *níor bharrsad ar mbriathroine;*
> *ní fearr tuigse do throd rinn*
> *bog do chuidse don chointinn.*
> (*SIB* iii, q. 62)

[My words have not outdone any understanding
that was an unblemished/faultless understanding;
your dispute with me was not better with regard
to understanding – your part in the contention was
feeble.]

Fear Feasa's '*Créad dá sealbhuinn damh an dán*' is an example
of a poem that chose considerable amplification of a slight and
well-worked theme. It opens with self-praise (*SIB* iii, qq. 1–11)
and balances this with contentious fault-finding with the 'other'
poet (*SIB* iii, qq. 12–24). Lessons in grammar and diction, the
rules and the texts (*SIB* iii, qq. 25–34) follow. Human interest
is sustained with personal vilification, achieved with analogies
in the form of mini-apologues, drawn from natural fauna (dog,
bird), and natural phenomena (echo) (*SIB* ii, qq. 35–43). An
elaboration, by way of an extended dialogue within the poem,
occurs, in which the poet remembers a previous encounter with
the 'other' poet. They were then master and student, and he
compares himself and his work with that of the former student,
attacking and defending alternately (*SIB* iii, qq. 44–49). Enu-
merating the 'faults' and 'barbarisms' of the 'other', the poet
employs the 'you' and 'I' formula (*SIB* iii, qq. 50–63). Final
quatrains emphasize the 'other' poet's folly in contending with
poets (or a poet, namely Fear Feasa) who are more qualified
than he, and bringing further obloquy on himself, and degrad-
ing the standard of legitimate debate among equals (*SIB* iii, qq.
64–68).

UNFOUNDED CLAIMS

Fear Feasa's poem consists of at least three discrete themes, which have been twisted [woven] (*snighthe*) together by him, to create the 'yarn' (both senses) of this multi-textured composition. The two main themes are in the opening quatrain: the poet and his skills; the unfounded criticisms of the inexpert versifier. An expert poet reproves an inexpert one for meddling in the question of qualifications. The theme of entitlement to criticize is sustained throughout the sixty-eight quatrains.[104] The assumption of superiority by this poet over the other is, in part – and typically – explained by one having been master to the other (q. 45, see above, p. 230). This relationship is anticipated in quatrain two:

> *Dá roinntí dán an domhain*
> *ar oidibh ar adhbhoruibh*
> *nocho tháir do thuigse bhog;*
> *ní náir duitse do dhearmod.*
> (*SIB* iii, q. 2)

[If the poems of the world were apportioned to masters and novices, your feeble competence might not emerge; it is no shame to you to be forgotten.]

However, this poem ensures that the inferior work of that student/poet is not forgotten, nor in this particular instance, the shoddy work of his father, Brian:[105]

> *I n-a bheathaidh dá mbeadh soin*
> *t'athair beag Brian an bhaothroidh*
> *sár ar laoidhibh ní léamhadh;*
> *dán aoinfhir ní oirléaghadh.*
> (*SIB* iii, q. 19)

[Were your lowly father, the foolish Brian, alive, he would not dare to criticize lays – he read aloud no man's poem.][106]

A third theme is in the elaboration of the invective used against the 'other' poet, a subtheme that makes an entire poem in itself, but which is skilfully entwined around the other topics to maintain a vituperative and memorable momentum in this long work. At all events, the first ten quatrains are all about 'I' (abounding in first person singular pronouns, first person singular verbs, and references to what 'I' do, have, say, claim, and so forth), and how the poet rates himself, with references to his poem '*Mór an feidhm deilbh an dána*'. This little ten-quatrain composition could stand alone as a defence of '*Mór an feidhm deilbh an dána*', if that were all that were required.

Quatrain eleven poses the rhetorical question, echoing that in the first quatrain (*Créad dá sealbhuinn . . . ?*), and could effectively start a new poem:

> An tan nach teilgfinn[107] acht daoi
> 's nach méadóchuinn acht mórshaoi,
> ó nach saith as dleisde dul,
> gar mheisde an mhaith do mholadh?
> (*SIB* iii, q. 11)

> [Since I would rebuke only a dunce and I would enhance only a master, (and) since that is not wrong, one is bound to continue (with the poem, or with the praise); what harm is there in praising the good?]

The dramatis personae are present in this quatrain: the ignorant – the 'other' poet and his fellows; the wise – Fear Feasa and his peers.

Quatrain eleven allows a pause in the composition. It re-establishes the *inventio* and prepares ground for the next thirteen quatrains (12–24). These are addressed to 'you', the other party to the dialogue. Verbs in the second person singular (and those using the plural in the sense of singular) carry the charge of this attack on the weak, presumptious poet of the *inventio*. The evidence of his own work – his hideous boastful anger (*led dhoirr n-iolghránna n-aidhbhsigh*, q. 12d), – proclaims that he is not among those of knowledgeable inspiration (q. 12), and his anger was not the creative frenzy of the poet (*ní fearg dhéinmhe do dhásacht*, q. 13d). He takes first place among the ignorant, and he is their sole teacher,[108] noble compositions are not found among them: '*Do chuiris iad a n-umhlacht / ná taitnionn re tuathumhlacht / deilbh shaoroige rú na ribh; / is tú as aonoide uaisdibh*' [. . . through boorishness, a noble composition does not appeal to them or to you, you are their sole teacher ('you are the sole teacher in charge of them')] (q. 14). Strong epithets of dispraise, '*a thrudoire*' [stammerer] (q. 17, q. 21d),[109] '*a amadán*' [fool] (q. 29d), are employed:

> *D'éis do labhra, a los goimhe*
> *ní dubhairt tú, a thrudoire,*
> *acht ní as eagal ar rádh ribh*[110]
> *ad dhán 'n-a theagar thuaithbhil.*
> (*SIB* iii, q. 17)

[Stammerer, despite your talk motivated by malice, you said nothing in your poetry – a misshapen collection – but that which you risk being said of you.]

This weak poet accuses Fear Feasa – unjustly and without grounds – of follies that may well be associated with his own work. The quatrain anticipates the mini-apologue in quatrains thirty-six, thirty-seven and thirty-eight, where a barking dog frightens himself with his own noise. The first dog (q. 37) is the angered poet himself – he is a rabid dog in pursuit of those who would surpass him:

> *Le hadhbhar nú gan fhachain*
> *níor bharr aonshaoi m'ealathain;*
> *truagh saoithe óm thagra 'n-a ttocht,*
> *'s madra gaoithe dá ngreasocht.*
> (*SIB* iii, q. 37)

[No wise man ever got the better of my art, with cause
or without reason; it is a pity that master-scholars have
been silenced as a consequence of my disputation, with
a mad dog inciting them.]

The senseless noise made by the weak poet, on the other hand,
is that – anticipated above (q. 17) – of the silly dog barking at
nothing, which in turn frightens him:

> *Amhasdrach dá eagla féin,*
> *do-ní an madra le mícbéill;*
> *nó go dtarraing air an t-olc*
> *dá thail ní fhaghbhaim annsocht.*
> (*SIB* iii, q. 38)

[The mad dog foolishly barks at his own fear;[111] I take
no pleasure in his inclination (to do this) until he draw
evil on himself.]

This same fruitless howling in the wilderness is a characteristic
the poet associates with the bittern alone in the wasteland:

> *Búireadh an buineán*[112] *léana*
> *a n-ionadhaibh uaithmhéala,*
> *gi bé aitreabh i n-a n-an*
> *ní faicthear é ach go hannamh.*
> (*SIB* iii, q. 39)

[Let the bittern call in frightful places; whatever habitat
he occupies, he is but rarely seen.]

Extending this notion of the isolation and oddity of the weak
poet in his remonstrations about the strong poet's work, the
analogy of the echo is used: the great noise made by the echo
of a whisper in an area where the least sound will be magnified.
It makes no difference to the nonsense of the original sound
(q. 40). At quatrain forty, the series of mini-apologues finishes

and the poet turns again to address the weak poet directly, *tusa*. This noisy 'other' is, as we have just seen, a foolish poet whose claims about Fear Feasa's poetry is the barking of a foolish dog frightening himself; his calls from the desert of his talent are the lonely cries of the bittern; the repeated sound of his criticism is echo of a frivolous nonsense (qq. 37–40). Indeed, it was unknown whether this poet were alive or dead until he drew attention to himself with his witless criticism of Fear Feasa:

> *Tusa do bheith beo nó marbh*
> *ní fios* . . . .
> *gur thairnngis léim m'fheirge ort*
> *led ghéim ngeirge dam ghreasocht.*
> (*SIB* iii, q. 41)

[It was not known whether you were alive or dead . . . . . until you drew the rush of my anger on you, inciting me with your crow-like squawk.][113]

Like the bittern, this other poet entertains but meanly away from the gatherings of peers, '*iosdadh cúthail do chleachtais / fada uait na hoireachtais*' (q. 42ab). A pity, suggests Fear Feasa, that he is not prevailed upon to go to the centre of Ireland at a point where the five provinces meet[114] that his ignorance might be displayed (q. 43). Echoing the sense of quatrain seven in his '*Mór an feidhm deilbh an dána*' (see above, p. 211), Fear Feasa regrets that his interlocutor is not equipped to dispute with him:

> *Saoth lem meanma dar mó móid*[115]
> *nach saoi a-tá ad chuid don chuspóid;*
> *olc linn ar malairt dá mhéid*
> *sinn do labhairt led leithéid.*
> (*SIB* iii, q. 44)

[It distresses my spirit which increases (my) desire, that your part in the dispute is not held by a master-scholar;

I regret, however great the exchange, that I have to
address the like of you.]

Instead of the empty bluffing of the gambler, Fear Feasa hides
about him the '*ga bolga*' – Cú Chulainn's famous javelin – an
instrument that would hurt the quatrains of this other poet:[116]

A-tá gléas an gha bolga
dá dtiocfadh haoi d'ionnarba,
gléas mhairbheas roghoimh do rann
'n-a fhailgheas oraibh agam.
(*SIB* iii, q. 46)

[Hidden from you, I have the contrivance of the *ga
bolga* about me, by which your poetry would be des-
troyed; an instrument that kills the excessive malice of
your quatrains.]

Along with the literal and figurative meanings in this quatrain
concerning the trick of the *ga bolga*[117] and the destruction of
poetry with it are the host of allusive references to the literary
tradition of satire and of the vexed questions about inspiration
and application.   Fer Dia, in the saga of *Táin Bó Cuailnge*,
feared to encounter Cú Chulainn because of the enchanted
javelin Cú Chulainn possessed, the *ga bolga* – the only advant-
age he had over Fer Dia. Fear Feasa possesses a like instrument
for the destruction of the other poet: his mastery of composi-
tion and his ability in satire.   The poem revels in the possibilities
surrounding literary and literal readings of *ga*, the javelin, the
satiric onslaught; of *bolga*, the epithet attached to that javelin,
the *bolg* (blister) raised by satire on the human face, the *bolg fís*
– the mythic bubbles of inspiration.[118]

Aoi (*SIB* iii, q. 46b)[119] can refer widely also to the varieties of
inspiration and composition discussed endlessly by the poets.[120]
In this case, while the poet might disembowel the weak poet

with his sharp thrusts, the literary game that both poets are playing suggests the richer hinterland of, for instance, an episode from *Táin Bó Cuailnge* as the background to this exchange, and indeed, the whole literature of satire and its rules. The 'game' is once again referred to in quatrain fifty-six:

> *Más í an imirt as éigse,*
> *más í an chaint a choimhéidse,*
> *beag mo shainnt i slimbeirt sonn,*
> *an chaint 's an imbeirt agom.*
> (SIB iii, q. 56)
>
> [If playing is literary learning, and if discourse is its pre-servation (= what maintains it), little do I covet mean play here (in this regard), I (already) have both the speech and the play.][121]

The pedagogical and reiterative quatrains of the poem, those referring to the rules of composition, and to the faults, are sandwiched between the other elements of the 'dialogue'. Quatrains twenty-five to thirty-five give brief mention to some of the rules known to all the poets. Questioning a fellow-poet, of almost any standing, about the basics of word formation, orthography and syntax in the manner outlined in these quatrains is not indicative of a realistic exchange. Poems about writing, about composition, and concerning the matters that might be emphasized to students, contain such rhetorical questions and self-contained dialogue. Fear Feasa's list of questions include queries about the nature of a verb in *da-* (q. 25); the forms of the diphthongs *ifín* and *amharcholl*; the letters that made *eabha*, *óir* and *uilleann* (q. 26); the characteristics of the two 'n's, the *ceann-fo-chrois* of the manuscript (q. 27b). The attacks on the 'other's' lack of knowledge are punctuated by insults such as '*a dhaoi lochtach*' [incorrect dolt] (q. 27c).

The references to instructions concerning the correct use of the alphabet and the orthographical requirements of learnèd writing are familiar from *Auraicept na n-Éces*, from works such as Gofraidh Fionn Ó Dálaigh's '*Madh fiafraidheach budh feasach*', from the anonymous '*Feadha an oghaim aithnidh damh*', and pre-eminently – in the later period – from the compilation of pedagogical material, edited by modern scholars, under such titles as *Irish Grammatical Tracts* and *Bardic Syntactical Tracts*.[122]

Quatrain twenty-six upbraids the weak poet for failure to recognize the characteristics of the diphthongs:

> *Ní haithne dhuit mar is dleacht*
> *ifín amharcholl d'éifeacht,*
> *náid na feadha is cóir 'n-a gcionn*
> *eabha ná óir ná uillionn.*
> (*SIB* iii, q. 26)
>
> [You do not know, as is proper, the characteristics of the diphthongs *iu*[123] and *ai*; nor the letters which ought to accompany *e(a)(o)*, *o(i)* nor *u(i)*.]

And so it goes through the next eight quatrains, listing elements from the canons of correct usage, punctuating them with aspersive asides on the poet who is not familiar enough with the rules: the dual quality of 'n', the scribal use of the *ceann-fo-chrois* (q. 27); the names of the vowels, the inflections, the consonants (q. 28); the number of the unstressed particles, '*is ceisd oirbhse, a amadán*' [it is a question for you, fool] (q. 29d); delenition (*an cadádh*, q. 29); and the elements that support vowels (*na conganta*) (q. 30).[124] This weak poet fails even to achieve emphasis in his poetry by his lack of learning ('*ní reiche, . . . na neithe a-tá a ttréasfhacal*', q. 32cd).

In effect, the eight quatrains that outline the weak poet's shortcomings are in apposition to the single quatrain, which summarizes the foregoing and creates the compositional pause in this particular working of the theme. Quatrain thirty-three comprehensively sums up the lack of learning, declaring that the poet, clearly, had not studied the basic texts:

> *Níor thógbhais eisdibh aiceacht*
> *Agallaimh ná Úraiceapt*
> *acht, mearfuil tar chéill dod char,*
> *[dod] réir theannchuir na ttuathadh.*
> (*SIB* iii, q. 33)

[You took no lesson out of them – the *Agallamh* nor the *Uraiceapt* – confusion putting you beyond sense; the instruments of the layman are at your disposal (not those of the learnèd man).]

These virtuoso flourishes, almost meaningless in their ostensible purpose – the reprimanding of a fellow, equally skilled poet – function at a high order of literary practice, and are well placed in respect of the *inventio* of the composition. They are also pleasurable examples and mnemonic aids to students.

MORE ERRORS

In pursuit of the same goals – the embellishment of a genre composition and in the reiteration of the schools' rules – are quatrains fifty to sixty-three. The burden of these, again relieved by scathing asides, is the classic list of 'faults'. Imputing these to the 'other' poet in a personalized way equates with the best practice of the mediaeval masters, Matthew of Vendôme, Geoffrey of Vinsauf and John of Garland.

Infractions of the metrical rules[125] are well covered in the texts that are represented in *IGT* V 'Metrical Faults',[126] which begins, 'Herewith the faults most commonly met in every poetic composition . . . ' (*Aig seo na lochta is coitcheand in gach aisdi don dán . . .*). A list of thirty-nine errors follows, and that number does not exhaust those treated in the text itself.[127] These are not the only lists available to the poet, and they are not the only lists used.[128] Matters outside of language, and referring to 'weaknesses' in composition, misapplication of figures, and so forth, feature in the poems discussed here and are directly comparable to those matters occurring in the manuals of the *artes*. Irish masters seem to be drawing on sources that have not survived in Irish manuscripts, except in the evidence of their application, which subsists in the poems themselves.

The poet who is the target of Fear Feasa's ingenuity is too tolerant of his own faults, or so he (Fear Feasa) has heard '*dochuala . . .*' [I heard . . .] (q. 50a).[129] Quatrains fifty-one to fifty-four attack by defending – Fear Feasa lists the faults that are *not* to be found in his poetry. The implication (a form of *litotes, deminutio*, where emphasis is given to a negative to draw covert attention to the positive) is that they *are* found in the 'other' poet's works. The master's work displays no evidence of '*gnás*' [banality, platitude], '*caoiche*' [rhymes between identical words], '*ionannas*' [monotony], '*searbhrádh*' [harsh, discordant utterance],[130] '*gnúis gharg*' [rough countenance] (q. 51). Staying with his own work, quatrain fifty-two declares that no discordance (*gnúis gharbh*, q. 52a),[131] or rough repair measures, are found in his work; no uneven weave (*inneach as éadaingean*, q. 52b)[132] distorts its finish (*[an] snas ar a sníomh*, q. 52c). It is to be described as a fresh, pure, spinning, '*is glas an sníomh an sníomhsoin*' (q. 52d). Keeping his own work to the fore, the poet addresses the 'other', telling how he (the latter) never read any inaccuracies (*claoinfhighe* [false weave], q. 53b), nor softness (*maos*, q. 53d), in his – Fear Feasa's – work '*i ndréacht dom dhréachtoibh*' [in any poem of my poetry] (q. 53d). His poems are well written, and accord with the rubrics:

A-táid na molta i modh chóir,
ní fhuil ailm i n-áit éagcóir,
ní fhuil onn acht 'n-a ionadh,
[i] sonn ní fhuil oibrioghadh.
(*SIB* iii, q. 54)

[The adjectives are used correctly, *a* is not in the wrong
position, the letter *o* is in its place, and (the adverb)
sonn is not used as a verb.]

Quatrain fifty-five returns to 'you', addressing the 'other'
poet, putting the faultless poetry of his own making in direct
comparison with the misshapen efforts of the other. This
allows that the quatrains fifty-one to fifty-four (above) were
anticipatory of this more direct attack:

Do [shnáth] meallach nó gan mheall,[133]
do [shnáth] géar neamhúr neimhghearr,
cainnt bhorrfaidh gan eagna n-uill,
freagra orthaibh ní obruim.
(*SIB* iii, q. 55)

[Your yarn, lumpy or smooth, your yarn virulent, stale,
prolix (uncurtailed); bombastic/exaggerating[134] utter-
ance without great wisdom, I do not work at a response
to them.]

The 'other' poet is not worthy of the true poet's attention nor
do his empty works deserve a response. Of course, the whole
poem is a response to the 'inferior work'.

PARADOX

This is the delightful contradiction within this suite of poems,
in which the poets lash out at each other in, it is argued, feigned
horror at the other's sloppy work, and shameless display. The
paradoxical essence of the exchange keeps a lively thread of

absurd humour and unresolved tension running through the poems. It also creates a considerable sense of inconsequence in the effect of the works themselves. Contingency and ambivalence are so skilfully worked into this category of poem, and into other bardic compositions, that commentators are tempted to set to one side the ambivalence as read and to attempt to extract the factual, or realistic, thread in the work.

Paradox and ambivalence are the stuff of the exchange between Fear Feasa and the other poet: despite the stand against responding to such unpoetic material (see above, p. 243), an analytical 'response' is forthcoming; wise men will understand that the 'other' is neither a scholar (*sgoláir*, q. 57c), nor a teacher (*oide*, q. 57c); and that his poetry is matter of shame among poets, '*ronáir t'oige idir éigsibh*' (q. 57d). His weak poem (*dán fann*, q. 58) is ornamented only by rhyme. So unschooled indeed is this work that quatrain fifty-nine delivers the ultimate damning verdict:

> [*Éabhadh] gan cheart gan chuma;*
> [*cuma is] eidir eatorra*
> *mairg, a Dhé, dán dod dhán*[135]
> *ní dán é agus ní habhrán.*
> (*SIB* iii, q. 59)

> [The dipthong *ea/eo/eu* incorrect and shapeless, the difference does not matter to you; pity God, any of your poems, it is not a *dán* and it is not an *abhrán*.[136]]

The paronomastic use of *cuma* in this quatrain, paralleled in the quatrain by similar uses of the various meanings in *dán*, satisfies many ornamental requirements and shows the mastery of the poet. The matters complained of are neither new nor easily dismissed, they belong to the usual list: unsupported descriptives (*focail tréithe gan taca*, q. 60a); weak expressions used as foundations (*focail bhoga bunata*, q. 60b); joyless

barbarism (*focal barbardha as bheag sult*, q. 61a); particles
of little importance (*mionfhocal nach mór tábhacht*, q. 61b);
foolish forms, which are shameful to mention (*foirm bhaoth
as ronár do reic*, q. 61c); 'these characterize the (your) soggy
doggerel' (*ad rabhán maoth is meinic*, q. 61d).[137] *Rabhán*
here makes an ingenious metaplasmic couple with *abhrán*
of quatrain fifty-nine, above. It satisfies doubly, in that the
abhrán can be equated with *rabhán*, though the *abh[mh]rán*
itself was not doggerel.

The weak poet has but little of the necessary ability or
training for legitimate debate with equals, '*bog do chuidse don
chointinn*' (q. 62d). His status is on a par with the lowest order
of performer:[138]

> *A bhaird gan an mbairdneacht féin,*
> *a abhlóir bhig,*[139] *a bheigéir,*[140]
> *mar shruth ngarg gidh teann a-taoi*
> *do gheall lem bard do-bhéarthaoi.*[141]
> (*SIB* iii, q. 68)
> [*Bard*,[142] without even bardic skill,[143] petty clown
> beggar; though you be strong like a harsh stream, you
> would yield pride of place to my *bard*.]

The poem concludes in four quatrains of direct attack on the
'other' poet, of which the foregoing is the final one. It is the
third strand of the poem offered, the other two strands being,
respectively, the defence of the work of the poet who speaks,
and the quatrains concerning the faults. The combination is
one that occurs in Matthew of Vendôme:

> Ignorance of the meaning of words is productive of
> more harm than all of the other offenses of learning,
> which number ten, namely these: involvement in
> obscure brevity (whence Horace: *Striving to be brief, I
> become obscure*) a digression in superfluous verbosity;

the construction of pared discourse; the wandering
of a bobbling mentality; craggy complications of
meaning; unlimited confusion of discourse; sterility of
untrained talent; the indecorous rattle of a headlong
tongue; a mutilated confusion of words; ignorance of
the meaning of words (*AV*, §IV.25, pp. 99–100; *LAP*,
p. 186).

And again in Geoffrey of Vinsauf:

In the beginning, therefore, you should clean the poem
itself of filth and root out its vices. What, of what
kind, and how many the things are which vitiate the
flow of speech, gather now from a few examples: *Ecce
deae aethereae advenere.* Hiatus of the vowels shudders
through this passage. Art gave this law to the vow-
els: namely, that their juxtapositions should not be
frequent. Juxtaposition it endures, but it forbids fre-
quency; and here, since they are frequent, the sound of
the vowels is disfiguring and heightens the hiatus.
Tu, Tite, tuta te virtute tuente tueris. So, the same letter
is a disgrace when it is shamelessly repeated. But a less
insistent repetition is a becoming ornament.
*Cum non sit ratio rationis de ratione, hinc non est ratio
praeberre fidem rationi.* So the same word defiles when
so often repeated and so pointlessly. A moderate repe-
tition of words is a color, but too much of anything is
without true color.
Sometimes similar endings of words serve as
ornament; but the frequency of the same sound in
these words so joined is unseemly: *Infantes, stantes,
lacrimantes, vociferantes.*
These four effects consitute a vice.
A fifth infection is when something comes suspended
in too long a construction.

A sixth is added when the violation of normal word order is awkward, as in *Luci misimus Eli.*

Lo, I have given you a comb, with which if they be combed, your poems may gleam . . .

. . . when you consider the appearance of a word, to see if perchance some lurking worm befouls it, let not the ear nor the mind alone be judge. Let the triple judgment of mind, ear, and usage decide it (*PN*, pp. 102–103; *LAP*, pp. 256–257).

And in John of Garland:

There are, then, six vices to avoid in a poem. The first is incongruous arrangement of parts; the second, incongruous digression from the subject; the third, obscure brevity; the fourth, incongruous variation of styles; the fifth, incongruous variation of subject matter; the sixth, an awkward ending . . . (*PP*, pp. 84–85).[144]

Conclusion: The death of poetry?

From at least the thirteenth century poets decried the 'end of patronage';[1] their abandonment by lords; the changing of times, which meant the end of traditional respect, and noble hospitality; the failure of 'new men' to appreciate old values, particularly the merits of the poets and of their 'art'. The death of patronage was axiomatic on the death of the lord.[2] It was part of the elegiac praise of the dead lord to declare that with his passing departed all love of the arts, all protection of the artist and the death of hospitality. These tropes are the commonplace of praise throughout Europe in Latin and in the vernaculars.

Occasionally a poet 'abandoned' poetry. He was accused of doing so if his compositions seemed to others to fall below the required standard, or to mix registers. It has been shown that accusation by other poets that his work failed to 'measure' up belong to a category of composition, the least earnest part of which was the accusation. 'Abandoning poetry' in these instances meant banishment from the company of learnèd poets.[3]

Poets left the life of professional teacher/poet to enter the Church in another professional capacity. Some poems indicate that their authors were writing in the spirit of those who associated profane verse with the folly and levity of youth, and their declared intention is to write serious devotional verse henceforth. This itself sometimes may indicate the ordination of the poet in some ecclesiastical grade.[4] At all events, it occurs in the existing works as a trope and exploited as such in pursuit of all kinds of poetic *inventio*.

The study presented here makes a gesture towards an expansion of our understanding of the bardic aesthetic in the light of contemporary instructions in the written arts. Formal Irish syllabic verse seemed to retain the sense of composition – recognizable from the manuals produced during the High Middle Ages – right down the early modern period. Our understanding of this rich background colours our perception of what constitutes, and what contributed to, the poets sense of their tradition of composition. Our sense of the 'end of the tradition', meaning the abandonment by the poets – from the end of the sixteenth century – of the rigid discipline of the aesthetic we have discussed here, can be enlarged by rereading the poets' verdict on what they were abandoning in the light of what might have been involved for them in teaching and in giving instruction. The *Poetria Nova* enjoined upon the poet never to go straight to composition but to sift and sort and arrange and compose the mind and the spirit inwardly for the task so that the matter is ready for committal to ink before the attempt is made to write at all:

> Let the mind's inner compass circumscribe the whole area of the subject matter in advance . . . Ever circumspect, assemble the whole work *in the stronghold of your mind*, and let it be first in the mind before it is in words. When a plan has sorted out the subject in the secret places of your mind, then let Poetry come to clothe your material with words . . . (*PN*, p. 35; emphasis added).

The fortress of the mind, the secluded place where the *inventio* itself is 'found', is the proper abode of the poet until he is ready to embark on the path to the poem:

> Arrangement's road is forked: on the one hand, it may *labour up the footpath of art*; on the other, it may follow *nature's main street* . . .
> More sophisticated than natural order is artistic order, and far preferable, however much permuted

> the arrangement may be . . . Now in the area of this
> technique may seem to be dark, the path rugged, the
> doors closed, the problem knotty . . . There will
> be found the means by which you may cleanse the
> shadow from the light, the foot on which you may
> traverse the rugged ground, the key with which you
> may open the doors, the finger with which you may
> loose the knots . . . (*PN*, p. 36; emphasis added).

The paths, doors, problems, darkness, light, keys, and 'feet', upon which to travel this ground, are matters of utter familiarity to the Irish classical poets. When aesthetic taste took a divergent path from scholastic formalism to other trends, many of them neo-classical styles and adaptations of and mannered varieties of classic works, Irish literature and poets could be expected to maintain an energetic engagement with such literary movements. It has long been acknowledged that Irish devotional writing came well within the aesthetic norms of contemporary Europe. Irish contributions to the currents of courtly love and – on the oral level – participation in the general ballad tradition of Britain and Europe has never been at issue.

Only in the arena of Irish bardic poetry has the literary enterprise been seen to have retained an anachronistic interest in outdated modes and to have been insulated from contemporary trends. Poets' seeming engagement with changes in literary fashion, therefore, have uniformly been read as laments, or resigned and embittered comment on changing fashions. These 'fashions' are similarly seen to emanate principally from the contemporary political climate.[5] Compositions on change in literary modes, on the decline of patronage, on the departure of lords, on all the 'endings' that seem to overwhelm the turn of the sixteenth into the seventeenth century are similarly accounted for by the 'end' of the Irish lordships. Social, political and economic changes doubtless have their influence on all the material composed in any given period, and had their influence during this period in Ireland. Emphasis is given in this discussion, however, to the literary nature of expressions of change. And the inherent continuity to be expected in a learnèd tradition where the 'world', as it was constituted in existing literature, was the universe with which the learnèd writer was equipped to deal.

With this in mind, we might look again at the poet Eochaidh Ó hEoghusa's (d. 1616), declared intention to release himself from the bondage of his strict training:[6]

> *Ionmholta malairt bhisigh;*
> *tárraidh sinde 'san amsa*
> *iomlaoid go suarrach sona,*
> *do-chuaidh a sochar dhamhsa.*
> (*IBP*, p. 127, q. 1)
>
> [A change for the better is to be commended: I have found at this time an exchange poor but fortunate, which has turned out profitable for me.[7]]

The proverbial style of the opening introduces a classic poem. The poem is at once a poem about poetry, a subtle and humorous tribute to the earl of Tyrconnell, and a declaration of abandonment – by the poet – of the strictures of the schools for the sake of a greater popularity. The *inventio* is that the poet may venture into common easy styles now that the earl of Tyrconnell is away (*o tharla a Saxaibh uainne* [since he is away from me in England], q. 10d), and will not be there to ridicule this easy new style. His [the earl's] learning is such that a poem, difficult even for the poet, is easy for him:

> *Mac Aodha, aigneadh fosaidh,*
> *fear ler robhog ar ccruaidhne,*

ní cás dúinn dénamh tapaidh,
ó tharla a Saxaibh uainne.
(*IBP*, p. 128, q. 10)

[Son of Aodh, steady mind, a man for whom my
difficult (effort) is too easy; I have no difficulty about
a hasty composition,[8] since he is away from me in
England.]

The simpler style to be embraced – according to this *inven-
tio* – will accrue to the profit of the poet, in achieving a wider
audience/readership because of a less intimidating (less learnèd)
style. The oxymoronic '*iomlaoid go suarrach sona*' secures the
tone of the poem, creating the unstable or contradictory tone
of irony from the outset. This is underlined by the form of the
composition itself, which follows the school norms. Narrow
is contrasted with broad, light with heavy, dark with bright,
easy with difficult. The composition, a slight matter of twelve
quatrains, closes with an exaggerated *dúnadh* – underlining the
irony of the treatment – with a final line fully mirroring the
opening: '*ionmholta malairt bhisigh*' (q. 12d).

The poet has deserted well-trodden paths to composition.
Praise is now secured by embracing an easier, less exacting style:

Do thréig sind sreatha caola
foirceadal bhfaobhrach ffrithir
ar shórt gnáthach grés robhog,
is mó as a moltar sinde.
(*IBP*, p. 127, q. 2)

[I have deserted the subtle rankings[9] of keen, intense
teachings;[10] for a common sort of easy art which brings
me more praise.]

The subtle series of learned instructions that are to be aban-
doned are the rules of schooled composition – in favour of a
less constrained kind of work, which earns more praise. Indeed,

the opaque and intriguing composition, which is learned and produced by long study and heartbreaking application to the rules, is no longer wanted now, a source of improvement to the poet's health:

Beag nach brisiodh mo chroidhe[11]
gach dán roimhe dá gcumainn:
is mór an t-adhbhor sláinte
an nós so táinig chugainn.
(*IBP*, p. 129, q. 11)

[Every poem I composed hitherto used almost to break my heart; this new fashion that has come to us is a great cause of health.]

The poet's opaque and finely wrought poems are met with horror and the protest of many that such works did not deserve esteem:

Le dorchacht na ngrés snoighthe
do bhínnse ag tuilliodh gráine:[12]
fa hí ughachta mhóráin
ná dhíol róghráidh ar ndáinne.
(*IBP*, p. 128, q. 3)

[I used to incur horror with the obscurity of the ornamented forms; many attested that my poetry was not worthy of esteem.]

Henceforward, it is the '*dán bog ar bhél na slighiodh*' [simple verse on the open road] for him, since it seems to be in favour. Ó hEoghusa is specific at quatrain five:

Dán bog ar bhél na slighiodh,
ós é anois siorthior oraind,
cuirfeadsa dhíom na fiacha
go ccead d'iarla Chlann gConaill.
(*IBP*, p. 128, q. 5)

[Free and easy verse on the open road! – since that is
what is asked of me, I will discharge the debts, by leave
of the earl of Clann Chonaill.[13]]

THE BROAD ROAD

Quatrain six holds the centre of the poem and provides a ful-
crum for the *inventio* – the desertion of the narrow ways for
the wide road: instead of adhering to the narrow, restricted
paths of composition, Eochaidh Ó hEoghusa declares that he
is taking the high road. The apologue in this composition
is alluded to rather than spelled out. A poem '*Bíodh aire ag
Ultaibh ar Aodh*'[14] by Eochaidh Ó hEoghusa, for Aodh Mág
Uidhir (d. 1600), gives the full story of the philosophers in the
rain (*Tríocha feallsamh fada ó shoin . . .*):

> '*Déanaim-ne aimhghlic amhail
> sinn féin' ar na feallsamhain
> 'beag díol na cruinne dár gcéill;
> ná bíom 's an uile acht d'éinmhéin.*'
>
> *Dá ndéanamh féin mar gach bhfear
> do b'é a gcríoch dul fa dheireadh,
> tuigse an bheatha mar do bhuaidh,
> fa uisge an cheatha i gcéaduair.*
> (*DD*, p. 239, qq. 34, 35)

['Let us be similarly foolish,' said the philosophers; 'the
world has little value for our wisdom; let us not be but
at one with the rest.'
In doing themselves as all men (had done) – since the
world's perception triumphed – they ended up finally
by going out at once into the shower of rain.]

This apologue, the conceptual centrepiece of Eochaidh
Ó hEoghusa's poem, '*Ionmholta malairt bhisigh*', is merely
alluded to in quatrain six:

Mo gheallsa ar bhuga ar mhaoile
ní bhérdaois daoithe an bheatha:
do-chuaidh mé, maith an tuicsi,
le cách fá uisge an cheatha.
(*IBP*, p. 128, q. 6)

[The dunces of the world would not beat me in softness
and artlessness; I have gone out in the rain like the rest
– a wise course.]

This nod in the direction of the, presumably, well-known tale
seems also to indicate that Ó hEoghusa's readers would recall
his, presumably, earlier use of this apologue. Its use here is in
apposition to the explanation of the parable of the apologue in
the quatrains following, where he describes how he has, like the
foolish philosophers, followed the world into the simpler style
of composition:

Do thréig mé – gá mó sonas? –
mo shlighthe docra diamhra:
dá ccluine cuid dár ndáinne,
beanfaidh gáire as an iarla.
(*IBP*, p. 128: q. 7)[15]

[I have abandoned – what greater luck? – my hard mys-
terious ways: if he hear some of my verse (poetry), it
will make the earl laugh.]

This, we might now surmise, is the poet declaring his intention
to abandon the formal style – the style described in a manual
such as the *Poetria Nova*, with its steep inclines and narrow ways
– in favour of the easy style on the broad highway.

The literal reading,[16] is highly attractive both visually and
historically and has been popular for some time. In a more
literary reading, such as presented here, the poet speaks to his
fellows in the knowledge that they, at least, understand the
references to their presumed scholarly sequestration, to their

professional embracing of the narrow ways, of the convoluted paths, and their contemplation of their works in the dark recesses of the mental 'stronghold'. The dwindling favour found by this kind of composition, and the waning of the literary appetite for such work, gives rise to works seemingly alluding to the change of aesthetic rather than to a specific comment on any kind of cultural abandonment.

Eochaidh Ó hEoghusa's desertion of the formal style is not inaugurated with this highly structured poem. He is, he claims, prevented from exploiting public approval to its utmost – in providing simple poems – for fear of the earl's ridicule. The historiographical image of the earl, Rudhraighe Ó Domhnaill (Rory O'Donnell, d. 1608), does not usually involve his characterization as one who might be appealed to in matters of literary aesthetics. As one who was probably taught by a master/poet in the manner of the schools, it may well be imagined that the earl was as familiar with the methods and curriculum as the poet himself, though his career took him to politics and war, rather than to teaching and composition.

The poem, structurally, turns at this point in a mirror image of itself. The diptychous form suits the necessity to amplify, encouraged in the manuals of composition. Quatrain seven repeats the poet's assertion that he has deserted the dark and mysterious ways. Quatrain two has already made this quite clear. Quatrain three notes that the majority is now in favour of the simple style; in quatrain eight, the poet dreads the judgement of the earl, whose verdict would not favour the new mode. Quatrain four promises poems that would not confound anyone in the world; the approval of all those – 'daoithe an bheatha' (q. 6b) – has overwhelmed the poet this year since he adopted the easy style. He would exploit this newfound popularity but that he fears the earl:

Is iomdha tré dhán bhfallsa
lán dom annsacht a mbliadhna:
do thuillfinn tuilleadh ceana
muna bheith eagla an iarla.
(*IBP*, p. 128, q. 9)
[Many are full of affection for me this year because of
lazy composition; I would earn more regard but for fear
of the earl.[17]]

While the poet suggests that he might acquit his obligations
with the more acceptable, simple style of composition (q.
5cd), he could do so only with the permission of the earl. Quatrain
ten indicates that this permission is unlikely. The compliment
to the earl is explicit. Difficult composition is easy to the earl,
only his absence (in England) allows the poet to dare a more
lazy style (see above, n. 6). Health and fortune are increased
with the desertion of the difficult, mysterious style required by
the earl. The poet's heart has been broken in the effort to follow
the requirements of the narrow path. Now the earl must do as
the philosophers of old (and as the poet seeks to do), accept the
false judgement of the majority in spite of his own discernment;
he must go into the rain:

Dá lochtaighe triath Bearnais
énrand dá ndealbhthor linde
budh iomdha ag cor 'na aghaidh –
ionmholta malairt bhisigh.
(*IBP*, p. 129, q. 12)
[If the lord of Bearnas find fault with any quatrain that
is made by me, there will be many opposed to him: a
change for the better is to be commended.[18]]

This neatly completes a poem that could, with equal
pleasure and cogency, be read (heard) from quatrain twelve
backwards. Ó hEoghusa, clearly, has not exploited the more

popular form in this composition. His poem may be a reflex of a changing taste in literature, an altered aesthetic that swept Europe in a two-pronged development: the re-establishment of classical Latin and Greek (involving the displacement and disparagement of mediaeval scholastic aesthetics), and the elevation of European vernaculars into languages thought capable of sustaining a literary aesthetic.[19]

Around the same time, a poem attributed to Fear Flatha Ó Gnímh, '*Cuimseach sin, a Fhearghail Óig*', suggests that he accuses a fellow-poet, Fearghal Óg Mac an Bhaird, of a similar desertion. The poem accuses Mac an Bhaird of behaving as though skill in poetry were an inborn talent and not an art[20] to be worked at with masters and manuals and practice, though Mac an Bhaird received the same strict schooling as did the author. The well-known quatrains accuse Mac an Bhaird of composing his poetry while riding a garron or a nag.

> *Cuimseach sin, a Fhearghail Óig,*
> *fuarois tiodhloicthi ón Tríonóitt;*
> *gan feidhm ndaghoide ar do dhán*
> *ag deilbh ghlanoige ar ghearrán.*
> (*IBP*, p. 118, q. 1)
>
> [This is convenient, Fearghal Óg, you received gifts from the Trinity; fashioning fresh texts (while mounted) on a garron, without the effect of a good teacher on your poetry.[21]]

The term *gearrán* refers to a small working horse. The term entered English as 'garron'. It is differentiated from *capall* 'horse' in the way that 'nag' is from 'horse'. In a similar fashion, the poetry composed by Fearghal Óg is to be ranked with the inferior sort of work. The well-wrought school-poem is the *capall* of composition; the easy jingle, casually composed, is the *gearrán*.[22]

Ó Gnímh lists a number of well-known fourteenth- and fifteenth-century poets[23] and reminds his fellow-poet that, far from the casual composition he (Fearghal Óg) now seems to favour, these masters practised deep contemplation, exclusion of distraction, and mental preparation (just as recommended by Geoffrey in the *Poetria Nova*). He himself still approaches his work according to the rules, presumably drilled into him in the schools:

> *Misi féin dá ndearnoinn dán,*
> *maith liom – lughoide ar seachrán –*
> *bac ar ghriangha um theachta as-teagh*
> *leaptha diamhra 'gar dídean.*
> (*IBP*, p. 119, q. 9)

[As for myself, should I make a poem, I like – my distraction is the less for it – a block on the sunlight coming in, secluded quarters to protect me.[24]]

This is the solitary stronghold of the mind where the images and *inventio* leading to the creation of an accomplished poem are conjured and contemplated before being committed to writing. Poets such as Donnchadh Mór Ó Dálaigh (d. 1244 [AFM]) (q. 3a) or Giolla Brighde Mac Con Midhe (*fl.* 1260s) (q. 3b) never composed a poem on the road:[25]

> *Donnchadh Mór bu mhillsi dán,*
> *Giolla Brighde is beó iomrádh,*
> *dias do thobhoigh grádh dá ngaois,*
> *dán ar conair ní cheapdaois.*
> (*IBP*, p. 118, q. 3)

[Donnchadh Mór whose poetry was sweetest, Giolla Brighde who lives in fame, two who won high rank for their wisdom, they used not compose poetry on the road.[26]]

In this literary joust, neither poet has, of course, embraced the simpler style they now praise. The whole discussion is still conducted within the syllabic formulae they were trained in, and with the knowing wit of the insider. Nevertheless, our understanding of the significance of our poets' adherence to the mediaeval preceptive doctrines of writing has rarely extended to our abandoning our favourite images of the poet and his milieux. In the light of what we have considered above, it is difficult to imagine how a contemporary reader/listener would have understood that Fearghal Óg was composing, literally, on horseback,[27] or conversely, that Ó Gnímh actually sequestered himself in a darkened room to produce his poetry, rather than retiring to the recesses of his mental world to compose his mind for the work in hand.

We now understand these poets to have engaged in an informed, poetic, witty discussion about the general abandonment of the mediaeval prescriptive arts, leading to the discrediting of their particular genres of formal poetry. This abandonment was common throughout Europe, and signified a change in educational practices and literary styles, which came perhaps a little later in formal Irish poetry than in other literary uses of the language, but which provided a very strong base for the literary modes that succeeded it.

Notes

In citing works in the notes, full titles have generally been used. Works frequently cited have been identified by the following abbreviations. See also the list of abbreviations on pp. ix–xi.

'Aesthetics': Breatnach, P. A. 2001. 'The Aesthetics of Irish Bardic Composition', *Cambrian Medieval Celtic Studies* 42 (Winter 2001), pp. 50–72.

AFM: O'Donovan, J. 1990 [1851]. *Annals of the Kingdom of Ireland etc.* 3rd. ed. Dublin.

Auraicept: Calder, G. [1917] 1995. ed., *Auraicept na n-Éces: The Scholars' Primer. Being the texts of the Ogham tract from the Book of Ballymote and the Yellow Book of Lecan, and the text of the Trefhocal from the Book of Leinster.* [Edinburgh] Dublin.

Dán Dé: McKenna, L. 1922. ed., *Dán Dé: The Poems of Donnchadh Mór Ó Dálaigh, and the Religious Poems in the Duanaire of the Yellow Book of Lecan.* Dublin.

Irish Royal Charters: Flanagan, M. T. 2005. *Irish Royal Charters: Texts and Contexts.* Oxford.

'Linguistic Terminology': Ó Cuív, B. 1965. 'Linguistic Terminology in the Mediaeval Irish Bardic Tracts'. In *Transactions of the Philological Society*, pp. 141–164.

'Linguistic Training': Ó Cuív, B. 1973. 'The Linguistic Training of the Mediaeval Irish Poet.' In *Celtica* 10, pp. 114–140.

'Literary Creation': Ó Cuív, B. 1963. 'Literary Creation and Historical Tradition', in *Proceedings of the British Academy* xlix [Sir John Rhŷs Memorial Lecture], pp. 233–262.

'Privileges': Gwynn, E. J. 1942. 'An Old-Irish Tract on the Privileges and Responsibilities of Poets', in *Ériu* 13, pp. 1–60, 220–236.

'Prolegomena': Quiggin, E. C. 1911–12. 'Prolegomena to the Study of the Later Irish Bards 1200–1500', in *Proceedings of the British Academy* v, pp. 89–143.

Rhetoric, Hermeneutics, and Translation: Copeland, R. 1991. *Rhetoric, Hermeneutics, and Translation in the Middle Ages.* Cambridge.

Téamaí Taighde: Breatnach, P. A. 1997. *Téamaí Taighde Nua-Ghaeilge*. Maigh Nuad.
'The Classics in Celtic Ireland': Bieler, L. [1971] 1979. 'The Classics in Celtic Ireland', in R. R. Bolgar, ed. *Classical Influences on European Culture AD 500–1500*; pp. 45–55. Cambridge.
The Early Irish Linguist: Ahlqvist, A. 1983. *The Early Irish Linguist: An Edition of the Canonical Part of the* Auraicept na nÉces. Helsinki.
'The Irish Language': Ó Cuív, B. 1976. 'The Irish Language in the Early Modern Period', in T. W. Moody, F. X. Martin, and F. J. Byrne, eds. *A New History of Ireland, iii: Early Modern Ireland 1534–1691*, pp. 509–545. Oxford.
The Medieval Art of Love: Camille, M. 1998. *The Medieval Art of Love: Objects and Subjects of Desire*. London.
The Partisan Voice: Klein, K. W. 1971. *The Partisan Voice: A Study of the Political Lyric in France and Germany, 1180–1230*. The Hague and Paris.

NOTES TO INTRODUCTION, PP. XV–XXVI

1 E. Knott, 'Filidh Éireann go hAointeach', *Ériu* 5 (1911), pp. 50–67. See also, M. O Riordan, 'Professors, Performers and "Others of Their Kind": Contextualizing the Bardic Poet', *The Irish Review* 23 (1998), pp. 73–88, for discussion of this poem, and for other instances of similar seasonal festivals in Ireland and in continental Europe.

2 This arrangement, referred to in the Middle Ages as the *fonduk/fondaco* was, indeed, common in trading towns. P. Spufford in *Power and Profit: The Merchant in Medieval Europe* (London, 2002), pp. 16–22, describes how specialist suppliers, traders, craftsmen, and other groups of related commercial activities were to be found together in designated areas of the city and in specific streets.

3 'Filidh Éireann go hAointeach', ll. 61–92, pp. 56–58.

4 A similar arrangement is indicated by the entry for the year 1387 in the Annals of Ulster when Niall Óg Ó Néill 'built [a house]

in Emhain Macha to recompense the [learned] companies of Ireland therein' (*do dhil damh Erenn ann*). The poet Tadhg Óg Ó hUiginn (d. 1448) recorded that his patron Orlaidh Ní Cheallaigh made a house for the 'companies' on one of her festive occasions. See, in *AithDD* i, no. 11, st. 31, p. 43, '*Bean ré cobhair na gcoinneamh / teagh fa a gcomhair do cumadh*'. In a similar fashion in mediaeval Burgundy – on a more vast scale but in the same spirit – the thirteenth-century duke of Burgundy laid on some thirty thousand ells of fabric to cover the courtyard of his castle in order to house the company he invited to the festivities he organized to ingratiate himself with King Charles V in 1387. This temporary roofing was necessary to accommodate the several hundreds of guests, including entertainers who were attending the week-long festivities in honour of his nuptials (see B. Tuchman, *A Distant Mirror: The Calamitous Fourteenth Century* (Harmondsworth [1978] 1985, p. 467). The arrangements made for the meeting of Henry VIII of England and Francis I of France at the Field of the Cloth of Gold are legendary (see S. Anglo, *Images of Tudor Kingship*, (London, 1992), pp. 1, 25, 30.

5 Recently explored in P. A. Breatnach, 'Aesthetics'.

6 In *Poetry of the Carolingian Renaissance* (London, 1985), pp. 1–80, P. Godman continually draws attention to the fallacy of treating the poetry of Walahfrid, Gottschalk, and others, as having a direct biographical significance (pp. 36–43). Godman's discussion of the flourishing of the Carolingian court under Charlemagne, and of its changing nature under Louis the Pious and Charles the Bald, follows the thread of consistency in the literature, as ever-renewed generations of writers and poets built their poems and styles on that which had preceded them.

7 In a footnote concerning the king-list in the tenth-century versified biblical history *Saltair na Rann* and its political import, M. Herbert ('Sea-divided Gaels?: Relationships between Irish and Scots *c.* 800–1169', in B. Smith, ed., *Britain and Ireland 900–1300: Insular Response to Medieval European Change* [Cambridge, 1999], p. 90) emphasizes her sense of the literary nature of such material

as king-lists as follows: 'I take the view that the exigencies of the metrical form of the list militates against the proposition that the placement of the king of Alba in the list means that its compiler had links with that kingdom.'

8   Needless to say, standards varied according to individual ability and talent and taste. The best of any period was of a uniformly high standard and the bardic syllabic compositions adhered to recognizable styles and formulae which dominated formal composition for four hundred years.

9   For a brief outline of the influence of the successive waves of non-Irish languages in Ireland and on the Irish language, see M. Ó Murchú, *The Irish Language* (Dublin, 1985), pp. 19–24. For the unifying function of Latin as a literary language among the mediaeval English and French, see M. Worley, 'Using the *Orumulum* to Redefine Vernacularity', in F. Somerset and N. Watson, *The Vulgar Tongue: Medieval and Postmedieval Vernacularity* (Pennsylvania, 2003), pp. 19–30; esp. pp. 23–27.

10 See B. Ó Cuív, 'Literary Creation', pp. 233–262; 251, 255.

11 *Dán díreach*, referring to the formal syllabic metres used by literary writers, are to be found in material from pre-Norman times. The distinctive praise-poetry genres in syllabic metres, which became common in the twelfth century and were taught in the schools under the tutelage of *ollaimh*, are those commonly understood today as 'bardic poetry'. See A. Mac an Bhaird, '*Dán díreach agus Ranna as na hAnnála 867–1134*', *Éigse* 17 (1977–1979), pp. 157–168).

12 See D. MacManus, 'The Bardic Poet as Teacher, Student and Critic: A Context for the Grammatical Tracts', in C. G. Ó Háinle and D. E. Meek, *Unity in Diversity: Studies in Irish and Scottish Gaelic Language, Literature and History* [Léann na Tríonóide: Trinity Irish Studies I] (Dublin, 2004), pp. 97–123.

13 Irish familiarity with Donatus, and learnèd Hiberno-Latin commentary on Donatus, such as that by Sedulius Scottus (B. Löfstedt, ed., *Sedulius Scottus in Donati Artem Maiorem* [Corpus Christianorum, Cont. Med. 40b] [Turnhout, 1977] p. 374, cited

in E. Poppe, 'Reconstructing Medieval Irish Literary Theory: The Lesson of *Airec Menman Uraird maic Coise*' (in *Cambrian Medieval Celtic Studies* 37 [1999], pp. 33–54), p. 50, show that Irish scholars were familiar with the terms and concepts that formed the background to the learnèd tradition common to European literature, in Latin and in the emerging vernaculars.

14 Literary imitation of first lines, locutions, topics, treatments and so forth, is a commonplace of the corpus of Irish syllabic poetry. Aspects of this literary phenomenon, its nature and implications have been studied in P. A. Breatnach, *Téamaí Taighde, 'Traidisiún na hAithrise Liteartha'*, pp. 1–63. There he examines examples of poetic imitation in identical first lines, in close imitations, in echoing, and in pastiche.

15 See P. A. Breatnach, 'Elegy of Aodh Ruadh Ó Domhnaill (d. 1505)', *Éigse* 35, pp. 27–52, for a typical example of the genre. In his edition of the poem, Breatnach lists the themes associated with the genre (p. 31) and refers to these features in other bardic poems in the informative notes accompanying the edition.

16 See E. Knott, *TDall* i/ii, i, pp. liv–lvii.

17 No attempt has been made to skew translation to suit a theory, but, on the contrary, the effort has been to escape from any pre-judged notion of what the poet ought to mean in the light of the understood 'factual' background.

NOTES TO CHAPTER ONE, PP. 1–23

1 The greater part of Irish verse since the seventh century had been syllabic, i.e. it was verse in which the line was defined by the number of syllables; in our period (1250–1650), the strictest form of syllabic verse was termed *dán díreach*.

2 Later (High Middle Ages) translations of classical legends are among 'the earliest vernacular translations of classical literature in existence' (W. B. Stanford, 'Towards a History of Classical Influences in Ireland', *Proceedings of the Royal Irish Academy* [1970], pp. 15–91; pp. 33, 37).

3 H. Waddell, *Medieval Latin Lyrics* (London, 1952), and her *The Wandering Scholars* (London, 1954). See also P. Godman, *Poetry of the Carolingian Renaissance*, pp. 53–56; p. 278–306. The Irish poets noted by Godman, 'Hibernicus Exul', Bernowin, Cadac-Andreas, Sedulius Scottus, Colman, John Scottus, take their place among those with whom they found themselves in the various courts and convents of the Continent. Their education and literary bent chimed in harmony with their fellows. Sedulius Scottus excelled many of his fellow-poets in his exploitation of irony and parody. His career in Europe is described by Godman (p. 56) as being typical:

> To each of the sons of Louis the Pious Sedulius addressed verses extolling his descent from Charlemagne and praising his achievements, but neither Lothar nor Louis the German nor even Charles the Bald – the much-vaunted promoter of letters – counts as the major patron of Sedulius' work. Sedulius wrote for several audiences, and with an eye to the main chance. In this respect his example is typical of poets active in the third quarter of the ninth century not only in Middle Francia but also throughout the Carolingian realms, including the West Frankish kingdom of Charles the Bald.

4 Irish Latin scholarship is usefully synopsized by C. Doherty, 'Latin Writing in Ireland, *c.* 400–1200', in S. Deane, A. Carpenter, J. Williams, eds., *The Field Day Anthology of Irish Writing* i (Derry, 1991), pp. 61–140. And see B. I. Jarcho, '*Die Vorläufer des Golias*', *Speculum* 3 (1928), pp. 523–579. The implications, for the later period, of Kuno Meyer's statement, following, should be borne in mind throughout this study:

> Ireland had become the heiress of the classical and theological learning of the Western Empire of the fourth and fifth centuries, and a period of humanism was thus ushered in which reached its culmination during the

sixth and following centuries, the Golden Age of Irish civilisation. The charge that is so often levelled against Irish history, that it has been, as it were, in a backwater, where only the fainter wash of the larger currents reaches, cannot apply to this period (K. Meyer, *Ancient Irish Poetry* (London, 1913), p. ix).

M. T. Flanagan, in 'The Contribution of Irish Missionaries and Scholars to Medieval Christianity' (in B. Bradshaw and D. Keogh, eds., *Christianity in Ireland: Revisiting the Story*, (Dublin, 2002), pp. 30–43, reassesses, positively, the current sense of the Irish contribution to both Christianity and scholarship in mediaeval Europe. Flanagan emphasizes the stress placed on the acquisition of Latin learning in early Christian Ireland, and notes that by the seventh century, the surviving materials indicate levels of a 'confident attainment' (p. 31), and goes on to describe aspects of Irish innovation in the presentation of material for pedagogic and mnemonic purposes (pp. 31–34) indicating an 'intensity of engagement' (p. 35) with the Bible (with the Latin translation – the principal source of Christian writing and commenatary) which involved continuous (efforts at) awareness of, and engagement with, British and continental European scholars and scholarship (pp. 41–44).

5 D. Ó Corráin, 'Irish Origin Legend and Genealogy' (in T. Nyberg, ed., *History and Herioc Tale* [Odense]), p. 52. See also, V. Law, in 'Memory and the Structure of Grammars in Antiquity and the Middle Ages' (in M. de Nonno, et al., *Manuscripts and Tradition of Grammatical Texts from Antiquity to the Renaissance* i [Cassino, 2000], pp. 9–57), notes (p. 25) commentaries by Murethach and Sedulius showing how Irish scholars were aware of, and participated in, the latest trends in scholarship. And see R. Hofman, 'The Irish Tradition of Priscian', in ibid., pp. 257–287. E. Poppe, in 'Reconstructing Medieval Irish Literary Theory: The Lesson of *Airec Menman Uraird maic Coise*', *Cambrian Medieval Celtic Studies* 37 (1999), pp. 33–54, asserts that '. . . vernacular and Hiberno-Latin texts share the same

cultural background' in the period roughly between the seventh to the thirteenth century (p. 33).

6 See, for instance, D. Kelly, *APP*, p. 149; E. Faral, *LAP*, p. 48.

7 Ireland, Iceland and Provence seem to have taken this step quite early in the mediaeval millennium. See A. Ahlqvist, *The Early Irish Linguist*, p. 19. J. O. Ward, in *CR*, notes how mediaeval material such as this, emerging from a teaching, learning, and *studium* milieu, gathered introductions, glossarial material, interpolated notes, further redactions of the same material, and so on, respective elements of which became separated from each other and survived for different reasons, and in different contexts. The isolation of the 'canonical' part of what can appear under a given title is often almost impossible.

8 D. Kelly, in *APP*, outlines the literary circumstances in which European countries produced vernacular grammars and prosodies based on Latin patterns and, while accepting the individuality of materials produced in different languages, makes the following point (p. 146): '[Second,] the extant treatises are quite elementary, even when written in Latin, being more nearly comparable to Latin treatises on elementary grammar and versification than to the twelfth-century and thirteenth-century arts of poetry and prose, as such.'

9 See G. Calder, ed., *Auraicept*.

10 See D. Ó hAodha, '*An Bhairdne i dTús a Ré*', in P. Ó Fiannachta, eag., *An Dán Díreach*, Léachtaí Cholm Cille xxiv (1994), pp. 9–20; p. 17. And compare, D. Kelly, in *The APP* (p. 149), where he summarizes the emergence of the 'second rhetoric' as follows: 'The vernacular languages posed problems which Latin grammar and poetics did not address: a different language with elements like the article lacking in Latin, different features in versification, new genres, the exclusive use of rhyme and cadence, a lay public and poet. There emerged from this a second, vernacular grammar, rhetoric, and poetic modeled on the first and appended to it, but with different subjects, forms, and genres.'

11 G. Murphy, *Early Irish Metrics* (Dublin, 1961), p. 7.

12 *Auraicept*, p. ix: '. . . but if the *Trefhocal* be included, it treats also of poetry in the strict sense'. See also *The Early Irish Linguist*, pp. 17–18; R. MacLaughlin, 'In Lebor Ollamain' (forthcoming), shows that what appears to be an *accessus*-style document which may have, like others of its kind, become a textbook in itself; and see D. McManus, *A Guide to Ogam* (Maynooth, 1991). See *DIL*, s.v. *trefhocal*, for the range of meanings of this term and its connections with the rules of satire. The *Trefhocal* text connected with *Auraicept na n-Éces* contains the rules governing the sense of belonging to a fraternity of poets working in the vernacular, and the appropriate rewards for work of certain standards (*Auraicept*, ll. 2219–2254, pp. 166–168). And see L. Breatnach, 'The "Caldron of Poesy" ', in *Ériu* 32 (1981), pp. 45–93; idem, *Uraicecht na ríar: The Poetic Grades in Early Irish Law* (Dublin, 1987); idem, 'Sedulius Scottus, St Gall Stiftsbibliothek 73, and Latin in the Irish Laws', in *Proceedings of the Irish Biblical Society* 16 (1993), pp. 123–124.

13 See *The Early Irish Linguist*, p. 32; *CR*, p. 59.

14 The three terms, *fili*, *Gaedel*, *Laitneoir*, are found throughout.

15 The latest redaction of the word of God, for instance, was also seen as the most authoritative: in the seventh century, Muslims identified Muhammad as the final prophet of God, 'whose instructions replaced all previous ones', J. Herrin, *The Formation of Christendom* (London, 2001), p. 9.

16 Cf. V. Law, 'Memory and the Structure of Grammars', p. 36; and see *CR*, pp. 71, 203–205.

17 In the context, *trefhocal* can refer to a type of poetry or to a poem; in this instance the reference is to a long syllabic poem on the faults of composition and remedies for them.

18 A *trefhocal* text appearing in the Book of Leinster, edited by G. Calder in *Auraicept*, pp. 258–269, lists the twelve errors, and the twenty-four defences, and follows with '*Haec sunt exempla praecedentium*', with stanzas exhibiting erroneous forms and appropriate forms.

19 R. Hofman, 'The Irish Tradition of Priscian', p. 279.

20 In fact, Kelly's statement that the troubadours were the first 'consciously to raise the vernacular to a formal literary language' (p. 172) indicates that his sense of developments in Ireland and Scandinavia is not strong. See S. N. Tranter, 'Divided and Scattered, Trussed and Supported: Stanzaic Form in Irish and Old Norse Tracts', in H. L. C. Tristram, ed. *Metrik und Medienwechsel: Metrics and Media* (Tübingen, 1991), pp. 245–272, where the metrical terminology in mediaeval Irish sources and those of Iceland are compared. Tranter stresses the importance of the influence of writing in the case of the Irish *artes poeticae*:

> In that the Irish *artes poeticae* differ radically from those of the control culture Iceland, we can define them as having been basically writing-influenced. Though we cannot thus prove beyond doubt that the form of the poetry itself was writing-influenced, our analysis supports this view far more strongly than it does the contrary. . . . On one plane, the Conversion brought the Irish into increased contact with Latin learning. This brought with it the specific forms of analysis outlined above, and favoured the establishment of hierarchical models of structure, both social and artistic, both of poets and of poems. . . . In addition, concomitant to this intellectual borrowing, the Irish imported the medium of the parchment manuscript. This allowed analysis of form not merely on the basis of the audible, but also on a visual basis. Indeed, since writing was the preserve of the initiates, visual analysis was accorded a higher status than aural analysis. The layman heard rhymes; the cleric could also count syllables on the page (p. 271).

In further support of this view, it might be noted that Irish is, and throughout its known history would appear to have been, a stress-timed language in which syllabic verse is accoustically ineffective. Its impact would seem to have been purely visual.

21 R. I. Best, O. Bergin, and M. A. O'Brien, eds., *The Book of Leinster* (Dublin, 1954), p. xvi.

22 ibid., p. xvi.

23 ibid., pp. xv– xvii; and see T. Ó Concheanainn, 'LL and the Date of the Reviser of LU', *Éigse* 20 (1984), pp. 213–214.

24 S. Forste-Grupp, 'The Earliest Irish Personal Letter', in K. Chadbourne, L. J. Maney and D. Wong, eds., *Proceedings of the Harvard Celtic Colloquium (April 27–30)*, xv (1995), pp. 1–11. M. T. Flanagan, in *Irish Royal Charters*, notes (p. 23) the appearance of Latin charters in the European formulae in twelfth-century Ireland (15 copies extant): 'The adoption of the European Latin charter would appear, therefore, to be linked to the introduction of continental reformist structures and monastic observances into Ireland during the twelfth century. From the late eleventh century onwards the Irish church underwent a transformation, one of the main aims of which was to bring it more into conformity with medieval Christendom.' Like other imports, however, the Irish made their own contribution to the formulae (ibid., pp. 23–24): 'These [reforming] houses may be presumed to have promoted the use of the European Latin charter, and, in the first instance, to have drafted the charter-texts in conformity with the contemporary practices of diplomatic and presented them for approval and authentication to Irish kings. But although the diplomatic of the texts may have been prescribed by contemporary European norms, Irish kings were not simply passive agents in that process, but proved fully able to exploit the new charter-form to enhance their own prestige and political objectives.'

25 For the history and contexts of the emergence of these related arts, see M. Camargo, *Ars Dictaminis, Ars Dictandi* (Turnhout, 1991); and M. G. Briscoe and B. H. Jaye, *Artes Praedicandi* and *Artes Orandi* (Turnhout, 1992), respectively.

26 MS Auct. F. III.15 was among several presented by an Oxford scholar Thomas Allen (1540–1632) to the Bodleian Library in 1601 (P. Ó Néill, 'An Irishman at Chartres', *Ériu* 48 [1997],

pp. 1–35). P. Ó Néill describes this manuscript in detail, its provenance and its contents. The evidence overwhelmingly suggests Irish students studying in Paris and annotating works as teaching materials for their return.

27 P. Ó Néill, 'An Irishman at Chartres', 4–8.

28 ibid., p. 12.

29 ibid., p. 19.

30 'apoconu' here is mismatched with the definition following it: it should probably read 'apocope' and refer to that subtractive feature, or more likely, to the term that more correctly matches the definition 'zeugma'.

31 P. Ó Néill, 'An Irishman at Chartres', p. 24.

32 ibid., p. 24.

33 M. T. Flanagan's *Irish Royal Charters* makes it quite clear that Irish kings and political leaders considered themselves to be on a par with any of their European counterparts. Irish political leaders participated in the written culture that produced formulaic charters and other similar documents whenever that seemed feasible or appropriate. Religious foundations on the Continent with strong Irish links, like St Gall and Bobbio, were familiar with Latin charter-style material and formulae from the seventh and eighth centuries (p. 13). Flanagan, points out how the modern sense of 'pre-Norman' and 'post-Norman' readings of Irish history have tended to occlude any sense of continuity, cultural, literary or otherwise:

> They [the charters] constitute an additional genre of source material, offering a different range of information to the better-known annals, regnal lists, genealogies, and dynastic propaganda tracts of pre-twelfth-century Ireland, and this is especially so in the case of those charters issued by Irish kings that predate Anglo-Norman incursion into Ireland. *Their value is augmented by the fact that they are couched in the formulae of the characteristic European Latin charter-tradition of the twelfth century*

and are therefore directly comparable with charters of Anglo-Norman provenance issued in Ireland. . . . The advent of the Anglo-Normans did indubitably generate dramatic changes in Irish society, but here were also continuities. Those elements of continuity, however, have tended to be submerged and obscured by the dissimilarities and non-comparability of pre- and post-Anglo-Norman primary sources. *The Latin charters issued by Irish kings in the twelfth and early thirteenth centuries, in that they are directly comparable with Anglo-Norman charters, highlight some of the correspondences between Irish and Anglo-Norman society, and are thus invaluable also in enabling a more balanced appraisal of the Anglo-Norman impact on twelfth-century Ireland* (pp. 3–4; emphasis added).

34 Among the MS sources used by H. R. Fairclough in his Loeb edition of Horace, is the Codex Bernensis (available for the *Ars poetica* to l. 441) written by an Irish scribe at the end of the ninth century (H. R. Fairclough, ed., *Horace: Satires, Epistles and Ars Poetica* [Harvard, 1970], p. xxv). And see L. Bieler, 'The Classics in Celtic Ireland', p. 48:

> . . . The case of Horace is different. In the transmission of Horace's poems the Irish do seem to have played a leading part during the eighth and ninth centuries. A substantial portion of Horace's *œuvre* is contained in a ninth-century codex in Irish script (Berne 363) which is connected with the circle of Sedulius Scottus; and the fact that Horace was known to Columbanus is possibly suggestive of a tradition of Horatian studies in Ireland from the sixth century onwards.

M. T. Flanagan, considering the possible influence of German imperial charter formulae on Irish charters, notes two Irish masters of cathedral schools within the empire:

Indeed, an Irishman, David *Scottus* who was master of the cathedral school of Würzburg before 1110, travelled as *capellanus* in the entourage of the German emperor, Henry V, on his Italian expedition of 1111 and wrote a now lost account of the emperor's manoeuvres against Pope Paschal II, while another Irishman, Carus of Nuremberg, acted as *capellanus* for Emperor Conrad III (1138–52) (*Irish Royal Charters*, p. 183).

The particular connections which the Mac Carthaighs had with the *Schottenklöster* of southern Germany and Austria and the influence of imperial court culture and diplomatic on documents connected with the Mac Carthaigh family and those institutions which it patronized in the eleventh and twelfth centuries are discussed in detail by M. T. Flanagan, ibid., pp. 181–212. The extent to which Ireland was a participant in mainstream European culture, in many cases through its ecclesiastical links, all of which represented links of scholarship at the time, is a matter that is dealt with by her in some detail. All the contacts that she describes are those same links that kept Irish scholars in tune with trends and movements in ecclesiastical and secular learning, which seem to have prevented a cultural isolation or isolationism in Irish learning in Ireland.

35 From the earlier part of the twelfth century, communities of monks and regular canons under continental rules had been established in every province. Cistercian monks were established in Mellifont from the mid-twelfth century. Establishments such as these, caused rules and other related literature to be disseminated in Ireland and, frequently, the immediate presence of foreign monks too. Bernard of Clairvaux sent French monks to Malachy at Mellifont in 1142. For a modern synopsis of how matters stood in the High Middle Ages, especially on the implementation of reform, see J. A. Watt, 'The Irish Church in the Middle Ages', in B. Bradshaw and D. Keogh, eds., *Christianity in Ireland: Revisiting the Story* (Dublin, 2002), pp. 44–56. The classic descriptions of the mediaeval Irish Church

in Ireland are found in A. Gwynn, *The Twelfth-Century Reform*, vol. I, in P. J. Corish, ed., *History of Irish Catholicism* ii (Dublin, 1968); G. Hand, *The Church in the English Lordship 1216–1307*, *History of Irish Catholicism* ii, 3 (Dublin, 1968); A. Gwynn, *Anglo-Irish Church Life in the 14th and 15th Centuries, History of Irish Catholicism* ii, 4 (Dublin, 1968); C. Mooney, *The Church in Gaelic Ireland in the 13th to 15th Centuries, History of Irish Catholicism* ii, 5 (Dublin, 1969).

36 Copeland, in *Rhetoric, Hermeneutics, and Translation*, p. 178, notes the following: 'If it is a truth of historical practice that hermeneutics often borrows the tools of rhetoric, so we have seen how the obverse is also true: *grammatica*, in antiquity the debased term against which rhetoric had to defend its disciplinary superiority, can in the Middle Ages, restore to rhetoric its proper identity as a praxis.'

37 The word 'troubadour' comes from the Provençal *trovar*, which, it has been argued, means 'to find', 'to write tropes', 'to compose' (F. Jensen, *The Earliest Portuguese Lyrics* [Odense, 1978], pp. 23–24). Irish [bardic] poetry and the works of the troubadours, the trouvères, and the Minnesingers overlap in very significant areas. They also part company at significant junctures. One of the points of contact is the centrality of *inventio* in the learnèd tradition of the mediaeval tracts on Latin composition, and the reflexes of that in the vernacular tradition of the troubadours. Irish vernacular composition straddled both traditions.

38 J. J. Murphy, in *RMA*, outlines the extent of the debate in the schools in the Middle Ages (pp. 192–193):

> The twelfth and early thirteenth centuries witnessed a lengthy debate over the matter of the 'classification of the sciences'. A number of writers attempted to distinguish the exact relations between grammar, rhetoric, and logic. Dialecticians were especially interested in the problem, since all three members of the traditional *trivium* dealt with the use of words, and they naturally wished to define the proper sphere of each discipline

in order to clarify dialectic itself. The complexities of
this debate . . . [addressing, as it attempted to do, the
implicit grammatical controversy between unity and
diversity] did have a widespread and profound effect
on the course of medieval rhetorical development . . .

39 The amibiguity in the poets' literary personae is explored in M.
O Riordan, 'Professors, Performers and "Others of Their Kind"':
Contextualizing the Bardic Poet', *The Irish Review* 23 (1998), pp.
73–88.

40 P. A. Breatnach, in 'Aesthetics', undertakes (p. 54) to 'observe
the manner in which an awareness of what is termed the
"environment of discourse" created by the inheritance of
medieval rhetorical theory, can lead us towards a more complete
and satisfying appreciation of the inherent aesthetic qualities
of an early modern Irish bardic system'. The sense of a shared
environment of discourse would include a shared sense of the
'cultural script'.

41 Taking a different view of this, P. Mac Cana, in 'The Rise of the
Later Schools of *Filidheacht*', (*Ériu* 25, pp. 126–146) suggests (p.
138) that:

> The truth would seem to be that the continuity of the
> tradition of *filidecht* was never completely ruptured,
> but that the organization itself experienced several cen-
> turies of unsettled, changing conditions culminating
> in the cultural crisis of the twelfth century. During
> this time monastic scholars, most of them laymen, no
> doubt, became increasingly absorbed in the study of
> native historical tradition and, secondarily, of native
> literary sources in general.

See, also, P. Mac Cana, 'Praise Poetry in Ireland before the Nor-
mans' (*Ériu* 54, pp. 11–40), which notes panegyric works (from
the seventh century on) which exhibit features considered typ-
ical of the later 'bardic' poetry and, in general, highlights areas of
continuity in the preNorman–postNorman tradition rather than

the contrary. The article also includes interesting parallels and divergences in the Welsh tradition.

42 See, for instance, M. Roston, *Sixteenth-Century English Literature* (New York, 1982), pp. 34–54; B. King, *Seventeenth-Century English Literature* (New York, 1982), pp. 20–28.

43 See L. Breatnach, 'An Mheán-Ghaeilge', in K. McCone, et al., eag., *Stair na Gaeilge in ómós do Pádraig Ó Fiannachta* (Maigh Nuad, 1994), pp. 221–333. And see M. Ó Murchú, *Léirmheas ar Stair na Gaeilge*, *Éigse* 30 (1997), p. 187, who suggests that the continual socio-political unrest of the eleventh and twelfth centuries, with constantly shifting centres of power and influence, provided conditions in which a new Gaelic koiné might have been expected to emerge; that, in conformity with this emerging koiné, a new literary norm would seem to have evolved, possibly in some influential centres of learning; that, in any case, it is scarcely plausible to suggest that the new literary norm could have been consciously developed as a defensive response to the Anglo-Norman intervention.

44 B. Ó Cuív, 'Linguistic Training', pp. 116–117.

45 Some details of these controversies are discussed in D. Bracken, 'Authority and Duty: Columbanus and the Primacy of Rome', *Peritia* 16 (2002), pp. 168–213; and in P. Ó Néill, '*Romani* Influences on Seventh-Century Hiberno-Latin Literature', in P. Ní Chatháin and M. Richter, eds., *Ireland and Europe: The Early Church (Irland und Europa: die Kirche im Frühmittelalter)* (Stuttgart, 1984), pp. 280–290.

46 S. Ó Tuama in *An Grá in Amhráin na nDaoine* (Baile Átha Cliath, [1960] 1978) suggests that Norman French would have been the normal language of Anglo-Norman settlers in Ireland, of their households, of the newly arrived Franciscan and Dominican friars to Ireland, and the language heard spoken by Irish scholars at Oxford and at Paris. He surmises as follows on the cultural make-up of the Anglo-Norman household in Ireland and in England (pp. 258–259):

*Ba í an Fhraincis an phríomhtheanga labhartha i Sasana,
ar ndóigh, roimh c. 1250, ní amháin ag na huaisle is ag
an aos cultúrtha, ach ag mórchuid de na gnáthdhaoine
chomh maith. . . . Ní foláir áfach nó ba í an Fhrain-
cis an príomhfhórsa cultúrtha sa tír go dtí lár na haoise
sin, cibé scéal é (c. 1350). Ceoltóirí agus amhránaithe
Francacha is mó a bhíodh i gcúirt an rí san aois sin féin.
Conas a bhí in Éirinn? Is deimhnitheach gurb í
an Fhraincis an teanga nádúrtha a bhí ag na huaisle
Normannacha a bhí i gceannas fhormhór na tíre seo,
1170–c. 1300. Is deimhnitheach leis, is dócha, gurb í an
Fhraincis a bhí ag a gcuid filí,* jongleurs, *agus ceoltóirí.
Ní fios áfach, conas a bhí ag a gcuid saighdiúirí, giollaí,
etc. Is dealraithí, áfach, go mbeadh Fraincis acu, cibé acu
ba í nó nárbh í a bpríomhtheanga labhartha í. Is geall
le deimhnitheach gurb í an Fhraincis príomhtheanga
labhartha na n-ord iasachta – na Proinsiasaigh,
Dominicigh, etc. – a shroich an tír seo i lár an tríú haois
déag. Is geall le deimhnitheach, leis, gurb í an Fhraincis
an teanga labhartha a chuala na hÉireannaigh go léir, a
bhí ag freastal ar Oxford sa tríú haois déag (lasmuigh de
chúrsaí léinn an choláiste), agus cibé méid eile a bhí ag
freastal ar Ollscoil Pháras.*

47 B. Ó Cuív, 'Literary Creation', p. 253.
48 See B. Cunningham, *The World of Geoffrey Keating: History, Myth
and Religion in Seventeenth-Century Ireland* (Dublin, 2000), pp.
24–31.
49 E. C. Quiggin, 'Prolegomena', pp. 89–91.
50 Referring thus to Irish translations, 'But these translations, or
rather free adaptations' ('Prolegomena', p. 90) – Quiggin may
not have taken sufficient note of the sense of the mediaeval
approach to translation that strove to avoid the *fidus interpres*
(*Rhetoric, Hermeneutics, and Translation*, pp. 168–171). Nessa Ní
Shéaghdha (in 'Translations and Adaptations into Irish', *Éigse*
16 [1984], pp. 107–124; p. 107) notes, 'Straightforward or literal

translation was not the practice in these early days in Ireland; neither, for that matter, was it the practice on the continent of Europe, where vernacular paraphrases and summaries generally preceded full translations.' In characterizing the adaptations and translations as 'remarkably idiosyncratic', and also as characteristic of the independence inherent in the Irish literary enterprise, Ní Shéaghdha, quoting E. G. Quin, *Stair Ercuil ocus a Bás: The Life and Death of Hercules* [Irish Texts Society 38] (Dublin, 1939), accepts his formulation: 'the adapter is by no means a slavish follower of his original' (referring to a later text). R. Copeland suggests that translation itself was an arena of 'hermeneutical action' in the Middle Ages: 'What does account for the nature of medieval translation is a rhetorical motive of textual appropriation, akin to that of Roman translation, but which the Middle Ages finds in a newly empowered force and broadened scope of hermeneutical action' (*Rhetoric, Hermeneutics, and Translation*, p. 175). Cf. W. B. Stanford, in 'Towards a History of Classical Influences in Ireland', *Proceedings of the Royal Irish Academy* 70 C (1970), pp. 15–91; p. 37, referring to some pre-Norman translations of classical historical legends, states:

> All in all these translations (in so far as one can judge from English versions) give the impression of having been made out not by carefully and methodically instructed scholars but by fluent writers with a wide but at times inaccurate knowledge of classical history and mythology, combined with a lively imagination of their own and a proud confidence in the Irish techniques of storytelling.

This strand of methodology in respect of adaptation or of translation has not been taken into account, either, by R. P. Parr (*AV*, p. 11) in his account of the controversy between Matthew of Vendôme and Arnulf: 'Arnulf's interest in Ovid and Lucan suggests the same desire to *avoid tradition* and bring to poetry its natural facility for extensive variety of implied meaning.' (Emphasis added.) And cf. Matthew of Vendôme, *Ars Versificatoria*: '*Nec etiam aliquis verbo verbum proponat reddere fidus interpres*' (*LAP*, IV §1, p. 180; *AV*, IV §1, p. 93).

51 L. McKenna, ed., *Dán Dé*, p. xi. McKenna's analysis clearly understands the references, apart from those directly related to the Gospel account, to mirror aspects of contemporary Irish society. The intention of the excerpt quoted here is to indicate (McKenna's point) the prevalence of the certain biblical and scriptural themes in bardic devotional poetry, and to note the treatment given to such material.

52 T. Ó Dúshláine, in *An Eoraip agus Litríocht na Gaeilge, 1600–1650: Gnéithe den Bharócachas Eorpach i Litríocht na Gaeilge* (Baile Átha Cliath, 1987), referring to the influence of styles and topics in contemporary Counter-Reformation devotional literature on writing in Irish, particularly, in the contemplative tradition, remarks as follows (p. 179):

> *Ar an iomlán tá genres difriúla na filíochta cráifí sin faoi réir ag na teicnící céanna míúine agus tá filíocht chráifeach na Gaeilge ag teacht sa mhéid sin leis an bhfilíocht chomhaimseartha Eorpach. Thagraíos do go leor samplaí Eorpacha thuas d'fhonn na cosúlachtaí a thabhairt amach agus d'fhonn an fhilíocht Ghaeilge a shuíomh ina comhthéacs ceart Eorpach.*

53 Isolation, suggested in 'Prolegomena', pp. 90–91, for example.

54 Cf. P. Mac Cana, 'The Rise of the Later Schools of *Filidheacht*', p. 141.

55 The exclusion to the margins of cultural and political life of the majority of the Irish population following the Treaty of Limerick (1691), and the literary or cultural consequences of this, lies outside the scope of this study.

NOTES TO CHAPTER TWO, PP. 24–56

1 John of Garland's *Parisiana Poetria* aimed to equip the writer with the 'technique for treating any subject whatever, in prose, quantitative verse, or rhymed syllabic verse' (*Vtilitas est scire tractare*

quamcumque materiam prosayce, metrice, et rithmice) (T. Lawler, ed., *PP*, ll. 6–7).

2 See *PP*, ll. 92–123; and this volume p. 53.

3 The matter is synopsized as follows by R. Copeland (*Rhetoric, Hermeneutics, and Translation*, p. 160):

> Augustine's definition of invention as an exegetical procedure is a prototype for one important conception of invention in late medieval rhetorical poetics. In the medieval *artes poetriae, inventio* is an extractive operation, as in its classical sense, a deliberation about a subject, about the potentials of 'what to say' by drawing on a topical reserve. But in these rhetorical poetics, *inventio* can often assume the existence of a textual legacy, an inherited tradition of written authority which will provide a topical reserve.

4 The rich literary hinterland from which the continental and British manuals developed, being as they were a codification for students of modes and formulae hundreds of years old, is well described in P. Godman, *Poetry of the Carolingian Renaissance*, (London, 1985), pp. 1–80. The styles, the topics, the methods, the cathedral school milieu (replaced to some extent by that of the emerging universities in the later period), the court of Charlemagne – of legendary status by the twelfth century – were part of the foundations upon which later scholars such as John of Garland and the others built their treatises. Panegyric, elegy, praise of place, disputes among scholars, poems of exile, are all represented in the works of the poets who were associated at one time and another with the courts of Charlemagne, Louis the Pious and Charles the Bald.

5 R. Copeland, in *Rhetoric, Hermeneutics, and Translation* (p. 59), gives a detailed analysis of the relationship between the mediaeval *artes poetriae* and the ancient classical traditions of Plato and the strands of rhetoric, dialectic, logic and their relationship with mediaevel hermeneutics which is ultimately relevant for our discussion, but not immediately appropriate to this study.

6 The sense that the Anglo-Norman invasion could have presented a unitary cultural threat is belied by the contemporary norms. A wider view of literary and political identity prevailed even in areas sharing a common literary language (for the literary language of Irish poetry, see D. McManus, '*An Nua-Ghaeilge Chlasaiceach*', in K. McCone, et al., *Stair na Gaeilge in Ómós do Pádraig Ó Fiannachta* [Maigh Nuad, 1994], pp. 335–445), such as that employed by the troubadours of Southern France, Italy, Spain and Portugal. The troubadours shared Provençal as a language but the political identity was divergent. They expressed themselves not in the 'common *romana lingua*, but in clearly distinct linguistic systems as well as in the supranational Occitan literary *koiné* . . .' (E. Schulze-Busacker, 'French Conceptions of Foreigners and Foreign Languages in the Twelfth and Thirteenth Centuries', *Romance Philology* 41 [1987], pp. 24–47; p. 26). Common literary language meant also common themes: courtly love, political and religious debate, and laments for the dead. Ireland and Scotland shared a literary language but did not share an identical political culture. And cf. M. Ó Murchú, '*Stair na Gaeilge*, Léirmheas', *Éigse* 30 (1997), pp. 171–195; p. 187 (see ch. 1, no. 43).

7 *LAP* lists works on the written arts from the tenth century (pp. 47–51). Faral provides comparative concordances of lists of rhetorical features occurring in the most well known of the prescriptive treatises – including the three listed above – derived from (pseudo-Ciceronian) *Rhetorica ad Herennium*, figures of diction, of tropes, and of figures of thought (pp. 52–54). Faral also synopsizes the contents of each treatise. The works of the three, Matthew of Vendôme, Geoffrey of Vinsauf, and John of Garland, are compared in respect of their teachings (pp. 58–98). A brief synopsis is provided in the present chapter of the salient features of *Ars Versificatoria* (Matthew of Vendôme), *Poetria Nova* (Geoffrey of Vinsauf), and *Parisiana Poetria* (John of Garland), giving a roughly sketched background for material that is too wide in scope to be discussed in any detail here.

8 The details of Matthew of Vendôme's life outlined here are taken from *LAP*, pp. 3–12.

9 *LAP*, p. 2, n. 3.

10 E. Faral edited the copy of *Ars Versificatoria* found in Glasgow, Hunterian Museum 511 (Faral, 'Le manuscrit du "Hunterian Museum" de Glasgow', *Studi Medievali* a. 9. 2ª serie [1936], pp. 18–119). R. P. Parr's translation is based on the text printed in *LAP*. The synopsis following is based on both of those published texts.

11 This follows the translation by Parr (*AV*).

12 *AV*, pp. 8–9. Matthew of Vendôme clearly attacked an individual identifed as Arnulf/Rufinus in the *Ars Versificatoria*. The fame or infamy of the controversy was referred to by Eberhard the German in his *Laborintus* in the following century (*AV*, p. 8).

13 The sense of a pool of known texts and of a community of scholars is palpable from poets such as Hugh Primas. In his poem about the Cathedral School at Reims, he summarized the 'rules' of literary gamesmanship, contrasting the virtue of sacred learning with the vanities of secular – probably not in earnest – thus:

> Here's [*sic*] there's no Platonic teaching:
> one true God is all the preaching.
> All that's here is true religion.
> *But in the schools of disputation*
> *there is argument and discord;*
> *some have strayed and some are scattered;*
> *what some state the others counter;*
> *someone's vanquished, someone's victor;*
> *all's refuted by the teacher.*

F. Adcock, *Hugh Primas and the Archpoet* (Cambridge, 1994), pp. 46–47, ll. 50–64; emphasis added.

14 *LAP*, §60, 'Reminder' notes to the teacher/reader that the use of individual 'known' names are as *aides-mémoires*;

> So, to keep the special name from outweighing
> the other individuals of the same circumstance,

age, dignity, office or sex, let what is said about the Supreme Pontiff, Caesar or other individuals who follow, be understood as attributed so that the special name, taking the place of the general name, calls to mind what is relevant. . . . For these proper names take the place of general names (*LAP*, §§ 60–61, p. 132; *AV*, p. 40).

See also M. Camille, *The Medieval Art of Love*, commenting on a rubricated drawing of the children of Venus in a German manuscript (*c.* 1500) (p. 87):

The hot-blooded redness that suffuses this whole drawing of the children of Venus is the most potent pictorial marker of sexual license, visible on the faces of all Venus's ruddy children.

Matthew of Vendôme, similarly, continually emphasizes the redness, ruddiness of skin, hair, eyes, of this Arnulf/Rufinus as a signifier of his vicious and concupiscent nature. The sobriquet Rufinus, itself, rhetoricizes the relation with this putative rival/enemy, Arnulf. The use of elements of this given name 'ruf' also signifies a literary play rather than an actual state of affairs. See also a poem attributed to Hugh Primas in which a certain 'red-haired' person [*rufus erat*] is accused of taking unfair advantage of the poet; the red one is thought to be Arnulf of Orléans (F. Adcock, *Hugh Primas and the Archpoet* [Cambridge, 1994], pp. 3, 62). The sense of a pool of known texts and of a community of scholars is palpable from poets such as Hugh Primas.

15 *AV*, §53, pp. 33–35.

16 See above, n. 14, where red, rubicundity and Rufinus are all linked in lasciviousness; Thais too is red and wanton.

17 W. M. Purcell, in *Ars Poetriae: Rhetorical and Grammatical Invention at the Margin of Literacy* (Columbia, South Carolina Press, 1996), notes (p. 6) the devolution (or evolution) of the originally

oratorical arts into the technical drill of writing and composition in the schools' curriculum:

> The *artes poetriae* are intended to instruct students in the composition of prose and poetry, not oratory. Their techniques center on the reworking of existing themes and stories rather than creating original orations that respond to particular circumstances. Many of the techniques used to rework those themes, however, did originate in classical rhetorical theory. Classical rhetoric may therefore be aptly utilized in understanding the doctrine found in *ars poetriae*, but only if the differences that this theory brings to this type of written composition are recognized.

18 See ch. 7, n. 16 and ff.

19 A comprehensive synopsis of the contents of the manual is found in *LAP*, pp. 106–108. It is not proposed to go through the entire manual here, but to give a sense of the contents and to concentrate on matters that have a bearing on the modes and methods evident in bardic poetry.

20 In §73, Matthew suggests that 'the main exercise of poetic talent consists of descriptive skill . . .' (*AV*, p. 42).

21 *LAP*, p. 118; *AV*, p. 27.

22 *LAP*, §74, p. 135; *AV*, p. 43.

23 '*Tabhrum an Cháisg ar Chathal*', a poem attributed to the thirteenth-century Muireadhach Albanach Ó Dálaigh, addresses the king of Connacht, Cathal Ó Conchubhair (d. 1224) in respect of his supposedly 'red' (lit. purple) hand. The '*corcra*' in this case is distinct from the ruddiness of Venus (see above, n. 14) and probably refers to some birthmark or has a figurative meaning of 'noble'. In the poem it is used (i) as a vehicle to create a contrast between his delicate white skin and the crimson arm with which he was born; (ii) to carry a sustained discussion of the skill of this hand at shooting; and (iii) to permit the use of many kinds of colour in the poem. (*IBP*, pp. 104–107).

24 *LAP*, I §§83–106, pp. 137–146; *AV*, pp. 46–54.

25 Irish literary tradition is familiar with triads; *trefhocal* itself (the 'three words' – in the context of the *Auraicept* – a series of metrical mnemonic stanzas explaining the metrical and rhetorical rules for the student); and see F. Kelly, 'Thinking in Threes: The Triad in Early Irish Literature'. [Sir John Rhŷs Memorial Lecture] *Proceedings of the British Academy* 125 (2003), pp. 1–18.

26 'Listener' in this context refers to the student hearing the lecture.

27 *LAP*, III §1, p. 167; *AV*, p. 79.

28 Whether the teacher should, or should not, use examples of his own invention was another source of controversy. *Irish Grammatical Tracts* illustrated points with couplets and quatrains from known and esteemed masters. See D. McManus, 'The Irish Grammatical and Syntactical Tracts: A Concordance of Duplicated and Identified Citations', *Ériu* 48 (1997), pp. 165–187; and idem, 'Varia IV, IGT Citations and Duplice Entries: Some Additional Identifications', *Ériu* 51 (2000), pp. 193–194.

29 *LAP*, III §18, p. 172, §§18–44, pp. 172–177, §45, p. 177; *AV*, p. 84, pp. 84–90; again, under their Greek or Latin terms, *LAP*, III §47, p. 178; *AV*, p. 91.

30 *LAP*, IV §1 p. 180.

31 *IGT*, V (Met. Faults), p. 259, n. 3. See L. McKenna, *BST*.

32 *LAP*, IV §5, p. 181; IV §§10–12, p. 181–182; IV §12, pp. 182–183; *AV*, IV, pp. 94–96.

33 In G. Calder, *Auraicept*, avoidance of error is metaphorically dealt with by the concepts of defence and protection against errors in writing and grammar – *slacht* and *dídean* – ll. 1944, 1963, 1978; *sciath* and *anacal* – ll. 2043–2044. These occur in the section concerning '*trefhocal*' – a series of metrical mnemonic stanzas explaining the metrical and rhetorical rules for the student.

34 Matthew's examples come from Avianus, Statius, Ovid, Lucan (*AV*, p. 105).

35 See J. J. Murphy, *TMRA*, pp. 29–31. Faral notes as follows: '. . . *il est certain que la* Poetria Nova, *oeuvre authentique de Geoffroi de*

Vinsauf, a été composée sous le pontificat d'Innocent III . . . Ce que nous pouvons connaître avec certitude de la date et des circonstances de la vie de Geoffroi de Vinsauf . . . et c'est ceci: qu'il était Anglais, qu'il vint à Rome et qu'il composa son poème aux environs de l'année 1210' (LAP, p. 16).

36 Faral refers to Geoffrey as *'Anglais'*. The fluidity of identity between Normans and Anglo-Normans at this time, especially while French remained the vernacular of the Normans in England, may account for the vagueness about Geoffrey's nationality. For the purposes of composition, Matthew of Vendôme, teaching the elements of description, noted the salient attributes in respect of race and nation: 'Extrinsic attributes, however, are divided into those which are derived from one's race, fatherland, age, kindred or sex. There is a difference, however, between one's fatherland and race, because one's race is determined according to origin of its language; one's fatherland, according to its original locality' (*LAP*, I §82, pp. 136–137; *AV*, I §82, p. 44). See J. Gillingham, 'The English Invasion of Ireland', in B. Bradshaw, A. Hadfield and W. Maley, eds., *Representing Ireland: Literature and the Origins of Conflict, 1534–1660* (Cambridge, 1993), pp. 24–42, where he argues, convincingly, for the supplanting of the terms 'Norman', 'Anglo-Norman' and 'Cambro-Norman' with the term 'English', which, he claims, was the contemporary choice. The term 'English' was not chosen in the discussion presented here, because to do so would (it was feared) cause inappropriate confusion between the term for the language with the term for the people.

37 *TMRA*, p. 30.

38 The edition and translation of Horace used in this work is that of H. R. Fairclough, *Horace: Satires, Epistles and Ars Poetica*. The immediate source of any reference is not necessarily discernible in the case of mediaeval writers. See S. A. Barney, et al., *The Etymologies of Isidore* (Cambridge, 2006), pp. 10–14. Barney

notes the 'complacently derivative' character of Isidore's compendium, and comments on the impossibility of knowing – for the most part – whether Isidore's sources and references are first-hand or otherwise. Isidore addressed the matters of grammar, tropes, schemes and rhetorics of writing and many other matters, and was hugely available and popular from the seventh to the sixteenth centuries. Relevant for our purposes is the fact that the earliest dissemination of Isidore, outside of Seville and Saragossa, seems to have been in 'Gaul and Ireland' (p. 24), and that the earliest MS fragments (of the *Etymologies*) are in the Irish foundation of St Gall.

39 The *Rhetorica ad Herennium* (hereafter *AdHer*) summed up its treatise on figures as follows:

> Indeed I have shown how in every type of cause one ought to find ideas (*invenire oporteat*). I have told how it is proper to arrange these. I have disclosed the method of delivery. I have taught how we can have a good memory. I have explained the means by which to secure a finished style. If we follow these principles, our Invention will be keen and prompt, our Arrangement clear and orderly, our Delivery impressive and graceful, our Memory sure and lasting, our Style brilliant and charming. In the art of rhetoric, then, there is no more. All these faculties we shall attain if we supplement the precepts of theory with diligent practice (*AdHer*, §59 [68], p. 410).

There is no need to note here how much in debt the mediaeval manuals were to this first-century treatise. A consise summary of the most well-known mediaeval writers and works is available in Barney, et al., *Etymologies of Isidore*, pp. 10–17.

40 The edition and translation of Cicero used in this work is that of H. Caplan, *AdHer*.

41 *TMRA*, p. 31; and see R. W. Mathisen, 'Epistolography, Literary Circles and Familiy Ties in Late Roman Gaul', *Transactions of*

the American Philological Association III (1981), pp. 95–109, which provides further context for the correspondence of Sidonius Apollinaris.

42 Geoffrey of Vinsauf's *Poetria Nova* is translated by Jane Baltzell Kopp in *TMRA*, pp. 32–108. Baltzell Kopp's translation of Geoffrey's text will be referred to hereafter as *PN*. The text is a version in English of the Latin published in *LAP*, pp. 197–262. References to both follow.

43 The death of Pope Innocent III is noted in the Annals of Inisfallen, *s.a.* 1216.3: *Obitus domini Innocentii Pape*; as is the death of Pope Honorius 1226.2; of Pope Gregory 1241.2; and the general council called by Pope Clement V in France, to which the bishops of Cashel, Killaloe, Lismore, Emly and Cloyne were invited in person (*ad quod personaliter fuerunt citati . .*) and to which they neither went, nor sent proxies, out of fear (*propter timendum quod eisdem eueniet inconueniens . . .*).

44 *TMRA*, p. 43, n. 27. The lists of rhetorical devices, figures of thought and diction are too long and repetitive to be reproduced in any comprehensive way in this study. It should be noted, also, that definitions can be mutually contradictory or dublicative. A useful list from the pseudo-Ciceronian *Rhetorica ad Herennium* (*c.* 85 BC – sometimes attributed to Cornificius (E. R. Curtius, *European Literature and the Latin Middle Ages*, transl. from German by W. R. Trask [London, 1953], p. 66) – is to be found as an appendix in *RMA*, pp. 365–374. A contemporary list with illustrations is found in John of Garland, *Parisiana Poetria* (*PP*, pp. III–135). A more recent description and analysis of the manual and of the figures is found in W. M. Purcell, *Ars Poetriae: Rhetorical and Grammatical Invention at the Margin of Literacy*. See also Barney, et al., *Etymologies of Isidore*, pp. 55–88.

45 Taking an extreme view of the subject, P. Valesio (in *Novantiqua: Rhetorics as a Contemporary Theory* [Indiana University Press, 1980], pp. 21–22) makes the following declaration:

Thus in any form of behavior involving human language . . . it is never a question – or at least, never

primarily and directly a question – of pointing to ref-
erents in the 'real' world, of distinguishing true from
false, right from wrong, beautiful from ugly and so
forth. The choice is only between what mechanisms to
employ, and these mechanisms already condition every
discourse since they are simplified representations of
reality, inevitably and intrinsically slanted in a partisan
direction. These mechanisms always appear (so much
more convincingly if the discourse is more polished and
well organized) to be gnoseological, but in reality they
are *eristic*: they give a positive or a negative connota-
tion to the image of the entity they describe in the very
moment in which they start describing it.

In fact, Valesio is repeating what Matthew and Geoffrey are
teaching in their treatises: the art itself, born of disputation and
persuasion, inherits the eristic habits of its origin, and is put to
service as formulaic, formalized mode of address, description,
and so forth.

46 Geoffrey is quite graphic in his use of the metaphor of the path
of the arts:

Arrangement's road is forked: on the one hand, it may
labour up the footpath of art; on the other, it may follow
nature's main street. . . .
More sophisticated than natural order is artistic
order, and far preferable, however much permuted
the arrangement may be. . . . Now in the area of
this technique may seem to be *dark*, the path rugged,
the *doors* closed, *the problem knotty* . . . . There will
be found the means by which you may cleanse the
shadow from the light, the *foot* on which you may
traverse the rugged ground, the *key* with which you
may open the doors, the finger with which you may
loose the *knots* . . . (*PN*, p. 36; emphasis added).

47 In the realm of the visual arts, M. Camille's analysis of the iconography of love emphasizes the degree of obliquity in the relation of the art to reality (*The Medieval Art of Love*, p. 59 and passim).

48 Not all the surviving manuscript material concerning metrical tracts and matters dealing with prosody are published, but among the most significant published editions are: *Auraicept na n-Éces, Bardic Syntactical Tracts, Irish Grammatical Tracts, Mittelirische Verslehren*, and *Uraicecht na Ríar: The Poetic Grades in Early Irish Law*.

49 Extant compositions by Gofraidh Mac an Bhaird, Fear Feasa Ó'n Cháinte and Eochaidh Ó hEoghusa (see pp. 183ff.), disputing the relative merits of their respective compositions, hint at the existence of an established terminology covering matters of style and composition, along with those concerned with metrical and linguistic matters alone (and with the, seemingly, related matters of status and reward).

50 That mediaeval Irish literary schools followed a long and strict curriculum there can be no doubt. Some (parts) of their manuals of instruction on language and metrics are extant, but comparable texts on style and content, if they ever existed, would not appear to have survived. The central hypothesis of the present work is that the curriculum did include formal instruction on content and that that instruction was to a considerable degree influenced by the literary teaching that was part of the common Western European heritage of the Middle Ages, and which has been formalized in the works of Matthew of Vendôme, Geoffrey of Vinsauf and others. The hypothesis will be tested against postulated manifestations of the influence of such teachings on Irish compositions. P. A. Breatnach suggests a limited evidence for such influence (see above, p. 13) and indeed, points to evidence of it in a seventeenth-century work. In a study of literary imitation 'Traidisiún na hAithrise Liteartha', P. A. Breatnach (in *Téamaí Taighde*, pp. 1–63), citing examples of poetic imitation in identical first lines, in close imitations, in echoing, and in pastiche, queries whether Irish

poets whose teaching, he suggests, unlike that offered in the continental *artes poetriae* – as far as surviving manuscripts show – covered only matters of language and metre, were taught to imitate other poets. It is suggested here that the entire corpus displays characteristics emanating from a sensibility and training very close to that taught in continental and British schools, and that it did involve conscious imitation of masters. See also, D. Dilts Swartz, 'Unwise and Unlovable', *Proceedings of the Harvard Celtic Colloquium* 5 (1985), pp. 128–144.

51 Students attached themselves to masters rather than to institutions in the period when the schools flourished and before they became structured as universities.

52 *Arrmainti*: for *arrumainte/i*, a variant of *argumaint(e/i)* 'argument', is a borrowing of the Latin *argumentum* (see *DIL*, s.v. *argam[a]int*). M. Ó Murchú outlined this lexical development for me.

53 Cf. E. Poppe, 'Reconstructing Medieval Irish Literary Theory: The Lesson of *Airec Menman Uraird maic Coise*', *Cambrian Medieval Celtic Studies* 37 (1999), pp. 33–54 on *scél, fabula* and *historia*.

54 '*An stair imorro foillsiugad na nethedh do reir firinne do-rinnedh . . .*', in B. Ó Cuív, '*Scél: Arramainte: Stair*', *Éigse* 11 (1964–1966), p. 18. B. Ó Cuív associates the Irish extract with Macrobius, (*fl.* 399–422), possibly from his *Saturnalia*. It is likely, in the Irish Christian context, that the source is the reflex of Macrobius in Isidore's *Etymologia*, rather than from the pagan Macrobius directly. From Isidore's *Etymologia*, E. R. Curtius synopsizes:

> History relates real events; fables tell of things which never happened and never could happen because they are contrary to nature. Between the two there is an intermediate genre: a report of things which are possible even if they did not happen. Isidore calls this genre *argumenta* (E. R. Curtius, *European Literature and the Latin Middle Ages*, p. 452).

55 Lists of 'required reading', of tales, for instance, which were compulsory elements in the students curriculum exist. See P. Mac Cana, *The Learned Tales of Medieval Ireland* (Dublin, 1980), pp. 7–19, 41–65 and passim.

56 'Perhaps the most important thing to say of both John's *Poetria* and all three of Geoffrey's works is that they represent what was being taught in Paris at the end of the twelfth century and well into the thirteenth' (T. Lawler, *PP*, p. 328).

57 *LAP*, pp. 263–320. The *Documentum* is a prose treatise, covering material dealt with in the *Poetria Nova*. It is an *attribution probable* of Geoffrey's, according to Faral (ibid., pp. 23–24). See also Appendix Two, in *PP*, pp. 327–332, for extracts from a manuscript version of the *Documentum* which is somewhat longer than that published in Faral.

58 *PP*, p. xi. Irish students frequented Oxford and Cambridge from the twelfth and thirteenth centuries, as they did the other mediaeval universities. They were expelled briefly from Oxford in 1252 and in 1267 for rioting (*NHIviii, s.a.*). On the other hand, members of the ecclesiatical Ó Gráda family took degrees in canon law at Oxford in successive generations in the fourteenth century, and this was not exceptional or remarkable (J. A. Watt, 'Gaelic Polity and Cultural Identity', *NHIii*, p. 338). And see A. B. Emden, *A Biographical Register of the University of Oxford to AD 1500*, 3 vols (Oxford, [1957] 1989), passim.

59 A 'poetic academy' was said to exist at Toulouse in the fourteenth century, where the publication of *Leys d'Amors* classified the distinctions between *canso* and *vers*, classifications that had been understood from the twelfth and thirteenth centuries. (V. Law notes that the *Leys d'Amors* was a cumulative work, entrusted to Guilhem Molinier, 'appearing in several versions between 1332 and 1356' (V. Law, *The History of Linguistics in Europe from Plato to 1600* [Cambridge, 2003], p. 202). It may be significant that John of Garland taught in that city in the early thirteenth century, where a tradition of poetry in the vernacular was strong

and where the sense of an academy of poetry subsisted. See ch. 5, n. 28; and see V. Law, *The History of Linguistics*, pp. 201–204.

60 *PP*, pp. xi–xii. Lawler cites L. J. Paetow (ed. and transl. *Two Medieval Satires on the University of Paris: 'La Bataille des VII ars' of Henri d'Andeli and the 'Morale scolarium' of John of Garland* [Memoirs of the University of California] vol. 4, nos. 1 and 2. [Berkeley, 1927]) as his source for the details of John of Garland's life. The information on John of Garland presented here is based on Lawler's publication. The references that follow from *PP*, are by page, by chapter and by line according to the context.

61 J. J. Murphy suggests that John failed in his attempt to provide a comprehensive collation of all the prosodic, metrical and rhetorical material commonly available to the student/poet at the time:

> The chronology of this preceptive movement is interesting. It begins, rather hesitantly, with Matthew of Vendôme about 1175, reaches a peak – its most 'rhetorical' stage – with Gervase of Melkley and Geoffrey of Vinsauf around 1210, begins to falter with the abortive attempt at collation by John of Garland two decades later, and sputters out almost cynically shortly after mid-century with Eberhard the German (*RMA*, pp. 161–62).

See *LAP*, pp. 336–377, for an edition of Eberhard's *Laborintus* (*c.* 1280).

62 See D. Luscombe, *Medieval Thought* (Oxford, 1997), pp. 61–133, for discussion of the break-up of the mediaeval scholastic consensus.

63 *PP*, p. 230, n. 75; pp. 242–243; p. 247, nn. 314–318.

64 *PP*, p. xvi.

65 The influence of the schools of Orléans and the University of Paris is emphasized by Faral, who notes that the three authors of the treatises dealt with here (and Eberhard the German) attended the schools of Paris (University of Paris) and, in the case of Matthew, (the schools of) Orléans as well as Paris:

Il est notable que la plupart des auteurs d'arts poétiques les aient fréquentées. Matthieu de Vendôme a étudié et enseigné à Orléans, puis à Paris; Geoffroi de Vinsauf à Paris; Évrard l'Allemand à Paris, puis à l'Orléans; Jean de Garlande à Paris (LAP, pp. 99–103; p. 101).

See B. Ó Cuív, 'An Appeal on Behalf of the Profession of Poetry', *Éigse* 14 (1971–1972), pp. 86–106 ('*Damhnaidh dúind cóir, a chléirche*'), where reference is made to the University of Paris as arbitrator in matters concerning the poet at the time. Irish students participated in the ferment of activity of the French schools, see P. Ó Néill, 'An Irishman at Chartres', *Ériu* 48 (1997), pp. 1–35; and see above, p. 9.

66 Mediaeval Irish writers used the Ciceronian division – originally used for oratorical matters and performance – of place, time, occasion, manner and facilities. The subdivisions of the characteristics of argument, had become – by the Middle Ages – a formula of beginning.

67 'Tragedy' and 'comedy' in this context meant works by poets dealing respectively with grave matter and 'low ' matter – meaning material suitable for the 'low' style.

68 Cf. G. Calder, *Auraicept*, pp. 56, 146.

69 Different lists are given in the treatise in chapter 4 and in chapter 6; these seem merely to give a hint of what is meant in using them.

70 *PP*, pp. 235–236.

71 This chapter (in *PP*) is very much based on material found in Geoffrey of Vinsauf's *Documentum* (*PP*, p. 241, n. 4; p. 246, nn. 286–288). In this treatise, the theory of beginnings refers specifically to narrative poetry (p. 241, n. 12), but the 'narrative' can be at the service of a number of different styles, including elegy, encomium and so forth.

72 The distinction of this chapter is an editorial decision of Lawler – 'There is no indication in the text of the beginning of Chapter Four, but I have begun it here in accordance with the plan announced at the beginning . . . ' (*PP*, p. 242).

73 *dictamen* embraced *epistola* and *littere* (*PP,* p. 253, n. 265).

74 *PP,* p. 243, nn. 10–13. See M. O Riordan, 'A Poet on Horseback? The Mediaeval *Ars Poetica* and the Bardic Poem', in J. Carey, M. Herbert, K. Murray, eds., *Cín Chille Cúile: Texts, Saints and Places. Essays in Honour of Pádraig Ó Riain* (Cork, 2004), pp. 354–366.

75 This secluded place is the barricaded cell of the bardic poet. Whether or not it involved a physical sequestration is not a matter that can be proved conclusively either way. It is certain that the figurative seclusion indicated here was practised. References to physical isolation are probably to be read as figurative. This kind of seclusion is discussed in more detail below.

76 The threefold division envisaged is like that also discussed in L. Breatnach, 'The "Caldron of Poesy"', *Ériu* 32 (1981), pp. 45–93; and in P. L. Henry, 'The Caldron of Poesy', *Studia Celtica* 14–15 (1979–1980), pp. 114–128; p. 121. John of Garland's expansion on the 'meaning' of 'style' is relevant:

> Notice, by the way, that 'style' is used metaphorically. For a style is the middle section of a column, on which rests the epistyle, and whose lower section is called the base. 'Style', then, in this sense is 'the poetic quality', or an 'uprightness' preserved throughout the body of the matter. Sometimes it means the poem itself. Style means the office of a poet . . . . Finally, style means the pen we write with. [*Item notandum quod 'stilus' dicitur transumptiue. Est enim stilus medietas columpne, cui supponitur epistilium, cuius inferior pars dicitur basis. Est ergo, 'stilus' in hoc loco, 'qualitas carminis' uel 'rectitudo' seruata per corpus materie. Stilus dicitur aliquando carmen ipsum. Stilus dicitur officium poete, . . . Stilus etiam dicitur graphium quo scribimus.*] (*PP,* p. 88 5, ll. 86–93)

Cf. L. Breatnach, ibid., where the cauldrons of 'poetry and learning' (p. 52) – though of a much earlier date (ninth century) –

seem to have some of the sense of John's discussion of the *stilus*. The 'uprightness' [*rectitudo*] of the *stilus* recalls the *uas toíb* of the cauldron (ibid., p. 62, l. 8) with possible parallels for the contents of each cauldron in the division into columns of John's schema (*secundum Tullium* 'following Cicero') (*PP,* pp. 36–38, 2, ll. 90–115).

77 *PP*, p. 41 [fig. 4].

78 'A History reports an event which has taken place long before the memory of our age' (*PP* 5, ll. 321–22).

79 The *Parisiana Poetria* supplies examples of many types of formal writing, including that of a letter from a pope to an emperor; a call to Crusade; a summons to an ecclesiastical court (*PP,* 7, ll. 1–246). General rules (*generalis doctrina*) about the drafting of other kinds of documents – grants, charters, manumissions and so forth – are outlined. John of Garland notes how different courts have different preferences in respect of the conventions of presentation and drafting: 'A court secretary . . . should keep custom in mind, since various courts have various customs; and preference, since frequently enough a secretary must abandon his accustomed style if his master prefers another (*Notarius . . . consuetudo, quia diuerse curie diuersas habent consuetudines; voluntas, quia pro voluntate domini sepius mutat stilum consuetum notarius*)'. Examples of deeds, indentures, summonses and similar forms follow (*PP,* 7, ll. 255–258; ll. 258–383). This group also includes petitions and formulae for such incidentals as a letter on the granting of ordination (ll. 455–465); for a convert to Catholicism (ll. 434–448); the grant of an indulgence (ll. 449–454).

NOTES TO CHAPTER THREE, PP. 57–105

1 *DD*, pp. 352–355, '*Mairg chaitheas dlús re dhalta*'.

2 *AithDD*, p. xxxii.

3 In a poem attributed to Gofraidh Mac an Bhaird in the late sixteenth century, '*Cuimhnigh, a Mháire, an cunnradh do*

cheanglabhar', a certain Gofraidh Fionn (Ó Dálaigh?) is referred
to in the following terms:

> . . . *Gofraidh Fionn fáidh ar dtreibheine*
> *seinfhile do-cháidh ós chionn gach sgolaidhe*
> (*AithDD* i, p. 76, no. 19, q. 6)

[Gofraidh Fionn, the sage of our tribe, an old poet
who surpassed every scholar]

A Gofraidh Fionn (Ó Dálaigh?) is listed, for instance, in the late
sixteenth-century poem by Fear Flatha Ó Gnímh, '*Cuimseach sin,*
a Fhearghail Óig', q. 7:

> *Ní gluaisti le Gothfroidh Fionn*
> *dán ar nach dénadh dítheall;*
> *re blaosgach do bhiadh folamh*
> *riamh dob aonsgoth ealadhan.*
> (*IBP*, p. 119)

[Gofraidh Fionn proceeded with no poem on
which he did not expend effort; he was always the
very flower of art, (even) with regard to an empty shell.]

See E. Knott and G. Murphy, *Early Irish Literature* (London,
1966), p. 76. The same metaphor of the empty shell, the fruitless
nut (*(gan) chnaoi ccaoich* . . .), is used in praise of the work of
Aodh Ruadh Ó Dálaigh (d. 1420) q. 4; and cf. P. A. Breatnach,
'Moladh na Féile' (in *Téamaí Taighde*), p. 104, n. 21.

4 L. Mac Cionnaith, *DD*, pp. 228–235, '*Beir eolas dúinn, a*
Dhomhnuill'.

5 The edition of Gofraidh Fionn's poem, '*Beir eolas dúinn, a*
Dhomhnuill' used here is that published in *DD*, p. 228–235, no.
74. An earlier edition of the poem appeared in L. McKenna,
GFOD. The metre, which will not be discussed here, is
deibhidhe; see E. Knott, *Irish Syllabic Poetry* (Cork, 1928), pp.
18–20.

6 L. McKenna identifies that Domhnall who is addressed as Mág
Carthaigh of Clár Gaillimhe in quatrain 69, as 'Domhnall Glas',
lord of Cairbre (*GFOD*, p. 341). The conservative form Mac

Carthaigh, rather than the later Mac Cárthaigh, is chosen in this study as that generally seemingly chosen by Gofraidh Fionn.

7 K. W. Nicholls, 'The Development of Lordship in County Cork, 1300–1600', in P. O'Flanagan, and C. G. Buttimer, eds., *Cork History and Society: Interdisciplinary Essays on the History of an Irish County* (Dublin, 1993), pp. 156–211; p. 159. Nicholls's chapter is the most comprehensive recent account of the emergence of strong local lordships in the former kingdom of Desmond.

8 See Annals of Inisfallen, *s.a.* 1390:

> *Donall Og ma Carraig, .i. a macsomh, .xxxi. annis regnauit, agus ni thanig a comhaimsir ris fein () Gall na Gaegheal dob fearr dealbh na daenacht, na ba treise na b'()rca eneach agus eangnamh, na dob fhearr a icht agus firine ina aimser fein. Mortuus est a Caslen Locha Lein agus a anocudh annsa Manister ceadna air buaidh atrige agus crabaid; agus ni raibh annson aimser echt a commor sin.*

Domhnall had succeeded his father Cormac Mac Carthaigh who died in 1359 after a 34-year reign – his reign was to last 31 years. The two reigns together covered well over half a century. Cormac Mac Carthaigh came to power in the aftermath of the wars of Edward Bruce in Ireland (1315–1318) and in succession to his brother Diarmuid, who was killed in 1325 by Nicholas FitzMaurice and by the son of the bishop of Ardfert, among others, at an assize court being held in the monastery of Tralee (Annals of Inisfallen, *s.a.* 1325/1328 [1320].2, p. 434).

9 K. Nicholls, *Gaelic and Gaelicized Ireland in the Middle Ages* (Dublin, 2003), pp. 25, 189.

10 See M. T. Flanagan, *Irish Royal Charters*, pp. 185–186, for the donation by Ó Briain and the subsequent endowment of the Romanesque chapel there, Cormac's Chapel, by Cormac Mac Carthaigh in 1134. The description of mediaeval Cashel following is based mainly on J. Bradley, 1985, 'The Medieval Towns of Tipperary', in W. Nolan and T. G. McGrath, eds., *Tipperary: History and Society* (Dublin, 1985), pp. 34–59; esp. pp. 42–45.

11 The Eoghanacht dynasties were theoretically derived from the eponymous Eoghan Mór (or from his grandfather Mugh Nuadhat), but literary sources usually favoured the mythical saga which gave the Eoghanacht their origins in the descendants of Conall Corc, the prince who 'discovered' Cashel in the fifth century, see F. J. Byrne, *Irish Kings and High-Kings* (Dublin, [1973] 2001), p. 177.

12 *The Annals of Tigernach*, vol. 2, transl. W. Stokes. [Reprinted from *Revue Celtique* 1896–1897] (Llanerch, 1993), *s.a.* 1134: '*Uball a mbiad mir duine samail gach cloiche agus si trebennach, cor'bo snam dona heachaib ar margadh Chaisil . . .*' (p. [150] 364).

13 J. Bradley, 'The Medieval Towns of Tipperary', p. 35.

14 P. Connelly, *Irish Exchequer Payments 1270–1446* ii, (Dublin, 1998), pp. 427–467.

15 J. Bradley, 'The Medieval Towns of Tipperary', pp. 44–45.

16 Further details are in C. A. Empey, 'The Norman Period: 1185–1500', in W. Nolan and T. G. McGrath, eds., *Tipperary: History and Society*, pp. 71–91; p. 75. See and cf. M. Potterton, *Medieval Trim: History and Archaeology* (Dublin, 2005) for a comprehensive and comparable account of Trim in the same period.

17 K. Nicholls, 'The Development of Lordship in County Cork', p. 164.

18 The poem '*Mór ar bfearg riot a rí Saxan*' (60 qq.) was written by Gofraidh Fionn for Maurice fitzMaurice (Maurice fitz Thomas, the first earl), the second earl of Desmond (d. 1356), older brother of Gearóid/Gerald the third earl (*IBP*, pp. 73–81). See other poems by Gofraidh Fionn for contemporary notables published in *GFOD*, and see *AithDD*, i, p. xxxii, for lists of other lords for whom Gofraidh Fionn wrote poems.

19 *GFOD*, pp. 509–514.

20 A site which is said, according to folklore, to be haunted by him every seventh year.

21 See, for instance, *Irish Royal Charters* (chapter 1, n. 36, above), for the traditional links between the Mac Carthaighs and the Empire.

22 In the Annals of Inisfallen (*s.a.* 1217.2), note, for example: '*Rí Saxan d'eag agus mac ri Frangc do thidacht a Saxanaib*' [The king of England (Jean sans Terre/John Lackland d. 1216) died and the son of the king of France came to England (Louis)].

23 F. X. Martin's apt formulation expresses the interrelationships: '. . . Ireland, a separate realm under its own King John [John, lord of Ireland], within the Angevin "empire" of federated statelets, Normandy and Anjou, Aquitaine, Brittany, in association with Scotland and the Welsh territories, all in a family consortium under a patriarchal Angevin king of England. . . . The significance of John's expedition in 1185, as part of a plan to make him king of Ireland, will be appreciated only if we continue to see Ireland in the context of the Angevin "empire". Likewise, it is only in that same context that we can make sense of the activities and ambitions of Norman lords who held lands in France, England, Wales, and Ireland . . .' (F. X. Martin, 'Overlord becomes Feudal Lord, 1172–85', in *NHIii*, p. 126). And see J. Watt, 'The Anglo-Irish Colony under Strain', in ibid., p. 376, who notes Irish troops in Scotland (1335), Calais (1346) and Rouen (1419).

24 *DD*, p. 453, L. McKenna states cautiously, *agus é 'n-a aois leinbh* [while he was still a child]; cf. ch. 3, n. 18, above.

25 A curious echo(?) of this formulation *dhá chineadh*/'two races': *duo sunt in Momonia . . .*/'there are two in Munster', occurs in a speech that was cited in a case of defamation brought by James, earl of Ormond, against Richard Wye, bishop of Cloyne, in 1380. The bishop had substituted the usual preface of the mass with a statement of his own: . . . *duo sunt in Momonia qui destruunt nos et bona nostra viz. Comes Ermonia et Dessemonie cum eorum sequacibus quos in fine destruet Dominus per Christus dominum nostrum amen.* [. . . there are two in Munster who destroy us and our goods, namely the Earl of Ormond and the Earl of Desmond with their followers, whom in the end the Lord will destroy, through Jesus Christ Our Lord amen.] The earl of Desmond seems not to

have pursued the case, but the earl of Ormond did, resulting in the excommunication of the bishop. The proceedings of the case outlined in surviving documents suggest that a responsive and well-organized system of cathedral court (the cathedral court at Cashel was the scene of the trial though the offence took place in Dublin) justice operated at the time. The sense of this being a parallel universe to that occupied by Domhnall Óg and his poet, engaged in their march on Cashel, is a distortion created by misunderstanding the poetry. In a further document associated with this tale of defamation, William, vicar-general of Emly who conducted the trial, sent his 'praeconis' (herald, crier) to notify others of the excommunication. This herald's name is given as Maynys O'Moyn (E. Curtis, *Ormond Deeds etc.* [London, 1934], pp. 158–182; p. 179). This herald and his master shared the world of Domhnall Mac Carthaigh and Gofraidh Fionn Ó Dálaigh.

26 'Conall Corc son of Lugaid . . . son of Ailill Fland Bec is descended, according to the genealogies, from Éogan Mór, eponymous ancestor of the Éoganacht, and so from Éber son of Míl. He was famous in Irish tradition as the founder of the kingdom of Cashel and of the Éoganacht dynasty' (M. Dillon, 'The Story of the Finding of Cashel', *Ériu* 16 [1952], pp. 61–73; p. 61).

27 The numbers here are representative and are not to be taken literally. The resonance of Latin *centurion* is to be noted in the formulaic *taoiseach céid*. More relevant for our purposes here is the echo of the mediaeval tale *Cathréim Chellacháin Chaisil*. D. Ó Corráin, in '*Caithréim Chellacháin Caisil*: History or Propaganda?' (*Ériu* 25 [1974], pp. 1–69), dates the tale to sometime in the early to mid-twelfth century:

> I feel it can be ascribed more exactly to the years from 1127 to 1134 when Cormac Mac Cárthaig was consensus king of Munster.

The 'historical romance' (ibid., p. 1) is a ghostly presence behind Gofraidh Fionn's poem for Domhnall Mac Carthaigh. The text of *Caithréim Cellacháin Caisil* referred to in this study is that provided as an electronic text (G100030) by *CELT: Corpus of Electronic Texts: A Project of University College Cork*, based on A. Bugge, ed., *CCC*. D. Ó Corráin's conclusions as to the nature of the the twelfth-century saga *CCC* (ibid., pp. 63–64), can be referred to in respect of the historical sensibility displayed in Gofraidh Fionn's poem for Domhnall Mac Carthaigh. Ó Corráin specifically links the approach taken by the author of the *Caithréim* to that taken by a bardic poet:

> Firstly, I have no doubt that the author of *CCC* was an Irish secular man of learning who served Meic Carthaig in the same way as the later bardic poets served their patrons and his approach to history is one of a piece with theirs.... There is ... good reason to believe that the writer's purpose was to produce a saga glorifying Cellachán and thus his descendants. The purpose of the exercise is political propaganda and, if such is to be effective, it must be credible in one way or another. Yet the text is full of the wildest chronological errors and the grossest blunders. However, these notions derive from our ideas of history and there is no good reason to believe that they ever crossed the mind of the compiler of *CCC*.

Domhall Mac Carthaigh's journey, as depicted by Gofraidh Fionn, shadows and echoes that of Ceallachán, in many ways, just as it does that of Conall Corc. While the matter will not be discussed in detail here, notice will be taken, from time to time, of matters that seem to derive from *CCC*.

28 *CCC*, §7: '*Is andsin ro eirgheder na vii. tuatha déc gu des-urrlamh do coimrigad Cheallachain. & tucsad a ghairm righ & ro altaigset don fhír-Dhia fhurorda a fhaghail*'. The names of the 'best' of that seventeen follow, and these *flatha* gave their allegiance to Ceallachán. This group of seventeen is referred to as the 'electors' of Ceallachán, in D. Ó Corráin, ibid., p. 62.

29 Ammrai [Amram], father of Moses, is listed among the proper names in *Saltair na Rann*, E. Knott, 'An Index to the Proper Names in *Saltair na Rann*', *Ériu* 16 (1952), p. 104.

30 The archangel with which the Story of the Finding of Cashel was associated was Victor (M. Dillon, 'The Story of the Finding of Cashel', pp. 2–4). Gofraidh Fionn does not exploit this connection in his conclusion, and adheres to his own, presumably, personal favourite, Michael. From a later period, a faded remnant of what must have been an elaborate and vibrant painting of St Michael is to be found in the sixteenth-century Ardamullivan Castle, Co. Galway (a detail of which is published in K. Morton, 'Irish Medieval Wall Painting', in J. Ludlow and N. Jameson, eds., *Medieval Ireland: Barryscourt Lectures I–X* (Cork, 2004), pp. 311–349, pl. 1, p. 312. The sixteenth/seventeenth-century poet Aonghus Ó Dálaigh, concluded many of his compositions with a quatrain of entreaty or of praise to Archangel Michael.

31 E. R. Curtius, *European Literature and the Latin Middle Ages*, p. 69n.

32 *Rhetoric, Hermeneutics, and Translation*, p. 160.

33 F. J. Byrne, *Irish Kings and High-Kings*, pp. 291–298.

34 M. Dillon (in 'The Story of the Finding of Cashel', pp. 62, 63, 68) accepts Conall Corc as a historical character about whose life the sagas and folk-tales related to his name developed.

35 V. Hull, 'Conall Corc and the Kingdom of Cashel', in *Zeitschrift für Celtische Philologie* 18 (1930), pp. 420–421; idem, 'The Exile of Conall Corc', *Proceedings of the Modern Language Association of America* 56 (1941), pp. 937–950; idem, 'Conall Corc and the Corco Luigde', in *Proceedings of the Modern Language Association of America* 62 (1947), pp. 887–909.

36 *Rhetoric, Hermeneutics, and Translation*, p. 160.

37 See D. Ó Corráin, '*Caithréim Chellacháin Chaisil*: History or Propaganda?', pp. 63–64.

38 Gofraidh Fionn Ó Dálaigh made selective choices to suit the requirements of his *inventio*. He 'found' elements in *CCC* and in the adventures of Conall Corc which he exploited. He did

not choose to follow other fertile elements, from, for instance, the stories surrounding the 'Finding of Cashel' (see Byrne, pp. 182–192) including the snow, the twenty-four electors, the swineherds, Lios or Ráth na nUrlann, Aoimheann's birds, the Pictish princess and the Scottish connection, all present in versions of the Conall Corc saga.

39 See E. Knott, *TDall* i, pp. liv–lvii, where she outlines the frequency of metonymic epithets for kings and lords in bardic praise-poems. Knott classifies, in a manner reminiscent of the manuals themselves, the epithets accorded a lord into six groups with subgroups in the following broad categories: (i) warlike; (ii) rank; (iii) metaphorical (including animals and other creatures, mythical and actual);   plant-terms;   natural   phenomena; epithets 'conveying notions of brilliance'; metaphorically significant items reminiscent of power, etc., like *slat* 'wand'; miscellaneous containers of glory or indicators of power (*teach séad* 'treasure-house'); descriptions of the lord's warlike nature; (iv) figurative or metonymical; (v) metonymy of the body; (vi) epithets linked to ancestry. The qualifying adjectives and phrases and contexts of these epithets creates another group of features.

40 The metaphorical device of synecdoche is extremely popular with Irish bardic poets, especially in the device part for the whole (*pars pro toto*), container for contained (see E. Knott, ibid.), and so forth. Its emotional effect is amplified when the synecdochical phrase is in apposition to a vocative. For nominative inflection in the vocative, see O. Bergin, 'Nominative and Vocative', *Ériu* 9 (1921), pp. 92–94.

41 By way of comparison, note the modern usage in a compilation such as *Burke's Peerage* [106th edn, ed. C. Mosely (1999)]. Eleanor Knott has synopsized clearly the use of animal and plant and other metaphors in the service of epithet (*TDall* i, pp. li–lvi).

42 The celebrated ascetic preacher Savonarola, in a sermon noted in 1493, referred to the teaching of the *bottega* – the workshops

and training schools of the painters in fourteenth- and fifteenth-century Italy: '. . . What does a pupil look for in the master? I'll tell you. The master draws from his mind an image which his hands trace on paper and it carries the imprint of his idea. The pupil studies the drawing and tries to imitate it. Little by little, in this way, he appropriates the style of his master' (cited in F. Ames-Lewis, *The Intellectual Life of the Early Renaissance Artist* [New Haven and London, 2000], p. 36).

43 The notion of the poet composing entirely in the dark – some versions have him with a stone on his stomach – and the mysteriously creative process involving rituals with light and memory and secluded huts has become part of the general conception of the Irish bardic poets and their schools and methods of teaching. This study emphasizes the metaphoric nature of many statements made by poets in respect of their learning and practice. It is hoped that the exotic and unscholastic, not to say unscholarly, methods outlined in many descriptions of poets' practice, most notably that put forward by O. Bergin (*IBP*, pp. 5–9), drawing on the Introduction to the *Memoirs of the Marquis of Clanrickard*, and echoed since by every generation of scholars who have examined the poetry, can be shown to be unlikely, to say the least of it. Recent work by D. McManus, 'The Bardic Poet as Teacher, Student and Critic: A Context for the Grammatical Tracts', in C. G. Ó Háinle and D. E. Meek, eds., *Unity in Diversity: Studies in Irish and Scottish Gaelic Language, Literature and History* [Léann na Tríonóide: Trinity Irish Studies I] (Dublin, 2004), pp. 97–123, has enlarged upon and foregrounded the sense of the poet as student, teacher and critic.

44 The following definitions and range of meanings are selected from *DIL*, s.v. *eól*: **I (a)** knowledge (of a person or thing); acquaintance (with person or thing); experience (in); skill; **I (b)** lore, history; **I (c)** that which is known or familiar, esp. of places, accustomed surroundings, home; **(d)** information, direction, guidance; right way; **II** as adjective: knowing, acquainted with, versed in;

éolach: knowing, learned, skilled (in), acquainted with **(b)** esp. knowing, acquainted with a locality (way, place, person etc.); **(c)** hence as subst. a guide; **(d)** known, familiar.

eólas, eulas: *IGT* §38 (a) knowledge, information, esp. knowledge gained by experience or practice . . .; **(b)** experimental proof, experience; **(c)** esp. knowledge of the way (place), guidance; *beirid eólas do*: leads, guides; *Beir eolas dúinn*, guide us, lead us; **(d)** a way, direction, path, opening;

seól: [sail] **(d)** course: **(e)** manner, way, means, expedient;

seólad: **(b)** [act of sailing] course, manner (*trésan seoladh sin*, by this means);

seólad: **(d)** the act of showing the way, guidance; 'The first couplet of a *rann* is called the seoladh'

seólad: (e) the act of directing, training, instructing;

seólaid: sails, steers (as a transitive); **(c)** shows the way, guides **(d)** directs, trains, teaches;

seólaid: (intransitive) (a) sails, advances, proceeds; **(b)** instructs;

seólta: well-directed, educated, skilled.

45 *IGT*, for example, under §§151–159, '*Na samhlaighthe feasda*', lists and declines in every case a select number of nouns to act as examples of usage. Concerning the noun *tuata*, for instance, the exposition results in some twenty-four expressions, of which the noun *tuata* is the head noun.

46 See n. 44, above.

47 F. J. Byrne, *Irish Kings and High-Kings*, p. 174. *Saltair Chaisil*, the Psalter of Cashel, was probably a compilation of historical, pseudo-historical and genealogical material. It was reputedly put together by the archbishop of Cashel, Cormac Mac Cuilleanáin (d. 903), who was also responsible for the encylopaedic *Sanas Cormaic* or Cormac's Glossary. The collection, *Saltair Chaisil*, is known now only through what are thought to be extracts from it in a fifteenth-century manuscript (Laud, 610 in the Bodleian Library, Oxford) (E. O'Curry, *Lectures on the Manuscript Materials of Ancient Irish History* Dublin, (1861) [1995], p. 19). And see M. Dillon, *Lebor na Cert* (Dublin, 1962), pp. xiii, xx; and B. Ó

Cuív, *Catalogue of Irish Manuscripts in the Bodliean Library and Oxford College Libraries* 2 vols. (Dublin, 2001), i, pp. 62–87.

48 This ancestor Corc was enchanted into forgetfulness too in Scotland, according to the saga of his adventures: when the daughter of the king of Scotland was given to Corc, druidical incantations were put upon him so that for seven years he should forget Ireland (V. Hull, 'Conall Corc and the Corco Luigde', p. 895).

49 F. J. Byrne, *Irish Kings and High-Kings*, pp. 166–167.

50 In the pseudo-Ciceronian *Rhetorica ad Herennium*, §36, it is urged that the device of 'frankness of speech', or reproval, or any kind of statement that is not oblique or unambiguous praise, be used with care and subtlety:

> . . . Frankness of Speech when, talking before those to whom we owe reverence or fear, we yet exercise our right to speak out, because we seem justified in reprehending them, or persons dear to them, for some fault.

The amelioration of the 'frankness' is comprehended within the use of this figure. It can be palliated with flattering statements – 'as a result, the praise frees the hearer from wrath and annoyance' (*AdHer*, p. 351). In short, the flexibility of the device of Frankness of Speech (*licentia*) is assured by the latitude allowed in its use:

> This figure, called Frankness of Speech will, as I have shown, be handled in two ways: with pungency, which, if too severe, will be mitigated by praise; and with pretence, . . . which does not require mitigation, because it assumes the guise of Frank Speech and is itself agreeable to the hearer's frame of mind' (*AdHer*, p. 355).

This device is commonplace in poems that purport openly to criticize or to complain to or about a lord – examples of its use in such contexts will be dealt with later.

51 *tarlinn*, in *DIL*, s.v. 'to leave wine for small beer'.

52 This is not to argue that Gofraidh Fionn Ó Dálaigh was taught from Geoffrey's manual or anything of the sort; merely that Geoffrey's work, and the manuals like it, give instructions that appear to be followed in the type of composition created by Gofraidh Fionn, and that though comparable written instructions for the use of Irish poets seem not to have survived, that their existence can be inferred in the evidence of the poetry itself.

53 An interesting discussion of the nature of the apologue, *exemplum*, *úirsgéal* and so forth is to be found in L. P. Ó Caithnia, *Apalóga na bhFilí* (Baile Átha Cliath, 1984), pp. 7–48. Note in Ó Caithnia, ibid., pp. 7–8) –

Ag na filí féin bhí 'sgéal', 'uirsgéal', 'foisgéal', 'fáithsgéal', 'sgéal fabhail', 'sdair', 'eisiompláir', 'samhail', agus 'macasamhail' agus a thuilleadh eile fós mar a chífimid. Is láidir má dhein siadsan aon idirdhealú idir ciall agus feidhm na dtéarmaí sin. Tá, mar shampla, 'sgéal' ag Aonghus Fionn Ó Dálaigh in AOD 48, 'uirsgéal' in AOD 49, 'sdair' in AOD 50 agus 'eisiompláir' in AOD 51. Is mór é m'amhras ná gurbh ionann ar fad leis brí na dtéarmaí sin go léir. Ach is é an focal 'sgéal' is minice ag na filí go fada mór: chomh líonmhar go rábach, a déarfainn, le suim na dtéarmaí ar fad eile le chéile. Agus b'annamh gan aidiacht á cháiliú acu nó ginideach tuarascála de shórt éigin. Bhíodh 'scéal fabhail' acu, 'scéal ionadh', 'scéal go bhfairbhríogh', nó bheadh sé 'neamhghnách', 'foirfe', 'oirirc', 'diaga', 'fíor', agus mar sin. . . . Deireadh file gur scéal ar a leithéid seo nó siúd a bhí aige – ní i dtaobh éinní, ná mar gheall air: 'sgéal ar m'aithghin', 'ar Mhuire', 'ar Chathbhadh Draoi', 'ar ghabháltas nGréig' agus mar sin de. Ba chuma riamh leo fad scéil: níor bhain sin lena chinéal. Ba mhinic nár mhó ná rann iad – tagairtí ar éigean mar a chífear go tiubh sa bhailiúchán seo. Ina choinne sin gheofar scór rann nó breis i gcuid eile acu. . . .

54 Geoffrey's instructions describe a characteristic noted by Kuno Meyer – finding the Japanese comparison more compelling – when referring to the Irish syllabic poetry of an earlier period:

> Like the Japanese, the Celts were always quick to take an artistic hint; they avoid the obvious and the commonplace; the half-said thing to them is dearest (K. Meyer, *Ancient Irish Poetry* (London, 1913), p. xiii).

Whatever similarities can be adduced in respect of Celtic/Japanese cultural traits, a source of such elliptic or allusive style can be found much nearer home in the literary styles practised in the European and Irish schools in the mediaeval period.

55 The underlying compliment is doubled here, Domhnall faces the challenge of Moses crossing the Red Sea; he is well able for it, being from a seafaring race (see below, n. 62).

56 In the nature of things, the apologue did not need to be explained, nor, indeed, did the formulae require that the poet spell out either the comparison or the lesson to be taken, though, as a feature of amplification, the explication often formed a central part of a poem. L. P. Ó Caithnia, *Apalóga na bhFilí*, pp. 7–8 (see n. 53) makes this point very well. Geoffrey of Vinsauf praised the use of the hint as much as the explication (see above, p. 87).

57 This, often achieved by 'militarizing' the scenario, is something we have noted in the treatise of John of Garland, and a feature that is taken for granted in many of the treatises. See above, p. 56.

58 The painter in mediaeval Europe was taught a similar method for composition in the two-dimensional art form; the growing influence of theory on the production of artworks in paint, and the re-established references to classical painters and sculptors, gradually 'raised' the status of a career in painting from the mechanical arts to the liberal arts (F. Ames-Lewis, *The Intellectual Life of the Early Renaissance Artist*, pp. 34–38).

59 If 'caladh Dairbhre' refers to the place known more recently as An Caladh, in English now Portmagee, this was the point from which crossings to the island were normally made in earlier times.

60 Cuan Béirre was in all likelihood the earlier name for the important harbour known more recently in Irish as Cuan Bhaile an Chaisleáin, and in English as Beare Haven (Berehaven etc.). It, therefore, corresponds exactly to Caladh Dairbhre to the north-west in defining the south-westerly limits of Domhnall Óg's territory/hegemony and the direction from which he was being urged to turn as he set out on his expedition to Cashel. The map of Ireland *c.* 1350 in S. J. Connolly, *The Oxford Companion to Irish History* (Oxford, 1998), p. 610, shades this precise territory between the almost symmetrically positioned Beare Island and Valentia Island, as that governed by Mac Carthaigh.

61 This itinerary was worked out in modern terms by M. Ó Murchú, who has kindly permitted me to use it here.

62 Annalistic accounts draw attention to the maritime nature of what by the fourteenth century was Mac Carthaigh territory. His power and that of his neighbours, related families, and ancestors was built on maritime prowess and control of coastal regions. In 1315, Mac Carthaigh's Book (S. Ó hInnse, *Miscellaneous Irish Annals* [Dublin, 1947]) records that a member of the Ó Mathúna family came from Béarra with four longboats [*longa fada*] containing his people including the women to Inis Cairbre and laid siege to Diarmuid Mór Ó Mathúna and others for the greater part of the summer. Diarmuid Mór's son, in turn, hauled a boat [*bád*] from Baile Roisid strand to Dún Mánais and went with the crew to Inis Cairbre. He sent for more of his people in relays to the Island, where he stayed. He and his people defeated the Ó Mathúnas who came in the longboats.

As might be expected in a coastal region, the Annals of Inisfallen cite many instances of fleets (*cabhlaigh*) being outfitted and naval expeditions being launched, notably in 1119 when Ciarraí Luachra was invaded by a member of the Ua Briain and a company from Thomond, only to be defeated by Mathghamhain and the men of Ciarraí (Annals of Inisfallen, *s.a.* 1119.4); a fleet by Ua Muircheartaigh, 'king of Loch Léin', came to Loch Léin (*s.a.* 1126. 13); in 1127 a fleet under the direction of the same people attacked Scattery Island in the Shannon; and in the same year Cormac, son of Mac Carthaigh, put a fleet on Loch Derg [1127.15]. In 1209 Fínghin Mac Carthaigh led an expedition against Ó Muircheartaigh in Magunihy (Magh gCoinche), and defeating him, made a naval circuit of Uíbh Ráthach, which culminated in the killing of cattle and people on Dairbhre (Annals of Inisfallen, *s.a.* 1209.2), cf. Ó hInnse, *Miscellaneous Irish Annals*, p. 87; Fínghin Mac Carthaigh was killed in the same year by the Uí Shúilleabháin and he was succeeded as king of Desmond by Diarmuid, his brother (*s.a.* 1209.3).

More relevant, the most vivid descriptions of naval battles are to be found in the saga *Caithréim Chellacháin Chaisil* (see above, p. 66, and see D. Ó Corráin, '*Caithréim Chellacháin Chaisil*: History or Propaganda?', pp. 1–69), which almost certainly informs this composition of Gofraidh Fionn.

63 Dingle and Tralee traded wool and hides against French and Spanish wine and cloth in the beginning of the fourteenth century (T. J. Barrington, *Discovering Kerry, Its History, Heritage and Topography* [Dublin, 1976], pp. 60–61). Foundations of Dominicans and Franciscans were already a century old in south-west Kerry at the time Domhnall was to undertake this journey. Between 1302 and 1306 the annual income of all ecclesiastical benefices in Ireland was assessed and taxed at one-tenth: the total income from the diocese of Ardfert was £178 16s 6d; it was seventh in the diocese of Cashel, with Lismore at £711 in first rank, and Ross at £47 last.

64 By the beginning of the thirteenth century, the lands belonging to the Mac Carthaigh had been garrisoned by Meiler fitz Henry, J. Otway-Ruthven notes as follows:

> A westward expansion in Desmond seems to have been going on for some years before this, facilitated by quarrels between the sons of Donnell (Domhnall) Mac Carthy, who died in 1206. The actual course of

the movement is by no means clear, but by about 1214 it seems that a string of castles had been erected along the line of the river Maine, and at Killorglin near the mouth of the Laune, protecting a settlement in the lands in north Kerry which had been granted to Meiler fitz Henry in 1200, while two more were erected in the neighbourhood of Killarney, and a further group along the coast from Kenmare to Galley Head (J. Otway-Ruthven, *A History of Medieval Ireland* [New York (1968) 1993], p. 86).

65 Domhnall Óg Mac Carthaigh's branch of the family might remember what happened in 1306: *Domnall Og mac Domnaill Ruaidh Meg Carrthaigh do gabail do Domhnall Mael mac Domnaill Guid Cairbrig ag fagbhail Corcaidhi, agus a tabairt leis go Baile I Moinigh da tig fein, agus a dicheannadh arna beith aimsear aige a n-iarand, agus dabo mor an sgel-sin ag Gaedilaibh Ereann* [Domhnall Óg . . . Mac Carthaigh was captured by Domhnall Maol . . . leaving Cork, and he was taken to Baile Í Mhoinigh (by him) to his own house and beheaded after being kept in irons for some time, and that was a big event for the Gaeil of Ireland] (S. Ó hInnse, ibid., p. 106, *s.a.* 1306).

66 See also, D. Sweetman, 'The Hall-House in Ireland', in J. R. Kenyon and K. O'Conor, eds., *The Medieval Castle in England in Wales* (Dublin, 2003), pp. 121–132. The destruction of Irish castles and dwellings in the course of time creates images of the past characterized by ruins and mean dwellings. P. Spufford makes the relevant point that extensive buildings, fortresses on which no expense had been spared, ambitious dwellings for new rulers, projects that outlived their originators, have disappeared with very little trace throughout the territories of the most famous mediaeval continental rulers. Rulers frequently cannibalized the older buildings of their predecessors – whether family or enemies – to rebuild in the latest style. War, natural disasters and abandonment destroyed buildings of which only descriptions or depictions in manuscript illustrations survive.

Of the magnificent buildings in which Philip the Good of Burgundy entertained, only the footings can be discerned, 'all the rest has vanished' (P. Spufford, *Power and Profit: The Merchant in Medieval Europe* [London, 2002] pp. 67–73; p. 73). Continuity in use of the site is often the only hint that anything other than the present, possibly mean building, had ever existed, where some great fortress might have had stood.

67   The discussion presented here accepts C. Doherty's suggestion: 'I might say first of all that I am going forward on the basis that major churches and monasteries in Ireland were urban and functioning as towns from at least the tenth century if not earlier; and, in the case of Armagh, from as early as the seventh century. Also that some smaller churches formed the core of "pre-village" or "village" nucleations' (C. Doherty, 'Settlement in Early Ireland: A Review', in T. Barry, ed., *A History of Settlement in Ireland* [London and New York, 2000] pp. 50–80; p. 57). Theories concerning the abrupt change to life in Ireland and to the development of its human geographical patterns following the Anglo-Norman invasions mirror those concerned with the culture in general, which we have seen, and questioned, earlier.

68   C. Doherty, 'Exchange and Trade in Early Medieval Ireland', *Journal of the Royal Irish Society of Antiquaries* 110 (1980), pp. 67–89; and C. Doherty, 'Settlement in Ireland, A Review', pp. 50–80.

69   As C. O Lochlainn ('Roadways in Ancient Ireland', in J. Ryan, ed., *Féil-sgríbhinn Eóin Mhic Néill: Essays and Studies Presented to Professor Eoin MacNeill* [Dublin, (1940) 1955], pp. 465–474; p. 465) notes briefly:

> Rarely do we read of roads being made or repaired. Only in the law tracts are such works mentioned, and then only to enumerate the advantage or worth of roads and the penalties for their neglect. . . . Advancing from legendary or early Christian times to the period of the Norse raiders, we find them at once able to march a day's or even two days' journey from the sea, making predatory incursions from such places

as Linn Duachaill or Áth na gCasán and returning with their plunder. Later still the Norman invaders find a country apparently so well provided with roads that they have little difficulty in moving bodies of heavily clad mailed warriors north, south, east and west without the preliminary military work of making roadways.

The network of roads, the five principal *Slí* noted in literature, covered the island. C. O Lochlainn, following Slighe Dhála Mic Umhóir al. Bealach Muighe Dála (a boundary of North Munster), noting how the road from West Munster to Tara was called Bealach Mór in Osraighibh by Keating, suggests that the following modern towns lay on the route, Roscrea, Monahincha and Aghaboe ('stated to be on that road' [p. 471]), giving the modern journey: Roscrea, Dunkerrin, Moneygall, Toomevara, Shanbally, Nenagh, Kilcolman, Carraigatogher, Ballina (Killaloe), Castleconnell, Annacotty, Limerick, Mungret, Kildimo, Kilcornan, Askeaton, Foynes, Tarbert. C. O Lochlainn notes:

It is obvious that such important seats of government as Caiseal and Durlas must have had good road connections with the furthermost part of their realms and there is every likelihood that the roads so well used by the Normans, and later by the Elizabethan generals, were recognised routes of long standing (p. 471).

70 'Long before the Anglo-Norman "invasion" considerable urban settlements had grown up at such important religious centres as Kildare and Clonard, and then in the later medieval period this tradition lived on in such episcopal cities as Armagh' (K. Nicholls, 'Gaelic Society and Economy in the High Middle Ages', in *NHIii*, p. 399).

71 Among the colours used to decorate the walls of Cormac's Chapel in Cashel were the expensive pigment azurite used for blue, mined locally in Tipperary and still found at Tynagh; malachite for green, also mined locally in Tipperary, and the luxury item

vermilion (M. McGrath, 'The Wall-Paintings in Cormac's Chapel at Cashel', *Studies* 64 [1975], pp. 327–332). Evidence of mediaeval wall paintings, architectural details accentuated with paint, painted carvings and other painted decorations, exists for some sixty-five sites in Ireland. Most of the evidence dates from the early twelfth century to the fifteenth; one to the seventh century (Clonmacnoise). K. Morton's article 'Irish Medieval Wall Painting' indicates a polychromatic Ireland in the High Middle Ages, with a developed and engaged, artisanal and craft culture. Notice of mining operations did not form part of the landscape features that bardic poets addressed in their art. No manual of writing considered an industrial site involving menial labour appropriate either for description or reference in a poem of the 'high' or 'middle' style.

72 That part of west Limerick through which Gofraidh Fionn urged Domhnall Óg to travel with his seventeen companies comprised exactly the area forming the manorialized cantreds of Anglo-Norman settlement in the thirteenth and fourteenth centuries (M. Keegan, 'The Archaeology of Manorial Settlement in West County Limerick in the Thirteenth Century', in J. Lyttleton and T. O'Keeffe, eds., *The Manor in Medieval and Early Modern Ireland* [Dublin, 2005], pp. 17–39).

73 Some sense of the richness of the 'topical reserve', textual legacy , and literary resonances evoked by the citing of these names can be gathered from F. J. Byrne's brief account of the Eoghanacht mythology:

> Áine of Knockaney in Limerick, the seat of the Eóg-anacht Áine; Aíbell of Craig Liath in Thomond, . . . Anu, mother of the gods, whose breasts are represen-ted by the Paps mountains on the Kerry border. The Mountain of the Fair Women, *Sliab na mBan Fionn* – Slievenamon south-east from Cashel – known in the early literature as Síd ol Femun, the *síd* beyond the plain of Femen, was the residence of Bodb, king of the Tuatha Dé Danann. . . .

> Sometimes women of the Otherworld are human-
> ised as the wives of kings. Such are Aímend, daughter
> of Óengus Bolg of the Corco Loígde, the mother of the
> Eóganacht dynasties and the wife of Corc of Cashel,
> and Mór Muman, daughter of the historical west Mun-
> ster king Áed Bennán and queen to successive kings of
> Cashel. . . . (F. J. Byrne, *Irish Kings and High-Kings*,
> pp. 165–201).

74 From 1314 the Dominicans had a separate vicar-provincial for Ireland with permission to send two students each to Oxford, Cambridge and London as well as one to Paris and to other places (T. J. Barrington, *Discovering Kerry*, p. 54–55).

75 Compare the modern usage of a Scottish peer, for instance, the twelfth duke of Argyll (1937–2001), 'Ian Campbell, 12th Duke of Argyll, Earl of Campbell and Cowal, Viscount of Lochow and Glenyla, Baron of Inverary, Mull, Movern and Tiree, heredit- ary Master of the Royal Household of Scotland, Admiral of the Western Coast and Isles and Keeper of the Great Seal of Scotland. Chief of the Clan Campbell, with the title Mac Cailein Mór' (cf. *DD*, p. 441, q.v.). This comparison was kindly provided by M. Ó Murchú.

76 'The Eóganachta who ruled Munster until the middle of the tenth century were distributed strategically throughout the province. The Eóganacht Chaisil, although dwelling around the rock of Cashel, seat of the high-kingship of the province, had no prerogative claim to that office. Geographically they were outliers, the most easterly of the dynastic groups. Their closest blood-relations were the Eóganacht Airthir Chliach and the Eóganacht Glendamnach. The former were on the western borders of Tipperary and controlled the important church of Emly, whose patron Ailbe is one of the so-called 'pre-Patrician' saints. The more powerful Eóganacht Glendamnach were seated to the south-west on the upper Blackwater near Fermoy: the Glendamain from which they took their name is the modern village of Glanworth. The Eóganacht Áine Cliach at Knockaney

(Cnoc Áine) in Limerick were close neighbours of the Eóganacht Airthir Chliach in the Golden Vale, an area which is a veritable palimpsest of half-submerged tribes. Somewhat isolated but powerful in Desmond were the Eóganacht Raithlind of the Lee valley: their ruling sept, the Uí Eachach Muman, were themselves divided into the Uí Lóegairi to the west and the Cenél nÁeda, now Kinalea barony between Cork and Kinsale; the neighbouring barony of Kinelmeaky derives its name from a further sub-sept, the Cenél mBécce. In the far west, ruling in Iarmuma or Iarluachair (the region to the west of Sliab Luachra, the mountainous barrier between the modern counties of Cork, Kerry and Limerick), were the Eóganacht Locha Léin at Killarney' (F. J. Byrne, *Irish Kings and High-Kings*, pp. 176–177; especially the useful map on pp. 173–174).

77 This itinerary, which was worked out in modern terms by M. Ó Murchú, was successfully undertaken by car (by me) in February 2006 (additional help with transport and directions was given by M. Ó Cearúil, M. Murphy, and B. and E. Ó Ríordáin).

NOTES TO CHAPTER FOUR, PP. 106–136

1 Poems of this kind are common in the published corpus of bardic poetry. The themes and tropes of this complex subgenre are generally taken at face value and given a literal rather than a literary reading. The more literary approach is applied here, which, while it does not negate the insights to be gained from a literal interpretation, offers another, perhaps, equally compelling, view. The (probably tenth-century) text *'Airec menman Uraird mac Coise'* attributed to the poet Urard mac Coise (d. 990) and concerning his dealings with the 'king of Tara', Domhnall mac Muircheartaigh (d. 980), is an example of an early complaint/reconciliation theme. The poet was despoiled of material goods by the king's men. The text is cited by P. Sims-Williams and E. Poppe as an example of a text that may support a non-literal reading:

> Urard's precedent is clearly invented, and thus fictitious, and it is an interesting question whether this

is also meant to legitimise the creative invention of a past. *Airec menman* does not teach conduct proper for a king, as its embedded narrative would do on its own; rather it teaches a proper way of understanding the meaning and implication of a performance of (pseudo-)historical narrative, and offers important, although admittedly limited, evidence for non-literal interpretations of texts of this genre (P. Sims-Williams and E. Poppe, 'Medieval Irish Literary Theory and Criticism', in *CHLC*, pp. 291–309; pp. 306–307).

See also, E. Poppe, 'Reconstructing Medieval Irish Literary Theory: The Lesson of *Airec Menman Uraird maic Coise*', *Cambrian Medieval Celtic Studies* 37 (1999), pp. 33–54.

The story about the composition explaining the 'strategem' in the title may also fall into the category of 'razo', which refers to the tale which becomes an explaining preamble to the composition. Cf. W. E. Burgwinkle, *RTS*, pp. 12–13; 38–47.

2 Countless examples of such poems from the corpus of mediaeval Latin verse, usually couched in terms of appeals for material support, survive. The appeals of the Archpoet, and of Hugh Primas, to respectively – for example – the Arch-chancellor Rainald and to notables in the court of Frederick Barbarossa, and to various unnamed ecclesiastics and others, are among those known from the goliardic tradition (P. Dronke, [Introduction] in F. Adcock, *Hugh Primas and the Archpoet* [Cambridge, 1994], pp. 17–22). The prescriptive tracts noted above, especially that of John of Garland, took special care to teach the art of irresistible appeal – for material support – to patrons, professors, sponsors, lords and other persons of influence.

3 Poems such as '*Ón aird thuaidh thig an chobhair*', by Tadhg Óg Ó hUiginn, for the lord of Tír Eoghain, Niall Ó Néill (d. 1403), have always attracted a literal reading, where quatrains are examined for references to the events that are purportedly addressed in the poem (see *AithDD* i, pp. 54–59, esp. in reference to q. 13).

4 In Irish literature the status of the poet, his 'privileges and responsibilities' constitute a subgenre in itself. Texts such as those edited by E. J. Gwynn, 'An Old-Irish Tract on the Privileges and Responsibilities of Poets', *Ériu* 13 (1942), pp. 1–60, 220–236; M. Joynt, *Tromdámh Guaire* (Dublin, 1941); R. Thurneysen, 'Zu irischen Texten . . .', *Zeitschrift für Celtische Philologie* 12 (1918), pp. 398–399; L. Breatnach, *Uraicecht na Ríar: The Poetic Grades in Early Irish Law* (Dublin, 1987) and the innumerable internal references to the poets' arrogance, to their demanding nature, to their powers of punishment by satire and so forth, are to be understood as lying behind many of the claims made by poets of despoliation. The antonomastic names of Amhairgin, Aithirne, Dallán Forgaill, and other mythological and historical characters, evoke the mixture of learning, arrogance, wisdom and mischief which the poets cultivated as part of their literary identity. This study understands – while not denying the possible reflexes of pre-literary qualities and characteristcs – the greater part of these claims and postures to form part of a literary identity. Names of rare, or even fictional, alphabets in *In Lebor Ogaim* are, for instance, qualified by personal names (D. McManus, *A Guide to Ogam* [Maynooth, 1991]; R. McLaughlin, 'Metres, in *Mittelirische Verslehren III*', *Ériu* 55 [2005], pp. 119–136; p. 127), which may also have had an antonomastic function in the service of memorization. The same occurs in names of metres that accreted the personal name of a character 'associated with poetry, language and writing' – especially with satire (R. McLaughlin, 'Metres', p. 128).

5 The nature of *transsumptio* is discussed in some detail in W. M. Purcell, *Ars Poetriae: Rhetorical and Grammatical Invention at the Margin of Literacy* (Columbia, South Carolina Press, 1996), pp. 71–83.

6 Referring to the different, but related, troubadour convention of verse ridicule (of a ruler), K. W. Klein notes, as follows:

> Invectives against a ruler must be dissociated from the concept of the 'good ruler' and its negation.

The purpose of personal invective is not to correct, but to ridicule and insult. As a technique it has a long tradition, extending back to the Graeco-Roman period. The poet exaggerates features of the ruler and makes wild accusations about his conduct – the wilder, the better. The audience, as well as the poet, recognizes the improbabliity of the charges. In Bertran de Born's invectives against Alfonso II of Aragon, none of the charges have any historical validity (K. W. Klein, *The Partisan Voice: A Study of the Political Lyric in France and Germany, 1180–1230* [The Hague and Paris, 1971], pp. 64–65).

7 In '*Déanum shíodh mbunaidh, a Bhriain*', a thirteenth-century poem for Brian Mág Shamhradháin (L. McKenna, *LMS*, pp. 21–31), though the poem complains of the lord's remoteness from him, quatrains thirteen to fifteen make it very clear that the earth responds positively and directly to Mág Shamhradháin – fruit, fish, and so forth, flourish.

8 Surviving Irish schools' poetry by named poets and dedicated to secular or ecclesiastical lords does not provide examples typical of the varieties of anti-clerical complaint common in continental and English sources of the High Middle Ages, though there are examples of anti-clerical verse, especially from the eighteenth and nineteenth centuries. On the other hand, the Middle Irish satire on monks and literary men *Aisling Meic Con Glinne* [The Vision of Mac Con Glinne] is of a piece with the most robust examples of anti-clerical material in mediaeval European literature.

9 D. Innes, ed. and transl. [based on W. Rys Roberts], *Demetrius, On Style* [Loeb Classical Library XXIII] (Cambridge, Mass., and London, 1995), pp. 312–321. This originally Greek material, from a reworking in the first century AD of material probably dating from two centuries before, contains material common to the earlier Latin treatises on rhetoric and composition underlying what developed into the more well-known treatises in Latin, with which the mediaeval authors (noted above) were more than

familiar. Demetrius favoured a four-style theory: grand, elegant, plain and forceful. Each one is discussed, ending with a brief look at its faulty twin. Similar material is found in *Rhetorica ad Herennium* (*c.* 82–86 BC) though here the three-style division is favoured. At least one mediaeval Latin version of Demetrius's *On Style* exists (B. V. Wall, *A Medieval Latin Version of Demetrius; De Elocutione* [Washington, 1937]). The text presented by D. Innes is based on a tenth-century manuscript with supplementary material from a further forty-four derivative manuscripts. Other independent versions exist in fourteenth-century manuscripts. The manuscript evidence suggests that Demetrius's text, in Latin, and possibly in Greek, was much in vogue in Europe from the tenth to the fourteenth centuries (D. Innes, *Demetrius, On Style*, pp. 332–335).

10 'The MS is particularly remarkable as being the earliest extant example of a *Duanaire*, i.e. an official book which each of the more important reigning families in Ireland possessed and in which were enshrined the Bardic eulogies of the family. Its scribe – or at least the scribe who wrote the opening pages of it – was Ruaidhrí Ó Cianáin, . . . He seems to have been a well-known person in his day to judge by the eulogistic phrases in which his obit under the date 1387 is recorded in the Annals' (*LMS*, pp. vii–viii). While the extant *duanaire* appears to be incomplete, it is not known now if an original complete *duanaire* to Tomás Mág Shamhradháin is contained within the work which now exists. It is a collection of poems to predecessors of Tomás and to later members of the family and to others connected with them (*LMS*, p. viii).

11 *LMS*, pp. 152–167 [poem no. xix], pp. 420–421.

12 The tone of master/mentor to pupil is a commonplace of such poetry. The twelfth-century English poet/teacher Hilary the Englishman opened a poem to a pupil as follows: 'Beautiful boy, unparalleled boy, / I pray look kindly / At this letter sent by your suitor / *See, read, and follow what you have read*' (T. Stehling, transl., *Medieval Latin Poems of Male Love and*

Friendship [Garland Library of Medieval Literature 7] [New York and London, 1984], pp. 68, 69; emphasis added).

13 *bar* has been emended here (at the suggestion of M. Ó Murchú) to the normalized *bhar*, in keeping with the normalization of the text by McKenna.

14 Note the 'I [am]': [*is*] *mé*, followed by 'you [are]': [*is*] *tú*, structure here. It is to be noted throughout the body of bardic poetry. The most well known of these 'I am : you are' declarations is that by Muireadhach Albanach Ó Dálaigh in a poem for Richard de Burgo, '*Créd agaibh aoidhigh a gcéin*': '*Beag a fhios agad, dar leam,/ cia misi d'fhearaibh Éireann;/ spéis am dhánuibh dhlighe dhe,/ Ó Dálaigh Midhe meise*' (*IBP*, no. 20, q. 17, p. 90). An earlier Latin version of this Poet (I), Lord (You) exchange, occurs in the declaration made by Henry d'Avranches to the Emperor Frederick. The contents of poem are condensed as follows by E. R. Curtius (*European Literature and the Latin Middle Ages*, transl. from German by Willard R. Trask, [London, 1953], pp. 485–486):

> But this is nothing in comparison with the self-complacency of Henry of Avranches . . . to Frederick II . . . . Its contents are as follows: request for a favorable hearing (11–12); . . . . I am the best poet of our day and I leave the desert of prose to others (19–21); I address myself to you at the instigation of the Bishop of Winchester (22–27a); you gather around you the best masters of all arts (27b–44); . . . . the world of values is divided into intellect, things, words (*voces*); the sphere of intellect is ruled by God, that of things by you [Frederick II], that of words by me [Henry d'Avranches] (55–66); hence in my realm I too am king (66–69); . . . . you surpass all rulers as the sun the stars (90–101). And now the inference:
>
> *Cum tua sic alios premat excellencia reges*
> *Simque poesis ego supremus in orbe professor,*
> *Dicendi, licet equivoce, sumus ambo*
> *monarchi*

> *Et summum reputo, quod in hoc communico*
> *tecum.*

15 'Low style' of course refers to the vocabulary and topics not to a perceived level of obscenity nor of a lower standard of literary worth or composition.

16 While McKenna has emended *each* and *breath* here, M. Ó Murchú suggests that it is unnecessary: *breath* is a recognized older variant (see *DIL*, s.v. *breth*); therefore *each* is g. plu. making internal rhyme with *breath*. For the form *breath*, see also *DD*, p. 96, no. 31, q. 20cd (*breath*: *leath*).

17 The eristic roots of the rhetorical method survives in this mannered way, in the quasi-logical presentation of matter.

18 *bam* has been emended here (at the suggestion of M. Ó Murchú) to the normalized *bham*, in keeping with the normalization of the text by McKenna (see above, n. 13).

19 Achall, near Teamhair, and used by Ó Fialán here as a metonym for Teamhair.

20 *cró* has many meanings, including L. McKenna's 'steading'; the polysemous *cró* included the meanings 'fold' and 'pen' as well as the shape of a battle group and of an enclosure of any kind. The shades of all these meanings are intentionally present in Ó Fialán's couplet, at once invoking a sense of herds, folds and flocks in this dispute about cattle (middle style) and poems; and maintaining the high style by allowing the military sense to predominate. Cf. D. Greene, '*Cró, Crú,* and Similar Words', *Celtica* 15 (1983), pp. 1–9.

21 *PN*, pp. 78, 79.

22 Irish learning was familiar with these concepts:

> The critical concepts *historia* and *fabula* were widely used from late-classical Antiquity; there discussed by Hiberno-Latin scholars such as Sedulius Scottus (*In Donati artem maiorem* p. 80), and in a note in a fifteenth-century manuscript triad *scél* ('fabula'), *arramainte* ('argumentum') and *stair* ('historia') is

briefly defined in the vernacular, with reference to
Macrobius and to the acceptance or rejection of
these different modes in theology and philosophy (P.
Sims-Williams and E. Poppe, 'Medieval Irish Literary
Theory and Criticism', p. 303).

23 *PP*, p. 254, nn. 333–372.

24 Describing one motivation to expressions of renewal, in the
context of troubadour works, W. E. Burgwinkle remarks on the
convention of the proverbial vacillating of the troubadour and
his 'lady':

> Nothing is so fatal to prestige as inaction. The
> troubadour must continually renew his standing by
> expanding his repertoire to new fields, new ladies,
> new patrons; and the lady/patron must also turn
> her attentions to whatever new figure blazes upon
> the cultural scene.   The poems are thus replete
> with references to other ladies to whom the poet
> almost, but not quite, succumbed; or to whom he
> did succumb, but for which he must now repent.
> The razo author, in turn, explains the poet's very
> necessary forays into enemy (i.e. rival) territory as
> merely unfortunate incidents, failings toward the one
> true lady; and he raises these crises to the level of
> melodrama by providing us with the names of each of
> these rivals, the names of their powerful husbands,
> and their standing at court.   Thus he explains the
> poets' [*sic*] ambiguous references to crimes and
> scandal-mongers, indecision and masochism, as the
> literal consequences of straying from one's lady/lover
> at the same time that he exposes the poet's lady as but
> another interested patron (*RTS*, pp. xxvi–xxvii).

25 Explored briefly in M. O Riordan, *The Gaelic Mind and the
Collapse of the Gaelic World* (Cork, 1990), pp. 119–140.

26 See *DIL*, s.v. *losgann*, it is a lizard, a toad, a frog, a salamander; possibly also a version of the griffin (half eagle, half lion). Some kind of possibly amphibious creature may sometimes be intended, or it may express the notion of the fire-proof, lizard-like salamander. In the light of the qualifying *lasrach* in q. 7, the sense here may best be expressed as 'dragon' – with his fiery breath.

27 This crux creates a 'fulcrum' in the sense used above (p. 116). This crucial sense of pivot or hinge in the poetry is a matter for further elaboration on another occasion.

28 See P. A. Breatnach, 'The Chief's Poet', *Proceedings of the Royal Irish Academy* 83 (1983), pp. 40–51; and, for further details on the Ó Fialáin family of poets, see p. 75, n. 187.

29 'Love is not love/Which alters where it alteration finds', Shakespeare's verdict held good for the earlier poet, both were following Ciceronian principles of love and friendship, though the kind of love expressed in poems such as this was deliberately elusive in its depiction of the nature of that love/friendship. T. Stehling, in *Medieval Latin Poems of Male Love and Friendship* (p. xviii), notes:

> . . . These bonds of male friendship were often strong and intimate, and they were idealized by medieval culture.   Cicero, Ambrose, Augustine, Aelred of Rievaulx and Thomas Aquinas treated friendship between men as a privileged relationship between human beings superior even to the relationship of husband and wife.

Reflexes of the Ciceronian elevation of friendship and love permeated all the literary expressions of love, fellowship, and cameraderie, and coloured the rhetorical treatment of such themes. See below, ch. 6, n. 13.

30 The normalized form of this word would be *amhlaigh* (M. Ó Murchú).

31 The text of this *rann* is probably corrupt but unfortunately no other copy of the composition seems to have survived. The interpretation here assumes *ro thréag*, for the MS [*rod*] *thréag*, which

is now scarcely legible in a *ceann-fa-eite* position. The possible solution of the textual difficulty has been suggested to me by M. Ó Murchú.

32 The play on the senses of betrayal and abandon in *tréig/tréigean* involves features common to *traductio* and to *paronomasia*.

33 *ag triall* has the sense of 'journeying' (verbal noun of *triallaid*) which fits the semantic range of *rian*, which signifies 'road' or 'track'.

34 Cf. above, p. 50.

35 Many other features are not mentioned here, those concerning metre, and the rules governing rhyme, assonance and so forth, for instance the repetition of the parenthetic cheville in each of the quatrains thirty-two, thirty-three, thirty-four, matching the alternating *creach* and *airg*, is another layer of adornment.

36 Breaking Mág Shamhradháin's name in this way by introducing words between the Mág and the Samhradhán is a form of *tmesis*. It is hugely effective in the vocative case and always has an emotive force.

37 The most comprehensive account of declarations of devotion to secular lords in bardic poetry is to be found in Breatnach, 'The Chief's Poet', pp. 37–79. The interpretation of the expressions of bardic love is teased out by Breatnach in the context of the appointment of professorships. The discussion presented here adds to that context the literary exploitation of love-themes in the pursuit of the amplified, and diverting, *inventio*.

38 Compare the two themes coming together in an anonymous poem (cited in T. Strehling, *Medieval Latin Poems of Male Love and Friendship*, p. xxxi; and probably from the eleventh century):

> I can't live without you, and I can't live with you;/ *Fear prevents the one, love the other.* O would that without you or with you I could live, / But I would rather live with you than without. [emphasis added]

39 Another poem from *Duanaire Mhéig Shamhradháin* by an unknown poet – to Brian Mág Shamhradháin (d. 1298), father

of Tomás of the present composition – also sought reconciliation with the lord. L. McKenna's note reads: 'The poet (whose name is not given) seeks reconciliation' (*LMS*, p. 403). This composition '*Déanum shíodh mbunaidh, a Bhriain*' begins with the lover's requests/demands: '*togaibh an malaigh nduinn [dúinn], ná falaigh an súil gcuirr gcaoimh*' [raise the dark brow, do not hide the round gentle eye] (*LMS*, p. 21, q. 1cd); '*Ná falaigh orainn t'ucht geal; . . . ná falaigh an gruadh ndearg damh, [a] learg do ghabh snuadh na subh*' [Do not hide your bright breast from me . . . do not hide the red ruddy cheek from me, surface that took its complexion from the hue of the berries] (*LMS*, p. 23, q. 2acd);

> *Mo bhéal red bhéal tana teann*
> *mar adéar, a mhala mhall;*
> *teanntar an corp rabhán riom,*
> *a fhoilt fionn na gcabhán gcam.*
> (*LMS*, p. 23, q. 3)
> [Press my lips to your slender lips as I shall say, stately brow; let the very fair body be pressed to me; fair hair of the curled hollows.]

The poet advances to the menace of complaint after this opening, finishing from quatrain nine to thirty-five in a frenzy of praise. This poem, to Tomás's immediate ancestor, may have inspired Ó Fialán's poem, or he may have written both.

NOTES TO CHAPTER FIVE, PP. 137–158

1 The most extensive study of this phenomenon is S. Ó Tuama, *An Grá in Amhráin na nDaoine* (Baile Átha Cliath, [1960] 1978). Each of the subgenres of the love-ballad, as it evolved, are discussed in his work. Ó Tuama identified the songs of the troubadours among the examples of such work. Irish bardic poetry and troubadour poetry have not often been associated with each other, though the overwhelming influence of continental modes on post-Norman Irish writing is readily

acknowledged by Ó Tuama (in a restatement of the material from *An Grá in Amhráin na nDaoine* in a later work): '. . . it is indubitably true that medieval Irish learned lyrics (1350–1650), as well as Irish popular song, bear an overwhelming evidence . . . of medieval continental influence. Even where it can be established that certain love themes existed already in Old Irish literature, when one encounters them again in post-Norman times (in both literary song and folk-song) they seem to be fitted out anew in French or Provençal dress. . . . as described in the *Leys d'Amor*' (S. Ó Tuama, *Repossessions: Selected Essays on the Irish Literary Heritage* [Cork, 1995], p. 167). It is of interest to this discussion to note Ó Tuama's comment in respect of the love-traditions in Irish songs, that, if the learnèd conventions of love were practised in the literary modes, that the oral version of those themes must, necessarily, have been practised too:

> . . . Sa tslí gurb é ba dhóichí ar fad le duine – is gan fianaise na dtéamaí grá in amhráin na Gaeilge féin os a chomhair – má bhí na dánta léannta grá á gceapadh in Éirinn c. *1400*, nach foláir nó go raibh na cineálacha eile ar fad á gcleachtadh um an taca sin chomh maith (S. Ó Tuama, *An Grá in Amhráin na nDaoine*, p. 256).

See also, S. Ó Tuama, *An Grá i bhFilíocht na nUaisle* (Baile Átha Cliath, 1988); and M. Mac Craith, *Lorg na hIasachta ar na Dánta Grá* (Baile Átha Cliath, 1989).

2 These are referred to in general as *amhráin na ndaoine* in S. Ó Tuama, *An Grá in Amhráin na nDaoine*, passim.

3 The phenomenon thus identified (nobleman amateur) in Irish literary commentary is noted also by W. E. Burgwinkle in his study of troubadour songs. Noblemen, who were independent of lordly patronage – who could hardly appeal to fellow lords for material support in this way – employed the same techniques in their poetry/songs as those regarded as professional troubadours depending on lordly patronage. Assigning literal interpretations to literary tropes in such cases highlights the absurdity arising

from too literal a reading of the works of either group. This is discussed in *RTS*, pp. xxvi–xxix.

4 T. F. O'Rahilly's *Dánta Grádha: An Anthology of Irish Love Poetry (AD 1350–1750), with an Introduction by R. Flower* ([T. Ó Rathile] [1924]; rev. and corr. 1926, Cork) gave currency to the expression, *dánta grá* for lyrics that O'Rahilly had referred to earlier – and perhaps historically more correctly – as *laoithe cumainn*. This distinction was brought to my attention by M. Ó Murchú.

5 M. S. Mac Craith, 'Gaelic Ireland and the Renaissance', in G. Williams and R. O. Jones, eds. *The Celts and the Renaissance: Tradition and Innovation* (Cardiff, 1990), pp. 57–89.

6 Particularly striking are examples from the late sixteenth and early seventeenth centuries by the poet Eochaidh Ó hEoghusa. Works of his are cited in J. Carney, *The Irish Bardic Poet* (Dublin, 1967). The relationship between lord and poet is further explored in P. A. Breatnach, 'The Chief's Poet', *Proceedings of the Royal Irish Academy* C 83 (1983), pp. 37–79; and, in the context of the mutual obligations of hospitality, in P. A. Breatnach, 'Moladh na Féile' (in *Téamaí Taighde*), pp. 97–129.

7 In respect of the decline of troubadour lyrics: 'Already in the middle of the 13th century, one voice – that of Joan Garcia de Guilhade – is heard, lamenting the decline of *trovador* art and of true love . . .' (F. Jensen, *The Earliest Portuguese Lyrics* [Odense, 1978], p. 19). The Albigensian Crusade, likewise, is credited with the destruction of the context for the troubadour lyrics: '. . . the loss of its frame of reference following the Albigensian Crusade' (*RTS*, p. xxiv).

8 The flowering and decline of the troubadour culture in Portugal and Northern Spain is summarized in this citation in Jensen, *The Earliest Portuguese Lyrics*, p. 21:

> An even greater simplification is proposed by J. Filgueira Valverde who operates with a ternery division: 1) 1189–1232, a time of Provençal imitation, 2) the period of Fernando III, Alfonso X and Denis

(1232–1325), and 3) from the death of Denis (1325) to that of Barcelos (1354), a period of transition.

With the death of Denis in 1325, Galician-Portuguese poetry begins a period of decline occasioned by ongoing changes in the social make-up and the literary taste of the country. The new Iberian dynasties were no longer patrons of *trovador* art, and the rising bourgeois classes showed little inclination for the *cantigas*. Gradually, a new literary taste had come to the forefront: the novels of chivalry had become the fashion of the day. This was accompanied by a growing disinterest in courtly-love lyrics in neighboring regions and by the waning of the Galician-Portuguese hegemony as the lyrical medium of the Peninsula.

9   The historiographical furore in the recent past, which centred on 'revisionist' and 'revanchist' readings of Irish history, brought contrasting readings of Irish syllabic poetry in its train.   A renewed interest in early modern Irish literature – poetry and prose – was a welcome side effect of this debate.   There is no intention here to revisit the debate itself, the matter has been summarized most effectively by C. Carroll, in her article 'Early Modern Ireland', in S. Deane and B. Mac Suibhne, eds., *Field Day Review 2005* (Dublin, 2005), pp. 205–215. A comprehensive outline of the relevant standpoints is also provided in M. Mac Craith, '*Litríocht an 17ú hAois: Tonnbhriseadh an tSeanghnáthaimh nó Tonnchruthú an Nuaghnáthaimh?*' *Léachtaí Cholm Cille* 26 (1996), pp. 50–79.

10   *RTS*, p. xxxi.

11   V. Law outlines the development of troubadour glossaries and grammars and the compilation of *Leys d'Amors*, in *The History of Linguistics in Europe from Plato to 1600* (Cambridge, 2003), pp. 201–204.

12   E. Schulze-Busacker, 'French Conceptions of Foreigners and Foreign Languages in the Twelfth and Thirteenth Centuries',

Romance Philology 41 (1987), pp. 24–47; p. 26. The practice of the most ornate and 'inaccessible' style of troubadour composition, the *trobar clus*, and its related styles in less arcane registers, was common across political frontiers:

> For some time Provençal played the rôle of a common literary language in the spiritual culture of the *noblesse* of South France, Italy, Spain, and Portugal, especially for lyrical poetry. This explains why in the first half of the thirteenth century the Catalan Ramon Vidal and the Provençal Uc Faidit, who wrote in Umbria, composed grammars of troubadour Provençal. And not less in Dante's *De vulgari eloquentia* a prominent witness of a cultural open-mindedness which was not diked in by language frontiers (B. Bischoff, 'The Study of Foreign Languages in the Middle Ages', *Speculum* 36 [1961], pp. 209–224; p. 211).

And Jensen emphasizes the use of Provençal by Catalonian poets:

> The importance of Cataluña in the transmission of Provençal lyrics to the Peninsula should not be overlooked. Close historical links and a great linguistic similarity facilitated an exchange across the border of these two regions, and so imbued were the Catalan troubadours with the poetic ideals of Southern France that they themselves wrote their poems in Provençal . . . (F. Jensen, *The Earliest Portuguese Lyrics*, pp. 185–187).

13 M. Ó Murchú clarified this distinction.

14 This use of language, analogous in some respects to the *trobar clus* of Provençal, is sometimes represented as in S. Ó Tuama's expression 'a majestic mandarin-type language which remained the standard literary medium throughout Ireland and Gaelic-speaking Scotland for some four hundred years' (Ó Tuama, *Repossessions*, p. 162). In neither case is the language

essentially different from the normal standard contemporary language; a distinction must be made between what might be obscure to a modern reader/ear and what might have been obscure to contemporaries. A deliberately archaic and abstruse style was more characteristic of the Irish historians than of the poets. Bardic compositions are often obscure to modern eyes/ears because of inadequacies of transmission (poor MSS, etc.), and because of a persistent resort to an unfamiliar metonymy. Grammar and lexicon are in general straightforward enough and, in particular, there is little evidence of lexical purism or archaism. Poets' pride in their own dark compositions, the difficulty of their craft and so forth, have more to do with the mystification of their learning and with the exigencies of suiting lexicon to metre, deliberate use of ambiguity and so forth, rather than to any inherent difficulty or intrinsic esoteric qualities. The skills learned by and taught by the poets were imparted in the contemporary equivalent of the grammar school.

15 Physically, territories forming part of the poets' world were normally the named places of Ireland and of Gaelic Scotland (M. B. Ó Mainnín, ' "The Same in Origin and Blood": Bardic Windows on the Relationship between Irish and Scottish Gaels, c. 1200–1650', *Cambrian Medieval Celtic Studies* 38 [1999], pp. 1–51). Ó Mainnín's article explores the shared literary territory, and the shared aesthetic sensibilities created by the common literary language (cf. p. 139, above). And see also, W. McLeod, *Divided Gaels: Gaelic Cultural Identities in Scotland and Ireland, c. 1200–c. 1650* (Oxford, 2004); note, M. B. Ó Mainnín, review of W. McLeod, *Divided Gaels: Gaelic Cultural Identities in Scotland and Ireland, c. 1200–c. 1650, Speculum* 81, no. 3, pp. 889–891.

16 G. Murphy ('Bards and Filidh', *Éigse* 2 [1940], pp. 200–207) discusses the terms *druid, filid* [pl.], and *baird* [pl.], taking these terms, and their cognates, back to the descriptions of classical authors of the Celtic peoples. His suggestion is that

the *fili* became indistinguishable from the earlier *bard*, and that subsequently the *bard* and the poetic measures associated with his grade became the norms of praise-poetry in syllabic metres from the High Middle Ages on. The classic work on the grades of *file* in Old and Middle Irish material is L. Breatnach, *Uraicecht na Ríar* (Dublin, 1987). This work includes discussion of the title text, and of related texts such as *Uraicecht Becc*, *Bretha Nemed*, and *Míadślechta*. The relevant parts (for the discussion here) of these texts concentrate on the presentation of seven grades of *file*/poet. Breatnach concludes that the seven grade system is derived from the seven ecclesiastical grades and is a relatively recent development (i.e. in the Old Irish period) (Breatnach, ibid., pp. xi–xii). The grades and their privileges and attainments are listed in ibid., pp. 102–115.

17 In the Middle Ages the hard work and 'schooled' character of that style that was part of the educational drill (originally ridiculed in contrast perhaps to the learnèd and literary productions of the classical man of letters) became a commonplace boast of the metrical versifier over the rhythmic songster:

> Underlying this is the concept that metrical composition is a very difficult, or rather the most difficult, kind of literary work. This was generally held. To be sure, Horace and Quintilian . . . had distinguished between *versificator* and *poeta*, Petronius . . . had censured that nuisance the versifier, but this had not penetrated. Only occasionally do we find a protest against purely scholastic poetry (E. R. Curtius, *European Literature and the Latin Middle Ages*, transl. from German by Willard R. Trask [London, 1953], p. 249).

18 Taking the literal view, Jensen divides the grades of Ibero-Gallican troubadours as follows:

The poetic-musical culture did not belong exclusively to any one class of society; kings, noblemen and commoners all took an active part in it, though normally at different levels of artistic pursuit. Three distinct categories are discernible: *trovadores, segreis* and *jograis* or, in more archaic terms: *trobadores, segreres* and *jograres* (or *joglares*). The *trovador*, usually of noble birth, is the person who writes original works, inventing both *palavra* and *som*, the former referring to poetry and the latter to music. Of independent means, he writes for pleasure and not for gain. . . . [For] the *segrel*, poetry is a profession, and he expects to receive gifts in return for his work. The *jogral*, who is at the bottom of the artistic ladder, is essentially an entertainer who plays musical instruments and sings, but who does not normally write original poetry or compose new melodies (F. Jensen, *The Earliest Portuguese Lyrics*, p. 23).

Note, however, that a translation of a text covering the distinction between *jogral* and *segral* involves the strategic avoidance of defining the 'trobadors' below, it is covered in the expression 'poets' in the translation:

In his answer to Guiraut Riquier's *Supplicatió*, Alfonso X defines the roles of the *joglar* and the *segrel* as follows:

> *Hom apela joglars*
> *totz sels dels esturmens*
> *e ditz als trobadors*
> *segriers per totas cortz.*
> (F. Jensen, *The Earliest Portuguese Lyrics*,
>   pp. 28–29)

[All those who play instruments are called *jograis*, and are called *segreis* the poets who visit the courts.]

Many translations of Irish syllabic poetry exhibit some of this selectivity in locutions referring to the poet, his retinue, a scholar,

and so forth. Echoes of the ambiguity surrounding the approp-
riate translation or expression of *bard/file* – as with *jograis* and
segreis – often result in terms being applied to suit a translator's
sense of the relative status of either.

19 E. Schulze-Busacker, 'French Conceptions of Foreigners and
Foreign Languages in the Twelfth and Thirteenth Centuries', p.
33.

20 See, for instance, A. Mackay, with D. Dichtburn, ed. *Atlas of
Medieval Europe* (London and New York, 1997), pp. 153–154.

21 The author of the thirteenth-century Provençal 'Romance of Fla-
menca' was familiar with high-value artefacts from Ireland: given
as a gift by 'William' to his host is a leather belt with a silver buckle
of French workmanship and '. . . *El cuers, ques ben dels vers yrlans,
Val en cest aür un tesaur . . .*' [. . . with this belt of real Irish
leather . . . it is a treasure much extolled . . .] (M. J. Hubert, *The
Romance of Flamenca: A Provençal Poem of the Thirteenth Cen-
tury* [Princeton, 1962], pp. 140, 141). And see below, ch. 6, n.
26. M. Potterton's detailed study of Trim, Co. Meath, from the
eleventh/twelfth to the sixteenth century gives some idea of the
complexity of identities, intermarriages, levels of urbanization,
heterogeneousness and varieties of influence which co-existed in
later mediaeval Trim (idem, *Medieval Trim: History and Archae-
ology* [Dublin, 2005]). Irish men of letters were an integral part
of the most influential stratum of Irish society and were amen-
able to the ambient political and intellectual currents. See W.
Childs and T. O'Neill, 'Overseas Trade', in *NHIii*, pp. 439–491.
See also, P. Spufford, *Power and Profit: The Merchant in Medieval
Europe* (London, 2002), for the general tenor of European trade,
traffic, postal services and routing in the High Middle Ages.

22 Summarizing the career of Henry of Avranches, J. C. Russell notes
how Latin and the cultivation of Latin letters at many levels was
the norm for a 'clerk'/poet on a three-pence-a-day (normal allow-
ance for a court chaplain) retainer at the court of King John (Sans
Terre), *c.* 1245:

Master Henry's career emphasizes the international and clerical character of Mediaeval Latin civilization. Although his poetry is seldom scholarly, he composed in Latin in four countries, found his audiences largely among churchmen, experienced the hospitality held one or more ecclesiastical preferments. Writing in Latin he appealed to few nobles below emperor or king; his superiority over that of the French jongleur is evident. Even French, widely current as it was, admitted only to England, parts of Italy, and the Levant; Latin was universal. Master Henry might hold a clerkship at Rome, a canonry at Avranches, and at the same time serve as Dean of Maastricht or write for Henry III. Few such sinecures were open to the jongleur who usually sang first and received his reward later (J. C. Russell, 'Master Henry of Avranches as an International Poet', *Speculum* 3 [1928], pp. 34–63; p. 53).

23 Schools for accounting and the requirements of merchants developed in thirteenth- and fourteenth-century Italy (the *abbachista*) they concentrated on numeracy, literacy, and grammar, and were emulated elsewhere (P. Spufford, *Power and Profit*, pp. 29–20). Irish schools, which emphasized literary matters, were hardly likely to have been behind them in the principal literary language of Europe. Ireland's writers participated as fully as possible in the norm of international literary fashion in the twelfth and thirteenth centuries (and subsequent centuries) and Irish poets who worked in the syllabic metres were not different. W. P. Ker's comment on the participation in international trends by Adamnán, the eighth-century biographer of Colm Cille, is a good corrective to the notion that 'vernacular' means 'isolated', or that physical isolation, such as that experienced by island dwellers, indicates literary eccentricity, impoverishment or unintentional exoticism:

The quaint things in his [Adomnan's *Life of Columba*] language, it may be remarked, are not to be put down forthwith to the credit or otherwise of the Celtic genius. Adamnan was an Irishman (from Donegal), and he shared in the common Irish love of rhetoric and ornamental words. He did not, however, go beyond the rules or invent new devices for himself. The Irish love of rhetoric was not much different from the florid fashions of other people at that time; what is native and characteristic in Adamnan must be looked for in his substance and his sentiment more than in his phrasing (W. P. Ker, *The Dark Ages*, [London, (1904) 1955], p. 148).

24 S. Ó Tuama summarizes the poet's education thus:

The poet's principal function . . . became eulogistic; and most of his seven years rigorous training – in syllabic metres, Irish history and literature, Latin poetry and so on – was directed towards that end (S. Ó Tuama, *Repossessions*, p. 162).

25 Pursuit of 'personal creative insight' in the poetry of this period leads S. Ó Tuama to make the following statement:

It is true that in a few isolated instances, a bardic poet . . . manages to develop in a praise-poem a personal creative insight, thereby transforming and recasting the traditional eulogistic material. But the risk of losing patronage by not properly conforming to the role allotted to them in Irish society must have actively discouraged even bardic poets of real quality from pursuing the near-impossible quest of shaping high art out of formal elegy (ibid., p. 163).

W. P. Ker, referring to the artistry of a poem such as that addressed to the sword of Cearbhall, makes the contrasting point: 'The proportions are right; the unities are preserved. The ideas are not new, but they are made to seem important for the time – that is, they succeed in literature' (W. P. Ker, *The Dark Ages*, p. 332).

26 C. H. Haskins, 'Latin Literature under Frederick II', *Speculum* 3 (1928), pp. 120–151; pp. 141–146.

27 The nature and function of the vida and the razo is dicussed in by W. E. Burgwinkle (*RTS*, pp. xvii–xxiv). Burgwinkle notes how razos often concluded 'as is written here, as you shall hear', indicating that the poems themselves, and the matter of vida and razo accreting to them – while they might have been enjoyed aurally – were conceived of as written and committed to writing (p. xviii). See also, P. Dronke (in F. Adcock, *Hugh Primas and the Archpoet* [Cambridge, 1994], pp. xvii–xxii), in which he briefly discusses the nature and (un)reliability (for biographical details) of vidas and razos.

28 The problem of defining the types of genre represented in the Provençal poetry addressed in K. W. Klein (in *The Partisan Voice: A Study of the Political Lyric in France and Germany, 1180–1230* [The Hague and Paris, 1971], p. 34) is similar to that which occupied Irish poets, and commentators. The 'poetic academy in Toulouse' is, similarly, understood to have existed because of repeated references to it, and because of the tradition subsisting there of vernacular learning:

> Although the types were not carefully defined until the *Leys d'Amors*, written in 1388 in the poetic academy in Toulouse, the classifications were understood by the poets of the twelfth and thirteenth centuries, although some quarreled over the distinction between *canso* and *vers*. The genre with the most restrictions as to form, and the one in which form was the most important, was the *canso*. . . . None of the other genres was considered to be of such high quality, nor as difficult to write. The form in which the political lyric was written was the *sirventes*, the exact definition of which has become a problem of no small proportions for modern scholars. The *sirventes* was a catch-all genre, a grabbag

of opinions, polemics, insults, the transcription of per-
sonal experiences, moral commentary, advice to rulers,
praise of kings, and exhortations to the Crusades.

V. Law notes that the *Leys d'Amors* was a cumulative work,
entrusted to Guilhem Molinier, 'appearing in several versions
between 1332 and 1356' (V. Law, *The History of Linguistics*, p. 202).
The latest discussion of genre and voice in Galician-Portuguese
lyric poetry is that by W. D. Paden, 'Principles of Generic
Classification in the Medieval European Lyric: The Case of
Galician-Portuguese', *Speculum* 81 (2006), pp. 76–96.

29 Similarities in the area of reward, demand, status and so forth
between troubadour court verse and Irish court verse, are briefly
illustrated in M. O Riordan, 'Professors, Performers and "Others
of their Kind": Contextualizing the Bardic Poet', *The Irish Review*
23 (1998), pp. 73–88.

30 One is reminded of the comment by B. Ó Cuív concerning
'certain conventions', see above, p. 16.

31 No more than with the claims of the troubadour are such allusions
to 'dark', 'closed', and 'difficult' to be taken literally. The current
state of knowledge about, and familiarity with, the corpus of late
mediaeval Irish literature is not such that a definitive assertion
about deliberate obscurity could be made.

32 B. Bischoff ('The Study of Foreign Languages in the Middle Ages',
p. 212) notes as follows:

> . . . We see from extant texts or learn from the titles
> of others that the more seriously and systematically
> mediaeval language studies were pursued the more
> they derived their principles from Latin grammar.
> I have already mentioned Uc Faidit, who in the
> thirteenth century wrote his *Donat Proensal*. About
> the same time the Englishman, John Basingstoke,
> the friend of the great translator, Robert Grosseteste,
> wrote a *Donatus Grecus*. . . . After so many analogies,
> it seems not improbable that the first strictly mediaeval

grammar, the Old High German 'grammatica patrii sermonis' that Charlemagne had ordered compiled closely followed the model of Donatus.

See also V. Law, *The History of Linguistics,* pp. 203–204, where the contents and scope of the *Leys d'Amors* are outlined, showing clearly the dependence of the Occitan work, on the materials on which all the Latin grammar masters drew.

33 Klein's work is noted here principally to show how the work of the troubadours is analysed in a manner similar, heretofore, to that offered for Irish bardic poetry, though, superficially, the arts practised by both groups would appear to be wholly divergent.

34 'Indulgence', an expression used in respect of goliard demands in J. H. Hanford, 'The Progenitors of Golias', *Speculum* 1 (1926), pp. 38–58; pp. 39–40.

35 *RTS* (p. xxxi) describes aspects of the troubadour song as follows: '. . . the guarantors of the nobility of a system of courtly patronage, and political autonomy that made of the Hispano-Catalan-Italiano-Provençal region a privileged locus for the elaboration of a unique system of art and ethics'.

36 'Gender confluence' is the term applied by W. E. Burgwinkle (*RTS*, p. xxxii) to the deliberate obscuring of sexual identity in troubadour songs. The matter of gender in troubadour song has most recently been discussed, and a system of 'key-word' identification for genre and voice has been devised by W. D. Paden in 'Principles of Generic Classification in the Medieval European Lyric: The Case of Galician-Portuguese', pp. 76–96. Note Paden's observation: 'The entire corpus of *cantigas d'amigo* and *cantigas d'amor* constitutes a vast dialogue between fictional lovers' (ibid., p. 84). The razos and vidas that were attached to the songs during the thirteenth century and afterwards and that became part of literary packaging of the earlier compositions,

. . . allowing a voice from outside the lyric to circulate within it, choosing which details to accentuate, explaining references, creating connections with historical events, both monumentalizes and destroys the pretensions of the songs. . . . The coded messages of praise and threat that characterize the lyrics were referentialized: the gender confluence in the person of the lady or patron was dissipated or ignored; and the 'self-fashioning' techniques of the troubadour anxious to create from textual elements in circulation a unique persona which would bring him material or political success were reduced to the plaints of an unsatisfied lover (*RTS*, p. xxxii).

T. Stehling (transl. *Medieval Latin Poems of Male Love and Friendship* [Garland Library of Medieval Literature 7] [New York and London, 1985], p. xvii) notes the popularity of literary nicknames and other literary games at Charlemagne's court during the heyday of Alquin there.

37 See, particularly, K. Simms's studies on houses, land-use and so forth, as evidenced in Irish bardic poetry; K. Simms, 'Native Sources for Gaelic Settlement: The House Poems', in P. J. Duffy, D. Edwards, and E. FitzPatrick, eds., *Gaelic Ireland c. 1250–c. 1650: Land, Lordship and Settlement* (Dublin 2001), pp. 246–267; and idem, 'References to Landscape and Economy in Irish Bardic Poetry', in H. B. Clarke, J. Prunty, and M. Hennessy, eds., *Surveying Ireland's Past: Multidisciplinary Essays in Honour of Anngret Simms* (Dublin, 2004), pp. 145–168.

38 P. A. Breatnach, 'The Chief's Poet', esp. pp. 37–51.

39 There is a similarly freighted vocabulary to cover seemingly identical concepts in troubador lyrics, for instance: ' "Onors, onramens" can refer to gifts of property and goods as well as to abstract "honor" ' (*RTS*, p. 13, n. 2); Gifts, awards, payment, honour, dignity, etc., also had its own connotative and denotative lexicon: ' "*pretz, prez, pres*" (prĕtium) value, worth, merit, nobility; dignity, prestige; fame; (good) name; *bon* [pretz] virtue' (T. G. Bergin and R. T. Hill, eds., *Anthology of the Provençal Troubadours*, 2nd edn., 2 vols. [New Haven and London, 1973], p. 210). For further discussion of the equally

richly connotative Irish vocabulary concerning terms for the mutual obligations of hospitality, see P. A. Breatnach, 'Moladh na Féile' (in *Téamaí Taighde*), pp. 97–129.

40 Accounts of the life of Eochaidh Ó hEoghusa, and of the Ó hEoghusa family, are found in C. McGrath, 'Í Eoghusa', *Clogher Record* 2 (1957), pp. 1–19; and in J. Carney, *The Irish Bardic Poet*. In 1611 Eochaidh Ó hEoghusa was granted (by the Crown) 210 acres near Enniskillen (P. A. Breatnach, 'The Chief's Poet', p. 66).

41 P. Mac Cana, 'The Rise of the Later Schools of *Filidheacht*', *Ériu* 25 (1974), pp. 126–146. P. A. Breatnach notes how members of the Ó Fialáin family were noted in the annals as *airchinnigh* as well as poets (P. A. Breatnach, 'The Chief's Poet', p. 75, n. 187). See W. E. Burgwinkle's comment on this – the petitioner of independent means – phenomenon among the troubadours, above, ch. 5, n. 3.

42 The following account in J. H. Hanford, 'The Progenitors of Golias', pp. 42–43, of the supposed traits of the goliard mirror the paradoxical image of the Irish poet. The image presented below injudiciously mixes the identity of the poet with the poem:

> These traits [of goliardic verse] are essentially a product of the conditions and tradition of Latin minstrelsy. It has long been recognized that the writers of goliardic verse fulfilled a function analogous to that of the vernacular minstrel or jongleur as purveyors of literary entertainment for the learned and ecclesiastical world. It is impossible to generalize about a group so varied, but some of its members, certainly, abandoning whatever academic or ecclesiastical ambitions they may once have had, assumed the part of professional entertainers and spent not only their restless youths, but their whole lives in ministering to the lighter hours of that vast international body of individuals of every variety of taste and temper to whom the flexible church Latin of the Middle Age was a second mother tongue. They often went even further, divesting

themselves of their clerical inheritance and adapting their talents to the amusement of lay audiences until they became indistinguishable in habit and character from the ordinary minstrel or jongleur. In so far, however, as they adhered to Latin and sought a purely ecclesiastical patronage, they represent a distinct line with a technique and attitude which is quite their own. Placed, as they were, in the position of dependents [sic] on a household or institution, yet sharing with their masters an academic training which set them above the multitude, partaking of the quality of domestic fool on the one hand and of learned laureate on the other, they have as stock in trade a combination of extravagant flattery, graceless almsbegging, and the affectation of intellectual superiority. Under special privilege of indulgence they satirize individuals and classes, at once flaunt and deprecate their waywardness of life, and revelling in impudence, proceed even to the mocking of those solemnities which are the profession of their patrons and have perhaps been their own. All this in the name of entertainment pure and simple. The spirit of reform is something different, though the two elements may and do become interfused.

See and compare H. Waddell, *The Wandering Scholars* (London, 1954); C. H. Haskins, *Studies in Mediaeval Culture* (New York, 1929); and F. Adcock, *Hugh Primas and the Archpoet*.

43 *RTS*, pp. xxvii–xxv; T. G. Bergin and R. T. Hill, *Anthology of the Provençal Troubadours*, pp. xix–xxv.

44 Irish *crosántacht* might be mentioned in this connection, though the prose passages that characterize its occurrence are hardly explications. In many instances, the same prose passages are the source of puzzlement as to the 'meaning' of what might have been a fairly routine piece of verse. See A. Harrison, *The Irish Trickster* (Sheffield, 1989); and P. Mac Cana, '*Croesaniaid* and

Crosáin: Literary Outsiders', in G. H. Jenkins, ed., *Cymru a'r Cymry 2000 : Wales and the Welsh 2000* (Aberystwyth, 2000), pp. 19–39.

45 *TDall* i, p. xvi (and see above, p. 165). The entry in the D. Murphy, ed., *Annals of Clonmacnoise* (Dublin, 1896), *s.a.* 1351 (p. 298) on the festival held by William O'Donogh Moyneagh O'Kelly serves as a razo-style introduction to the poem by Gofraidh Fionn Ó Dálaigh, '*Filidh Éireann go hAointeach*'. Though not part of the discussion to be presented here, prose tales, and even annalistic accounts in Irish, which conclude with formulae such as 'as the poet said', might bear exploration in this context. The formula introducing the troubadour 'sirventes', concluding the introductory or explanatory razo (often accreting to the song generations later), is frequently: 'And for all these reasons x composed this sirventes which says: . . . ' (*RTS*, pp. xxx–xxi, p. 69 and passim). See, for example, and compare the razo-style introduction to a quatrain by Maoilín Óg Mac Bruaideadha (whose book was used as a source for events in Thomond by the Four Masters), AFM, *s.a.* 1559, pp. 2102–2104.

46 Attention is drawn here to the sense, in Jensen, of graduation from prospective lover to established official wooer and so forth (analogous to the notion of the progress of the poet from tyro to *ollamh flatha*); the suggestion that there is a socio-political reality supporting this particular conceit, in either case, is not belied in the present study, but it is not understood as a necessary context. See, for instance, below, ch. 6, n. 30. Paden's analogous sense, however, of the *cantigas d'amor* as a 'vast dialogue between fictional lovers' is preferred.

47 P. A. Breatnach, accepting the spousal theme as code for appointment/marriage, suggests that expressions of spousal intimacies are nonsensical where a 'marriage' (appointment) is unlikely:

> On the other hand for a poet as a mere casual visitor to address a patron in terms of intimacy such as we have encountered in the case of Ó Fialáin, for instance, would surely be a nonsense. This suggests that the

basic image of a poet as spouse applied properly speaking where the relationship between the parties was a fairly firm one; when developed and sustained in a composition the theme indicates that the author coveted a special, perhaps official, status in the house of the patron addressed ('The Chief's Poet', p. 43).

Compare the 'female' role of the poet 'pregnant' with a satire in the discussion of 'Mac Bronn', below, ch. 6, n. 2.

48 Taking a wide (and a more socio-economic than literary) view of the participation of independent wealthy individuals – such as Bertran de Born (works noted from c. 1180–1194) in the full literary panoply of the troubadour, W. E. Burgwinkle comments:

The other explanation for wealthy lords' dabbling in poetic themes about economics and advancement through love is that the troubadour's classic techniques for ensuring his usefulness, poetic praise and public censure, are equally applicable to issues of political alliance. In Bertran de Born's calls for an active gift economy, in his condemnation of hoarding and consumption, in his public announcements of the rising and falling fortunes of the barons of Aquitaine as they switch their allegiance from one Plantagenet to another, we see the potential for the conflation of amorous and political metaphors fully exploited. Bertran's lord is his lover, and he trumpets his own usefulness as public relations expert in much the same way that Raimon de Miraval does when he tells his lady/patrons that he can make them or break them. When lords/patrons/allies disappoint him by retiring from the marketplace (i.e. the practices of gift-giving and waging war), Bertran decries their cowardice. His own well-being, both material and moral, depends upon the symbiotic relation of patron and poet, master and slave, in which he holds them. Lest any of them forget, he goads them with love songs that turn poisonous and critiques that end with a kiss. Love, he has discovered, is stronger as metaphor than as reality, and is stronger still when paired with a blade. Are we really to believe, in razo 12, that the most powerful lords of Europe (Richard-the-Lionhearted, Geoffrey of Brittany, Raimon V of Toulouse, and King Alphonse of Aragon) are all vying for the attentions of Bertran's imaginary lover, Maeuz of Montaingnac, as the razo author pretends? How much more satisfying to accept the song . . . on its original allegorical level rather than follow the razo author's lead. Where Bertran tells us that his lady wants neither '. . . Poitiers nor Toulouse, Brittany nor Saragossa' and goes on from there to castigate lazy and inactive lords, the razo author sees each of these regions as representing a potential suitor. In fact, Bertran has constructed a series of synecdoches that do indeed refer to each region's principal lord, but with political implications that allow for the literal and allegorical to apply simultaneously: 'she' (being Bertran or his castle, Autafort) has no desire for the man or pretensions to his land. Bertran is only demanding that a lord exercise his function in the public sphere and keep the economy moving through gift exchange and war. The courts of Northern Italy may have had ideological reasons for insisting on reducing love to a simple battle between the sexes, and so, for that matter, might the romantic critics who popularized the courtly lyric in the nineteenth century; but should we follow them in their biased readings, even when the razos so clearly deconstruct that fiction in other, more subtle ways? (*RTS*, pp. xxvi–xxix)

NOTES TO CHAPTER SIX, PP. 159–180

1   The pseudo 'legal' basis for the ensuing 'case' recalls the original context for the rhetorical devices that became the small-change of literary soufflés like this. Ó hUiginn needed no special negative experience of English law to construct his poems, normal experience of Irish law as conducted by brehons would have sufficed. He may have used experience of a Crown court to amplify the ambit of his references and to enlarge the relevant lexical base. Irish law, conducted by the graduates of traditional law-schools, was a vital and documented resource in the sixteenth century: O'Doran brehons in Upper Ossory, for instance, were involved (in 1579) in the settlement of the ownership of Clonboran Castle and estate between the disputing parties, the FitzPatricks and the Butlers of Ormond (D. Edwards, 'Collaboration without Anglicisation: The MacGiollapadraig Lordship and Tudor Reform', in P. J. Duffy, et al., *Gaelic Ireland*, pp. 87–88, 90).

2   A reflex, or a variety of this theme is explored in D. Greene, 'Mac Bronn', *Éigse* 5 (1947), pp. 231–235. '*Mac Bronn*' seems to refer to a subdivision of verse satire, the chief characteristic is its communication in secret or to only one person (ibid., p. 231). In a poem from the Book of the Dean of Lismore, '*Dá ghabhladh dhéag insan dán*', to an otherwise unidentifiable Donnchadh Óg Albanach, the term seems to refer to the unborn vituperation of satire. The poet refers to the urge to satirize growing within him as a '*drochthoircheas*' [an evil pregnancy] (q. 1a). The satire has no mother, carried as it is by the poet, though it has a father: '*Ní dual máthair ag mac bronn; / fios a athar fhuil agam*' [It is not customary for a *mac bronn* to have a mother; I know its father] (q. 3ab). In this case the father is '*tighearna uasal éigin*' [a certain noble lord] (q. 16b). The poet has spent nine months concealing spite (q. 4c); it is time to give birth. This conceit builds on the gender-confluent relationship between poet and lord; their relationship can lead to a pregnancy, in this case of satire, to which the poet gives birth, but of which the faithless lord is father. Tadhg Óg, in the poem '*Fada an ráitheise romham*' is similarly restrained

for a season, the unsatisfactory relationship in the lord's house is giving life to a satire, but in this case, the poet choses the locked tongue device.

3 The Archpoet, having misbehaved at a festival in Vienna, found himself skulking similarly: 'Amid the throngs of nobles and their hangers-on, including all manner of actors, minstrels, each expecting a donation, comes the Archpoet skulking. He has misbehaved and is out of favour . . .' (J. H. Hanford, 'The Progenitors of Golias', *Speculum* I (1926), pp. 52–53). And compare the Archpoet's appeal to Arch-chancellor Rainald (*c.* 1164), the *inventio* in this poem is the Archpoet presenting himself as another Jonah, swallowed up by vice and turpitude, seeking forgiveness and a re-establishment of patronage, using the trope of the gossiping 'others' spreading untrue stories about his excesses:

> Peacemaker and quarrel-settler
> sir, please treat your poet gently;
> don't believe the stupid prattlers;
> now my lusts are quelled completely . . .'
> (F. Adcock, *Hugh Primas and the Archpoet*, pp. 81–85)

4 These are like the jealous suitors who surround the love-object of the troubadour, even when the slighted husband is not the cause of difficulty: 'The lady is not guarded by a jealous husband, nor spied upon by his entourage of flatterers (Prov. *gilós* and *lauzengiers*), but there are enemies at large, depicted mostly as rivals or slanderers and referred to vaguely as "they" (3rd. pers. pl. verbs) . . .' (F. Jensen, *The Earliest Portuguese Lyrics* [Odense, 1978], pp. 193–194). In a lyric by Bertran de Born to his 'lady' (Maeutz of Montaingnac – a cover name, either for another poet, or a fellow noble) these jealous 'others' are fostering distrust and mischief (*RTS*, p. xxviii) (emphasis added):

> Lady, I defend myself; *may no evil come to me*
> *Over what those false-flatterers have said about me.*

> I beg you for mercy. *Let no one be able to cause trouble*
> *Between me and your fine, true, loyal,*
> *Humble, pure, refined and pleasing body,*
> *By the telling of lies, my lady.*
> (*RTS*, p. 52)

The exploitation by troubadours of the term *senhor* to mean lady/lord is discussed in some detail in W. D. Paden, 'Principles of Generic Classification in the Medieval European Lyric', esp. pp. 82–83.

5 Bertran de Born's satirical lyric to his weak allies included the lines:

> I keep my opinions under lock and key
> Even though they have gotten me into big trouble . . .
> (*RTS*, p. 64)

6 The threat of a troubadour can involve his untimely revealing of the secret liaison to the disadvantage of the lady and the poet, but his chagrin permits him to hurt himself in this way. The threat to the 'others' might be expressed as follows, as it was by Bertran de Born:

> You false, envious, lying flatterers,
> Now that you've caused trouble between me and My-
> Lord
> I would advise you to leave me alone.
> (*RTS*, pp. 52, 54)

7 Another echo of the eristic origins of the rhetorics of composition.

8 Cf. the Archpoet's address to his lord as 'quarrel-settler', above, n. 3.

9 Cf. Tadhg Dall's poem, '*A thechtaire théid ar sliabh*', and n. 1 above; and below, ch. 7, n. 13. See also, above, n. 3.

10 Compare this use of *transitio* already noted in Gofraidh Fionn Ó Dálaigh's poem for Domhnall Óg Mac Carthaigh.

11 These are the 'lovers' who might attempt the seduction of the troubadour's secret lover.

12 The concessionary nature of *paromologia* often exploits the sting of the lesser admission (or its exaggerated form) to draw attention to the greater wrong being suffered by the plaintiff.

13 Shakespeare's sonnet 'Let me not to the marriage of true minds', captures the sense of unchanging love demanded in this trope: 'Love is not love/ Which alters where it alteration finds'. This 'love', 'friendship', 'amity', is familiar in European writing since its formulation in Cicero's *de Amitica*: Mutability is always seen as an evil and an unworthy trait in the rhetoric surrounding composition, though innuendo and ambiguity were prized qualities in composition. Compare above, ch. 4, n. 29. M. Mac Craith takes a different view of this in his evaluation of the works of the seventeenth-century poets Piaras Feiritéar and Pádraigín Haicéad: 'Feiritéar and Haicéad *are also unique in that they both wrote poems to their male friends:* poems that are not merely verses composed for friends but are deliberate, self-conscious celebrations of friendship' (M. Mac Craith, 'Gaelic Ireland and the Renaissance', in G. Williams and R. O. Jones, eds., *The Celts and the Renaissance: Tradition and Innovation* [Cardiff, 1990], pp. 57–89; p. 67; emphasis added). The exchange of gifts between men, including poems, often mimicked the dowry system in espousals or the exchange of gifts between male and female lovers. Regarding the survival of love-tokens that were exchanged between men, M. Camille, in *The Medieval Art of Love*, pp. 12–13, notes:

> Marriage was a form of gift exchange, in which men bound themselves to each other in kinship bonds using the circulating currency of women as conduits of exchange. Men also gave gifts to one another. Scholars of the troubadour lyric have shown how, despite their fictive address to a woman, these poems could be addressed just as easily to powerful lords, making them part of the power-play between men, celebrating masculine status. The Limoges casket [*c.* 1180] with its enameled roundels of warriors on

the lid as well as its troubadour subjects on the front panel, might just as easily have been a gift to a noble lord from his vassal, in which the male giver was equating his own position, *vis-à-vis* his lord, with that of a lover subject and bound to his lady. It is not so much a record of a personal relationship as a public statement about power.

14 This bargain is very common in religious verse, where the poem is a token of the poet's devotion and is to be exchanged for the favour of the deity or of some saint.

15 Compare a similar use of the subjunctive mood below, ch. 7, n. 107.

16 *historia* and satire are distinct, though because of its frequent tone of ridicule, the contents of satirical writing are often held to have a factual base, and so to partake of the nature of *historia*. This is not always the case, unclarity about fact and fiction, and the sense that a notional dispute or scandal is always partly true, creates an untenable link between the poems of dispute and 'reality'.

17 See P. A. Breatnach, 'The Chief's Poet', *Proceedings of the Royal Irish Academy* C 83 (1983), pp. 37–79, passim.

18 'The bloody cousinhood' described the nobility of Naples in the internecine warfare following the death of King Robert in 1343 (P. Spufford, *Power and Profit: The Merchant in Medieval Europe* [London, 2002], p. 77).

19 Details and sources of Knott's biographical sketch of Tadhg Dall are in *TDall* i, pp. xiv–xxxii; *TDall* ii, Appendices.

20 The chronology of Tadhg Dall's life and work would suggest that a fifteen-year-old Tadhg Dall was composing poems for contemporary lords (Knott suggests that the persons for whom he wrote flourished between 1560 and 1590). The fragility of all the information about Tadhg Dall, the poet, is worth bearing in mind.

21 Death by murder attaches itself to two other Irish writers of the seventeenth century. The scholar, antiquary and poet Dubhaltach Mac Fhirbhisigh, was murdered, it was understood, by

one Thomas Crofton (N. Ó Muraíle, *The Celebrated Antiquary Dubhaltach Mac Fhirbhisigh (c. 1600–1671)* [Maynooth, 1996], pp. xv, xix, 282–285, 296). The tragic death of Mac Fhirbhisigh, who was reputedly an octogenarian, accreted tellings and embellishments, until by the nineteenth century, he was another victim of Oliver Cromwell. Geoffrey Keating, the noted seventeenth-century author, was, according to one tradition, murdered by Cromwellians (A. de Blácam, *Gaelic Literature Surveyed* [Cork and Dublin, 1929], p. 243; cf. B. Cunningham, *The World of Geoffrey Keating: History, Myth and Religion in Seventeenth-Century Ireland* [Dublin, 2000]). Real and fictional death by murder seems to have had an association with the tradition of certain writers.

22 C. Léglu, 'Defamation in the Troubador *Sirventes*: Legislation and Lyric Poetry', *Medium Aevum 66* (1997), p. 28.

23 Of interest in this debate is the use of the term *dán díreach* to describe the kind of poetry practised by Tadhg Dall.

24 See B. Ó Cuív, 'Personal Names as an Indicator of Relations between Native Irish Settlers in the Viking Period', in J. Bradley, ed., *Settlement and Society in Medieval Ireland: Studies Presented to F. X. Martin, OSA* (Kilkenny, 1988), pp. 79–88.

25 See *TDall* i, p. xxii.

26 Ireland was no *terra incognita* among the troubadours. Even in the twelfth century, a troubadour listed Irishmen, unexceptionally, among Gascons, Poitevins and others. In a *planh* or elegy for the 'Young King' Bertran de Born (*fl. c.* 1180–1194), the troubadour noted the range of peoples who would mourn his death:

Lord, in your honor I wish to give up on joy;
All those who ever set eyes on you
Must now stand grief-stricken and mute
And may no joy ever transform that sorrow:
Bretons and Irishmen,
English and Normans,

Aquitainians and Gascons,
And Poitou suffers over it
As do Maine and Tours.
May all of France, up to Compiègne,
Be unable to hold back her grief,
And Flanders, from Ghent
All the way to Wissant;
Even the Germans weep!
When the men from Lorraine and Brabant
Hold their tournaments
They will be so saddened not to see you there.
The world isn't worth a penny
Or the drop of an acorn to me
Nor are those who are left within it.
(*RTS*, p. 88)

27 The Mac Néill letter which Knott quotes in her Introduction is, in its way, self-contradictory. Mac Néill explores the possibility of the name Uiginn deriving from Viking and finds it unlikely, one of the reasons being that 'It would be strange to find a man of Norse descent blossoming into Irish poetry in Mide early in the 10th century. His grandfather, the first Uicing, should have arrived at Clonmacnois with Turgesius!' On the other hand, Mac Néill's point about approaching poetic genealogies and the genealogies of poets with caution is well made: 'In general, I feel we must be cautious about accepting the pedigrees of the poet-historian families. They had every temptation to invent, and all the material' (*TDall* i, p. xxi).

28 Other named and noted (in the annals) members of the family are listed in *TDall* i, p. xxiii.

29 The poem '*Lios Gréine is Eamhain d'Ultaibh*' (*TDall* i, pp. 38–40, 18 qq.) is addressed to a dwelling of Shane O'Neill's. Tadhg Dall was about seventeen years old when Shane O'Neill died, according to Knott's chronology.

30 *IBP*, pp. 4–9; and cf. P. A. Breatnach ('The Chief's Poet', p. 71) who notes the tyro offerings of the poet Eochaidh Ó hEoghusa

to the successive lords Maguire, Cú Chonnacht (1566–1589) and Hugh (1589–1600). In the poem '*Anois molfam Mág Uidhir*' for Cú Chonnacht, the poet declares himself fit to praise his lord; the later lord, Hugh, is the addressee in '*Atám i gcás idir dhá chomhairle*'. The poet's dilemma here, apparently, is whether to abandon his studies and present himself, though a student, to Hugh Maguire as his poet. Breatnach acknowledges the dilemma presented by this 'evidence' as follows: 'There is no satisfactory way I know to resolve the contradiction in this evidence. It remains only to accept that Eochaidh acted for both patrons in an ollamh's capacity, having been appointed while still an apprentice, if self-opinionated, poet' (p. 71). A less literal interpretation of both works would lead us to suggest that the tyro-offering is the *inventio* chosen by Eochaidh Ó hEoghusa in the first case, and that the second case may have been a deliberate echo of that; the first poem being to the father, the second to the son. A further compliment might have been inherent in the assigning of similar *inventio* to both men.

31 Tadhg Dall's poem '*Molfaid Connallaigh clann Táil*' (*TDall* i, pp. 19–26, 54 qq.), an oblique rebuke/praise of Ó Domhnall, gives to understand (in qq. 46 and 47) that he was reared among the Ó Domhnaills. Features such as these in the poems are adornments of disappointed love, betrayed friendship, grounds for reconciliation and so forth. On the other hand, he may have spent his young childhood with Ó Domhnaills in Donegal and was schooled later with de Búrca.

32 *TDall* i, pp. 215–219, 27 qq.

33 One is reminded of P. Valesio's (*Novantiqua: Rhetorics as a Contemporary Theory* [Indiana University Press, 1980], p. 36) assertion in defence of the formality of rhetorical writing:

> Stylization also means heightening the contrasts. Thus, the intrinsic realism of rhetoric is not what goes by this name in the nineteenth-century literary rhetoric (still surviving) about realism: on the contrary, what rhetoric shows is that the basis on

which people 'really' think is a dialectic of heightened contrast, and not that ghost which is still bandied around, the life of people 'as they really are' – a shapeless, unverifiable entity that cannot be expressed in speech.

The modern concept of literary verisimilitude addresses the tension between reality and representation and allows that the latter may be neither real nor unreal, but plausible. Louis de Paor drew my attention to this modern version of the sense known in the mediaeval arts.

34 *TDall* i, pp. xxiv–xxv.

35 At about twenty-two years of age, by Knott's reckoning of Tadhg Dall's birth in *c.* 1550 (*TDall* i, p. xxiii).

36 *TDall* i, pp. 156– 159; 169–172 (nn. 22 and 23).

37 *TDall* i, '*Fearann cloidhimh críoch Bhanbha*', pp. 120–131, 69 [70] qq. The poem, dated to 1571x1580, is addressed to Seaán son of Oliver Mac William (*Iochtair*), seneschal of Connacht in 1575, d. 1580.

38 Such a poem was composed by Gofraidh Fionn Ó Dálaigh, (*GFOD*, p. 563) for Gearóid Iarla, third earl of Desmond, '*Iongaibh thú orm a Iarla*'; a similar use of the theme of despoliation, hurt, reconciliation, legal terms, and blame of others occurs in the fourteenth-century composition.

39 Something of the ambivalence attached to English terms like 'to borrow', which, historically, can involve a 'borrow to', and 'borrow from', are present in the expressions in Irish involving obligations, claims and dues, such as those exploited for these characteristics by Tadhg Dall here.

40 The same poet's moving elegy for Cathal Ó Conchubhair (*TDall* i, pp. 92–97, 37 qq. '*Déanam cunntus, a Chathail*') presents a different image entirely of the life and times of a worthy object of the poet's attention.

41 The *barántas*, 'warrant' poem is described by P. Ó Fiannachta (*An Barántas* [Má Nuad, 1978] , p. 11) as ultimately, a borrowing from

French or English sources. The term *barántas*, based on 'warrant', in the literary vogue to which it referred, is a jesting 'legal' document for which the a poet/jester attached to the court of Isabella d'Este at the end of the fifteenth century, was particularly renowned. Irish poets were adept in its employment:

Iasacht ón bhFraincis nó ón mBéarla is ea an focal
baránta, *agus is air atá an focal* barántas *bunaithe.* . . .
Is ionann a chiall agus ciall an fhocail warrant *sa*
Bhéarla sa chomhthéacs liteartha in a bhfuilimid ag plé
leis, ach gur bréagcháipéis nó scigcháipéis a bhíonn i
gceist. Sa mhéid gur bréagcháipéis é baineann sé le nós a
bhí coiteann go leor ó na meánaoiseanna anuas ar fud
na hEorpa; bhí an-taithí ag uaisle, agus ag geocaigh,
litreacha magúla agus saobhcháipéisí a sheoladh chun a
chéile. Bhí cáil ar leith, . . . *ar Il Matello, an óinmhid a*
bhí ag Isabella d'Este i Mantua ag deireadh an chúigiú
haois déag de bharr a litreacha scigiúla.

42 *TDall* i, pp. 262–264.
43 See below, n. 49.
44 Note John of Garland's examples of the washerwoman story in *PP* (p. 263, n. 24), and see above, p. 56; the fifteenth-century poem '*Bríathra cogaidh con chath Laighnech*' in *IBP* (pp. 154–157) exhibits characteristics consistent with a treatment in the low, or mixed style, with its deliberate mingling of 'low' elements (see above, p. 54), such as the kitchen implements, '*aighne is greidle*' [pot-ovens and griddles], 'low' animals '*gaillcherc*', '*ganndal*' ['foreign' (English, French?) hens and ganders], and even bacon and a pot-stand '*bagún is brannrad*' [*IBP*, p. 155, ll. 35–40], with the more 'high' style descriptions of the valiant lord. Clearly, a comic element is to the fore in this celebration of the depredations of An Calbhach Ó Conchubhair (d. 1458). The poem itself, in a metre not much represented in surviving manuscripts, cited in *IGT* (*Géill fa síthlaibh óir ghá n-iumchar, / ag ríghraidh fóid Almhan* [*IGT* §955] (cited in *IBP*, p. 154–155, ll. 43–44), is in a

freer version of the schools' metrical styles and may represent an infrequent survival of a once-popular metre.

45 See above, p. 52.

46 See above, p. 54.

47 See these 'others' above, chap. 5, nn. 3, 4.

48 See C. Ní Dhomhnaill, 'Closure in Bardic Poetry', *Celtica* 14 (1981), pp. 47–61.

49 The troubadour Bertran de Born routinely addressed his 'messenger Papiol' in his compositions:

> Papiol, go tell
> My-Lord about my song.
> For love of Sir Aimar
> I give up on waging war
> (*RTS*, p. 82).

This final verse of a song by Bertran de Born ends where Tadhg Dall started his poem: Go messenger and bring a message to my lover/patron. The burden of Bertran de Born's song has much else in common with Tadhg Dall's poem above – the loss of land/goods/love, treacherous friends and the mingling of apology, forgiveness, hurt, threat and praise:

> I am not so discouraged,
> Even though I have lost,
> Or do what I can
> To recover Autafort,
> Which I lost
> To the lord of Monfort
> Because he wanted it.
> And ever since I came before him
> Asking for forgiveness,
> And the count granting me pardon,
> Receiving me with a kiss,
> I don't have to suffer any further damage,
> Regardless of what he did to me before,
> Or praise any scandal-monger.

. . . . . .

This is what I want of a baron:
That he honor his pardon
And, if he takes something, that he returns it.
I want to ask the count
Who has my house
To lend it to me for safekeeping
Or just give it to me . . .
(*RTS*, pp. 81–82)

This demand by the poet (Bertran), 'This is *what I want of a baron . . .*' (emphasis added), is that of Tadhg Dall: '*is mór atá uaim ar a theacht*' [I want much of his coming] (*TDall* i, p. 159, q. 22).

50 In '*A theachtaire théid ar sliabh*', the poet urges his messenger to speak to his companion: '*labhair rém chompánach féin . . .*', q. 21c.

51 See *TDall* i, pp. xxix–xxx, and Knott's note on Ó hUiginn being a follower of O'Hara; see also how Cormac O'Hara (Ó hEadhra), lord of Léighne, is praised in respect of his fellowship and collegiality with the poet.

52 The use of the synecdochic *méirleabhar fhionn* followed by the apposite 'Uilliam' achieves full emotive effect.

53 See pp. 232, 233, and ch. 4, n. 14.

54 Gofraidh Fionn Ó Dálaigh's treatment of this theme of mutability and alteration in love, one remaining steadfast, the other changing, and the resulting necessity to renew the basis of their mutual love, is to be seen in '*Iongaibh thú orm a Iarla*' (*GFOD*, p. 563ff. [qq. 44–47]). The 'others', the legal terms, the proof (qq. 25–35), and other familiar treatments, are displayed in this lengthy fourteenth-century poem of recrimination and reconciliation for the earl of Desmond.

55 M. Ó Murchú (personal communication) makes the following observation on the expression *déar aille*: the phrase *déar aille* would appear to have been a standard expression of praise; cf., for example, *déar aille na n-aoigheadh é* (E. Knott, *Irish Syllabic*

Poetry, p. 23). *DIL* has a word *aille*, which it suggests may be an early borrowing of *alleluia*, and explains it as 'act of praising, giving thanks', etc. If the expression *déar aille* contained this word, it might be taken to mean 'tear of gratitude', and the line in *Irish Syllabic Poetry* might be translated as 'he is the one for whom guests weep in gratitude', literally, 'he is the guests' tear of gratitude'. However, *DIL* does not include this relatively well-attested expression in its citations under *aille*, and it may be that the editors did not believe that it contained the word. The other possibility is that *aille* in this expression is the g. sg. of *aill* 'cliff'. In the Aran Islands, the phrase *deora aille* was used of 'wind-blown flakes of sea foam'. That this was the literal meaning of the phrase in bardic poetry seems to be supported by the line '*mo dheór aille fhionnMhárta*' (*IBP*, p. 86, q. 9b), where the qualifying *fionn-Mhárta* could hardly be meaningfully associated with *aille* 'gratitude'; the line must literally mean 'my flake of sea foam in clear March [weather]'. Bergin, in this instance, translates *deór aille* here as 'cataract', which, while hardly satisfactory, suggests that he took *aille* to be the g. sg. of *aill*, as it is in the expression attested from the Aran Islands.

56 *TDall* ii, p. 263. Thadeus Higgin, listed by Fr Hugh Ward as one of his teachers when he made his 'declaration' as a student in the Irish College in Salamanca in 1612, may be this Tadhg Óg Ó hUiginn (P. A. Breatnach, 'An Irish Bollandus: Fr Hugh Ward and the Louvain Hagiographic Enterprise', *Éigse* 31 [1999], pp. 1–30; p. 1; and see n. 4). The poem '*A fhir théid go Fiadh bhFuinidh*', composed by Maol Muire Ó hUiginn – a devotional exile poem in syllabic metres – echoes the opening of his brother Tadhg Dall's poem, '*A theachtaire théid ar sliabh*' (T. F. O'Rahilly, *Measgra Dánta*, 2 vols. [Cork, 1927], ii, pp. 139–143, and p. 204n).

57 D. McCulloch, *The Reformation* (London, 2004).

58 His 'exile' poem '*A fhir théid go Fiadh bhFuinidh*' supposedly refers to his sojourns in France, Spain and Italy; he died in Antwerp.

NOTES TO CHAPTER SEVEN, PP. 181–247

1 D. McManus, in 'The Bardic Poet as Teacher, Student and Critic: A Context for the Grammatical Tracts' (in C. G. Ó Háinle and D. E. Meek, eds., *Unity in Diversity: Studies in Irish and Scottish Gaelic Language, Literature and History* [Léann na Tríonóide: Trinity Irish Studies I], pp. 97–123 [passim]) provides an account of the poet as teacher and critic, as evidenced in the poetry. His article notes outstanding examples of the poets as self-conscious purveyors of their own works and as emulators of their masters.

2 The varieties of register, style and intent in works such as the twelfth-century *Cath Cathardha* (ed. and transl. W. Stokes, *In Cath Cathardha: The Civil War of the Romans, an Irish Version of Lucan's Pharsalia* [Irische Texte, Vierte serie, 2. heft.] [Leipzig, 1909]); the collection of tales and lyrics linked with *Fiannaíocht*, for instance, E. Mac Néill, *Duanaire Finn: The Book of the Lays of Fionn* i [Irish Texts Society vol. 7] (London, 1908); G. Murphy, *Duanaire Finn: The Book of the Lays of Fionn* ii [Irish Texts Society vol. 28] (London, 1933); ibid., idem, iii [Irish Texts Society vol. 43] (Dublin, 1953); J. Carey, *Duanaire Finn: Reassessments* [Irish Texts Society, supplementary volume 13] (Dublin, 2003); the medical texts and so forth (see, for example, F. Shaw, 'Medieval Medico-Philosophical Treatises in the Irish Language', in J. Ryan, ed., *Féil-sgríbhinn Eóin Mhic Néill: Essays and Studies Presented to Professor Eoin MacNeill* [Dublin, (1940) 1995], pp. 465–474; pp. 144–157), constitute the rich literary life that existed apart from the specific literary style of bardic poetry, but inhabited the same cultural zone.

3 *MFBF.*

4 T. F. O'Rahilly (ed. Flaithrí Ó Maolchonaire, *Desiderius otherwise called Sgáthán an Chrábhaidh* [Dublin, 1955], p. xv), quoting Luke Wadding's report of Flaithrí Ó Maolchonaire, some time before 1618.

5 ibid., p. 2.

6 The antiquity of this formula is not disputed. A mid-twelfth-century version by the Archpoet typifies the later usage,

especially in matters pertaining to devotional practice or spiritual matters: *'Lingua balbus, hebes ingenio, / viris doctis sermonem facio; / sed quod loquor, qui loqui nescio, / necessitas est, non presumptio'* [Though dull of wit and prone to stammering, / I'm making a speech to men of learning. / What makes me speak without knowing how to / is not presumption but that I have to] (F. Adcock, *Hugh Primas and the Archpoet* (Cambridge, 1994), pp. 70–71).

7 The 'key' had another existence in the iconography of love popular in the illustrations of manuscripts in which love-poetry predominated. Illustrated copies of the mediaeval Romance of the Rose gave currency to a pictorial language of keys and locks; artefacts containing love-tokens and so forth made similar use of locks and keys. See M. Camille, *The Medieval Art of Love*, pp. 13, 42, 68, 112–113.

8 M. O Riordan, *The Gaelic Mind and the Collapse of the Gaelic World* (Cork, 1990), pp. 119–140; a moving example of its use (in the service of praise: the man once captured, is now released) is in *LMS* (no. 22, qq. 2–4), *'Ní beag an léansa ar Leath Cuinn'*, each strophe beginning with *léan* (*epanaphora/repetitio*) [ruin, misery] *'léan ar chliaruibh dho chongbháil'* [ruin on the maintenance of clerics/poets] (q. 3d).

9 See for example *LMS* (no. 6, q. 7), *'Olc beatha na gcoisidheadh each uaidh do na tiompánchaibh / ar sgéalaidheacht na féine'* [He gives a horse to the timpanists for stories about the Fianna]; the poem *'Tánag d'Fhánaid an einigh'* [I come from hospitable Fanad] mentions, as part of an elaborate compliment to Tomás Mag Shamhradháin (d. 1343), the inappropriate (overgenerous) awards given for inferior poetry (*LMS*, pp. 236–247; no. 27, qq. 2–8).

10 For instance, in D. McManus, 'The Bardic Poet as Teacher, Student and Critic: A Context for the Grammatical Tracts', pp. 106–109.

11 This poem is titled 'Art *versus* Nature', in *IBP*, pp. 118–119.

12 'Some Irish Bardic Poems', *Studies* 40 (1951), pp. 93–96; 217–222; 352–363), hereafter *SIB* i = pp. 93–96 (*Mór an feidhm deilbh an dána*); *SIB* ii = pp. 217–222 (*A fhir shealbhas duit an dán*); *SIB* iii = pp. 352–363 (*Créad dá sealbhuinn damh an dán*).

13 These are understood in D. McManus, 'The Bardic Poet as Teacher, Student and Critic: A Context for the Grammatical Tracts' (pp. 116–121), to be a claim and response sequence. L. McKenna's editions, likewise, highlighted their claim and response character. His editions were published, respectively and successively, under the following titles: 'A Poet Boasts of His Skill'; 'A Poet Attacks a Boastful Fellow-Poet'; 'A Poet Answers His Critic' (*SIB* i, ii, iii). Compare the discussion of the *ymrysonau* of the Welsh tradition in J. Hunter, 'Professional Poets and Professional Insults: *Ad Hominem* Attacks in Late Medieval Welsh *Ymrysonau*', *Proceedings of the Harvard Celtic Colloquium* 13 (1993), pp. 54–65. And see also, M.-A. Bossy, ed. and transl., *Medieval Debate Poetry: Vernacular Works* [Garland Library of Medieval Literature 52], (New York and London, 1987). Bossy's comments on the mediaeval fascination with debate that shaded into vituperative polemic and exchanges of conundrums is relevant here:

... Given certain cultural conditions, it [contests of words and of wit] may surge into an intense public fascination with symmetrical oppositions articulated in debate, a fascination promoting the development of numerous forensic themes and forms in literature (p. xi).

Bossy notes three particular factors supporting the growth of this particular subgenre, the growth of literacy, and its increasing focus on the medium *per se*: 'the fictiveness of the simulation is frequently foregrounded either in the narrative which frames the dialogue or in the dialogic exchange itself, for example the speakers blatantly adopt roles, embroil themselves in pedantic minutiae, and revel in logical inconsistencies . . .' (p. xii);

the increased practice of polemics in education with rhetoric becoming a keystone in the cathedral schools' curriculum; and the pervasiveness of legal education propagating the techniques of litigation (p. xiii).

14 *MFBF*.

15 Gofraidh Fionn focuses on the positive search for answers to the questions he puts, rather than on a system of warnings concerning errors, which is the mode of the *Trefhocal*. L. McKenna's notes detail references to instances of correspondence and paraphrasis of this material in *BST* and in *IGT*; both texts quoted Gofraidh Fionn's work frequently.

16 *BST*, and *IGT* V: Metrical Faults. See P. Sims-Williams and E. Poppe, 'Medieval Irish Literary Theory and Criticism', in A. Minnis and I. Johnson, eds., *The Cambridge History of Literary Criticism* ii (Cambridge, 2005), pp. 291–309.

17 The ubiquitous *Ars minor* of Donatus made all Christendom familiar with the formula of question and answer. Irish literature from the earliest period used this practice.

18 M.-A. Bossy's general comment on the debate genre fills out the context of the individually devised 'debate' created by a single poet, such as this by Gofraidh Fionn:

> The true interest of the debates resides in their variety, in their continual juggling of cultural references and categories. Theirs is a highly syncretic, kaleidoscopic literary mode. Everything is grist for their mills: popular sayings, learned examples, commonplace images and figures of speech, proverbial human types, objects and situations drawn from all walks of life, and especially motifs borrowed from other kinds of debates (M.-A. Bossy, *Medieval Debate Poetry: Vernacular Works*, p. xvi).

19 *DIL*, s.v. *solus*.

20 See D. McManus, 'The Bardic Poet as Teacher, Student and Critic: A Context for the Grammatical Tracts', pp. 111–113, on grading and the graduation poem.

21 Punctuation here is altered in accordance with suggestions made by M. Ó Murchú. The 'man' here (*a fhir*), asserting his knowledge, is the same man, essentially, as the '*fear* [*a fhir*]' of '*A fhir shealbhas duit an dán*', and of '*a fhir do thairg mo thochrádh*' (in the Fear Feasa Ó'n Cháinte 'response' '*Créad dá sealbhuinn damh an dán*' [*SIB* iii, p. 352, q. 1b]).

22 *Inntleacht* was long established in Irish (in Old Irish once spelled *inntsliucht* as though a compound of native elements) and may not have been felt as 'Latinate' by Gofraidh Fionn.

23 See *versibus digerere* [to arrange lines]; see below, n. 92; and compare below, Conclusion, n. 9.

24 This may be the reference to the 'judge' which Gofraidh Mac an Bhaird makes in respect of Fear Feasa Ó'n Cháinte's poem, but which does not mention a judge *per se*. See p. 225.

25 M.-A. Bossy notes the importance of training in polemics and dialectics in the new universities. The habits of teaching and learning that underpinned these disciplines were those taught while the tools of writing, grammar and rhetoric were being inculcated:

> To climb the ladder of academic success, a student must repeatedly prove his skills at dialectical dueling. He does so in particular during public examinations (*quaestiones* or *disputationes*), in which he jousts verbally against a fellow student or a master. . . . Consequently, the rhetorical and dialectical practices of the schools are routinely parodied in Latin verse debates and are often evoked in the vernacular debates (M.-A. Bossy, *Medieval Debate Poetry: Vernacular Works*, p. xiii).

See and compare, D. McManus, 'The Bardic Poet as Teacher, Student and Critic: A Context for the Grammatical Tracts', pp. 111–121.

26 These 'others' correspond to the envious troublemakers who surround the lord in poems of complaint and reconciliation. They

are, essentially, literary creations to lend texture and narrative coherence to poems. These 'others', too, are the faulty poets addressed in the poems that decry falling standards.

27 The metrical requirements of the style would also necessitate the use of these phatic breaks as chevilles. The nature of the chevilles in this case support the *inventio* of the poem, just as asides about the beauty of the lord, the neglect of the poet and so forth are employed in other poems at the service of other *inventiones*.

28 *DIL*, s.v. *ocht* lists a number of 'eights' which may be understood to underly this mnemonic ploy, most of them have a scriptural significance.

29 E. Poppe, and P. Sims-Williams, 'Medieval Irish Literary Theory and Criticism', pp. 291–299.

30 It may stretch the point a little to suggest that this notion has echoes of Genesis 2:19, '. . . for whatsoever Adam called any living creature the same is its name'.

31 See *DIL*, s.v. *rúac* (a) and (c).

32 The literary use of the apostrophe has been explored by M. Whelton in *'Teagmháil agus Tnúthán: Staidéar ar an Apastróp i bhFilíocht na Nua-Ghaeilge'*, unpublished PhD thesis, National University of Ireland, Maynooth, 2004.

33 The apostrophe here to the *aos ceirde* (q. 31) could be read as the poet's appeal to the students, but the irony which this would involve is not fully in keeping with the more earnestly didactic tone of the poem, and with the sense that their recourse is to himself; and it is not present in the further appeal made by the poet to the experts in quatrain forty-one *'ceist agam ar na h-eolchaibh / fagham uathaibh a n-aithne'* [my question to the experts, – let us get their precept from them] (q. 41bc).

34 Compare with quatrain 29c, *'as é soin snaidhm na haithne'*.

35 The apt phrase is that of W. M. Purcell, *Ars Poetriae: Rhetorical and Grammatical Invention at the Margin of Literacy* (Columbia, South Carolina Press, 1996), p. 147.

36 Cf. references to door and key, below, p. 250.

37 The editor, L. McKenna, seems to rise to the challenge in the notes he provided for his edition of the poem, in which he responds to the questions raised in the poem (*MFBF*, pp. 74–76).

38 Cf. n. 30, above.

39 The sense of this quatrain has been explicated by M. Ó Murchú. The, perhaps deliberate, homonymic clash between *aithne* 'acquaintance, knowledge' and *aithne* 'precept, commandment' cannot be conveyed in translation; here and elsewhere the meaning 'precept' appears to fit the immediate and overall context, cf. p. 194, above.

40 The sense of old and new, which Isidore of Seville commented upon (*Etymologica* VI i, using II Corinthians 5:17: '*vetera transierunt, ecce facta sunt* [*omnia*] *nova*' [E. R. Curtius, *European Literature and the Latin Middle Ages*, transl. from German by Willard R. Trask (London, 1953), p. 154]) is the prevailing vogue of twelfth- and thirteenth-century scholarship:

> Horace's *Ars Poetica* was commonly called his *Poetria*. So Geoffrey of Vinsauf, author of the *Poetria Nova* (*ca.* 1210), intends no more by his title than to say that he is putting forth a new poetics. In the same sense, it was usual to refer to Cicero's *De inventione* as *Rhetorica vetus* or *prima* or *prior*, to distinguish it from *Rhetorica ad Herennium*, which was known as *Rhetorica nova* or *secunda* or *posterior* . . . (ibid., p. 153).

41 For the nuances of *frioth* in *friothghobhláin*, cf. *friothchasán* (*DIL frithchassán*) and *friothród* (*DIL frithrót*). The meaning of *trivium* and *quadrivium*, the 'three ways' and the 'four ways', underlies all talk of paths to learning, approaches to wisdom, narrow and broad ways, and so forth, which are common in all the poems about poetry and learning. The sense of 'branch', 'way' and 'road' in this quatrain carries the charge of all these varied and accumulated connotations.

42 *SIB* i, ii, iii. A ninth-century example of this topic at the court of Charlemagne (by the poet Moduin of Autun) uses the conceit of

the young poet in a dialogue with the older poet. The *senex* and the *puer*. The younger poet patronizes the older, suggesting that his work is accomplished and that he might now retire in honour. The older poet replies with a scathing attack on the inferior work of the callow poet:

> Presumptious young man who aspire to be a poet, is it here
> that you plan to write uncouth poetry in your rasping style?
> What was your reason, stupid boy, for coming here to gaze
> upon the mighty palaces and lofty walls of new Rome?
> Here to no avail you stretch out your poem at great length,
> you say nothing of public events, your poetry satisfies no one,
> but is despised by all, most miserable poet.
> (P. Godman, *Poetry of the Carolingian Renaissance* [London, 1985], pp. 192–193; pp. 24–27)

43 This poem, titled 'Art *versus* Nature' (in *IBP*, pp. 118–119) is one of the better-known poems from the last decades of the sixteenth century and the early decades of the seventeeth century. Reference has already been made to the literal interpretation offered by many scholars as to the 'meaning' of this poem. The effort here is to furnish a further context for the poem, which adds to its texture and to its connotative richness.

44 This poem, titled 'The passing of the old order' (in *IBP*, pp. 120–123), has been similarly read as a factual comment on the times.

45 This fable was known in troubadour poetry, see R. Cormier 'The Maddening Rain: A Comparison of the Irish and Provençal Versions', *Éigse* 11 (1964–1966), pp. 247–251.

46 M.-A. Bossy notes the characteristics of the French literary *jeu parti*, which shares some of the characteristics of the exchanges

between the Irish poets (*Medieval Debate Poetry: Vernacular Works*, pp. 27–28).

47 L. McKenna edited the three poems – Ó'n Cháinte's '*Mór an feidhm deilbh an dána*'; Gofraidh Mac an Bhaird's '*A fhir shealbhas duit an dán*', and the presumed riposte to that response, Ó'n Cháinte's '*Créad dá sealbhuinn damh an dán*' – as an interdependent trio. They are read as such by D. McManus, 'The Bardic Poet as Teacher, Student and Critic: A Context for the Grammatical Tracts' (pp. III–II7), who reads a personalized animus in the works:

> Like many a personalised wrangle this probably generated more heat than light for the contemporary observer, but for us, looking in from the outside, it is highly illuminating, whether we take it in earnest or not. Indeed, with the exception of Gofraidh Fionn Ó Dálaigh's *Madh fiafraidheach budh feasach* . . . . there is probably no better insight to be had in the poetry, as opposed to the grammatical tracts, into the strict academic regime of the bardic schools (p. II7).

The reading urged in this study is that of the literary claims of such poems, belonging to an *iomarbháigh* tradition, analogous to the Welsh *ymrysonau*.   The collection *Iomarbháigh na bhFileadh* (L. McKenna, 1918), the collective *inventio* of which is the extolling of the north and south of Ireland by northern and southern poets in competition with each other, is only one manifestation of the genre.   The aspersions, reprimands and slightings abounding in that literary enterprise has many features in common with the contention concerning composition in the mini-*iomarbháigh* of the three poems looked at here.   Their essentially literary nature is identical and the echoes in them of earlier material and their survival – in turn – in later material is a testament to their lack of immediate topicality in any one instance.   This is the goal of all schools' composition, and success in those terms is what the participating poets sought and achieved.

48 Cf. Fear Feasa Ó'n Cháinte's '*linnte téachta 'n-a timcheal*' in '*Bean dá chumhadh críoch Ealla*' (*DD*, p. 223, 1d).

49 Two MS readings give *bhfuil* (*SIB* i, p. 96), which would change this line slightly to 'it is nothing but folly to compete with it'. On the other hand, *fios* (in line c) corresponds with *ainbhis* in line d.

50 This refers once again to the *slighe* or 'path' to learning, see above, n. 41.

51 R. McLaughlin, in an article 'Metres, in *Mittelirische Verslehren III*' (*Ériu* 55 [2005], pp. 119–136), notes, among other things, metres classified as *écoitchenna* [infrequent, or uncommon], as distinguished from *gnáthaisti* [common metres] (p. 127). Among those listed, under quite eccentric names, are §167 *snám súad* (p. 121), and §170 *meisce Rómáin* (p. 121), both of which may be obliquely referred to in this suggestion that the poet has swum through the oceans of learning. Similarly, reflexes of §183 *aí idan* (p. 121) might occur in references to pure poetry/verse below, p. 242. The use of personal names qualifying or identifying metres, particularly those in satire, may be relevant here too. See R. McLaughlin, ibid., pp. 127–129; and see above, chapter 4, n. 4.

52 The seven grades are the subject of much work and comment, among which see G. Calder, *Auraicept na n-Éces: The Scholars' Primer. Being the texts of the Ogham tract from the Book of Ballymote and the Yellow Book of Lecan, and the text of the Trefhocal from the Book of Leinster* ([Edinburgh, 1917] Dublin, 1995), p. 18, and passim, and L. Breatnach, *Uraicecht na Ríar: The Poetic Grades in Early Irish Law* (Dublin, 1987) (passim). D. McManus ('The Bardic Poet as Teacher, Student and Critic: A Context for the Grammatical Tracts', p. 111, n. 37) remarks that the full list of stages, such as is given here by Ó'n Cháinte, 'seldom appear in the poetry on their own'. Most recently, P. Sims-Williams and E. Poppe ('Medieval Irish Literary Theory and Criticism', pp. 294–295) synopsize the contents of the texts that would have formed a staple of the curriculum of the poets:

One eighth-century law tract, *Uraicecht na Ríar* ('The Primer of the Stipulations'), is devoted to the qualifications and privileges of the seven grades of *filid*, and three other tracts from the Old Irish period discuss these grades, or those of the *baird*, among other material concerning social status: *Bretha Nemed* ('Judgements of Privileged Persons' – in two main versions), *Míadslechta* ('Passages on Rank') and *Uraicecht Becc* ('Short Primer/Introduction [to *Bretha Nemed*?]'). *Uraicecht na Ríar* and *Uraicecht Becc* draw on and refer to *Bretha Nemed*, whereas *Míadslechta* is independent of it. In descending order, the hierarchy of *filid* in *Uraicecht na Ríar* and *Uraicecht Becc* are: *ollam, ánruth, clí, cano, dos, macfhuirmid* and *fochloc*, plus (in *Uraicecht na Ríar*) three sub-grades: *taman, drisiuc* ('briar-dog') and *oblaire*. The sub-grades are not true *filid* for even the first, the *taman*, 'does not have knowledge of letters' (*Uraicecht na Ríar* §18). The seven grades are common to the various texts (although *Míadslechta* uses the term *ollam* and *éces* interchangeably and *Bretha Nemed* places the *suí* 'sage' even higher than the *ollam*), but there is some variation in the details of the poets beneath the *fochloc*: *Míadslechta* places the *bard, fer cerda* and *cáinte* here. As already mentioned, the ranks of the *baird* (who are excluded from consideration in *Uraicecht na Ríar*, apart from the three 'sub-grades' noted above) are enumerated much more inconsistently and number between six and sixteen.

53 *Recte 'a n(daghbhoth)'*? 'of their fine huts'. D. McManus, 'The Bardic Poet as Teacher, Student and Critic', p. III emends to *dánbhoth* and translates: 'the rich productions of these (alone) are worthy of their (origin in a) composition hut'. The reading *dánbhoth* is supported by the rhyme with *ánsruth* (in which, correctly, the *á* is long). D. McManus (ibid., p. 98, n. 4) has more on

this line and on *dánbhoth*, its rhyming with *ánsruth*, etc., q.v. His emendations would appear to be based primarily on the metrical requirement, and the established precedent of a rhyme *dánbhoth* ~ *ánsroth*.

54 *troigh* meaning both 'step' and 'metrical' measure is echoed, perhaps, in Gofraidh Mac an Bhaird's reference to *dréimire* [a ladder], which the poet climbed to ignorance (*SIB* ii, q. 26d), see below, p. 222.

55 *deacht*, translated as 'exact' here, is found as an expression describing worked silver – a smithing term – in *DIL*, s.v. 1. *decht*. *Rian*, 'path', is a term used very frequently to indicate the approaches to knowledge. Cf. above, n. 41.

56 *DIL*, s.v. 3. *fochair*, notes another meaning for this term, of uncertain meaning but having to do with some level of learning. This may be one of the meanings here, that there are other grades that are part of learning, but that these are not as good as those the poet listed. However, much the same sense is conveyed by the more familiar *fochair* 'proximity', i.e. that there are other grades besides those mentioned.

57 The three manuals referred to above, p. 25ff, are themselves examples of all that they have to teach, and were deliberately structured thus.

58 *IGT* §164: '*imda fili ga foil oigi/ga figi a toigh oide d'Aodh*'. It is unnecessary to labour the popularity and ubiquity of the metaphors of weaving and composition and the sense of text, texture and so forth that informs this literary imagery. Cf. The seventeenth-century poet Dáibhí Ó Bruadair's '*uige is léir i'm dhóid anois*', in '*D'fhigh duine éigin roimh an ré so*' (*DÓB* iii, p. 76).

59 On the other hand, reference to fulling and the tucking/fulling mill, *úcáil* (see Ó'n Cháinte, '*Créad dá sealbhuinn damh an dán*', q. 23), brought in a term suitable for the 'low' style (see styles above, p. 52). Within the understanding of styles in this sense, the use of a low-trade reference to a low-grade poet was a perfect match of material with language. The 'high' and 'low' did not refer to ability or standard of composition.

60 Using any link with military matters immediately elevated the 'style' to the 'high' style. See above, p. 56.

61 Cf. Fear Feasa's insistence that only those qualified in the schools could adopt the title: see above, p. 207.

62 Cf. Fear Feasa's claim that Gofraidh Mac an Bhaird's work was dependent on air/breath: see below, n. 68.

63 Cf. Fear Feasa's lonely calling bittern, above, p. 236.

64 For *teach* in the sense of 'realm', see *DIL*, s.v. *tech* (III e): *na trí tighe* '?heaven, earth and hell', and compare, E. Knott, *Irish Syllabic Poetry 1200–1600* (Dublin, 1974), p. 36: '*saor na dtí dtoigheadh*' [architect of the the three realms], i.e., 'the Creator'. Here the realms of Irish may be law and history in addition to the art of poetry, an interpretation possibly acknowledged in Gofraidh Mac an Bhaird (*SIB* ii, q. 4); see below, p. 225. There are echoes also, however, of the 'three cauldrons of poesy' (L. Breatnach, 'The "Caldron of Poesy"', *Ériu* 32 [1981], pp. 45–93). Note also, the 'alliterative verse dedication that was inserted into a ninth-century Gospel-book of Irish provenance known as the Mac Durnan Gospels, which reads "Máel Brigte mac Tornáin teaches this Gospel through the tripartite world . . ."' (cited in *Irish Royal Charters*, p. 15): ['*Maelbridus Mac Durnani istum textum per triquadrum Deo digne dogmatizat*' (M. McNamara, 'Echternach and Mac Durnan Gospel: Some Common Readings and Their Significance', *Peritia* 6–7 [1987–1989], pp. 217–222)]. This tripartite division was popular in Isidore's notion of the map of the world, which gave Europe, Africa and Asia. The popularity of threefold divisions, identities and so forth was both familiar and common in factual, metaphorical and allegorical use and certainly familiar to the poets. 'Throughout the world' is at least one of the meanings in the ninth-century example here, and possibly is that understood in Fear Feasa's '*na trí tighe a-tá a nGaoidheilg*' (*SIB* i, q. 16b). D. McManus, 'The Bardic Poet as Teacher, Student and Critic: A Context for the Grammatical Tracts' (p. 120 and n. 55), has noted that there are clear indications that the first couplet of

this *rann* is corrupt and, on the basis of Mac an Bhaird's 'reply', implies that the correct reading should be something like: '*do ránag roighne ar gceard / na trí tighe i dtá an Ghaoidhealg*' [I made contact with the choicest of our skills, the three houses in which Irish is]. D. McManus's suggestion is in part supported by the variants for q. 16 (*SIB* i, p. 96); see also D. McManus, ibid., p. 99, n. 5, where he gives the line as '*trí tighe i dtá an Ghaoidhealg*'. The term, *trí tighe* as the three realms, was explicated for me by M. Ó Murchú.

65 See above, pp. 128, and see above, chapter 6, n. 4.

66 See *Meisce Rómáin*, and *Meisce Draigin meic Dorndorbied*, in the classification of metres from *Mittelirische Verslehren III* (R. McLaughlin, pp. 121, 122), and above, n. 51.

67 Cf. *DD*, p. 227: 73.35, '*ina ghríbh chuirthe caithiorghail*', in a poem by Fear Feasa Ó'n Cháinte, '*Bean dá chumhadh críoch Ealla*', on the death of Domhnall mac Airt Ó Caoimh (his lord), and of Aonghas mac Amhlaoibh Ó Dálaigh, his teacher (*c.* 1601–1610) (*DD*, p. 456).

68 Cf. Fear Feasa Ó'n Cháinte's ('*Créad dá sealbhuinn damh an dán*', q. 36) complaint about facile poets whose material is empty save for wind:

> *Mar badh tusa an tobar fís*
> *nach mór an t-adhbhar aithis*
> *do thoirm mar gach ndaoidh san dán*
> *'s gan d'fhoirm at (aoibh) acht anál.*

> [As though you were the well of knowledge! Is your clamour – like every other dolt in poetry – not a great cause of disgrace, and no form in your verse except that of wind (breath).]

This reference to *anál* serves also to anticipate the slur cast on the poetry later when Fear Feasa declares that the poetry of the 'other' lies somewhere between *dán* and *abhrán*, the latter associated with dependence on mere breath (q. 59).

69 Perhaps, thus: 'The education that I received is worthwhile if I direct my rebuke against them with the effect that they regret this comment, those who are ignorant of the arts' (explication, M. Ó Murchú).

70 This is a function of the literary jousting, which, no less than tournament jousting, created sham battles, which may occasionally have caused real injury and gave actual offence. Their nature is essentially in the former case, literary; in the latter, ritualistic.

71 *SIB* ii; D. McManus, 'The Bardic Poet as Teacher, Student and Critic: A Context for the Grammatical Tracts', pp. 111–117.

72 Cf. above, p. 215.

73 Conjecture as to the 'identity' of Rufinus in Matthew's treatise, while interesting in itself and possibly illustrative of academic politics of an earlier age, probably misses the main point, which is that the pedagogic object is best served by personalizing the lesson. Matthew makes this point quite clearly in his defence of using historical or actual personages in illustrative material, for which other names may be substituted as needed: 'The intelligence of the listener would be more eager to entrust things to its faithful memory, so that . . . it comprehend general knowledge through specific names, lest it presume an understanding diverse from the intention of the author and singular to itself. . . . So, to keep the special name from outweighing the other individuals of the same circumstance, age, dignity, office or sex, let what is said about the Supreme Pontiff, Caesar, or other individuals who follow, be understood as attributed so that the special name, taking the place of the general name, calls to mind what is relevant' (*AV*, §6–§60, p. 40). See L. Breatnach, *Uraicecht na Ríar* (p. 77), who notes the figure *antonomasia* in the use of Amhairgin Glúngheal as the named progenitor of the 'cauldrons' of poesy.

74 See and compare M.-A. Bossy (*Medieval Debate Poetry: Vernacular Works*, pp. xvii–xviii) on the nature of the *partimen*:

> The form of their debate [a late fourteenth-century Catalan verse contest between poets] enables them to

vie in poetical ingenuity, as well. Its genre, named *partimen* or, in French *jeu-parti* . . . calls for a symmetrical exchange of stanzas with the same meter and rhyme scheme. The poet who initiates the exchange defines an antithetical topic in the opening stanza. His partner then chooses one side or the other of the alternatives and defends it in the second stanza, replicating the rhymes of the first stanza. . . .

75 Matthew of Vendôme, too, knows of such trifling braggarts: 'Moreover, there are certain braggarts and triflers, who have an urge to awkward presumption and presume to caw and abuse the meaning of words in this fashion . . .' (*AV*, §42, p. 77). [*Amplius, sunt quidam trasonitae et nugigeruli qui, ex impetu praesumptionis inconcinnae praesumentes cornicari, verborum significationibus abutunter hoc modo . . .*] (*LAP*, §42), p. 166.

76 See above, pp. 5ff.

77 This, again, is the same 'man' of p. 187, and n. 21, above.

78 When Fear Feasa notes that there are other grades that are weak in art: '*gé táid foghráidh 'n-a bhfochair*', etc. (*SIB* i, q. 10a, p. 94), he allows for the existence, within the terms of the profession, for such inferiors. These, then, are stripped of status in the poem, which describes their works. This is one of the mechanisms for generating poetry, the amplification of an *inventio* that can carry yet another excursus on themes that are familiar.

79 Participation in the debate about writing is a function of these poems, which employ the disputatious *inventio* as a vehicle to discuss or to teach the elements of the art. See above, p. 205.

80 Henry of Avranches did not confine his attacks to Michael of Cornwall. J. C. Russell's study of Henry ('Master Henry of Avranches as an International Poet', *Speculum* 3 [1928], pp. 34–63; pp. 36–41) notes the following literary joust between Henry and one Peter Siler:

. . . Of Master Henry of Avranches's work, some 150 of his poems survive, a diatribe against him by a 'rival'

Michael of Cornwall, some documentary evidence from the Continent, and items from Exchequer rolls of the thirteenth century. . . . He was adept in vituperation. He tells on how entering at church at Angers he beheld two asses braying in the choir . . .: one was Peter Siler to whom he devotes a dozen pieces, all very acrimonious and frequently advising Peter to be silent (*silere*). Peter Siler was probably the fellow-poet Peter who with Master Henry carried a controversy to the Papal Curia . . . but his poetry is not known to have survived. Neither have we Master Henry's share of his controversy with Michael of Cornwall.

Theodulf's attack on Cadac-Andreas (an Irishman) at the court of Charlemagne in the ninth century (P. Godman, *Poetry of the Carolingian Renaissance*, pp. 10–13) bore the hallmarks of the literary feud, which itself was a genre topic, executed in a recognizable style.

81 Isidore of Seville's *Etymologies* provided a synopsis of the written arts formulae from the seventh century; and see above, chapter 2, n. 38.

82 See above, pp. 5ff.

83 Faults and licence enjoyed a mutually complementary relationship, see E. Curtius, *European Literature and the Latin Middle Ages*, pp. 42–47. Metaplasm, for instance, a fault, is an ornament in Gofraidh Fionn's '*Beir eolus dúinn*'.

84 Cf. Fear Feasa's quatrain 18c (*SIB* i, p. 95). Note his '*mo sproigeacht riu dá ronnar . . .*' (*SIB* i, q. 21c) and the quatrain: '*Do (shnámhas) iad tar a n-ais / srotha ionnalta an iomhais, / do ghlé mé m'oige eisdibh,/ oide mé 's as maighisdir*' (*SIB* i, q. 20).

85 The two words '*sproigeacht*' and '*oideacht*' are found in an exemplary expression in *IGT*, §24 ex. 841: '*Sona an flaith ó bhfuair sbroigeachd / maith do-chúaidh in chomhoideacht*'. The expressions '*adhbhar*' and '*cúis*' are resonant of legal terminology, both terms appear as technical legal terms and the poets made use of

such expressions as frequently as possible. Such terminolgy suits the 'debate' or 'case' for the prosecution being put forward here.

86 (*'Mór an feidhm deilbh an dána'*), *'an t-oigéan dorcha domhuin'* (*SIB* i, q. 2a); *'srotha ionnalta an iomhais'* (*SIB* i, 20b, pp. 93, 95).

87 *ascnamh* in q. 27b is a word that has a technical application in prosody meaning a form of conclusion known also as *dúnadh*.

88 The feature of *figura etymologica* is used as often as possible.

89 An example of showy clericity in the management of such rhetorical devices is demonstrated in the inscription of a love-token ring (fifteenth-century French) described by M. Camille (*The Medieval Art of Love*, p. 103): 'On the outside appear the words *une femme nominative a fait de moy son datiff par la parole genitive en depit de l'accusatiff* and inside, . . . is the inscription *m[on] amour est infiniti[v]e ge veu estre son relatif* . . .'

Irish poets lived in a world where a 'lover' might contemplate such an inscription, having received similar instruction in the techniques of stylish and effective writing.

90 Intricately linked to each other, this sentiment in this poem is echoed in Fear Feasa below, p. 235.

91 The reference to 'judge' here, while appropriate for the general claims being made in Fear Feasa's poem, is not referring to any overt assertion made by him, and while it may be a reflex from Gofraidh Fionn's poem '*Madh fiafraidheach, budh feasach*'; see above, p. 188; it may also be making explicit what is implied in Ó'n Cháinte's reference to '*na trí tighe a-tá a nGaoidheilg*' (*SIB* i, q. 16b) (see above, p. 225): *dlí ~ croinic ~ dán: breitheamh ~ croinicidh ~ fear dánal ollamh*. There may be a play on the various meanings of *ollamh*, but *balach* here may mean 'professional', thus 'practising lawyer', and *croinicidh* is very specific.

92 The expression *dán díreach* has not been conclusively explained. E. Curtius remarked that in the Middle Ages the absence of a satisfactory term for composition and the writing of 'metrical poetry', 'metrical poem' and 'to compose in meter', caused authors to refer paraphrastically *inter alia* to *versibus digerere*, *metrica facundia*, and *metrica amussi* [straight-edge metre] (E. R.

Curtius, *European Literature and the Latin Middle Ages*, p. 153). This last makes a very fine translation of *dán díreach*. *Versibus digerere* 'to arrange lines' describes very well what the poets themselves were proud to do.

93 See B. Ó Cuív, *Cath Maighe Tuireadh: The Second Battle of Magh Tuireadh* (Dublin, 1945); and see P. Mac Cana, *The Learned Tales of Medieval Ireland* (Dublin, 1980).

94 This translation assumes *do* to be the common unstressed from of the preposition *de*. If *do* is taken to be the 2sg. possessive, as McKenna (*SIB* ii, p. 220n.) takes it to be, the translation would differ slightly as follows: 'both claims represent [equally] your entitlement to recognition/status'. Explication here by M. Ó Murchú.

95 Though Gofraidh Mac an Bhaird bemoans the state of the schools here, it is important to note in quatrain sixty-four of Fear Feasa's '*Créad dá sealbhuinn damh an dán*' that Ó'n Cháinte claims to have excellent students who would not be deceived by another (this?) poet's nonsense: '*Mór an sruith oidis fhoirbhthe / mór bhfealmhac bhféith bhfaobhoirthe / as fhearr iná thú ar mo thréad / as gheall rem chlú do choimhéad*' [Many is the mature scholar of perfect training, many is the quiet incisive pupil among my flock who are better than you; they are a pledge for my reputation] (*SIB* iii, q. 64). Fear Feasa claims that he taught the attacking poet (Gofraidh Mac an Bhaird?) (*SIB* iii, q. 45), the latter's sly claim that schools were now without standards may be aimed at the former teacher, or at that claim. Teacher–pupil relations enjoyed a tropic world of their own, analogous to that of poet–patron. The claims may be made to give shape or form to the *inventio* requiring them. It is noteworthy, too, that Fear Feasa, writing around the early decades of the seventeenth century, should have boasted a full school of worthy scholars, whatever the facts of the matter.

96 *tuisle(adh)* also carries a sense of falling in the moral sense (*DIL*, s.v. *tuisled* d.), which is intended in a tropic discourse which associates vice in composition with moral turpitude. Again, attacking

the 'other', Rufinus, Matthew of Vendôme associates his putative weak learning with moral blindness and figurative blindness: 'There are some unlearned ones who usurp the office of correcting; and they, blind leading the blind, fall in a pit together, like Rufinus. But since in the kingdom of the blind, the king is a one-eyed man, and he has a people which trusts him; and they are perverted with the perverse, they redden with Rufus, and are made blind with the blind.' (*AV*, §42, p. 102 [*Sunt autem indisciplinati quidam, qui correctionis usurpant officium, qui, caeci caecos ducentes, cum eis in foveam cadunt, ut Rufinus. Sed, quia in regione caecorum rex est monoculus, et populum, qui sibi credat, habet, et cum perverso pervertunter, cum Rufo rufizant et cum caeco excaecantur*] (*LAP*, §42, p. 189).

97 Outlined in, M. O Riordan, *The Gaelic Mind and the Collapse of the Gaelic World*, pp. 282–285. And compare D. Ó Bruadair, combining the weaving metaphor with the metaphor of the game in '*D'fhigh duine éigin roimh an ré so*', '*D'fheartaibh an airdrígh d'athruigh na cártaoi . . .*' (*DOB*, iii, p. 90).

98 Cf. J. E. Doan, 'The Erotics of Backgammon in Provençal and Irish Poetry', *Proceedings of the Harvard Celtic Colloquium* 12 (1992), pp. 29–42. In a thirteenth-century love-debate (*jeu parti* involving questions and answers about two ladies of equal beauty), the troubadours Jean Bretel (d. 1227) and Jean de Grieviler (d. *c.* 1255) used the following metaphor (M.-A. Bossy, *Medieval Debate Poetry: Vernacular Works*, p. 153):

> John, a person who knows all the dice tricks
> Is likelier to become a streetcorner rogue
> Than one who doesn't know how to play . . .

99 Referring to John of Garland's poem that was intended to illustrate his treatise on composition, T. Lawler notes how John himself becomes caught up in the intricacies of his own devices: 'The Division is made to fit the scheme by some verbal trickery. In Rhetoric, as John's definition says, the Division contains a statement of the opponent's case. The poet, however, has no

real opponent in this sense. But the subject of the poem, since it deals with a battle, has an opponent, so John achieves a spurious "Division" by stating here what virtue's enemies are doing. Here the psychomachia alone is at issue: the World and the Flesh have no counterpart among the Saracen host' (*PP*, p. 245n. 207–284). The creation of an opponent to achieve 'division' is the very device used by the poets in the suite of attacks and responses identified in the three poems dealt with here.

100 D. McManus suggests that the modern mode of mutual criticism among academics is a corresponding ambience for these compositions (D. McManus, 'The Bardic Poet as Teacher, Student and Critic: A Context for the Grammatical Tracts', pp. 114–117).

101 The composition edited by R. A. Breatnach, 'A Poem on Rime in Scholastic Verse' (*Éigse* 3 [1943], pp. 36–51), is undated, but Breatnach points out that it agrees for the most part with comparable material in *IGT* I. The fifty-three quatrains of this poem detail the rules governing rhyme and may well have been known by heart, by the later poets at least. It is a straightforward pedagogical poem without the spice of controversy or disputation, and as such, is more like Gofraidh Fionn Ó Dálaigh's '*Madh fiafraidheach budh feasach*', and may be another ghostly presence behind the trio of poems in this suite.

102 The Welsh tradition of *ymrysonau* [poems of contention or competition], analogous to the Irish tradition of *iomarbháigh*, exhibits many characteristics of the poems under discussion here. Particularly interesting, in the light of D. McManus's suggestion that some poems (not necessarily those of the *iomarbháigh* subgenre) are 'graduation' pieces, or masterpieces in the sense of a completed apprenticeship (D. McManus, 'The Bardic Poet as Teacher, Student and Critic: A Context for the Grammatical Tracts', pp. 111–113), is J. Hunter's remark that the poets' own declaration – within the poems – that they are '*ymryson am radd*': 'contesting for a degree', is a realistic context for such poems (J. Hunter, 'Professional Poets and Professional Insults: *Ad Hominem* Attacks in Late Medieval

Welsh *Ymrysonau'*, pp. 53–54). The poems discussed here do not seem to refer particularly to the conferring of a degree on either participant, but this does not negate the overwhelming similarities of style and content between the *iomarbháigh* style poems discussed here and the *ymrysonau* discussed in J. Hunter (ibid., pp. 54–65). There is also the possibility that the three poems are by a single author, Fear Feasa, perhaps, creating the dispute which used the 'Mac an Bhaird' poem as device to allow elaboration of the original 'Ó'n Cháinte' composition. The surnames of the 'poets' may have played a part in the literary game evoking, as they do, aspects of the profession of poetry itself. (This reading of a single author was suggested to me by M. Ó Cearúil.)

103 These latter features are not the elements of the poem being focused on here.

104 The authority to teach/criticize/correct – matters addressed in D. McManus, 'The Bardic Poet as Teacher, Student and Critic: A Context for the Grammatical Tracts' – also exercised the ingenuity of the poets' English and continental counterparts. See and compare Matthew of Vendôme (see above, n. 96).

105 This reference to the poet's father, whether he is a poet 'Brian Mac an Bhaird' or not, is not at issue here – though the poem is enriched by the sense that it might be – is akin to the extension of the attack from the (other) poet to his relatives, lovers and so forth (J. Hunter, 'Professional Poets and Professional Insults', pp. 58–59). No works of Brian Mac an Bhaird have been identified, but that does not mean that he was neither a poet nor a teacher. See, for the Mac an Bhaird family, P. Walsh, ed. C. O Lochlainn, *Irish Men of Learning: Studies by Father Paul Walsh* (Dublin, 1947), pp. 151–159.

106 Since the final quatrain in this poem refers to the *bard*, possibly in the sense of reciter, there may be a suggestion in this quatrain (19) that even the foolish Brian was not reduced to reciting the work of others.

107 The conditional mood here, creating conditionality, contingency, and hypotheticality in the discussion, is to be compared with that noticed above, p. 162, and chapter 6, n. 15.

108 He is like Matthew of Vendôme's weak teacher, blind, leading the blind (see above, n. 96).

109 *trudaire* and *trudairecht* (*DIL*, sv.v.) are terms that refer to infelicities of speech, stammering, babbling, barbarity in speech, and so forth. They recall the background in oratory and eloquence that informed the arts of composition, and emphasize the literary contrivance of the composition.

110 Compare, Horace, *Mutato nomine de te fabula narratur* (*Satires* I 1, 69).

111 This may be an echo or a reflex of Quintus Curtius (d. *c.* 53) *History of Alexander* (over one hundred mediaeval MS copies of it survive, without the first two books), which has the proverbial '*canis timidus vehementius latrat quam mordet*' VII.iv.13 (J. C. Rolfe, transl. *History of Alexander*, Quintus Curtius) [Loeb Classical Library] 2 vols. (Harvard, 1946).

112 *béicire* is another term for the bittern (P. S. Dinneen, *Foclóir Gaedhilge agus Béarla: An Irish–English Dictionary* [Dublin, 1927], s.v. *béicire*).

113 Cf. Matthew of Vendôme's cawing poet, above, p. 213.

114 This suggestion may be intended to reflect some of the sense attaching to the performance of the satirical *glám dícind*, see H. Meroney, 'Studies in Early Irish Satire: i, ii, *Cis Lir Fodla Áire?*', *Journal of Celtic Studies* I (1950), pp. 199–226; idem, 'Studies in Early Irish Satire: iii *Tréfhocal Fócrai*', *Journal of Celtic Studies* 2 (1958), pp. 59–130, p. 65. And see V. Mercier, *The Irish Comic Tradition* (Oxford, 1962), pp. 119–127.

115 *dar mó móid* (*DIL*, s.v. *móit* c) may be *dar mo mhóid*; see *SIB*iii, p. 363, note on 44a. In that case the line could read 'It distresses my spirit, I swear, that your . . .'. Cf. L. McKenna, ed., *Iomarbháigh na bhFileadh* ii, p. 228 (London, 1918) (*DIL* s.v. *móit* a).

116 In '*Tairgidh mo sheachna, a shíol mBriain*', a sixteenth-century composition by Tadhg (mac Dáire) Mac Bruaideadha for Donnchadh Ó Briain, fourth earl of Thomond, the poet has about him similar concealed weaponry: '*A-tá oirchill arm nimhe . . . / ar ceilt fós fam thuinn-se as-tigh . . .; / Glac rann lé ngontar gruaidhe / mh'arm i n-aimsir anbhuaine . . .*', qq. 11ac, 12ab (R. McLaughlin, 'A Threat of Satire by Tadhg (mac Dáire) Mac Bruaideadha', *Ériu* 55 [2005], pp. 37–57; p. 48). These, the weapons of satire, are to be wielded against the lord in times of inflicted hardship.

117 Cú Chulainn's enchanted javelin is transposed here into *gae na haeire* (*DIL*, s.v. a. *gae*). The *ga* of satire is referred to in *Táin Bó Cuailgne* – '*Táinic Fer Diad leo-som tar cend a oinigh, uair ba husa laiss tuitim do gaib goile agus gaiscidh (agus eagnamha) ina tuitim do gaib aoire agus eugnaigh agus imdercctha*' [For the sake of his honour Fer Diad came with them, for he deemed it better to fall by shafts of valour and prowess and bravery than by the shafts of satire and reviling and reproach] (C. O'Rahilly, *The Stowe Version of Táin Bó Cuailnge* [Dublin, 1961], pp. 84; translation from idem, *Táin Bó Cúalnge from the Book of Leinster* [Dublin, 1967], p. 212). All the poets were familiar with the saga of the *Táin*.

118 See *DIL*, s.v. *bolg*, and, s.v. *Bolg*; and note the *balg fis* in q. 18 and q. 26 above, p. 222.

119 *Aoi* is rendered 'entrails' (one of its meanings) by L. McKenna, in *SIB* iii, p. 362.

120 See *DIL*, s.v. 2. *aí* 'poetic inspiration, learning, metrical composition'; E. J. Gwynn, 'An Old-Irish Tract on the Privileges and Responsibilities of Poets', *Ériu* 13 (1942), pp. 1–60, 220–236; K. Meyer, 'Three Poems in Bérla na Filed', *Zeitschrift für Celtische Philologie* 5 (1905), pp. 482–494; p. 483, §1; H. Meroney, 'Studies in Early Irish Satire: i, ii, pp. 199–226; iii, p. 65; C. Watkins, 'Indo-European Metrics and Archaic Irish Verse', *Celtica* 6 (1963), pp. 194–249; pp. 215–216. *Aí idan* is one of the uncommon metres noted in R. McLaughlin, 'Metres, in *Mittelirische Verslehren III*', p. 121.

121 This quatrain is very finely balanced on all the meanings of *imirt* in both its spellings here, of the element *beart* within it, used as a part of a compound here, hidden in *imirt* and visible in *slimbeirt*, and in the meanings of *caint* as speech, and discourse. The eristic shades of *airlabrae* (*DIL*, s.v.), with its senses of advocacy and eloquence, are recalled in this use of *caint*. The primer *Auraicept na n-Éces* follows the classical sense of composition in giving to understand that the whole matter is one of oratory in citing the twelve faults: '*da locht deg na hirlabra in sin*' (*Auraicept na n-Éces*, p. 148, l. 1943). It also reflects the fact that mediaeval teachings on style derived from the principles of classical rhetoric. Speech, discourse, play, trick, performance, game, and all their semantic range, are employed in this single quatrain. It is representative of the highly textured quatrains and the intense intertextuality characteristic of these poems, the surface of which can only be alluded to in this discussion.

122 R. A. Breatnach's edition of '*Feadha an oghaim aithnidh damh*' (R. A. Breatnach, 'A Poem on Rime in Scholastic Verse', *Éigse* 3 [1941–1943], pp. 36–51) collates the instructions given in this poem with the material in *IGT*. All the material referring to the correct use of the alphabet, the '*beithe, luis*', and other grammatical matters governing the creation of proper verse, is repeated, from the Middle Ages in *Auraicept na n-Éces* and the *Trefhocal*, to the grammatical work of Giolla Brighde Ó hEoghusa in the seventeenth century (P. Mac Aogáin, *Graiméir Ghaeilge na mBráthar Mionúir* [Baile Átha Cliath, (1968) 2001]). The details of the instructions or the grammatical importance of the information does not concern this discussion. It is used as material in the poems under review here, as substance for teaching, for rhetorical flourishes and for the amplification of the subject matter, in the service of *inventio* concerning teaching, learning and composition.

123 *IGT* I, §12, §14. And compare Gofraidh Fionn Ó Dálaigh, '*Madh fiafraidheach budh feasach*'; see above, p. 192.

124 *IGT* I, §18.

125 The word *claon* (*DIL*, s.v. *cláen*) is commonly used to describe metrical faults.

126 The manuscript from which this text was edited comes from a fourteenth-century scribe.

127 *IGT* V (Met. Faults), p. 259, n. 3.

128 Cf. B. Ó Cuív, above, p. 43.

129 It is to be noted throughout that, as in poems of complaint, the subjunctive mood, and the indirect source of damaging information, is used here too. Quatrain eighteen puts the case thus:

> *Dá ttuillinn mar nar thuillios*
> *guin m'aighthe tre fhábhuillfhios*
> *dom chailg do badh doiligh dul;*
> *mairg rom oiligh gan adhbhar.*
> (*SIB* iii, q. 18)
> [Were I to merit injury to my reputation through false knowledge – which I did not – attempting to wound me would be a troublesome process; woe to whom would insult me without cause.]

This sense of *potential* trouble, the conditional element in the quatrain, pervades the poem, but is easily forgotten in the smooth transition to the reality of the poem. Compare this with p. 120, above. Similarly with *do-chuala* [I have heard], the poet has heard, he does not know for sure, it may be untrue; however, assuming it is so, and he presumes so . . . and so on, to the further disparagement of the faulty poet.

130 Cf. above, p. 30 and ff.

131 *gnúis* (*DIL*, s.v. *gnúis*), along with its meanings of 'countenance', 'surface', 'face', it also means 'species' and is used figuratively as the expression connoting the sense of grammatical or poetic means of compensating faults in metre.

132 Cf. *DOB* ii, '*fá ghairbhe shnais an tlachta*' §3, p. 42.

133 *DIL*, s.v. *mellach*, and 2. *mellach*, give the meanings 'pleasant' and 'protuberant', 'knobby'. Both meanings are applicable here,

that the verse is pleasant, and also that the verse is unpleasant; misshapen or smooth. Both meanings, though contradictary in intent, are suitable here in both and several senses *at the same time* because the second phrase '*gan mheall*' (*DIL*, s.v. 2. *mell* 'confusion, error[?]') can also mean without lumps or disfiguring bumps.

134 Cf. the condemnation of bombast, above, p. 55.

135 Two meanings of *dán* are juxtaposed here: 'a poem of your poetry'.

136 In this context the differentiation would point to poems composed in the scholastic metres and syllabic count in the case of *dán*, and on rhyming vowels and regular stress rhythms in the case of the *abhrán*. See E. Knott, *Irish Syllabic Poetry*, pp. 1–20.

137 See *DOB* iii, p. 90: '*D'fhigh duine éigin roimh an ré so*' (Ó Bruadair probably knew most of the works noted here by heart) – '*ag déanamh robhán róibhriste . . .*' The poem itself opens with the weaving metaphor '*D'fhigh duine éigin*'.

138 See discussion of facets of the ambiguity surrounding the poet/performer in M. O Riordan, 'Professors, Performers and "Others of Their Kind": Contextualizing the Bardic Poet', *The Irish Review* 23 (1998), pp. 73–78.

139 The term *abhlóir*, used in the sixteenth and seventeenth centuries, came to mean an inferior poet/performer, often in comparison to the superiority of the one using the term, in respect of another. As *oblaire* (*DIL*, s.v.), it described a class of inferior poet; as *obláir* (*DIL*, s.v.), it referred to a lower level performer (sometimes interchangeable with *fuirseoir*, buffoon, clown or jester), and occurs in the literature in company with the list of jugglers, tumblers) and 'others of their kind' (see M. O Riordan, 'Professors, Performers and "Others of Their Kind": Contextualizing the Bardic Poet', pp. 73–88). It has also meant 'scorner' (*DIL*, s.v.) and this meaning is apposite too. A generation later the poet P. Haicéad (or a fellow-poet), in '*Ní mise an Cearbhall rod chlos*', used the term in a quatrain that abounds in allusions to all the material under discussion here:

Ní gabha 's ní ceard cóir
ní húcaire 's ní habhlóir
ní figheach i seólaibh slinn;
ní heólaidh aoinneach orainn.
(M. Ní Cheallacháin, *Filíocht Phádraigín Haicéad*
[Baile Átha Cliath, 1962], p. 7)

This quatrain recalls the quatrain in the Annals of Connacht, *s.a.*
1249.11 (and the Annals of Loch Cé, *s.a.* 1249), on the death of
Donnchadh mac Anmchadha Ua Giolla Pádraig:

Bid 'na tsaer, bid 'na tornoir
bid mo laeg ina lebroir;
bid se ag reicc fina is craicenn
mar a faicenn se semnoir.

The literary echoes are clear and the poem is an example of the
'low' style at work. The prefatory material to this little verse, foll-
owing the traditional obituary of Donnchadh Ua Giolla Pádraig,
has the quality of a razo: 'He [Ua Giolla Pádraig] used to go
in person as spy in the market-town in the guise of a beggar or
carpenter or turner or some other craftsman, *ut dicitur . . .*'

140 The poet may be a beggar because his works do not deserve
recompense.

141 Cf. above, p. 236.

142 The sense of *bard* in this context may be that of the lesser
'rhyming' poet, or even 'reciter', used here as an insult; it is
not consistently used thus, and must be understood here as the
ambivalent slur it is. This quatrain does not 'close' the poem in
the sense of providing a classical *dúnadh* and the poem itself
may be unfinished.

143 There may be a reference to the surname of the poet here, 'Mac
an Bhaird', *'gan an mbairdneacht féin'*.

144 John of Garland treats of the vices in many different contexts.
For the vices linked to the styles, see *PP* pp. 85–88, and see above,
p. 55. T. Lawler gives the Latin original on facing pages.

NOTES TO CONCLUSION, PP. 248–260

1 B. Ó Cuív, 'An Appeal on Behalf of the Profession of Poetry', *Éigse* 14 (1971–1972), pp. 86–106; P. A. Breatnach, 'A Poem on the End of Patronage', *Éigse* 31 (1999), pp. 79–88, some centuries apart, are just two of the kinds of appeal made by poets that their wonted status and income be maintained. Such appeals are stock-in-trade among all the European school poets, but their particular characteristics cannot be discussed in detail here.

2 See M. O Riordan, *The Gaelic Mind and the Collapse of the Gaelic World* (Cork, 1990), pp. 62–118.

3 There seems to be no subgenre of poems in which a poet begs to be considered among the company of poets. Though there are plenty of works in which the poet begs to be considered *ollamh* by a lord (see P. A. Breatnach, 'The Chief's Poet', *Proceedings of the Royal Irish Academy* C 83 [1983], pp. 37–79, passim).

4 This phenomenon is discussed briefly in M. O Riordan, 'Professors, Performers and "Others of Their kind": Contextualizing the Bardic Poet', *The Irish Review* 23 (1998), pp. 73–88; pp. 75–78. See B. Cunningham, *The World of Geoffrey Keating: History, Myth and Religion in Seventeenth-Century Ireland* (Dublin, 2000), pp. 24–31.

5 Recent writing on this topic is summarized in C. Carroll, 'Early Modern Ireland', in S. Deane and S. Mac Suibhne, eds., *Field Day Review* 1 (Dublin, 2005), pp. 205–215.

6 M. Mac Craith situates another poem of E. Ó hEoghusa, '*Ní mé bhur n-aithne, a aos gráidh*', within a courtly-love debate in the early seventeenth century. Mac Craith suggests that Irish poets were accultured into European literary modes by means of the 'middle' cultural nation of the Old English. He suggests that Ó hEoghusa was coaxed from his 'traditional' mode by his connections with the Anglo-Irish Nugent family ('Gaelic Ireland and the Renaissance', in G. Williams and R. O. Jones, eds., *The Celts and the Renaissance: Tradition and Innovation* [Cardiff, 1990], pp. 57–89; 69–70):

> All the protagonists in this harmless piece of fun
> were acquaintances of William Nugent. It is also
> remarkable that a professional poet such as Eochaidh
> Ó hEoghusa was prepared to join in the sport. . . .
> We have previously remarked that the work of the
> professional poets, by its very nature, shows very
> little openness to new ideas. Eochaidh himself was
> very much in the traditional mould. He considered
> his relationship to his patron Aodh Mág Uidhir
> as a marriage, an idea that was part of the poetic
> order's pre-Christian inheritance, but an idea to
> which Eochaidh himself was extremely attached . . .
> Eochaidh Ó hEoghusa may have been a traditional
> poet, every bit as traditional as Tadhg Dall Ó hUiginn,
> yet his work contains many indications of his being
> open to outside influences and to contemporary
> English literature. This may be partly due to personal
> disposition, but it must have been facilitated in no
> small way by his involvement in circles frequented by
> both Old English and Old Irish.

It is suggested in the present study that no such intermediate
medium was necessary to Irish literature, and that the Irish
tradition did not exclude independent, creative and innovative
participation in the major trends of European writing.

7 *iomlaoid* (*DIL*, s.v. *imlait*) also has the meaning 'mistake' or 'error';
suarrach sona can also have the oxymoronic meaning of mean-
spirited/happy. This ambivalence satisfies the *inventio*, which
requires that a qualified poet suggests that he is about to adopt
simple measures and transparent modes instead of the ornate, and
sometimes opaque, creations associated with artistic endeavour in
the traditional school modes.

8 The translation here differs slightly from that in Bergin, in that
the 'hasty composition' is substituted for Bergin's 'to be brave';
though both are correct in the context, I favour the reference to
composition in '*dénamh tapaidh*'.

9 This describes exactly the *sraithe* above, and see above, p. 187, and chapter seven, n. 92. The translation here differs very slightly from that in Bergin, in that 'subtle' is chosen over 'delicate', and 'teachings' rather than 'admonitions', as describing the kind of teaching to which the scholar-poets were exposed.

10 See *DIL*, s.v. *sreth*; and *DIL*, s.v. *cael*.

11 '*crad cride ecis*' [torment of a poet's heart] is the name of an Ogham alphabet in G. Calder, ed., *Auraicept na n-Éces: The Scholars' Primer. Being the texts of the Ogham tract from the Book of Ballymote and the Yellow Book of Lecan, and the text of the Trefhocal from the Book of Leinster* (Edinburgh [1917], Dublin, 1995), ll. 5895, and noted in R. McLaughlin, 'Metres, in *Mittelirische Verslehren III*', *Ériu* 55 (2005), pp. 119–136; p. 131. It was also used in its modernized form, Crádh Croidhe Éigeas, as a pseudonym, in revivalist style, by O. Bergin. This link with Bergin was brought to my attention by M. Ó Murchú.

12 The debate background, which has been outlined above, may lie behind the suggestion here that Ó hEoghusa, a renowned master, was the subject of ridicule for his composition.

13 Ó hEoghusa's own formulation here 'Clann Chonaill' is chosen over the Bergin 'Earl of Tyrconnell'.

14 In '*Bíodh aire ag Ultaibh ar Aodh*' (*DD*, pp. 236–240, to Aodh Mág Uidhir [d. 1600]), the apologue of the philosophers occurs in qq. 20–36. And cf. R. Cormier, 'The Maddening Rain: A Comparison of the Irish and Provençal Versions', *Éigse* 11 (1964–1966), pp. 247–251.

15 Cf. the troubadour Guiraut de Borneill (*fl.* 162–1199):

§8. So you see and understand,
You to whom my language is familiar,
That where once I used closed and covered words
I now make them good and clear.
§9. And toward this end I have made a real effort
That you might understand every song that I compose.
(Guiraut's ending is a reference to the fact that he previously wrote songs that were difficult to interpret [*trobar*

clus]. He might also mean that he used to compose songs that had multiple meanings and that encouraged alternate, often humourous and erotic readings . . . . His declaration of clarity is nonetheless belied by the not altogether clear context in which it is found [*RTS*, p. 25 (no. 8]).

Similarly, Eochaidh Ó hEoghusa's poem, while he asserts his abandonment of the difficult style of the schools, his work here, a lucid and fluent composition, is by no means simple and unschooled. It is an example of the best the schools' style had to offer.

16 See, for example, P. A. Breatnach, 'Aesthetics', p. 53.

17 This translation is slightly different to that in Bergin, 'lazy composition' taking the place of 'bad verse'.

18 The translation differs slightly from that in Bergin, in that 'lord' of Bearnas is substituted for 'chief' of Bearnas.

19 See, for instance, D. Robey, 'Humanist Views on the Study of Italian Poetry in the Early Italian Renaissance', in *CHLC*, pp. 626–647.

20 The conflict between art and nature had its origins in antiquity and each side secured adherents in every generation and trend. Debates between art and nature, war and peace, summer and winter, women and men, and so forth, were common in the debate literature itself. A poem such as this emerges from that background as much, if not more, than from any immediate factual cause.

21 The translation here differs slightly from that in Bergin, the term 'garron' is brought into English for reasons that become clear in the commentary.

22 Within the rankings of poets in the Provençal troubadour traditions, the use of a horse for travelling was a specific delineator of rank in some textual accounts. Outlining the ranked definitions of the various kinds of poet, versifier, singer, F. Jensen, *The Earliest Portuguese Lyrics* (Odense, 1978) (pp. 28–29), noted as follows:

The *segrel* is defined in these lines as a nomadic *trovador* wandering from court to court. A distinctive feature seems to be that he owned a horse; he is a *cavaleiro*. . . . As for travelling on horseback, this does not set the *segrel* apart from the *jogral* who moved about by similar means of transportation, and who also frequented the courts.

The departure from the secluded cell to the back of a garron is a suitable comment on the change in literary tastes, if that is what is being conveyed. The sense that transportation suitable to the rank of the poet – apart altogether from the propriety of composing in the open air – may wake echoes of the distinctions outlined in troubadour literature.

23   The poets are Donnchadh Mór Ó Dálaigh (d. 1244) (q. 3a); Giolla Brighde Mac Con Midhe (*fl.* thirteenth century) (q. 3b); Aonghus Ruadh Ó Dálaigh (*fl.* thirteenth century) (q. 5a); Sgolb (another member of the Ó Dálaigh family) (*fl.* fourteenth century) (q. 6a); Eoghan Mág Craith, 'An tÓrthóir' (fifteenth century) (6b); Gofraidh Fionn Ó Dálaigh (d. 1387) (q. 7a); Tadhg Óg Ó hUiginn (d. 1448) (q. 8b). Some of the famous poets listed are identified by their sobriquets or by-names. The use of nicknames within the literary cliques is well known from the troubadour circles and was popular too, for instance, in the Carolingian court, see, for example, M.-A. Bossy, *Medieval Latin Poems of Male Love and Friendship* (Garland Library of Medieval Literature, vol. 52, ser. A) (New York and London, 1987), pp. xvii–xxi.

24   The translation here differs slightly from that in Bergin, 'secluded quarters' is preferred to 'dim couches'.

25   These are poets cited again and again in *IGT* as headliners for scholars and poets. See D. McManus, 'The Irish Grammatical and Syntactical Tracts: A Concordance of Duplicated and Identified Citations', *Ériu* 48 (1997), pp. 165–187; and idem, 'Varia IV, *IGT* Citations and Duplice Entries: Some Additional Identifications', *Ériu* 51 (2000), pp. 193–194.

26 The translation here differs very slightly from that in Bergin, 'wisdom' instead of 'subtlety'; 'poetry' rather than 'verse'.

27 P. A. Breatnach, in 'Aesthetics', p. 53, remarks, 'That he should disobey the convention of composing while reclining in a dark cell should not altogether surprise us, in view of the exceptional character of his poetic talent.'

Select Bibliography

PRIMARY TEXTS

Adcock, F. 1994. *Hugh Primas and the Archpoet*. Cambridge.

Ahlqvist, A. 1983. '*The Early Irish Linguist: An Edition of the Canonical Part of the* Auraicept na nÉces. Helsinki.

Anderson, G. and W. 1963. Eds., *The Chronicles of Jean Froissart: In Lord Berner's Translation*. London.

Barney, S. A., W. J. Lewis and J. A. Beach. 2006. Eds., transl., intro. and notes, *The Etymologies of Isidore of Seville*. Cambridge.

Bergin, O. 1916–55. *Irish Grammatical Tracts*.. Supplement to *Ériu* 8 (Introductory); *Ériu* 8–10 (Declension); *Ériu* 14 (Irregular verbs and abstract nouns); *Ériu* 17 (Metrical faults).

Bergin, O. 1970. D. Greene and F. Kelly, eds., *Irish Bardic Poetry*. Dublin.

Best, R. I., O. Bergin and M. A. O'Brien. 1954. *The Book of Leinster*, vol. i. Dublin.

Bossy, M.-A. 1987. Ed. and transl., *Medieval Debate Poetry: Vernacular Works*. Garland Library of Medieval Literature, vol. 52 ser. A. New York and London.

Breatnach, L. 1981. 'The "Caldron of Poesy" '. *Ériu* 32: 45–93.

Breatnach, L. 1987. *Uraicecht na Ríar: The Poetic Grades in Early Irish Law*. Dublin.

Breatnach, P. A. 1986. 'Ar bhás Aodha an Einigh Mhéig Uidhir AD 1428'. *Éigse* 21: 37–52.

Breatnach, P. A. 1993. 'A Covenant between Eochaidh Ó hEódhusa and Aodh Mág Uidhir'. *Éigse* 27: 59–66.

Breatnach, P. A. 1999. 'A Poem on the End of Patronage'. *Éigse* 31: 79–88.

Breatnach, P. A. 2005. 'Elegy of Aodh Ruadh Ó Domhnaill (d. 1505)'. *Éigse* 35: 27–52.

Breatnach, R. A. 1941–1942 (1943). 'A Poem on Rime in Scholastic Verse'. *Éigse* 3: 36–51.

Breatnach, R. B. 1939 (1940). 'Oidheadh Chloinne Tuireann: A Sixteenth-Century Latin Fragment'. *Éigse* 1: 249–257.

Bugge, A. 1905. Ed., *Caithreim Cellachain Caisil, or the Wars between the Irishmen and the Norsemen in the Middle of the Tenth Century*. Oslo.

Burgwinkle, W. E. 1990. Razos *and Troubadour Songs*. Garland Library of Medieval Literature, vol. 71, ser. B. New York and London.

Byrne, F. J. 1964. 'Clann Ollaman Uaisle Emna'. *Studia Hibernica* 4: 54–94.

Calder, G. (1917) 1995. Ed., *Auraicept na n-Éces: The Scholars' Primer. Being the texts of the Ogham tract from the Book of Ballymote and the Yellow Book of Lecan, and the text of the Trefhocal from the Book of Leinster*. (Edinburgh) Dublin.

Caplan, H. 1981. Transl., *(Cicero) Ad Herennium: De Ratione Dicendi*. Harvard.

Carney, J. 1939 (1940). 'A Poem in Bérla na bFiled'. *Éigse* 1: 84–89.

Carney, J. 1943. *Topographical Poems by Seaán Mór Ó Dubhagáin and Giolla-na-naomh Ó hUidhrín*. Dublin.

Carney, J. 1950. 'De Scriptoribus Hibernicis'. *Celtica* 1: 86–103.

Carney, J. 1950. Ed., *Poems on the O'Reillys*. Dublin.

Ní Cheallacháin, M. 1962. *Filíocht Phádraigín Haicéad*. Baile Átha Cliath.

Chambers, F. M. 1979. 'Three Troubadour Poems with Historical Overtones'. *Speculum* 54: 42–54.

Connelly, P. 1998. *Irish Exchequer Payments 1270–1446*. 2 vols. Dublin.

Corcoran, T. 1928. *Education Systems in Ireland from the Close of the Middle Ages: Selected Texts with Introduction*. Dept. of Education, University College, Dublin.

Curtis, E. 1932. Ed., *Calendar of Ormond Deeds 1172–1350 AD*. Dublin.

Curtis, E. 1934. *Ormond Deeds: Being the Mediaeval Documents Preserved at Kilkenny Castle*. Dublin.

Dillon, M. 1962. Ed., *Lebor na Cert: The Book of Rights*. Irish Texts Society, vol. 46. Dublin.

Eriugena, John Scottus. 1987. *Periphyseon: Division of Nature.* Transl. I. P. Sheldon-Williams, revised by John O'Meara. Cahiers d'Études Médiévales: Cahier Spécial (3). Washington.

Fairclough, H. R. 1970. *Horace: Satires, Epistles and Ars Poetica.* Harvard.

Faral, E. (1924) 1962. *Les Arts Poétiques du xiie et du xiiie Siècle.* Paris.

Faral, E. 1936. 'Le manuscrit du "Hunterian Museum" de Glasgow'. *Studi Medievali* a. 9. 2ᵃ serie. 18–119.

Flanagan, M. T. 2005. *Irish Royal Charters, Texts and Contexts.* Oxford.

Forste-Grupp, S. 1995. 'The Earliest Irish Personal Letter'. In K. Chadbourne, L. J. Maney and D. Wong, eds., *Proceedings of the Harvard Celtic Colloquium (April 27–30),* vol. xv: 1–11.

Gilbert, J. T. 1879–1880. Ed., *Contemporary History of Affairs in Ireland, 1641–1652.* 3 vols. Dublin.

Godman, P. 1985. *Poetry of the Carolingian Renaissance.* London.

Gray, E. A. 1982. *Cath Maige Tuired = the Second Battle of Mag Tuired.* London.

Greene, D. 1947. 'Mac Bronn'. *Éigse* 5: 231–235.

Greene, D. 1972. Ed., *Duanaire Mhéig Uidhir.* Dublin.

Gwynn, E. (1903–1935) 1991. *Metrical Dindshenchas.* 5 vols. Dublin.

Gwynn, E. J. 1942. 'An Old-Irish Tract on the Privileges and Responsibilities of Poets'. *Ériu* 13: 1–60, 220–236.

Halliwell, S. 1995. Ed. and transl., *Aristotle: Poetics.* Loeb Classical Library XXIII. Cambridge, MA, and London.

Hamilton, H. C. (E. G. Atkinson and R. P. Mahaffy). 1860–1912. *Calendar of State Papers Relating to Ireland of the Reigns of Henry VIII, Edward VI, Mary, and Elizabeth, 1509–1603.* 11 vols. PRO London.

Hennessy, W. M., and B. MacCarthy. 1887–1901. Ed., transl., notes, *Annála Uladh: Annals of Ulster, otherwise Annála Senait: A Chronicle of Irish Affairs from AD 431 to AD 1540.* 4 vols. Dublin.

Henry, P. L. 1979–1980. 'The Caldron of Poesy'. *Studia Celtica* 14–15: 114–128.

Hubert, M. J. 1962. *The Romance of Flamenca: A Provençal Poem of the Thirteenth Century.* Princeton.

Hull, V. 1930. 'Conall Corc and the Kingdom of Cashel'. *Zeitschrift für Celtische Philologie* 18: 420–21.

Hull, V. 1941. 'The Exile of Conall Corc'. *Proceedings of the Modern Language Association of America* 56: 937–950.

Hull, V. 1947. 'Conall Corc and the Corco Luigde'. *Proceedings of the Modern Language Association of America* 62: 887–909.

Innes, D. C. 1995. Ed. and transl., based on W. Rys Roberts. *Demetrius On Style.* Loeb Classical Library XXIII. Cambridge, MA, and London.

Jackson, K. H. 1990. *Aislinge meic Con Glinne.* Dublin.

Jennings, B. 1953. Ed., *Wadding Papers, 1614–38.* Dublin.

Jensen, F. 1978. *The Earliest Portuguese Lyrics.* Odense.

Jolliffe, J. 1967. Ed. and trans., *Oeuvres de Froissart* (ed., J. M. B. Kervyn de Lettenhove) (25 vols, Brussels, 1867–1877). London (Henry Chrysted).

Joynt, M. 1941. *Tromdámh Guaire.* Dublin.

Kelly, M. 1848. Ed., John Lynch (1662), *Cambrensis Eversus.* 3 vols. Dublin.

Knott, E. 1910. 'An Address to David O'Keeffe'. *Ériu* 4: 209–231.

Knott, E. 1911. '*Filidh Éireann go hAointeach*'. *Ériu* 5: 50–69.

Knott, E. 1922–1926. Ed., *The Bardic Poems of Tadhg Dall Ó hUiginn 1550–1591.* 2 vols. Irish Texts Society, nos. 22–23. London.

Knott, E. 1928. *Irish Syllabic Poetry.* Cork.

Knott, E. 1974. *Irish Syllabic Poetry 1200–1600.* Dublin.

Lawler, T. 1974. *The* Parisiana Poetria *of John of Garland.* Ed., intro., transl., and notes. Yale University Press.

Lucas, A. M. 1995. *Anglo-Irish Poems of the Middle Ages.* Dublin.

Ludlow, J., and N. Jameson. 2004. Eds., *Medieval Ireland.* Barryscourt Lectures I–X. Cork.

Lynch, J. (1662) 1848. Ed. M. Kelly, *Cambrensis Eversus.* 3 vols. Dublin.

Mac Airt, S. 1944. Ed., *Leabhar Branach: The Book of the O'Byrnes.* Dublin.

Mac Airt, S. 1951. Ed., transl. and indexes. *The Annals of Inisfallen: MS Rawlinson B. 503.* Dublin.

Mac an Bhaird, A. 1977–1979. 'Dán díreach agus Ranna as na hAnnála 867–1134'. *Éigse* 17: 157–168.

Mac Aogáin, P. (1968) 2001. *Graiméir Ghaeilge na mBráthar Mionúir.* Baile Átha Cliath.

Mac Carthy, B. 1892. *The Codex Palatino-Vaticanus: no. 830 (text, translations and indices).* Todd Lecture Series, vol. 3. Dublin.

MacCarthy, D. 1867. *The Life and Letters of Florence MacCarthy Reagh, Tanist of Carbery, Mac Carthy Mór: With Some Portion of "The History of the Ancient Families of the South of Ireland".* London.

Mac Cionnaith, L. 1938. *Dioghluim Dána.* Dublin. (See also, McKenna, L.)

Mac Eoin, G. S. 1961. 'Dán ar Chogadh na Traoi'. *Studia Hibernica* 1: 19–55.

McErlean, J. C. 1910–1917. *Duanaire Dháibhidh Uí Bhruadair: the Poems of David Ó Bruadair.* 3 vols. Irish Texts Society 1910 vol. 11, 1913 vol. 13, 1917 vol. 18. London.

McKenna, L. 1918. *Iomarbháigh na bhFileadh.* London.

McKenna, L. 1919. 'Historical Poems of Gofraidh Fionn Ó Dálaigh'. *The Irish Monthly* January; successive pagings.

McKenna, L. 1919. Ed., *Dánta do chum Aonghus Fionn Ó Dálaigh.* With translation and notes. Preface by O. Bergin. Dublin and London.

McKenna, L. 1921. 'Poem to Maghnus O Conchobhair by Tadhg Mór Ó hUiginn'. *Irish Monthly* July: 279–298.

McKenna, L. 1922. Ed., *Dán Dé: The Poems of Donnchadh Mór Ó Dálaigh, and the Religious Poems in the Duanaire of the Yellow Book of Lecan.* Dublin.

McKenna, L., 1931. Ed., *Philip Bocht Ó Huiginn.* Dublin.

McKenna, L., 1938. Ed., *Dioghluim Dána.* Baile Átha Cliath.

McKenna, L. 1939–1940. *Aithdhioghluim Dána.* 2 vols. Irish Texts Society, vols. 37 and 40. Dublin.

McKenna, L. (1944) 1979. Ed., *Bardic Syntactical Tracts.* Dublin.

McKenna, L. 1947. Ed., *The Book of Maguaran: Leabhar Méig Shamradháin*. Dublin.

McKenna, L. 1947. 'A Poem by Gofraidh Fionn Ó Dálaigh'. In S. Pender, ed., *Essays and Studies Presented to Professor Tadhg Ua Donnchadha (Torna)*: 66–76. Cork.

McKenna, L. 1951. 'Some Irish Bardic Poems'. *Studies* 40: 93–96; 217–222; 352–363.

McKenna, L. 1952. 'A Poem by Gofraidh Fionn Ó Dálaigh'. *Ériu* 16: 132–139. (See also Mac Cionnaith. L.)

McLaughlin, R. 2005. 'A Threat of Satire by Tadhg (mac Dáire) Mac Bruaideadha'. *Ériu* 55: 37–57.

Mac Néill, E. 1908. *Duanaire Finn: The Book of the Lays of Fionn* i. (Irish Texts Society, vol. 7). London.

Mac Niocaill, G. 1961. Ed., *Notitae as Leabhar Cheanannais 1033–1161*. Baile Átha Cliath.

Mac Niocaill, G. 1963. 'Duanaire Ghearóid Iarla ('The "Poem-book" of Gerald, Earl of Desmond'). *Studia Hibernica* 3: 7–59.

Mac Raghnaill, F. 1976. Ed., Bonabhentura Ó hEodhasa OFM, *An Teagasc Críosdaidhe* (Antwerp 1611). Baile Átha Cliath.

Mhág Craith, C. 1967, 1980. Ed., *Dán na mBráthar Mionúr*. 2 vols. Dublin.

Meyer, K. 1894. *Hibernica Minora, being a Fragment of an Old Irish Treatise on the Psalter.* Oxford.

Meyer, K. 1905. 'Three Poems in Bérla na Filed'. *Zeitschrift für Celtische Philologie* 5: 482–494.

Murphy, D. 1896. Ed., *The Annals of Clonmacnoise*. Dublin.

Murphy, G. 1933. *Duanaire Finn: The Book of the Lays of Fionn* ii. Irish Texts Society, vol. 28. London.

Murphy, G. 1944. 'A Poem in Praise of Aodh Úa Foirréidh, Bishop of Armagh (1032–1056).' In S. O'Brien, ed., *Measgra i gcuimhne Mhichíl Uí Chléirigh*: 140–164. Dublin.

Murphy, G. 1953. *Duanaire Finn: The Book of the Lays of Fionn* iii. Irish Texts Society, vol. 43. Dublin.

Murphy, G. 1953–1955. 'Two Irish Poems Written from the Mediterranean in the Thirteenth Century'. *Éigse* 7: 71–79.

Murphy, J. J. 1971. *Three Medieval Rhetorical Arts.* University of California Press.

Nicholls, K. W. 1970. 'The Lisgoole Agreement of 1580'. *Clogher Record* 7: 27–33.

Ó Concheanainn, T. 1983. 'Dán Réitigh ó Fhearghal Óg Mac an Bhaird'. *Celtica* 15: 88–95.

Ó Concheanainn, T. 1984. 'Dán Molta ó Fhearghal Óg Mac an Bhaird'. *Celtica* 16: 73–85.

Ó Cuív, B. 1945. *Cath Muighe Tuireadh: The Second Battle of Magh Tuireadh.* Dublin.

Ó Cuív, B. 1954. 'A Poem on the Uí Néill'. *Celtica* 2: 245–251.

Ó Cuív, B. 1956–1957. 'A Poem in Praise of Raghnall, King of Mann'. *Éigse* 8: 283–301.

Ó Cuív, B. 1964–1966. 'Scél: Arramainte: Stair'. *Éigse* 11: 18.

Ó Cuív, B. 1969–1970. 'A Pilgrim's Poem'. *Éigse* 13: 105–109.

Ó Cuív, B. 1971–72. 'An Appeal on Behalf of the Profession of Poetry'. *Éigse* 14: 86–106.

Ó Cuív, B. 1973–1974. 'A Sixteenth-Century Political Poem'. *Éigse* 15: 261–276.

Ó Cuív, B. 1977. 'The Earl of Thomond and the Poets'. *Celtica* 12: 125–145.

Ó Cuív, B. 1981. 'An Irish Poet at the Roman Curia'. *Celtica* 14: 6–7.

Ó Cuív, B. 1983. 'A Poem for Fínghin Mac Carthaigh Riabhach'. *Celtica* 15: 96–110.

Ó Donnchadha, T. 1912. 'Cert Cech Rig co Réil'. In O. Bergin and C. Marstrander, eds., *Miscellany presented to Kuno Meyer*: 258–277. Halle. (See also, T. O'Donoughue.)

Ó Donnchadha, T. 1931. Ed., *Leabhar Cloinne Aodha Buidhe.* Baile Átha Cliath.

Ó Donnchadha, T. (1945?) Ed., *An Leabhar Muimhneach Maraon le Suim Aguisíní.* Baile Átha Cliath.

O'Donoghue, T. 1921–1923. 'Advice to a Prince'. *Ériu* 9: 43–54. (See also, T. Ó Donnchadha.)

O'Donnell, T. J. 1960. Ed., *Selections from the Zoilomastix of Philip O'Sullivan Beare.* Dublin.

O'Donovan, J. 1846. Ed., 'Annals of Ireland from the Year 1443 to 1468, translated from the Irish by Dudley Firbisse, or as he is more usually called Duald Mac Firbis, for Sir John Ware, in the Year 1666'. *Miscellany of the Irish Archaeological Society* i: 198–302. Dublin.

O'Donovan, J. 1852. *The Tribes of Ireland: A Satire by Aenghus O'Daly, with Poetical Translation by the late James Clarence Mangan*. Dublin.

O'Donovan, J. (1851) 1990. *Annals of the Kingdom of Ireland*. 3rd. ed., Dublin.

Ó Fachtna, A. 1953. *Parrthas an Anma, Antoin Gearnon*, OFM *a chum*. Baile Átha Cliath.

Ó Fiannachta, P. 1978. *An Barántas*. Maigh Nuad.

Ó Háinle, C. 1985. 'Flattery Rejected: Two Seventeenth-Century Irish Poems'. *Hermathena* 138: 5–27.

Ó Háinle, C. 2000. 'Teora Dréachta Adhmholta do Chuingidh Shíodha'. Eds., P. Riggs, B. Ó Conchúir, and S. Ó Coileáin, *Saoi na hÉigse: Aistí in ómós do Sheán Ó Tuama*: 1–22. Baile Átha Cliath.

Ó hInnse, S. 1947. *Miscellaneous Irish Annals (AD 1114–1437)*. Dublin.

Ó Macháin, P. 1986. 'Ar Bhás Chuinn Chéadchathaigh'. *Éigse* 21: 53–65.

Ó Muraíle, N. 2003. Ed., transl. and indexes, *Leabhar Mór na Genealach = The Great Book of Irish Genealogies . . .* compiled 1645–1666 by Dubhaltach Mac Fhirbhisigh. 5 vols. Dublin.

Ó Raghallaigh. T. 1930. Ed., *Duanta Eoghain Ruaidh Mhic An Bhaird*. Gaillimh.

O'Rahilly, C. 1961. Ed., *The Stowe Version of Táin Bó Cuailnge*. Dublin.

O'Rahilly, C. 1967. Ed., *Táin Bó Cúalnge from the Book of Leinster*. Dublin.

O'Rahilly, T. F. (T. Ó Rathile) (1924) Rev. and corr. 1926. *Dánta Grádha: An Anthology of Irish Love Poetry (AD 1350–1750)*. With an Introduction by R. Flower. Cork.

O'Rahilly, T. F. 1927. *Measgra Dánta*, 2 vols. Cork.

O'Rahilly, T. F. 1955. Ed., Flaithrí Ó Maolchonaire, *Desiderius, otherwise called Sgáthán an Chrábhaidh*. Dublin.

O'Sullivan, A. 1971–1972. 'Tadhg O'Daly and Sir George Carew'. *Éigse* 14: 27–38.

O'Sulllivan, A. 1987. Ed. and asst. P. Ó Riain. *Poems on Marcher Lords from a Sixteenth-Century Tipperary Manuscript.* London.

Paetow, L. J. 1927. Ed. and transl., *Two Medieval Satires on the University of Paris: 'La Bataille des VII ars' of Henri d'Andeli and the 'Morale Scolarium' of John of Garland*. Memoirs of the University of California, vol. 4, nos. 1 and 2. Berkeley.

Parr, R. P. 1981. Transl. from Latin with an Introduction, *Matthew of Vendôme: Ars Versificatoria*. Mediaeval Philosophical Texts in Translation, no. 22. Wisconsin.

Quinn, D. B. 'Calendar of the Irish Council Book, 1581–1586'. *Analecta Hibernica* 24: 1–90.

Quin, E. G. 1939. Ed. and transl., with notes, glossary, *Stair Ercuil ocus a Bás: The Life and Death of Hercules*. Irish Texts Society, vol. 38. Dublin.

Roberts, W. Rhys. 1902. *Demetrius, On Style: The Greek Text of Demetrius De Elecutione*, edited after the Paris manuscript with introduction, translation, facsimiles. Cambridge.

Rossetti, D. G. (1861) 2001. Transl., Dante Alighieri, *La Vita Nuova*. (London), Dover Publications, New York.

Russell, D. 1995. Transl., W. H. Fyfe, rev. by D. Russell, *Longinus on Style*. Loeb Classical Library XXIII. Cambridge, MA, and London.

Simms, K. 1977. 'The Concordat between Primate John Mey and Henry O'Neill (1455)'. *Archivium Hibernicum* 34: 71–82.

Stehling, T. 1985. Transl., *Medieval Latin Poems of Male Love and Friendship*. Garland Library of Medieval Literature, vol. 7. New York and London.

Stokes, W. (1896/97) 1993. Ed. and transl., *The Annals of Tigernach*. A facsimile reprint by Llanerch Publishers, vol. 2. Llanerch. (Reprinted from *Revue Celtique* 1896/97.)

Stokes, W. 1909. Ed. and transl., *In Cath Catharda: The Civil War of the Romans, an Irish Version of Lucan's Pharsalia*. Irische Texte, 4th series, vol. 2. Leipzig.

Thurneysen, R. 1891. 'Mittelirische Verslehren'. In W. H. Stokes and E. Windisch, eds., *Irische Texte*, 3rd series, vol. I. Leipzig.

Todd, J. H. 1846. 'Autograph Letter of Thady O'Roddy'. In J. O'Donovan, ed., *Miscellany of the Irish Archaeological Society* i: 112–125. Dublin.

Ní Uallacháin, Í. 2004. *Exempla Gaeilge: An Cnuasach Exempla Gaeilge sa LS 20978–9 i Leabharlann Ríoga na Bruiséile*. Dán agus Tallann, vol. II. Maigh Nuad.

Wall, B. V. 1937. *A Medieval Latin Version of Demetrius, De Elocutione*. Washington.

Waddell, H. 1952. *Medieval Latin Lyrics*. London.

Walsh, K. 1970. 'The "De Vita Evangelica" of Geoffrey Hardeby, OESA (*c*. 1320–*c*. 1385): A Study in the Mendicant Controversies of the Fourteenth Century'. *Analecta Augustiniana* 33: 151–261.

Walsh, P. 1928. 'An Irish Poem Addressed to Aodh Ruadh Ó Domhnaill (*Ataim inchóra re hAodh*)'. *Irish Ecclesiastical Record* 31: 583–588.

Webb, J. 1824. Ed. and transl., 'Histoire du Roy d'Angleterre Richard' (Jean Creton). *Archaeologia* 20.

SECONDARY TEXTS

Ames-Lewis, F. 2000. *The Intellectual Life of the Early Renaissance Artist*. New Haven and London.

Anglo, S. 1992. *Images of Tudor Kingship*. London.

Ariés, P., and G. Duby. 1988. Eds., *A History of Private Life: Revelations of the Medieval World*. Harvard.

Armstrong, J. 1985. 'A Glossarial Index of Nouns and Adjectives in *Irish Grammatical Tracts* i–v'. *Proceedings of the Harvard Celtic Colloquium* 5: 187–410.

Baldwin, J. A. 1997. 'The Image of the Jongleur in Northern France around 1200'. *Speculum* 72: 635–663.

Balogh, J. 1928. 'Rex a Recte Regendo'. Speculum 3: 580–582.

Barrington, T. J. 1976. Discovering Kerry, Its History, Heritage and Topography. Dublin.

Barry, T. 2000. 'Rural Settlement in Medieval Ireland'. In T. Barry, ed., A History of Settlement in Ireland. London and New York: 110–123.

Bergin, O., and C. Marstrander. 1912. Eds., Miscellany Presented to Kuno Meyer by his Friends and Pupils on the Occasion of his Appointment to the Chair of Celtic Philology in the University of Berlin. Halle.

Bergin, O. 1921. 'Nominative and Vocative'. Ériu 9: 92–94.

Bergin, O. 1938. The Native Irish Grammarian. Proceedings of the British Academy 24. London.

Bergin, T. G. and R. T. Hill. 1973. Anthology of the Provençal Troubadours. 2nd ed., revised, and enlarged by T. G. Bergin, with the collaboration of S. Olsen, W. D. Paden, JR, and N. Smith. 2 vols. New Haven and London.

Bieler, L. (1971) 1979. 'The Classics in Celtic Ireland'. In R. R. Bolgar, ed., Classical Influences on European Culture AD 500–1500. Cambridge: 45–55.

Binchy, D. A. 1929. 'The Irish Benedictine Congregation in Medieval Germany'. Studies 18: 194–210.

Bischoff, B. 1961. 'The Study of Foreign Languages in the Middle Ages'. Speculum 36: 209–224.

de Blácam, A. 1929. Gaelic Literature Surveyed. Cork and Dublin.

Bliss, A., and J. Long. 1987. 'Literature in Norman French and English to 1534'. In A. Cosgrove, ed., A New History of Ireland ii: Medieval Ireland 1169–1534: 708–736. Oxford.

Bolgar, R. R. (1971) 1979. Ed., Classical Influences on European Culture AD 500–1500. Cambridge.

Bracken, D. 2002. 'Authority and Duty: Columbanus and the Primacy of Rome'. Peritia 16: 168–213.

Bradley, J. 1985. 'The Medieval Towns of Tipperary'. In W. Nolan, and T. G. McGrath, eds., Tipperary: History and Society: 34–59. Dublin.

Bradley, J. 1988. Ed., *Settlement and Society in Medieval Ireland: Studies Presented to F. X. Martin, OSA.* Kilkenny.

Bradshaw, B. 1979. 'Manus "The Magnificent": O'Donnell as Renaissance Prince'. In A. Cosgrove and D. McCartney, eds., *Studies in Irish History: Presented to R. Dudley Edwards*: 15–84. Dublin.

Bradshaw, B., and D. Keogh. 2002. Eds., *Christianity in Ireland: Revisiting the Story.* Dublin.

Breatnach, L. 1988. 'An Aoir sa Ré Luath'. In P. Ó Fiannachta, ed., *An Aoir*. Léachtaí Cholm Cille, 18: 11–19. Maigh Nuad.

Breatnach, L. 1993. 'Sedulius Scottus, St Gall Stiftsbibliothek 73, and Latin in the Irish Laws'. *Proceedings of the Irish Biblical Society* 16: 123–124.

L. Breatnach, 1994. 'An Mheán-Ghaeilge'. In K. McCone, D. McManus, C. Ó Háinle, N. Williams and L. Breatnach, *Stair na Gaeilge, in Ómós do Pádraig Ó Fiannachta.* Maigh Nuad.

Breatnach, L. 2005. *A Companion to the Corpus Iuris Hibernici.* Dublin.

Breatnach, P. A. 1980. Review: *The Poems of Giolla Brighde Mac Con Midhe.* Ed. N. J. A. Williams. Irish Texts Society, vol. 51. *Éigse* 19: 411–426.

Breatnach, P. A. 1983. 'The Chief's Poet'. *Proceedings of the Royal Irish Academy* C 83: 37–79.

Breatnach, P. A. 1991. 'Die Entwicklung und Gestaltung des Neuirischen Rhythmischen Versmaßes'. In H. L. C. Tristram, ed., *Metrik und Medienwechsel: Metrics and Media* 289–299. Tübingen.

Breatnach, P. A. 1996. *A New Introduction to the Bardic Poems of Tadhg Dall Ó hUiginn (1550–1591).* Irish Texts Society. London.

Breatnach, P. A. 1997. *Téamaí Taighde Nua-Ghaeilge.* Maigh Nuad.

Breatnach, P. A. 1999. 'An Irish Bollandus: Fr Hugh Ward and the Louvain Hagiographic Enterprise'. *Éigse* 31: 1–30.

Breatnach, P. A. 2001. 'The Aesthetics of Irish Bardic Composition', *Cambrian Medieval Celtic Studies* 42 (Winter): 50–72.

Breatnach, R. A. 1967. *Great Books of Ireland.* Dublin.

Briscoe, M. G. (and B. H. Jaye). 1992. *Artes Praedicandi* (M. G. Briscoe) and *Artes Orandi* (B. H. Jaye). Typologie des Sources du Moyen Âge Occidental, fasc. 61. Turnhout.

Bromwich, R. 1974. *Medieval Celtic Literature: A Select Bibliography.* Toronto Medieval Bibliographies, vol. 2. Toronto.

Brooks, N. 1982. Ed., *Latin and the Vernacular Languages in Early Britain.* Leicester.

Buttimer, C. G., and P. O'Flanagan. 1993. Eds., *Cork History and Society: Interdisciplinary Essays on the History of an Irish County.* Dublin.

Butzer, P., M. Kerner and W. Oberschlep. 1997. Eds., *Karl der Grosse und sein Nachwirken: 1200 Jahre Kultur und Wissenschaften in Europa: Charlemagne and His Heritage: 1200 Years of Civilization and Science in Europe.* Turnhout.

Byrne, F. J. (1973) 2001. *Irish Kings and High-Kings.* Dublin.

Byrne, F. J. 1974. 'Senchas: The Nature of Gaelic Historical Tradition'. *Historical Studies* 9: 137–59.

Byrne, F. J. 1979. *1000 Years of Irish Script: An Exhibition of Manuscripts at the Bodleian Library.* Oxford.

Byrne, F. J. 1987. 'The Trembling Sod: Ireland in 1169'. In A. Cosgrove, ed., *A New History of Ireland ii: Medieval Ireland 1169–1534*: 1–42. Oxford.

Cahill, E. 1935. 'Irish in the Early Middle Ages'. *Irish Ecclesiastical Record* (5th ser.) 45: 363–76.

Camargo, M. 1991. *Ars Dictaminis, Ars Dictandi.* Typologie des Sources du Moyen Âge Occidental, fasc. 60. Turnhout.

Camille, M. 1998. *The Medieval Art of Love: Objects and Subjects of Desire.* London.

Carey, J. 1994. *The Irish National Original Legend: Synthetic Pseudo-History.* Quiggin Pamphlets on the Sources of Mediaeval Gaelic History, vol. i. Cambridge

Carey, J. 2003. *Duanaire Finn: Reassessments.* Irish Texts Society, supplementary volume 13. Dublin.

Carey, J., M. Herbert and K. Murray. 2005. Eds., *Cín Chille Cúile: Texts, Saints and Places. Essays in Honour of Pádraig Ó Riain.* Cork.

Carney, J. 1967. *The Irish Bardic Poet.* Dublin.

Carney, J. 1969. 'The Ó Cianáin Miscellany'. *Ériu* 21: 122–147.

Carney, J. 1987. ' Literature in Irish, 1169–1534'. In A. Cosgrove, ed., *A New History of Ireland ii: Medieval Ireland 1169–1534*: 688–707. Oxford.

Carr, A. D. 1992. 'The Patrons of the Medieval Welsh Poets in North Wales'. *Études Celtiques* 29: 115–120.

Carroll, C. 2001. *Circe's Cup: Cultural Transformation in Early Modern Writing about Ireland*. Cork.

Carroll, C. 2005. 'Early Modern Ireland'. In S. Deane and B. Mac Suibhne, eds., *Field Day Review 2005*: 205–215. Dublin.

Charles-Edwards, T. M. 2000. *Early Christian Ireland*. Cambridge.

Charles-Edwards, T. M. 2005. 'Early Irish Law'. In D. Ó Cróinín, ed., *A New History of Ireland i: Prehistoric and Early Ireland*: 331–370. Oxford.

Chaytor, H. J. 1946. *The Provençal Chanson de Geste.* London.

Childs, W., and T. O'Neill. 1987. 'Overseas Trade'. In A. Cosgrove, ed., *A New history of Ireland, ii: Medieval Ireland 1169–1534*: 439–491. Oxford.

Clanchy, M. T. 1997. *Abelard: A Medieval Life.* Oxford.

Clarke, H. B., J. Prunty and M. Hennessy. 2004. Eds., *Surveying Ireland's Past: Multidisciplinary Essays in Honour of Anngret Simms*. Dublin.

Connolly, S. J. 1998. *The Oxford Companion to Irish History.* Oxford.

Copeland, R. 1991. *Rhetoric, Hermeneutics, and Translation in the Middle Ages.* Cambridge.

Cormier, R. 1964–1966. 'The Maddening Rain: A Comparison of the Irish and Provençal versions'. *Éigse* 11: 247–251.

Cosgrove, A. 1979. 'Hiberniores ipsis Hibernis'. In A. Cosgrove and D. McCartney, eds., *Studies in Irish History: presented to R. Dudley Edwards*: 1–14. Dublin.

Cosgrove, A. 1987. Ed., *A New History of Ireland, ii: Medieval Ireland 1169–1534.* Oxford.

Cotter, F. J. 1994. *The Friars Minor in Ireland from their Arrival to 1400.* New York.

Cregan, Donal F. 1979. 'The Social and Cultural Background of a Counter-Reformation Episcopate, 1618–60'. In A. Cosgrave, and D. McCartney, eds., *Studies in Irish History*. Dublin.

Cronin, A. 1943/44. 'Printed Sources for Keating's *Foras Feasa*'. *Éigse* 4: 235–279.

Cronin, A. 1948 (1945/47). 'Printed Sources for Keating's *Foras Feasa*'. *Éigse* 5: 122–135.

Cunningham, B., and R. Gillespie. 1984. 'The East Ulster Bardic Family of Ó Gnímh'. *Éigse* 20: 106–114.

Cunningham, B. 1986. 'An Ulster Settler and his Irish Manuscripts'. *Éigse* 21: 25–36.

Cunningham, B. 1991. 'The Culture and Ideology of Irish Franciscan Historians at Louvain 1607–1650'. In C. Brady, ed., *Ideology and the Historians*. Historical Studies XVII: 11–30. Dublin.

Cunningham, B. 1999. 'The Source of Trí Biorghaoithe an Bháis: Another French Sermon'. *Éigse* 31: 73–77.

Cunningham, B. 2000. *The World of Geoffrey Keating: History, Myth and Religion in Seventeenth-Century Ireland*. Dublin.

Curtis, E. 1919. 'The Spoken Languages of Medieval Ireland'. *Studies* 8: 234–54.

Curtis, E. 1932. 'Extracts out of the Heralds' Books in Trinity College, Dublin, Relating to Ireland in the 16th Century'. *Journal of the Royal Society of Antiquaries of Ireland* 62 (vol. 2, 7th series): 28–49.

Curtius, E. R. 1953. *European Literature and the Latin Middle Ages*. Transl. from German by W. R. Trask. London.

Davies, N. 2000. *The Isles: A History*. London.

Deane, S., and B. Mac Suibhne. 2005. *Field Day Review 2005*. Dublin.

Dictionary of the Irish Language: Based Mainly on Old and Middle Irish Materials 1913–1976. 1983 compact edition. Royal Irish Academy. Dublin.

Dillon, M. 1952. 'The Story of the Finding of Cashel'. *Ériu* 16: 61–73.

Dilts Swartz, D. 1985. 'The Beautiful Women and the Warriors in the LL TBC and in Twelfth-Century Neo-Classical Rhetoric'. *Proceedings of the Harvard Celtic Colloquium* 5: 128–146.

Dinneen, P. S. 1927. *Foclóir Gaedhilge agus Béarla: An Irish-English Dictionary*. Dublin.

Doan, J. E. 1992. 'The Erotics of Backgammon in Provençal and Irish Poetry'. *Proceedings of the Harvard Celtic Colloquium* 12: 29–42.

Doherty, C. 1980. 'Exchange and Trade in Early Medieval Ireland'. *Journal of the Royal Irish Society of Antiquaries* 110: 67–89.

Doherty, C. 1991. 'Latin Writing in Ireland, *c.* 400–1200'. In S. Deane, A. Carpenter and J. Williams, eds., *The Field Day Anthology of Irish Writing*: 61–140. Derry.

Doherty, C. 2000. 'Settlement in Early Ireland: A Review'. In T. Barry, ed., *A History of Settlement in Ireland*. London and New York: 50–80.

Ní Dhomhnaill, C. 1981. 'Closure in Bardic Poetry'. *Celtica* 14: 47–61.

Ní Dhonnchadha, M. 1996. Ed., *Nua-léamha: Gnéithe de Chultúr, Stair agus Polaitíocht na hÉireann, c. 1600–c. 1900*. Baile Átha Cliath.

Dowling, P. J. (nd [1938]) *The Hedge Schools of Ireland*. Dublin and Cork.

Dowling, P. J. 1968. *The Hedge Schools of Ireland*. Cork.

Draak, M. 1967. 'The Higher Teaching of Latin Grammar in Ireland during the Ninth Century'. *Mededelingen de Koninklijke Nederlandse Akademie van wetenschappen, afd. letterkunde*. No. 4 (nieuwe reeks): 109–144. Amsterdam.

Dronke, P. 1994. 'Introduction'. In F. Adcock, *Hugh Primas and the Archpoet*: 17–22. Cambridge.

Dryburgh, P., and B. Smith. 2005. *Handbook and Select Calendar of Sources for Medieval Ireland in the National Archives of the United Kingdom*. Dublin and London.

Duffy, P., D. Edwards and E. FitzPatrick. 2001. Eds., *Gaelic Ireland: Land, Lordship and Settlement c. 1250–1650*. Dublin.

Elliot Van Liere, K. 2000 'Humanism and Scholasticism in Sixteenth-Century Academe: Five Student Orations from the University of Salamanca'. *Renaissance Quarterly* 53: 57–107

Emden, A. B. (1957) 1989. *A Biographical Register of the University of Oxford to AD 1500*. 3 vols. Oxford.

Empey, W. 1985. 'The Norman Period: 1185–1500'. In W. Nolan, and T. G. McGrath, eds., *Tipperary: History and Society*. Dublin: 71–91.

Flanagan, M. T. 1989. *Irish Society, Anglo-Norman Settlers, Angevin Kingship: Interaction in Ireland in the Late Twelfth Century*. Oxford.

Flanagan, M.-T. 2002. 'The Contributions of Irish Missionaries and Scholars to Medieval Christianity'. In B. Bradshaw and D. Keogh, eds., *Christianity in Ireland: Revisiting the Story*: 30–43. Dublin,

Frame, R. 1973. 'The Justiciarship of Ralph Ufford: Warfare and Politics in Fourteenth-Century Ireland'. *Studia Hibernica* 13: 45–46.

Frame, R. 1989. 'England and Ireland, 1171–1399'. In M. Jones and M. Vale, eds., *England and Her Neighbours: Essays in Honour of Pierre Chaplais*. London.

Franciscan Fathers, Dún Mhuire, Killiney. 1957. Eds., *Father Luke Wadding: Commemorative volume*. Dublin and London.

Fuhrmann, J. P. 1927. *Irish Medieval Monasteries on the Continent*. Washington.

Garrison, M. 1997. 'The English and the Irish at the Court of Charlemagne'. In P. Butzer, M. Kerner and W. Oberschlep, eds., *Karl der Grosse und sein Nachwirken: 1200 Jahre Kultur und Wissenschaften in Europa: Charlemagne and his Heritage: 1200 Years of Civilization and Science in Europe*: 97–123. Turnhout.

Geary, J. A. 1931. Ed., *An Irish Version of Innocent III's De Contemptu Mundi*. Washington.

Giblin, C. 1957. 'The *Processus Datariae* and the Appointment of Irish Bishops in the Seventeenth Century'. In Franciscan Fathers, Dún Mhuire, Killiney, eds., *Father Luke Wadding: Commemorative Volume*: 508–616. Dublin and London.

Gillingham, J. 1993. 'The English Invasion of Ireland'. In B. Bradshaw, A. Hadfield and W. Maley, eds., *Representing Ireland: Literature and the Origins of Conflict, 1534–1660*: 24–42. Cambridge.

Glasscock, R. E. 1987. 'Land and People, *c.* 1300'. In A. Cosgrove, ed., *A New History of Ireland ii: Medieval Ireland 1169–1534*: 204–239. Oxford.

Godden, M., and M. Lapidge. 1991. Eds., *The Cambridge Companion to Old English Literature*. Cambridge.

Graham, B. 1979. 'The Evolution of Urbanization in Medieval Ireland'. *Journal of Historical Geography* 5 ii: 111–125.

Graham, B. 2000. 'Urbanisation in Ireland during the High Middle Ages, *c.* 1100 to *c.* 1350'. In T. Barry, ed., *A History of Settlement in Ireland*: 124–139. London and New York.

Greene, D. 1983. '*Cró, Crú*, and Similar Words'. *Celtica* 15: 1–9.

Gunning, P. J. 1959. 'Sidelights on the Bishop of Raphoe from the Register of Pope Innocent III'. In T. O Donnell, ed., *Father John Colgan OFM 1592–1658: Essays in Commemoration of the Tercentenary of his Death*: 50–59. Dublin.

Gwynn, A. 1952. 'The Continuity of the Irish Tradition at Würzburg'. In *Herbipolis Jubilans: 1200 Jahre Bistum Würzburg*: 57–81.

Gwynn, A. 1968. 'The History of Medieval Ireland (review of A. J. Otway-Ruthven, *A History of Medieval Ireland* [London, 1968])'. *Studies* Summer 1968: 161–173.

Gwynn. A. 1968. 'The Twelfth-Century Reform'. In P. J. Corish, ed., *History of Irish Catholicism ii*, 1. Dublin.

Gwynn, A. 1968. 'Anglo-Irish Church Life in the 14th and 15th Centuries'. In P. J. Corish, ed., *History of Irish Catholicism ii*, 4. Dublin.

Hamburger, P. 1985. 'The Development of the Law of Seditious Libel and the Control of the Press'. *Stanford Law Review*: 661–765.

Hames, H. 2003. 'The Language of Conversion: Ramon Llull's Art as a Vernacular'. In F. Somerset and N. Watson, eds., *The*

Vulgar Tongue: Medieval and postMedieval Vernacularity: 43–56. Pennsylvania.

Hand, G. 1968. 'The Church in the English Lordship 1216–1307'. In P. J. Corish, ed., *History of Irish Catholicism ii*, 3. Dublin.

Hanford, J. H. 1926. 'The Progenitors of Golias'. *Speculum* 1: 38–58.

Harbison, P. 1975. 'The Twelfth and Thirteenth Century Irish Stone-Masons in Regensburg (Bavaria) and the End of the "School of the West" in Connacht'. *Studies* 64: 333–346.

Harrison, A. 1989. *The Irish Trickster*. Sheffield.

Haskins, C. H. 1928. 'Latin Literature under Frederick II'. *Speculum* 3: 120–151.

Haskins, C. H. 1929. *Studies in Mediaeval Culture*. New York.

Haskins, C. H. 1958. *The Renaissance of the Twelfth Century*. New York.

Hayes, R. 1948. 'Ireland's Links with Compostella'. *Studies* 37: 326–332.

Hayes McCoy, G. A. 1937. *Scots Mercenary Forces in Ireland, 1565–1603*. With an introduction by E. Mac Néill. Dublin and London.

Henry, F., and G. L. Marsh-Micheli. 1961–63. 'A Century of Irish Illumination (1070–1170)'. *Proceedings of the Royal Irish Academy* 62 C: 101–165.

Henry, F. 1970. *Irish Art in the Romanesque Period (1020–1170 AD)*. London.

Henry, F., and G. Marsh-Micheli. 1987. 'Manuscripts and Illuminations, 1169–1603'. In A. Cosgrove, ed., *A New History of Ireland ii: Medieval Ireland 1169–1534*: 781–815. Oxford.

Hennessey, M. 1985. 'Parochial Organisation in Medieval Tipperary'. In W. Nolan and T. G. McGrath, eds., *Tipperary: History and Society*: 60–70. Dublin.

Herbert, M. 1999. 'Sea-Divided Gaels?: Relationships between Irish and Scots c. 800–1169'. In B. Smith, ed., *Britain and Ireland 900–1300: Insular Response to Medieval European Change*. Cambridge.

Herrin, J. 2001. *The Formation of Christendom*. London.

Hofman, R. 2000. 'The Irish Tradition of Priscian'. In M. de Nonno, P. de Paolis and L. Holtz, eds., *Manuscripts and Tradition of Grammatical Texts from Antiquity to the Renaissance*: i, 257–287. 2 vols. Cassino.

Hogan, D., and W. N. Osborough. 1990. *Brehons, Serjeants and Attorneys: Studies in the History of the Irish Legal Profession*. Dublin.

Hogan, E. 1910. *Onomasticon Goedelicum: Locorum et Tribum Hiberniae et Scotiae*. Dublin.

Hogan, J. F. 1894. 'The Monastery and Library of St Gall'. *Irish Ecclesiastical Record* 15 (Jan.): 35–54.

Hogan, J. F. 1894. 'Art and Literature at St Gall'. *Irish Ecclesiastical Record* 15 (Apr.): 289–301.

Hogan, J. F. 1894. 'St Priminius of Reichenau'. *Irish Ecclesiastical Record* 15 (May): 403–417.

Hogan, J. F. 1894. 'The Irish Monasteries of Ratisbon'. *Irish Ecclesiastical Record* 15 (Nov.): 1015–1029.

Hore, H. F. 1858. 'Irish Bardism in 1561'. *Ulster Journal of Archaeology*, 1st ser. 6: 165–167; 202–212.

Hughes, A. J. 1994–1995. 'Land Acquisition by Gaelic Bardic Poets: Insights from Placenames and other Sources'. *Ainm* 6: 74–101.

Hunter, J. 1993. 'Professional Poets and Professional Insults: *Ad Hominem* Attacks in Late Medieval Welsh *Ymrysonau*'. *Proceedings of the Harvard Celtic Colloquium* 13: 54–65.

Jackson, W. T. H. 1960. *The Literature of the Middle Ages*. New York.

Jarcho, B. I. 1928. 'Die Vorläufer des Golias'. *Speculum* 3: 523–79.

Jennings, B. 1941. 'The Career of Hugh, Son of Rory O'Donnell, Earl of Tyrconnel, in the Low Countries, 1607–1642'. *Studies* 30: 219–234.

Jennings, B. 1944. 'Irish Students at the University of Louvain'. In S. O'Brien, ed., *Measgra i gCuimhne Mhichíl Uí Chléirigh*: 74–97. Dublin.

Keegan, M. 2005. 'The Archaeology of Manorial Settlement in West County Limerick in the Thirteenth Century.' In J. Lyttleton and T. O'Keeffe, eds., *The Manor in Medieval and Early Modern Ireland*: 17–39. Dublin.

Kelly, D. 1966. 'The Scope of the Treatment of Composition in the Twelfth and Thirteenth-Century Arts of Poetry'. *Speculum* xli: 261–278.

Kelly, D. 1991. *The Arts of Poetry and Prose*. Typologie des Sources du Moyen Âge Occidental, fasc. 59. Turnhout.

Kelly, F. 2003. 'Thinking in Threes: The Triad in Early Irish Literature'. Sir John Rhŷs Memorial Lecture. *Proceedings of the British Academy* 125: 1–18.

Kenney, J. F. 1929. *The Sources for the Early History of Ireland, i. Ecclesiastical.* New York.

Kenyon, J. R., and K. O'Conor. 2003. Eds., *The Medieval Castle in Ireland and Wales*. Dublin.

Ker, W. P. (1896) 1957. *Epic and Romance: Essays on Medieval Literature*. New York.

Ker, W. P. (1904) 1955. *The Dark Ages*. London.

King, B. 1982. *Seventeenth-Century English Literature*. New York.

Klein, K. W. 1971. *The Partisan Voice: A Study of the Political Lyric in France and Germany, 1180–1230*. The Hague and Paris.

Knott, E. 1952. 'An Index to the Proper Names in *Saltair na Rann*'. *Ériu* 16: 99–122.

Knott, E., and G. Murphy. 1966. *Early Irish Literature*. London.

Law, V. 1982. *The Insular Latin Grammarians*. Boydell Press: Woodbridge.

Law, V. 1995. *Wisdom, Authority and Grammar in the Seventh Century: Decoding Virgilius Maro Grammaticus*. Cambridge.

Law, V. 1999. 'Why Write a Verse Grammar?'. *Journal of Medieval Latin* 9: 46–76.

Law, V. 2000. 'Memory and the Structure of Grammars in Antiquity and the Middle Ages'. In M. de Nonno et al. *Manuscripts and Tradition of Grammatical Texts from Antiquity to the Renaissance*: i: 9–57. 2 vols. Cassino.

Law, V. 2003. *The History of Linguistics in Europe from Plato to 1600*. Cambridge.

Léeglu, C. 1997. 'Defamation in the Troubador *Sirventes*: Legislation and Lyric Poetry'. *Medium Aevum* 66: 28–41.

Lendinara, P. 1991. 'The World of Anglo-Saxon Learning'. In M. Godden and M. Lapidge, eds., *The Cambridge Companion to Old English Literature*: 264–281. Cambridge.

Lewent, K. 1963. 'The Catalan Troubadour Cerveri and his Contemporary, the Joglar Guillem de Cervera'. *Speculum* 38: 462–472.

Löfstedt, B. 1977. Ed., *Sedulius Scottus in Donati Artem Maiorem* (Corpus Christianorum, Cont. Med. 40b). Turnhout.

Ludlow, J., and N. Jameson. 2004. Eds., *Medieval Ireland: Barryscourt Lectures I–X*. Cork.

Luscombe, D. 1997. *Medieval Thought*. Oxford.

Lydon, J. 1987. 'The Impact of the Bruce Invasion 1315–27'. In A. Cosgrove, ed., *A New History of Ireland, ii: Medieval Ireland 1169–1534*. Oxford.

Lyons, M. A. 2003. *Franco-Irish Relations, 1500–1610: Politics, Migration and Trade*. Woodbridge, Suffolk.

Mac Cana, P. 1970. 'The Three Languages and the Three Laws'. *Studia Celtica* 5: 62–78.

Mac Cana, P. 1974. 'The Rise of the Later Schools of *Filidheacht*'. *Ériu* 25: 126–146.

Mac Cana, P. 1980. *The Learned Tales of Medieval Ireland*. Dublin.

Mac Cana, P. 2000. 'Croesaniaid *and* Crosáin: *Literary Outsiders*'. Ed. G. Jenkins, *Cymru a'r Cymry 2000: Wales and the Welsh 2000*: 19–39. Aberystwyth.

Mac Cana, P. 2004. 'Praise Poetry in Ireland before the Normans'. *Ériu* 54: 11–40.

McCarthy, T. J. H. 2002. 'Literary Practice in Eleventh-Century Music Theory: The *Colores Rhetorici* and Aribo's *De Musica*'. *Medium Aevum* 71: 191–208.

McCaughey, T. 2001. *Dr Bedell and Mr King: The Making of the Irish Bible*. Dublin.

McCone, K., D. McManus, C. Ó Háinle, N. Williams and L. Breatnach. 1994. Eds., *Stair na Gaeilge, in Ómós do Pádraig Ó Fiannachta*. Maigh Nuad.

Mac Craith, M. 1990. 'Gaelic Ireland and the Renaissance'. In G. Williams and R. O. Jones, eds., *The Celts and the Renaissance: Tradition and Innovation*: 57–89. Cardiff.

Mac Craith, M. 1996. 'Litríocht an 17ú hAois: Tonnbhriseadh an tSeanghnáthaimh nó Tonnchruthú an Nuaghnáthaimh?'. *Léachtaí Cholm Cille* 26: 50–79.

Mac Cuarta, B. 1993. 'A Planter's Interaction with Gaelic Culture, Sir Matthew de Renzy, 1577–1634'. *Irish Economic and Social History* 20: 1–17.

McCulloch, D. 2004. *The Reformation*. London.

Mac Eoin, G. 1960–1961. 'The Date and Authorship of Saltair na Rann'. *Zeitschrif für celtische Philologie* 28: 51–67.

McGrath, C. 1944. 'Eoghan Ruadh mac Uilliam Mac an Bhaird'. In S. O'Brien, ed., *Measgra i gCuimhne Mhichíl Uí Chléirigh*: 108–116. Dublin.

McGrath, F. 1979. *Education in Ancient and Medieval Ireland*. Dublin.

McGrath, M. 1975. 'The Wall-Paintings in Cormac's Chapel at Cashel'. *Studies* 64: 327–332.

McGrath, T. G., and W. Nolan. 1985. Eds., *Tipperary: History and Society*. Dublin.

McInnes, J. 1976–1978. 'The Panegyric Code in Gaelic Poetry and its Historical Background'. *Transactions of the Gaelic Society of Inverness* 50: 435–498.

McIntosh, A., and M. L. Samuels. 1968. 'Prolegomena to a Study of Medieval Anglo-Irish'. *Medium Aevum* 37: 1–11.

Mackay, A. with D. Dichtburn. 1997. Eds., *Atlas of Medieval Europe*. London and New York.

McLaughlin, 2005. 'A Threat of Satire by Tadhg (mac Dáire) Mac Bruaideadha'. *Ériu* 55: 37–57.

McLaughlin, R. 2005. 'Metres, in *Mittelirische Verslehren III*'. *Ériu* 55: 119–136.

McLaughlin, R. (forthcoming) 'Metres, in *Mittelirische Verslehren III'. Ériu* 55: 119–136.

McLeod, W. 2004. *Divided Gaels: Gaelic Cultural Identities in Scotland and Ireland, c. 1200–c. 1650*. Oxford.

McManus, D. 1991. *A Guide to Ogam*. Maynooth.

McManus, D. 1994. 'Teanga an Dána agus Teanga an Phróis'. *Léachtaí Cholm Cille* 24: 114–135.

McManus, D. 1997. 'The Irish Grammatical and Syntactical Tracts: A Concordance of Duplicated and Identified Citations'. *Ériu* 48: 165–187.

McManus, D. 2000. 'Varia IV, IGT Citations and Duplice Entries: Some Additional Identifications'. *Ériu* 51: 193–194.

McManus, D. 2004. 'The Bardic Poet as Teacher, Student and Critic: A Context for the Grammatical Tracts'. In C. G. Ó Háinle and D. E. Meek, *Unity in Diversity: Studies in Irish and Scottish Gaelic Language, Literature and History*. Léann na Tríonóide: Trinity Irish Studies I: 97–123. Dublin.

McNamara, M. 1987–1989. 'Echternach and Mac Durnan Gospel: Some Common Readings and Their Significance'. *Peritia* 6–7: 217–222.

McQuillan, P. 2006. '*Suairceas* in the Seventeenth Century'. S. Deane and S. Mac Suibhne, eds., *Field Day Review 2006* 2: 95–109. Dublin.

Mahon, W. J. 1987. *Contributions to the Study of Irish Lexicography*. Michigan.

Manning, B. 1980. 'The Origins of the Doctrine of Sedition'. *Albion* 12: 99–121.

Martin, F. X. 1979. 'Confusion Abounding: Bernard O'Higgin, OSA, Bishop of Elphin, 1542–1561'. In A. Cosgrove and D. McCartney, eds., *Studies in Irish History: Presented to R. Dudley Edwards*: 37–84. Dublin.

Martin, F. X. 1987. 'Diarmait Mac Murchadha and the Coming of the Anglo-Normans'. In A. Cosgrove, ed., *A New History of Ireland ii: Medieval Ireland 1169–1534*: 43–66. Oxford.

Martin, F. X. 1987. 'Allies and an Overlord, 1169–72'. In A. Cosgrove, ed., *A New History of Ireland ii: Medieval Ireland 1169–1534*: 67–97. Oxford.

Martin, F. X. 1987. 'Overlord Becomes Feudal Lord, 1172–85'. In A. Cosgrove, ed., *A New History of Ireland ii: Medieval Ireland 1169–1534*: 98–126. Oxford.

Martin, F. X. 1987. 'John, Lord of Ireland 1185–1216'. In A. Cosgrove, ed., *A New History of Ireland ii: Medieval Ireland 1169–1534*: 127–155. Oxford.

Martin, M. (1703) 1994. *A Description of the Western Islands of Scotland*. Edinburgh.

Martines, L. 1985. *History and Society in English Renaissance Verse*. Oxford.

Mathisen, Ralph W. 1981. 'Epistolography, Literary Circles and Familiy Ties in Late Roman Gaul'. *Transactions of the American Philological Association* 111: 95–109.

Mercier, V. 1962. *The Irish Comic Tradition*. Oxford.

Meroney, H. 1950. 'Studies in Early Irish Satire: i, ii. "*Cis Lir Fodla Áire?*"'. *Journal of Celtic Studies* 1: 199–226.

Meroney, H. 1958. 'Studies in Early Irish Satire: iii. "*Tréfhocal Fócrai*"'. *Journal of Celtic Studies* 2: 59–130.

Meyer, K. 1909. *A Primer of Irish Metrics*. Dublin.

Meyer, K. 1913. *Ancient Irish Poetry*. London.

Meyrick, L. D. 1993. *From the* De Excidio Troiae Historia *to the* Togail Troí: *Literary-Cultural Synthesis in a Medieval Irish Adaptation of Dares' Troy Tale*. Heidelberg.

Millett, B. 1976. 'Irish Literature in Latin, 1550–1700'. In T. W. Moody, F. X. Martin and F. J. Byrne, eds., *A New History of Ireland iii: Early Modern Ireland 1534–1691*: 561–586. Oxford.

Minnis, A., and I. Johnson. 2005. Eds., *The Cambridge History of Literary Criticism* ii. Cambridge.

Mitchell, B. 1988. *A New Genealogical Atlas of Ireland*. Baltimore, Maryland.

Moody, T. W., F. X. Martin and F. J. Byrne. 1982. Eds., *A New history of Ireland, viii: A Chronology of Irish History to 1976*. Oxford.

Moody, T. W., F. X. Martin and F. J. Byrne. 1984. Eds., *A New History of Ireland, ix; Maps, Genealogies and Lists*. Oxford.

Mooney, C. (C. Ó Maonaigh). 1959. 'Father John Colgan, OFM, his Work and Times and Literary Milieu'. In T. O Donnell, ed., *Father John Colgan OFM 1592–1658: Essays in Commemoration of the Tercentenary of his Death*: 7–40. Dublin.

Mooney, C. *The Church in Gaelic Ireland in the 13th to 15th Centuries*. In P. J. Corish, ed., *History of Irish Catholicism* ii, 5. Dublin.

Moran, B. T. 1991. *Patronage and Institutions: Science, Technology and Medicine at the European Court 1500–1750*. Woodbridge, Suffolk.

Morton, K. 2004. 'Irish Medieval Wall Paintings'. In J. Ludlow and N. Jameson, eds., *Medieval Ireland*, Barryscourt Lectures I–X: 311–349. Cork.

Mosely, C. 1999. Ed., *Burke's Peerage*. 106th edn. London.

Mullally, E. 1988. 'Hiberno-Norman Literature and Its Public'. In J. Bradley, ed., *Settlement and Society in Medieval Ireland: Studies Presented to F. X. Martin OSA*. 327–343. Kilkenny.

Murphy, G. 1932. 'Vergilian Influence upon the Vernacular Literature of Medieval Ireland'. *Studi Medievali* 5: 372–381.

Murphy, G. 1940. 'Bards and Filidh'. *Éigse* 2: 200–207.

Murphy, G. 1948. *Glimpses of Gaelic Ireland: Two Lectures*. Dublin.

Murphy, G. 1961. *Early Irish Metrics*. Dublin.

Murphy, J. J. 1974. *Rhetoric in the Middle Ages: A History of Rhetorical Theory from Saint Augustine to the Renaissance*. Berkeley.

Nader, H. 1979. *The Mendoza Family in the Spanish Renaissance 1350–1550*. New Brunswick.

Nicholls, K. W. 1985. 'Gaelic Landownership in Tipperary in the Light of the Surviving Irish Deeds'. In W. Nolan and T. G. McGrath, eds., *Tipperary: History and Society*. Dublin: 92–103.

Nicholls, K. 1987. 'Gaelic Society and Economy in the High Middle Ages'. In A. Cosgrove, ed., *A New History of Ireland ii: Medieval Ireland 1169–1534*: 397–438. Oxford.

Nicholls, K. W. 1993. 'The Development of Lordship in County Cork, 1300–1600'. In P. O'Flanagan and C. G. Buttimer, eds.,

Cork History and Society: Interdisciplinary Essays on the History of an Irish County: 156–211. Dublin.

Nicholls, K. W. 2003. *Gaelic and Gaelicized Ireland in the Middle Ages*. Dublin.

Nolan, W., and T. G. McGrath. 1985. Ed., *Tipperary: History and Society*. Dublin.

De Nonno, M., P. de Paolis and L. Holz. 2000. Ed., *Manuscripts and Tradition of Grammatical Texts from Antiquity to the Renaissance*. 2 vols. Cassino.

Nyberg, T. 1985. Ed., *History and Herioc Tale*. Odense.

Ó hAodha, D. 1991. 'The First Middle Irish Metrical Tract'. In H. L. C. Tristram, ed., *Metrik und Medienwechsel: Metrics and Media*: 207–244. Tübingen.

Ó hAodha, D. 1994. 'An Bhairdne i dTús a Ré'. In P. Ó Fiannachta, ed., *An Dán Díreach*. Léachtaí Cholm Cille, 24: 9–20. Maigh Nuad.

O'Brien, S. 1944. *Measgra i gCuimhne Mhichíl Uí Chléirigh*. Dublin.

Ó Buachalla, B. 1990. 'Cúlra is Tábhacht an Dáin *A Leabhráin Ainmnighthear d'Aodh*'. *Celtica* 21: 402–416.

Ó Caithnia, L. P. 1984. *Apalóga na bhFilí*. Baile Átha Cliath.

Ó Cathasaigh, T. 1984. 'Pagan Survivals: The Evidence of Early Irish Narrative'. In P. Ní Chatháin and M. Richter, eds., *Ireland and Europe: The Early Church (Irland und Europa: die Kirche im Frühmittelalter)*: 291–307. Stuttgart.

Ó Cíobháin, B. 1978. *Toponomia Hibernia* i, Barúntacht Dhún Ciaráin Thuaidh: Barony of Dunkerron North. Dublin.

Ó Cíobháin, B. 1984. *Toponomia Hibernia* ii, Paróiste Chill Chrócháin: Kilcrohane Parish 1 (Leath Thiar/West Half). Dublin.

Ó Cíobháin, B. 1984. *Toponomia Hibernia* iii, Barúntacht Dhún Ciaráin Theas: Barony of Dunkerron South; Paróiste Chill Chrócháin: Kilcrohane Parish 2 (Leath Thoir/East Half). Dublin.

Ó Clabaigh, C. 2002. *The Franciscans in Ireland, 400–1534: From Reform to Reformation*. Dublin.

Ó Concheanainn, T. 1973–1974. 'A Feature of the Poetry of Fearghal Óg Mac an Bhaird'. In *Éigse* 15: 235–251.

Ó Concheanainn, T. 1984. 'LL and the Date of the Reviser of LU'. *Éigse* 20: 213–14.

O Connell, P. 1996. 'The Irish College, Santiago de Compostela: 1605–1767'. *Archivium Hibernicum* 50: 19–28.

Ó Corráin, D. 1971. 'Mag Femin, Femen and Some Early Annals'. *Ériu* 21: 97–99.

Ó Corráin, D. 1974. '*Caithréim Chellacháin Chaisil*: History or Propaganda?'. *Ériu* 25, 1–69.

Ó Corráin, D. 1985. 'Irish Origin Legend and Genealogy'. In T. Nyberg, ed., *History and Herioc Tale*. Odense.

Ó Cróinín, D. 2005. 'Hiberno-Latin Literature to 1169'. In D. Ó Cróinín, ed., *A New History of Ireland i: Prehistoric and Early Ireland*: 371–404. Oxford.

Ó Cuív, B. 1963. 'Literary Creation and Historical Tradition'. *Proceedings of the British Academy* xlix (Sir John Rhŷs Memorial Lecture): 233–262.

Ó Cuív, B. 1967–1968. 'Some Developments in Irish Metrics'. *Éigse* 12: 273–290.

Ó Cuív, B. 1965. 'Linguistic Terminology in the Mediaeval Irish Bardic Tracts'. *Transactions of the Philological Society*: 141–164.

Ó Cuív, B. 1973. *The Irish Bardic Duanaire or 'Poem-Book'*. R. I. Best Memorial Lecture May 1973. Dublin.

Ó Cuív, B. 1973. 'The Linguistic Training of the Mediaeval Irish Poet'. *Celtica* 10: 114–140.

Ó Cuív, B. 1976. 'The Irish Language in the Early Modern Period'. In T. W. Moody, F. X. Martin and F. J. Byrne, eds., *A New History of Ireland iii: Early Modern Ireland 1534–1691*: 509–545. Oxford.

Ó Cuív, B. 1981. 'Medieval Irish Scholars and Classical Latin Literature'. *Proceedings of the Royal Irish Academy* 81 C: 239–248.

Ó Cuív, B. 1988. 'Personal Names as an Indicator of Relations between Native Irish Settlers in the Viking Period'. In J. Bradley, ed., *Settlement and Society in Medieval Ireland: Studies Presented to F. X. Martin, OSA*: 79–88. Kilkenny.

Ó Cuív, B. 2001. *Catalogue of Irish Manuscripts in the Bodleian Library and Oxford College Libraries*. 2 vols. Dublin.

O'Curry, E. (1861) 1995. *Lectures on the Manuscript Materials of Ancient Irish History*. Dublin.

O'Doherty, D. J. 1913. 'Students of the Irish College Salamanca (1595–1619)'. *Archivium Hibernicum* 2: 1–36.

O'Doherty, D. J. 1914. 'Students of the Irish College Salamanca (1619–1700)'. *Archivium Hibernicum* 3: 87–112.

Ó Dúshláine, T. 1987. *An Eoraip agus Litríocht na Gaeilge, 1600–1650: Gnéithe den Bharócachas Eorpach i Litríocht na Gaeilge*. Baile Átha Cliath.

Ó Fiach, T. 1971. 'Republicanism and Separatism in the Seventeenth Century'. *Léachtaí Cholm Cille* 2: 74–87.

O'Flanagan, P., and C. G. Buttimer. 1993. Eds., *Cork History and Society: Interdisciplinary Essays on the History of an Irish County*. Dublin.

O'Keeffe, T. 1998. 'Architectural Traditions of the Early Medieval Church in Munster'. In M. A. Monk and J. Sheehan, eds., *Early Medieval Munster: Archaeology, History and Society*. Cork.

O'Grady, S. H. (1926) 1992. *Catalogue of Irish MSS in the British Library (formerly British Museum)* i. First published by the British Museum. Dublin.

Ó Lochlainn, C. (1940) 1995. 'Roadways in Ancient Ireland'. In J. Ryan, ed., *Féil-Sgríbhinn Eóin Mhic Néill: Essays and Studies Presented to Professor Eoin MacNeill*: 465–474. Dublin.

Ó Macháin, P. 1991. 'The Early Modern Irish Prosodic Tracts and the Editing of "Bardic Verse"'. In H. L. C. Tristram, ed., *Metrik und Medienwechsel: Metrics and Media*: 273–287. Tübingen.

Ó Macháin, P. 1994. 'Tadhg Dall Ó hUiginn: Foinse dá Shaothar'. In P. Ó Fiannachta, ed., *An Dán Díreach*. Léachtaí Cholm Cille, 24: 77–113. Maigh Nuad.

Ó Mainnín, M. B. 1999. '"The Same in Origin and Blood": Bardic Windows on the Relationship between Irish and Scottish Gaels, c. 1200-1650'. *Cambrian Medieval Celtic Studies* 38: 1–51.

Ó Mainnín, M. B. 2006. Review of W. McLeod, *Divided Gaels: Gaelic Cultural Identities in Scotland and Ireland, c. 1200–c. 1650.* (Oxford, 2004), in *Speculum* 81, no. 3: 889–891.

Ó Maonaigh, C. (C. Mooney). 1962. 'Scríbhnoirí Gaeilge an Seachtú hAois Déag'. *Studia Hibernica* 2: 182–208.

Ó Muraíle, N. 1996. *The Celebrated Antiquary Dubhaltach Mac Fhirbhisigh (c. 1600–1671).* Maynooth.

Ó Murchú, M. 1985. *The Irish Language.* Dublin.

Ó Murchú, M. 1997. Léirmheas ar *Stair na Gaeilge Aistí in Ómos do Pádraig Ó Fiannachta,* eds., K. McCone, D. McManus, C. Ó Háinle, N. Williams and L. Breatnach (Maigh Nuad, 1994). *Éigse* 30: 171–195.

Ó Néill, P. 1984. '*Romani* Influences on Seventh-Century Hiberno-Latin Literature'. In P. Ní Chatháin and M. Richter, eds., *Ireland and Europe: The Early Church (Irland und Europa: die Kirche im Frühmittelalter)*: 280–290. Stuttgart.

Ó Néill, P. 1997. 'An Irishman at Chartres'. *Ériu* 48: 1–35.

Ó Néill, P. 2003. *Biblical Study and Mediaeval Gaelic History.* Quiggin Pamphlets on the Sources of Mediaeval Gaelic History, vol. vi. Cambridge.

Ó Ríordáin, S. P., and J. Hunt. 1942. 'Medieval Dwellings at Caherguillamore, Co. Limerick'. *Journal of the Royal Society of Antiquaries of Ireland* 72: 37–63.

O Riordan, M. 1990. *The Gaelic Mind and the Collapse of the Gaelic World.* Cork.

O Riordan, M. 1998. 'Professors, Performers and "Others of their Kind": Contextualizing the Bardic Poet'. *The Irish Review* 23: 73–88.

O Riordan, M. 2004. 'A Poet on Horseback?: The Mediaeval *Ars Poetica* and the Bardic Poem'. In J. Carey, M. Herbert and K. Murray, eds., *Cín Chille Cúile: Texts, Saints and Places. Essays in Honour of Pádraig Ó Riain*: 354–366. Cork.

Ordnance Survey Ireland. 2000. 1:50,000 map series. Dublin 7.

O'Sullivan, C. M. 2004. *Hospitality in Medieval Ireland 900–1500.* Dublin.

Ó Tuama, S. (1960) 1978. *An Grá in Amhráin na nDaoine*. Baile Átha Cliath.

Ó Tuama, S. 1995. *Repossessions: Selected Essays on the Irish Literary Heritage*. Cork.

Otway-Ruthven, J. (1968) 1993. *A History of Medieval Ireland*. New York.

Owen, M. E. 1992. 'Literary Convention and Historical Reality: The Court in the Welsh Poetry of the Twelfth and Thirteenth Centuries'. *Études Celtiques* 29: 69–85.

Paden, W. D. 2006. 'Principles of Generic Classification in the Medieval European Lyric: The Case of Galician-Portuguese'. *Speculum* 81: 76–96.

De Paor, Louis. 2000. ' "*Do Chor Chúarta ar gCridhe*": Léamh ar Dhán le hEochaidh Ó hEoghusa'. In P. Riggs, B. Ó Conchúir and S. Ó Coileáin, eds., *Saoi na hÉigse: Aistí in Ómós do Sheán Ó Tuama*: 35–53. Baile Átha Cliath.

Pender, S. 1947. *Essays and Studies Presented to Professor Tadhg Ua Donnchadha (Torna)*. Cork.

Poppe, E. 1999. 'Reconstructing Medieval Irish Literary Theory: The Lesson of *Airec Menman Uraird maic Coise*'. *Cambrian Medieval Celtic Studies* 37: 33–54.

Poppe, E., and P. Sims-Williams. 2005. 'Medieval Irish Literary Theory and Criticism'. In A. Minnis and I. Johnson, eds., *The Cambridge History of Litearicsm* ii: 291–309. Cambridge.

Potterton, M. 2005. *Medieval Trim: History and Archaeology*. Dublin.

Purcell, W. M. 1996. Ars Poetriae: *Rhetorical and Grammatical Invention at the Margin of Literacy*. Columbia, South Carolina Press.

Quiggin, E. C. 1911–12. 'Prolegomena to the Study of the Later Irish Bards 1200–1500.' *Proceedings of the British Academy* v: 89–143.

Rae, E. 1987. 'Architecture and Sculpture, 1169–1603'. In A. Cosgrove, ed., *A New History of Ireland* ii: *Medieval Ireland 1169–1534*: 736–780. Oxford.

Richter, M. 1995. *Studies in Medieval Language and Culture*. Dublin.

Robey, D. 2005. 'Humanist Views on the Study of Italian Poetry in the Early Italian Renaissance'. In A. Minnis and I. Johnson, eds., *The Cambridge History of Liteary Criticsm* ii: 626–647. Cambridge.

Roston, M. 1982. *Sixteenth-Century English Literature*. New York.

Rothwell, W. 1975–1976. 'The Role of French in Medieval Britain'. *Bulletin of John Rylands Library* 58: 445–466.

Russell, J. C. 1928. 'Master Henry of Avranches as an International Poet'. *Speculum* 3: 34–63.

Ryan, J. (1940) 1995. Ed., *Féil-sgríbhinn Eóin Mhic Néill: Essays and Studies Presented to Professor Eoin MacNeill*. Dublin.

Ryan, J. 1941. 'The Historical Content of the *Caithréim Ceallacháin Chaisil*'. *Journal of the Royal Society of Antiquaries of Ireland* 71, 89–100.

Ryan, J. 1946. 'The Convention of Druim Ceat (A.U. 575)'. *Journal of the Royal Society of Antiquaries* 61: 35–55.

Schultz, J. A. 1984. 'Classical Rhetoric, Medieval Poetics, and the Medieval Vernacular Prologue'. *Speculum* 59: 1–15.

Schulze-Busacker, E. 1987. 'French Conceptions of Foreigners and Foreign Languages in the Twelfth and Thirteenth Centuries'. *Romance Philology* 41: 24–47.

Ní Shéaghdha, N. 1984. 'Translations and Adaptations into Irish'. *Éigse* 16: 107–124.

Sedgwick, W. B. 1928. 'The Style and Vocabulary of the Latin Arts of Poetry of the Twelfth and Thirteenth Centuries'. *Speculum* 3: 349–381.

Seymour, St J. D. 1929. *Anglo Irish Literature 1200–1582*. Cambridge.

Shaw, F. (1940) 1995. 'Medieval Medico-Philosophical Treatises in the Irish Language'. In J. Ryan, ed., *Féil-sgríbhinn Eóin Mhic Néill: Essays and Studies Presented to Professor Eoin MacNeill*: 144–157. Dublin.

Silke, J. J. 1976. 'The Irish Abroad, 1534–1691'. In T. W. Moody, F. X. Martin and F. J. Byrne, eds., *A New History of Ireland iii: Early Modern Ireland 1534–1691*: 587–633. Oxford.

Simms, K. 1978. 'Guesting and Feasting in Gaelic Ireland'. *Journal of the Royal Society of Antiquaries of Ireland* 108: 67–99.

Simms, K. 1983. 'Propaganda Use of the *Táin* in the Later Middle Ages'. *Celtica* 15: 142–149.

Simms, K. 1994. 'An Eaglais agus Filí na Scol'. In P. Ó Fiannachta, ed., *An Dán Díreach*. Léachtaí Cholm Cille, 24: 21–36. Maigh Nuad.

Simms, K. 1998. 'Literacy and the Irish Bards'. In H. Pryce, ed., *Literacy in Mediaeval Celtic Societies*: 238–258. Cambridge.

Simms, K. 2001. 'Native Sources for Gaelic Settlement: The House Poems'. In Duffy, P. J., D. Edwards and E. FitzPatrick, eds., *Gaelic Ireland c. 1250–c. 1650: Land, Lordship and Settlement*: 246–267. Dublin.

Simms, K. 2004. 'Gaelic Miltitary History and the Later Brehon Law Commentaries'. In *Unity in Diversity: Studies in Irish and Scottish Gaelic Language, Literature and History, Trinity Irish Studies* 1: 51–67. Dublin.

Simms, K. 2004. 'References to Landscape and Economy in Irish Bardic Poetry'. In H. B. Clarke, J. Prunty and M. Hennessy, eds., *Surveying Ireland's Past: Multidisciplinary Essays in Honour of Anngret Simms*: 145–168. Dublin.

Sims-Williams P., and E. Poppe. 2005: 'Medieval Irish Literary Theory and Criticism'. In A. Minnis and I. Johnson, eds., *The Cambridge History of Literary Criticism* ii: 291–309. Cambridge.

Smith, B. 1999. Ed., *Britain and Ireland 900–1300: Insular Response to Medieval European Change*. Cambridge.

Sonnino, L. A. 1968. *A Handbook to Sixteenth-Century Rhetoric*. New York.

Somerset, F., and N. Watson. 2003. Eds., *The Vulgar Tongue: Medieval and postMedieval Vernacularity*. Pennsylvania.

Southern, R. W. 1970. *Medieval Humanism*. Oxford.

Southern, R. W. 1995. *Scholastic Humanism and the Unification of Europe*, i. Oxford.

Southworth, J. 1989. *The English Medieval Minstrel 1272–1327*. Suffolk.

Spufford, P. 2002. *Power and Profit: The Merchant in Medieval Europe*. London.

Stanford, W. B. 1970. 'Towards a History of Classical Influences in Ireland'. *Proceedings of the Royal Irish Academy* 70 C: 15–91.

Stanford, W. B. 1976. *Ireland and the Classical Tradition*. Dublin.

Stout, M. 2000. 'Early Christian Ireland: Settlement and Environment'. In T. Barry, ed., *A History of Settlement in Ireland*: 81–109. London and New York.

Sweetman, D. 2003. 'The Hall-House in Ireland'. In J. R. Kenyon and K. O'Conor, eds., *The Medieval Castle in England in Wales*: 121–132. Dublin.

Thurneysen, R. 1918. 'Zu Irischen Texten'. *Zeitschrift für Celtische Philologie* 12: 398–399.

R. Thurneysen, R. (1946) 1970. *A Grammar of Old Irish*. Revised, enlarged, transl., O. Bergin and D. Binchy. Dublin.

Tourneur, V. 1905. *Equisse d'une Histoire des Études Celtiques*. Bibliothèqe de la Faculté de Philosophie et Lettres de l'Université le Liège, fasc. xv. Liège.

Tranter, S. N. 1991. 'Divided and Scattered, Trussed and Supported: Stanzaic Form in Irish and Old Norse Tracts'. In H. L. C. Tristram, ed., *Metrik und Medienwechsel: Metrics and Media*: 245–272. Tübingen.

Troyan, S. D. 2004. Ed., *Medieval Rhetoric: A Casebook*. New York.

Tuchman, B. (1978) 1985. *A Distant Mirror: The Calamitous Fourteenth Century*. Harmondsworth.

Turville-Petre, T. 1977. *The Alliterative Revival*. Cambridge.

Turville-Petre, T. 1996. *England the Nation: Language, Literature, and National Identity, 1290–1340*. Oxford.

Valesio, P. 1980. *Novantiqua: Rhetorics as a Contemporary Theory*. Indiana University Press.

Waddell, H. 1954. *The Wandering Scholars*. London.

Walsh, P. 1947. Ed. C. O Lochlainn, *Irish Men of Learning: Studies by Father Paul Walsh*. Dublin.

Walsh, P. 2003. *Irish Leaders and Learning through the Ages*. Ed., N. Ó Muraíle. Dublin.

Walsh, T. J. 1973. *The Irish Continental College Movement: The Colleges at Bordeaux, Toulouse, and Lille*. Dublin and Cork.

Ward, J. O. 1995. *Ciceronian Rhetoric in Treatise, Scholion and Commentary*. Typologie des Sources du Moyen Âge Occidental, fasc. 58. Turnhout.

Waters, C. M. 2003. 'Talking the Talk: Access to the Vernacular in Medieval Preaching'. In F. Somerset and N. Watson, eds., *The Vulgar Tongue: Medieval and postMedieval Vernacularity*: 31–42. Pennsylvania.

Watkins, C. 1963. 'Indo-European Metrics and Archaic Irish Verse'. *Celtica* 6: 194–249.

Watt, J. A. 1987. 'Gaelic Polity and Cultural Identity'. In A. Cosgrove, ed., *A New History of Ireland, ii: Medieval Ireland, 1169–1534*: 314–351. Oxford.

Watt, J. A. 1987. 'The Anglo-Irish Colony under Strain'. In A. Cosgrove, ed., *A New History of Ireland ii: Medieval Ireland 1169–1534*: 352–396. Oxford.

Whelton, M. (2004): 'Teagmháil agus Tnúthán: Staidéar ar an Apastróp i bhFilíocht na Nua-Ghaeilge'. Unpublished PhD Thesis, National University of Ireland, Maynooth.

Williams, N. J. A. 1980. Ed., *The Poems of Giolla Brighde Mac Con Midhe*. Irish Texts Society, 51. Dublin.

Worley, M. 2003. 'Using the *Orumulum* to Redefine Vernacularity'. In F. Somerset and N. Watson, eds., *The Vulgar Tongue: Medieval and postMedieval Vernacularity*: 19–30. Pennsylvania.

General Index

abandon, abandoning poetry, the poet leaves his profession, 248; abandoning poetry for the Church, 248; abandonment, of the schools' style, in E. Ó hEoghusa, '*Ionmholta malairt bhisigh*', 252; of the 'narrow ways', in seventeenth-century poetry, 256

accusation, by poet of patron, 106

'action', and the imagination, in Matthew of Vendôme, 36

aesthetics, the 'shared aesthetic', 12, 13, 22

alphabet, Latin and Ogham, 3, 4; and orthography, in Fear Feasa Ó'n Cháinte's '*Créad dá sealbhuinn damh an dán*', 240

alteration, in love, in Tadhg Dall Ó hUiginn's '*Cóir Dé eadram is Uilliam*', 177

ambiguity, the studied ambiguity of the formal compositions, 146

amour courtois, in Irish poetry, 250

amplification, in '*Geabh do mhúnadh, a mheic bhaoith*', by Ádhamh Ó Fialán, 117; in '*Fada an ráitheise romham*', by Tadhg Óg Ó hUiginn, 161

Anglo-Norman, invasion of Ireland, 12; negative aspects, 13; impact, 15; Anglo-Normans, 26

anticipation, in Gofraidh Fionn Ó Dálaigh's '*Madh fiafraidheach budh feasach*', 200

appointment, the right/claim of the poet to appointment in Irish and troubadour tradition, 151; of an *ollamh*, 153

apposition, in Fear Feasa Ó'n Cháinte's '*Créad dá sealbhuinn damh an dán*', 240

ars dictaminis, arts of letter-writing, 8

art/arts, the rupture of the written arts, 13

ascription, of places to Domhnall Mac Carthaigh in Gofraidh Fionn Ó Dálaigh's '*Beir eolas dúinn, a Dhomhnuill*', 72, 102

aspersion, aspersive asides, in Fear Feasa Ó'n Cháinte's '*Créad dá sealbhuinn damh an dán*', 240

attonement, a device in '*Fada an ráitheise romham*', by Tadhg Óg Ó hUiginn, 162

attributes, physical and moral, of Domhnall Mac Carthaigh, in Gofraidh Fionn Ó Dálaigh's poem, '*Beir eolas dúinn, a Dhomhnuill*', 66

attribution, attributions of place to Domhnall Mac Carthaigh, to Domhnall Mac Carthaigh, in Gofraidh Fionn Ó Dálaigh's *Beir eolas dúinn, a Dhomhnuill*, 72

audience, communication, private, 6; performance, public, 6; readership, 6

authority, and its usurpation in Gofraidh Mac an Bhaird's '*A fhir shealbhas duit an dán*', 227

bairdne, in *Auraicept na n-Éces*, 4

bargain, the love-bargain, in '*Fada an ráitheise romham*', by Tadhg Óg Ó hUiginn, 163

begging, poets begging for terms, 153

biography, the life of the poet as read through his poems, Tadhg Dall Ó hUiginn, by E. Knott, 170

blame, 1; and recrimination in poems of blame/reconciliation, 106ff.

boasting, in Fear Feasa Ó'n Cháinte's '*Créad dá sealbhuinn damh an dán*', 235

bombast, of the inferior poet, condemned in Gofraidh Mac an Bhaird's '*A fhir shealbhas duit an dán*', 217

braggarts, trifling boasters among the inferior poets, 376

breathing, panting, breathing and air, the mark of the inferior poet, in '*Mór an feidhm deilbh an dána*', by Fear Feasa Ó'n Cháinte, and in Matthew of Vendôme, 373

canon, the canon of correct usage, in Fear Feasa Ó'n Cháinte's '*Créad dá sealbhuinn damh an dán*', 240ff.

Carolingian schools, 25

categorization, quinary categorization of invention in John of Garland, 48

'catena', mediaeval commentary, 3

change, and mutability in '*Fada an ráitheise romham*', by Tadhg Óg Ó hUiginn, 162

character, of the Irish poet, 93ff.

chevilles, and phatic breaks in Gofraidh Fionn Ó Dálaigh's

'*Madh fiafraidheach budh feasach*', 366

Christendom, Rome, and Avignon, 62

Christian, Latin literary culture, 1ff.; Christian Latin learning, 1ff.

cineál, in *Auraicept na n-Éces*, 4

circumlocution, in John of Garland, 50

Cistercians, in Mellifont in the twelfth century, 274

collapse, literature, cultural values, 183

colleges, continental seminaries, 182

colour, and metaphorical 'colour', in Gofraidh Fionn Ó Dálaigh's '*Beir eolas dúinn, a Dhomhnuill*', 91

columns, and metaphors for style in John of Garland, 53ff.

complaint, 1; as a foil for praise, 107ff.; progression from complaint, to accusation, to threat and to entreaty in '*Fada an ráitheise romham*', by Tadhg Óg Ó hUiginn, 161ff.

composition, 1; arranging in the mind before writing, 249ff.; Irish vernacular, 275ff.

conceptualizing, Matthew of Vendôme and the conceptualization of the subject, 67; compassing in the mind, before committal to writing, in Geoffrey of Vinsauf, 72ff.

conclusion, in Matthew of Vendôme, 38, 75

conditional, the provisional element in Fear Feasa Ó'n Cháinte's '*Créad dá sealbhuinn damh an dán*', 386 contingency, in Fear Feasa Ó'n Cháinte's '*Créad dá sealbhuinn damh an dán*', 244

contract, and the 'contractual service' of the poet and the lord, 153ff.; in Gofraidh Fionn Ó Dálaigh's '*Madh fiafraidheach budh feasach*', 189ff.

contrast, the good with the weak poets in '*Mór an feidhm deilbh an dána*', by Fear Feasa Ó'n Cháinte, 211

controversy, the pedagogic grounds of, 28ff.

correction, the office of correction and the teacher, in Matthew of Vendôme, and in Gofraidh Mac an Bhaird's '*A fhir shealbhas duit an dán*', 380

crafts, ignoble crafts of weaving, tucking, milling, etc., in Gofraidh Mac an Bhaird's '*A fhir shealbhas duit an dán*', 184ff.

criticism, the poet as critic, 181ff.

culture, cultural 'defence', 14; isolation, 22; emergence of the Christianized peoples in Europe, 24ff.; written Christian culture, 24

curriculum, mediaeval, 3ff.; trivium, 7; of the Irish schools of poetry, 44; the twelfth- and thirteenth-century 'classification of the sciences', 275

dán díreach, 1, 2, and the *ars poetriae*, 12ff.

daorbhard, in *Auraicept na n-Éces*, 4

darkness, metaphors in manuals, 250; in the description of art, 290

death, the death of the poet/poetry when the patron abandons him, in '*Geabh do mhúnadh, a mheic bhaoith*', by Ádhamh Ó Fialán, 121

debate, as a part of the *inventio*, in Gofraidh Fionn Ó Dálaigh's '*Madh fiafraidheach budh feasach*', 190; among the *cognoscenti*, in '*Mór an feidhm deilbh an dána*', by Fear Feasa Ó'n Cháinte, 211

defence, the trope of the defence of poets/poetry, 142; in '*Mór an feidhm deilbh an dána*', by Fear Feasa Ó'n Cháinte, 215; against 'others' in a debate poem, 215

degrees, of poetry, in Gofraidh Fionn Ó Dálaigh's '*Madh fiafraidheach budh feasach*', 208ff.

denigration, in '*Mór an feidhm deilbh an dána*', by Fear Feasa Ó'n Cháinte, 204

description, and the imagination, in Matthew of Vendôme, 36; of Domhnall Mac Carthaigh in Gofraidh Fionn Ó Dálaigh's '*Beir eolas dúinn, a Dhomhnuill*', 70; in Matthew of Vendôme, 71ff.

desertion, of the formal style threatened in E. Ó hEoghusa, '*Ionmholta malairt bhisigh*', 256; Fear Flatha Ó Gnímh accuses Fearghal Óg Mac an Bhaird of deserting the scholarly ways, 258

detractors, in '*Mór an feidhm deilbh an dána*', by Fear Feasa Ó'n Cháinte, 204

devotional works, of bardic poets, 17ff.; devotional literature, in Irish, 250 dialectic, in John Scottus Eriugena (*c.* 810–*c.* 877), *Periphyseon*, 25; in Fear Feasa Ó'n Cháinte's '*Créad dá sealbhuinn damh an dán*', 231; and the division of the written arts, 276

dialogue, in Gofraidh Fionn Ó Dálaigh's '*Madh fiafraidheach budh feasach*', 189ff.; in '*Mór an feidhm deilbh an dána*', by Fear Feasa Ó'n Cháinte, 204, 214ff.; the fictive dialogue in a debate poem, 215

diction, language appropriate to the 'lower' style in '*A theachtaire théid ar sliabh*', by Tadhg Dall Ó hUiginn, 174

disappointment, poets begging for appointment, 153ff.

discourse, 'environment of discourse', 276; and performance, in Fear Feasa Ó'n Cháinte's '*Créad dá sealbhuinn damh an dán*', 385

dispraise, in Fear Feasa Ó'n Cháinte's '*Créad dá sealbhuinn damh an dán*', 235

dispute, between lord and poet, 159ff.

door, and key, in Gofraidh Fionn Ó Dálaigh's '*Madh fiafraidheach budh feasach*, 202; door to knowledge in Gofraidh Fionn Ó Dálaigh's '*Madh fiafraidheach budh feasach*', 197; as a metaphor for obstacles to learning, 290; the metaphor of learning, 250

dynamic, in the poem, in '*Mór an feidhm deilbh an dána*', by Fear Feasa Ó'n Cháinte, 204

education, domination of Latin education, 6; Scandinavian, 6; Irish schools, 6; Welsh schools, 6; the Latin arts in Irish and Welsh schools, 7; influence of the trivium, 7; a grammatical analysis in an Armagh manuscript, 10; the trivium and the quadrivium in Irish scholarship, 10; continental formulae of composition, 11ff.; the mediaeval schools and the Irish poets, 22; the *artes poetriae*, 25ff.; the 'preceptive movement' in the schools of Western Europe, 26ff.; novelty in the presentation of old material, Matthew of Vendôme's claims, 27; and Matthew of Vendôme's pedagogical style, 35; the pedagogical thrust of Geoffrey of Vinsauf's *Poetria Nova*, 41; and the formal study of Irish langauge, 43; instruction concerning the use of language, metaphor, figures, etc., in Irish schools, 43; of Tadhg Dall Ó hUiginn, and his brother Maol Muire Ó hUiginn, 168; teaching and learning in Tadhg Dall Ó hUiginn's '*Cóir Dé eadram is Uilliam*', 177; going through the stages, in '*Mór an feidhm deilbh an dána*', by Fear Feasa Ó'n Cháinte, 206ff; the education of the earl of Tyrconnell, in E. Ó hEoghusa, '*Ionmholta malairt bhisigh*', 256; change in educational practices, and literary tastes in seventeenth-century Europe, 260; Irish students in Paris, 272

elegy, 1

elements of the poem, the eleven elements listed in Matthew of Vendôme, 70ff.

embellishment, in Gofraidh Fionn Ó Dálaigh's *'Beir eolas dúinn, a Dhomhnuill'* with the bystory of Moses, 95; in Fear Feasa Ó'n Cháinte's *'Créad dá sealbhuinn damh an dán'*, 241

encastellation, of Munster, 98

envy, charges of envy in poetry, 28

equivocation, in poems of blame, 109ff.

eristics, the eristic basis of the tropes of poems of dispute, 348; the origins of the debate in *'Mór an feidhm deilbh an dána'*, by Fear Feasa Ó'n Cháinte, 214

espousal, the lord and poet as spouse, 153ff.

exchange, of goods for poetry, in *'Geabh do mhúnadh, a mheic bhaoith'*, by Ádhamh Ó Fialán, 119

explication, prose explications or introductions to Irish syllabic poems, 154

fabric, and the weaving of text in *'Mór an feidhm deilbh an dána'*, by Fear Feasa Ó'n Cháinte, 204; in Gofraidh Mac an Bhaird's *'A fhir shealbhas duit an dán'*, 223

fame, accorded by the poet, in *'Geabh do mhúnadh, a mheic bhaoith'*, by Ádhamh Ó Fialán, 115

family, genealogical links protecting the patron in *'Geabh do mhúnadh, a mheic bhaoith'*, by Ádhamh Ó Fialán, 132

faults, and remedy, in *Auraicept na n-Éces*, 5; in Irish preceptive texts, 38; in Matthew of Vendôme, 30, 37; and their correct use as a sign of expertise, in Gofraidh Mac an Bhaird's *'A fhir shealbhas duit an dán'*, 218, 221ff.; in writing, 228ff., as disease, in Matthew of Vendôme, 37ff.; in John of Garland, 52; in Gofraidh Mac an Bhaird's *'A fhir shealbhas duit an dán'*, 221, 228ff.; in Irish poems, 184ff.

fear, man, the 'other' man, interlocutor, in Gofraidh Mac an Bhaird's *'A fhir shealbhas duit an dán'*, 218, 219, 224

feet, metaphorical, and metrical in manuals of composition, 250

file, in *Auraicept na n-Éces*, 2, 4

'finding' a theme, in *'Geabh do mhúnadh, a mheic bhaoith'*, by Ádhamh Ó Fialán, 119

folly, the folly of the lord, in *'Geabh do mhúnadh, a mheic bhaoith'*, by Ádhamh Ó Fialán, 124

forge, the forge of difficult questions, in *'Mór an feidhm deilbh an dána'*, by Fear Feasa Ó'n Cháinte, 210

form, and matter, of words, in Matthew of Vendôme, 34; in John of Garland's *Parisiana Poetria*, 46

forma tractatus/forma tractandi, in *Auraicept na n-Éces*, 5

frivolity, and trifling verse, in *'Mór an feidhm deilbh an dána'*, by Fear Feasa Ó'n Cháinte, 216; in Matthew of Vendome, 216

Gaeilge, Irish language, in *Auraicept na n-Éces*, 4

gaming and gambling, the bluffer's game in Fear Feasa Ó'n Cháinte's 'Créad dá sealbhuinn damh an dán', 238, 239; in Gofraidh Mac an Bhaird's 'A fhir shealbhas duit an dán', 227

gender, ambiguity of gender, in 'Geabh do mhúnadh, a mheic bhaoith', by Ádhamh Ó Fialán, 126; in the troubadour use of the senhal, 152; identity and confluence, 157ff.

genealogy, in the poem, in 'Geabh do mhúnadh, a mheic bhaoith', by Ádhamh Ó Fialán, 132

grades and rankings, in the Irish literary tradition, 141; among the troubadours, to be compared with those of file, bard, draoi, etc., 142

graduation, in schools of poetry, 187

grammar, Irish 'normative grammar', 15; rhetoric and poetic, vernacular, 2, 3; drills, in poems about poetry, 183

Hebrew, Greek and Latin, in Auraicept na n-Éces, 4

hermeneutics, mediaeval hermeneutics in the schools, 282

honour, the poet's honour in 'Geabh do mhúnadh, a mheic bhaoith', by Ádhamh Ó Fialán, 117

hospitality, the end of, in poetry about patronage, 248

hostage, the poet takes the lord's fame as hostage, in 'Fada an ráitheise romham', by Tadhg Óg Ó hUiginn, 162

humour, and levity in Gofraidh Fionn Ó Dálaigh's 'Madh fiafraidheach budh feasach', 194, 198

I and You, in 'Geabh do mhúnadh, a mheic bhaoith', by Ádhamh Ó Fialán, 123, 233; in Gofraidh Fionn Ó Dálaigh's 'Madh fiafraidheach budh feasach', 201; in Fear Feasa Ó'n Cháinte's 'Créad dá sealbhuinn damh an dán', 234

identity, Anglo-Norman and Norman identity in France and in England, 287; among those whose written language was Occitan, or Provençal, 282

ignorance, displaying the ignorance of the 'other' poet, in Fear Feasa Ó'n Cháinte's 'Créad dá sealbhuinn damh an dán', 237

imitation, literary imitation among the Irish poets, 265, 291ff.

indulgence, the right of the poet to be indulged, in Irish and in troubadour tradition, 151

inferior poets, in 'Mór an feidhm deilbh an dána', by Fear Feasa Ó'n Cháinte, 204ff.

inferior work, that of Fearghal Óg Mac an Bhaird, in Fear Flatha Ó Gnímh, 'Cuimseach sin, a Fhearghail Óig', 258

inflection, verbal inflection as a technique for enlarging the scope of variation in composition, 51

inspiration, the streams of, in Gofraidh Mac an Bhaird's 'A fhir shealbhas duit an dán', 222 interlocution, in Gofraidh Fionn Ó Dálaigh's '*Madh fiafraidheach budh feasach*', 187ff.

international ties, Ireland and the Latin states of Outremer, 62–64; and the Angevin Empire, 301

intertextuality, in the poems about poems, Fear Flatha Ó Gnímh and Gofraidh Fionn Ó Dálaigh, 203; in Gofraidh Mac an Bhaird's '*A fhir shealbhas duit an dán*', 225; in Fear Feasa Ó'n Cháinte's '*Mor an feidhm deilbh an dana*', 225ff.

intimacy, the vocabulary of poetic intimacies, 153

intoxication, a cause of error in inferior poets, and a possible reference to a rare metre from Irish lists, 215

invective, in Gofraidh Mac an Bhaird's '*A fhir shealbhas duit an dán*', 221; against the 'other' poet, in Fear Feasa Ó'n Cháinte's '*Créad dá sealbhuinn damh an dán*', 234

inventio, 12; and the 'textual legacy', 67; in '*Mór an feidhm deilbh an dána*', by Fear Feasa Ó'n Cháinte, 204, 205; in Gofraidh Fionn Ó Dálaigh's '*Beir eolas dúinn, a Dhomhnuill*', 67; in '*Geabh do mhúnadh, a mheic bhaoith*', by Ádhamh Ó Fialán, 115

Ireland, in troubadour works, Bertran de Born, 353

itinerary, Domhnall Mac Carthaigh's itinerary in Gofraidh Fionn Ó Dálaigh's '*Beir eolas dúinn, a Dhomhuill*', 95, 97ff.

judge, lord as judge between the poet and his enemies, 161; the lord as judge, in '*Fada an ráitheise romham*', by Tadhg Óg Ó hUiginn, 161; the judge of standards, in Gofraidh Fionn Ó Dálaigh's '*Madh fiafraidheach budh feasach*', 187; the master as judge, in Gofraidh Fionn Ó Dálaigh's '*Madh fiafraidheach budh feasach*', 189; the earl as judge of E. Ó hEoghusa's work, in E. Ó hEoghusa, '*Ionmholta malairt bhisigh*', 256

judgement, and the poet as judge, in Gofraidh Mac an Bhaird's '*A fhir shealbhas duit an dán*', 227; the false judgement of the majority, in E. Ó hEoghusa, '*Ionmholta malairt bhisigh*', 257

key, the golden key, the wooden key, 182ff.; the key that opens the door to learning, 290; the metaphor in manuals of composition, 250

Laitneoir, in *Auraicept na n-Éces*, 4

language, Latin literary, 12; language, register, 12; the 'consolidation' of the Irish literary language, 14; the 'cloaked' language of disreputable matter in John of Garland, 49; the language of the troubadours, 138; common literary language among the troubadours, as among the poets of Ireland and of Scotland, 139

lasciviousness, charges of lasciviousness in poetry, 28

Latin, and the vernacular, grammar and poetics, 1, 3; Latin learning among bardic poets, 18; choice of language for the mediaeval clerk, 144

legal, terminology in poem of reconciliation, in '*Fada an ráitheise romham*', by Tadhg Óg Ó hUiginn, 161; terms in, '*A theachtaire théid ar sliabh*', by Tadhg Dall Ó hUiginn, 172

licence, poetic licence, in Matthew of Vendôme, 37; licence and the faults, in Gofraidh Mac an Bhaird's '*A fhir shealbhas duit an dán*', 229

light, metaphors in manuals of composition, 250ff.

literal v. literary, literal 'truth', 16; reading of poems of complaint, 107ff.; literal reading of Gofraidh Fionn Ó Dálaigh's '*Beir eolas dúinn, a Dhomhnuill*' and its import in fourteenth-century Munster, 96ff.

literary, culture, the crisis of continuity after the Anglo-Norman invasion, 276; conventions in presentation and drafting, in John of Garland, 297; environment, of mediaeval Europe and its influence in Ireland, 108ff.; literary 'reality', 16

literature, Irish literature and continuity after the Anglo-Norman invasion, 13; translation, 13; Italian vogue in Elizabethan England, 13; literary 'conventions', 17; rhetorical conventions, 17ff.; French and German literary influences on bardic devotional poetry, 19; Arthurian tradition, 21; the native historical tradition

and the Anglo-Norman invasion, 276

lock, the locked and unlocked tongue, in '*Fada an ráitheise romham*', by Tadhg Óg Ó hUiginn, 160, 162

love, and the lover, in '*Geabh do mhúnadh, a mheic bhaoith*', by Ádhamh Ó Fialán, 131; expressions of love and its function, in Irish bardic poetry, 137ff.

love-poem, in '*Geabh do mhúnadh, a mheic bhaoith*', by Ádhamh Ó Fialán, 133

'magister', 3

marriage, of poet to patron, E. Ó hEoghusa, 390

master and student, the *inventio* of Gofraidh Fionn Ó Dálaigh's '*Madh fiafraidheach budh feasach*', 189; in Tadhg Dall Ó hUiginn's '*Cóir Dé eadram is Uilliam*', 177

material, for poetry, in the schools, in Matthew of Vendôme, 36; honourable and disreputable in John of Garland, 49

mediaeval universities, 4ff.

menace, in '*Fada an ráitheise romham*', by Tadhg Óg Ó hUiginn, 163

messenger, as go-between among lovers, 176

metrics, the superiority of metrical verse over that of rhythmic, 334

militarism, the trope of militarization in literature, 20; as a function of the *inventio*, in Gofraidh Fionn Ó Dálaigh's '*Beir eolas dúinn, a Dhomhnuill*', 94

mines, mining and the industrial landscape in Tipperary, 100

mixed speech ('cumasctha' [cumascda]), in *Auraicept na n-Éces*, 4

mnemonics, in poems about poetry, 183; in Gofraidh Fionn Ó Dálaigh's '*Madh fiafraidheach budh feasach*', 190; in Fear Feasa Ó'n Cháinte's '*Créad dá sealbhuinn damh an dán*', 241

morality, and the standards of writing, in Gofraidh Mac an Bhaird's '*A fhir shealbhas duit an dán*', and in Matthew of Vendôme, 380

murder, of troubadours, 166; of Tadhg Dall Ó hUiginn, 165; of Geoffrey Keating, 353

mutability, in the love relationship in Tadhg Dall Ó hUiginn's '*Cóir Dé eadram is Uilliam*', 177

mutuality, reciprocal regard and reward between poet and lord in '*Geabh do mhúnadh, a mheic bhaoith*', by Ádhamh Ó Fialán, 117ff.

naming, places in Gofraidh Fionn Ó Dálaigh's '*Beir eolas dúinn, a Dhomhnuill*', 101ff.

nonsense, and the inferior poet, in Gofraidh Mac an Bhaird's '*A fhir shealbhas duit an dán*', 227; and the barking dog in Fear Feasa Ó'n Cháinte's '*Créad dá sealbhuinn damh an dán*', 236

offence, given by the lord to the poet in '*Geabh do mhúnadh, a mheic bhaoith*', by Ádhamh Ó Fialán, 116; given by 'Uilliam Búrc' to the poet Tadhg Dall Ó hUiginn, in

Tadhg Dall Ó hUiginn's '*Cóir Dé eadram is Uilliam*', 176

ollamh, ollamh flatha, 155; Gofraidh Fionn, as *ollamh* in his '*Madh fiafraidheach budh feasach*', 200; status of *ollamh* in '*Mór an feidhm deilbh an dána*', by Fear Feasa Ó'n Cháinte, 205; in Tadhg Dall Ó hUiginn's '*Cóir Dé eadram is Uilliam*', 176; the primacy of the *ollamh* in poetic ranking, 142; *ollamhnacht flatha*, attainment of, 156; and the training of the poet, in '*Mór an feidhm deilbh an dána*', by Fear Feasa Ó'n Cháinte, 206

'other', in Fear Feasa Ó'n Cháinte's '*Créad dá sealbhuinn damh an dán*', 231; in Gofraidh Mac an Bhaird's '*A fhir shealbhas duit an dán*', 218; in '*Mór an feidhm deilbh an dána*', by Fear Feasa Ó'n Cháinte, 204, 208; in '*Fada an ráitheise romham*', by Tadhg Óg Ó hUiginn, 160; in the pedagogical poetry, in Gofraidh Fionn Ó Dálaigh's '*Madh fiafraidheach budh feasach*', 190

participation, in the intertextual debate about teaching and poetry and skill, in Gofraidh Mac an Bhaird's '*A fhir shealbhas duit an dán*', 220

patchwork, in the weave of the inferior poet in Matthew of Vendôme, 213

path, paths to poetry, in '*Geabh do mhúnadh, a mheic bhaoith*', by Ádhamh Ó Fialán, 126, 132; in '*Mór an feidhm deilbh an dána*', by Fear Feasa Ó'n Cháinte, 205;

the open road for the poet, in E. Ó hEoghusa, '*Ionmholta malairt bhisigh*', 253; the narrow v. the broad in E. Ó hEoghusa, and in Geoffrey of Vinsauf, 255; in manuals of composition, 250

patronage, lay and clerical, 6; artistocratic, bourgeois, 6; the end of patronage in Irish poetry, 388

pedagogy, in Fear Feasa Ó'n Cháinte's '*Créad dá sealbhuinn damh an dán*', 239; in Gofraidh Fionn Ó Dálaigh's '*Madh fiafraidheach budh feasach*', 190ff.

plaintiff, and defendant in '*Fada an ráitheise romham*', by Tadhg Óg Ó hUiginn, 161

poet, the Irish poet and his role(s), 13; as ruler in the realms of poetry, 65; as teacher and pupil, 110; as teacher, 112; the relationship in scholarship between Tadhg Dall and Uilliam Búrc in Tadhg Dall Ó hUiginn's '*Cóir Dé eadram is Uilliam*', 176; the inferior poet in '*Mór an feidhm deilbh an dána*', by Fear Feasa Ó'n Cháinte, 204, 206; the true poet and the false poet, in Gofraidh Mac an Bhaird's '*A fhir shealbhas duit an dán*', 220

poetry, praise-genres, 12, 15; modern historians and praise-poets, 16; literary 'conventions', 16; influence of French poetry on Irish poetry, 17; Irish devotional and profane poetry under the influence of continental modes, 18; contrast between Irish devotional poetry and Irish profane poetry in respect of continental influences, 18; '*dán díreach*', 22; the concept of 'populist realism', 22; court and bardic poetry, 26; post-Anglo-Norman invasion praise-poetry in Ireland, 26; the work of the inferior, in Fear Feasa Ó'n Cháinte's '*Créad dá sealbhuinn damh an dán*', 233; and literary imitation among the Irish poets, 265, 291; generating composition, in Gofraidh Mac an Bhaird's '*A fhir shealbhas duit an dán*', 376; poets, recognized masters among the poets, in Fear Flatha Ó Gnímh, '*Cuimseach sin, a Fhearghail Óig*', 259

politics, and the bardic poem, 61

praise, and blame in bardic poetry, 31; the mixture, in '*Fada an ráitheise romham*', by Tadhg Óg Ó hUiginn, 160

presumption, the vice of the weak poet, in '*Mór an feidhm deilbh an dána*', by Fear Feasa Ó'n Cháinte, 211

promiscuity, charges of promiscuity in poetry, 28

prosody, Irish vernacular, 3; elementary vernacular treatises in Latin, 2, 7

Provençal (Occitan), language, 282

proverb, proverbial opening in '*Fada an ráitheise romham*', by Tadhg Óg Ó hUiginn, 160; in support of invention, in John of Garland, 48

provisional tone, the use of conditional modes in '*Geabh do* mhúnadh, a mheic bhaoith', by Ádhamh Ó Fialán, 120

provocation, in 'Mór an feidhm deilbh an dána', by Fear Feasa Ó'n Cháinte, 214

quarrel, the lovers' quarrel, 159

questions, posed, in Fear Feasa Ó'n Cháinte's 'Créad dá sealbhuinn damh an dán', 239

razo, and vidas, in troubadour literature, 154; the 'razo' of Tadhg Dall, 165

realism, the concept of the realistic inventio in John of Garland, 73; of 'Fada an ráitheise romham', by Tadhg Óg Ó hUiginn, 163

reassessment, of the poet–lord relationship, in 'Geabh do mhúnadh, a mheic bhaoith', by Ádhamh Ó Fialán, 119

reciprocity, poem in exchange for 'friendship', in 'Fada an ráitheise romham', by Tadhg Óg Ó hUiginn, 162

reciter, and bard, in Fear Feasa Ó'n Cháinte's 'Créad dá sealbhuinn damh an dán', 382

recognition, seeking, the ollamh flatha and the troubadour, 157

reconciliation, as part of the poem of complaint, 107; and renewal, 157

red, rubicundity and the denotation of licentiousness in the naming of Arnulf/Rufinus, 284

reform, reformation, of the Irish Church in the twelfth century, 12–15; twelfth-century reform and the Anglo-Normans, 15; ecclesiastical, 15

refutation, refuting the claims of the 'other' poet to expertise, in debates, in Gofraidh Mac an Bhaird's 'A fhir shealbhas duit an dán', 224

religious orders, continental religious orders in Ireland, 12

renewal, renewal of love, in 'Fada an ráitheise romham', by Tadhg Óg Ó hUiginn, 160ff.; the necessity to renew praise in poetry, 111

repetition, in 'Geabh do mhúnadh, a mheic bhaoith', by Ádhamh Ó Fialán, 120

response, and claim, engendering response in 'Mór an feidhm deilbh an dána', by Fear Feasa Ó'n Cháinte, 205, 217; in Gofraidh Mac an Bhaird's 'A fhir shealbhas duit an dán', 220–223; in Fear Feasa Ó'n Cáinte's 'Cread da sealbhuinn damh an dan', 230; in the debate poems, 363

restraint, the locked tongue in 'Fada an ráitheise romham', by Tadhg Óg Ó hUiginn, 160ff.

reward for poetry, 6, 269

rhetoric, the third rhetoric, 2; the second rhetoric, 3; núa chrotha, 3; rhetorical treatise, mediaeval, 3ff.; in an Irish manuscript, 10; the First Rhetoric of the Ancients, 12; praxis, 12; European rhetorical modes in Irish profane poetry, 20; in John Scottus Eriugena (c. 810–c. 877), Periphyseon, 25; and John of Garland, 48; confusion between Latinized and Graecized forms, 35; contraries in support of invention in a binary system in John of Garland, 48; invention in John of Garland, 48; devices in the genres of praise and blame, 108ff.

rivalry, between poets for *ollamhnacht*, 153

Romance literature, and its influence on Irish poets, 17; on Welsh literature, 17

rules, of composition, in Gofraidh Fionn Ó Dálaigh's '*Madh fiafraidheach budh feasach*', 186

rumour, and lack of information about his beloved, in '*A theachtaire théid ar sliabh*', by Tadhg Dall Ó hUiginn, 173; and the anonymous 'others', in '*A theachtaire théid ar sliabh*', 175; the sowing of rumour to create discord, in '*Fada an ráitheise romham*', by Tadhg Óg Ó hUiginn, 160ff.

satire, 269; the failure of Tadhg Dall to satirize Uilliam Búrc in Tadhg Dall Ó hUiginn's '*Cóir Dé eadram is Uilliam*', 178ff.

schematization, of composition, 56

scholarship, Irish international links, twelfth-century, 11; lack of learning, in Fear Feasa Ó'n Cháinte's '*Créad dá sealbhuinn damh an dán*', 241

scholia, mediaeval glosses, 3

school, dispersal of the schools in Gofraidh Mac an Bhaird's '*A fhir shealbhas duit an dán*', 226; of '*filidheacht*', 2

scoil, in contrast to 'court' in '*Geabh do mhúnadh, a mheic bhaoith*', by Ádhamh Ó Fialán, 118

scripture, scriptural echoes, in Gofraidh Fionn Ó Dálaigh's '*Madh fiafraidheach budh feasach*', 194

seduction, poet of lord and lord of poet, 137

sequestration, references to it in E. Ó hEoghusa, '*Ionmholta malairt bhisigh*', 255; the stronghold of the mind in the *inventio* of Fear Flatha Ó Gnímh, '*Cuimseach sin, a Fhearghail Óig*', 259; of the poet at work, 296

sham, the sham battle in the debate poems, in Gofraidh Mac an Bhaird's '*A fhir shealbhas duit an dán*', 228

skill and training, in '*Mór an feidhm deilbh an dána*', by Fear Feasa Ó'n Cháinte, 205

slight, love slighted, in '*Geabh do mhúnadh, a mheic bhaoith*', by Ádhamh Ó Fialán, 128

smith, the smith and the smithy, in '*Mór an feidhm deilbh an dána*', by Fear Feasa Ó'n Cháinte, 210

sound, and syllable count, in *Auraicept na n-Éces*, 4

strangers, stranger-poets coming between the lord and his poet in '*Fada an ráitheise romham*', by Tadhg Óg Ó hUiginn, 161

student, the characterization of students for the purposes of 'invention' in John of Garland, 49

study, methods of study in poems about poetry, 183

style, 'high', 'middle' and 'low' style, in '*Mór an feidhm deilbh an dána*', by Fear Feasa Ó'n Cháinte, 372; military 'high' style, 55; in tragedy, in John of Garland, 56; the elevation of the tone into the 'high' style by the use of a military setting, in Gofraidh Fionn Ó Dálaigh's *'Beir eolas dúinn, a Dhomhnuill'*, 90; the 'lower' and 'middle' style, in *'A theachtaire théid ar sliabh'*, by Tadhg Dall Ó hUiginn, 173; the 'low' style, in Gofraidh Mac an Bhaird's *'A fhir shealbhas duit an dán'*, 184; the four styles in Demetrius' *On Style*, 322; the three styles in *Rhetorica ad Herennium*, 322; the 'low' style in a quatrain from the Annals of Connacht, 388

subtlety, in the art of composition, in *'Mór an feidhm deilbh an dána'*, by Fear Feasa Ó'n Cháinte, 212

summa, independent treatise, 3

teacher, and student, in Gofraidh Fionn Ó Dálaigh's *'Madh fiafraidheach budh feasach'*, 185; praise of the teacher, in *'Mór an feidhm deilbh an dána'*, by Fear Feasa Ó'n Cháinte, 211; the poet as teacher, 361; teachers in the cathedral schools, 13; in the universities, 13; the poet as teacher, in *'Mór an feidhm deilbh an dána'*, by Fear Feasa Ó'n Cháinte, 209

techniques, experimental techniques of the inferior poets, in *'Mór an feidhm deilbh an dána'*, by Fear Feasa Ó'n Cháinte, 212

tenure, in the case of an *ollamh*, 153

terminology, techincal terms in Gofraidh Fionn Ó Dálaigh's *'Madh fiafraidheach budh feasach'*, 190

terms, of address, 115

texts, textbooks in Fear Feasa Ó'n Cháinte's *'Créad dá sealbhuinn damh an dán'*, 241

theme, comparison of territories, Cashel v. Kerry, 65; of Mac Carthaigh leading his people, 65; of Moses, in the apologue of Gofraidh Fionn Ó Dálaigh's *'Beir eolas dúinn, a Dhomhnuill'*, 66; the discovery of Cashel, 65; the journey in Gofraidh Fionn Ó Dálaigh's *'Beir eolas dúinn, a Dhomhnuill'*, 66; the estrangement of poet and patron, 62

threat, in the poem of complaint, in *'Geabh do mhúnadh, a mheic bhaoith'*, by Ádhamh Ó Fialán, 120

three houses, the three houses in which Irish dwells, in *'Mór an feidhm deilbh an dána'*, by Fear Feasa Ó'n Cháinte, 213

threefold, division, in Matthew of Vendôme, Tragedy, Satire and Comedy, 34, 38; source of invention in John of Garland, 48

timelessness, the eternal truth of the well-wrought poem in Gofraidh Fionn Ó Dálaigh's *'Beir eolas dúinn, a Dhomhnuill'*, 104

tongue, cutting out of Peire Vidal's tongue, 166; the unguarded tongue, and the drunken word in *'Fada an ráitheise romham'*, by Tadhg Óg Ó hUiginn, 161; the cutting out of the satirist's tongue, 165; the cutting out of Tadhg Dall's tongue, 165; the cutting out of the tongue of Marcabru, the troubadour, 166

topicality, in poems about poems, in '*Mór an feidhm deilbh an dána*', by Fear Feasa Ó'n Cháinte, 369

translation, expressions for 'poet', 335; in Elizabethan England, 13; and adaptations, 26, 279; of the classics, 279

trobar clus, and the 'closed' troubadour poem, 332

troubadour, and Irish poet, 138ff.; decline in the troubadour arts, 139; *trovar*, and 'finding', 275, 281

truth, and reality in Matthew of Vendôme, 33

universities, English and continental, 182

urban, centres in Ireland, 100

Venus, the ruddy children of Venus, denoting licentious life, 284

vernacular, composition, 1; translations, 1; grammar, 2; vernacular arts of poetry, 5; Occitan, Italian, 6; literary vernaculars in the Middle Ages, 24; and Latin writings maintaining pace, 154; French in Norman England, 287

violation, of the poet's property, status, 106

vocabulary, the diction of the Irish school poem, 152; the troubadour vocabulary involving concepts of honour, etc., 342

vocative case, epithetic address, in '*Geabh do mhúnadh, a mheic bhaoith*', by Ádhamh Ó Fialán, 118

weaving, in the context of composition, in '*Mór an feidhm deilbh an dána*', by Fear Feasa Ó'n Cháinte, 204, 210; in Gofraidh Mac an Bhaird's '*A fhir shealbhas duit an dán*', 220, 228

yarn, text and texture in Fear Feasa Ó'n Cháinte's '*Créad dá sealbhuinn damh an dán*', 233

ymrysonau, the debate poems in Welsh, 363

You and I, in Fear Feasa Ó'n Cháinte's '*Créad dá sealbhuinn damh an dán*', 232, 237, 243

Index of Terms

The terms listed here are a simple reference tool for their use in this study only. They are not intended as definitions for the rhetorical terms. The references are not exhaustive.

abhlóir, and buffoonery, in Fear Feasa Ó'n Cháinte's *'Créad dá sealbhuinn damh an dán'*, 387

abhrán, in *'Mór an feidhm deilbh an dána'*, by Fear Feasa Ó'n Cháinte, 374

l'action [performance], in Geoffrey of Vinsauf, 40

adjective, 'inventing' adjectives in John of Garland, 50

admonishment, in Gofraidh Fionn Ó Dálaigh's *'Beir eolas dúinn, a Dhomhnuill'*, 93

adnominatio (*paronomasia, polyptoton*), in Gofraidh Fionn Ó Dálaigh's *'Madh fiafraidheach budh feasach'*, 196

aenigma [obscurity], in Matthew of Vendôme, 35

affection [reaction], in Matthew of Vendôme, 33

allegoria [allegory], in Matthew of Vendôme, 35

ambiguity [*acirologia and amphibologia*], in Matthew of Vendôme, 37

amplification, and abbreviation, in Geoffrey of Vinsauf, 40; in Gofraidh Fionn Ó Dálaigh's *'Madh fiafraidheach budh feasach'*, 186; in Fear Feasa Ó'n Cháinte's *'Créad dá sealbhuinn damh an dán'*, 232

anál, breath, breathing, panting, and inferior poetry in *'Mór an feidhm deilbh an dána'*, by Fear Feasa Ó'n Cháinte, 374

anaphora, in *'Mór an feidhm deilbh an dána'*, by Fear Feasa Ó'n Cháinte, 216

ánruth, 371

anticipation, prolepsis, in *'Mór an feidhm deilbh an dána'*, by Fear Feasa Ó'n Cháinte, 206

antiphrasis, in *'Mór an feidhm deilbh an dána'*, by Fear Feasa Ó'n Cháinte, 215

antonomasia, in Gofraidh Mac an Bhaird's *'A fhir shealbhas duit an dán'*, 218; in the service of memory in Matthew of Vendôme, 375

aor, satire (*satyra*), in John of Garland, 48, 54; in *'Geabh do mhúnadh, a mheic bhaoith'*, by Ádhamh Ó Fialán, 132; in Tadhg Dall Ó hUiginn's *'Cóir Dé eadram is Uilliam'*, 179; the satiric javelin, in Fear Feasa Ó'n Cháinte's *'Créad dá sealbhuinn damh an dán'*, 383

aos dána, those engaged in the arts, 197; inferior poets among *aos dana*, in *'Mór an feidhm deilbh an dána'*, by Fear Feasa Ó'n Cháinte, 212 apocope, 'apoconu' in MS Auct. F. III.15, 272

apologue, 21; in Gofraidh Fionn Ó Dálaigh's 'Beir eolas dúinn, a Dhomhnuill', 87; the mini-apologue in Fear Feasa Ó'n Cháinte's 'Créad dá sealbhuinn damh an dán', 232, 235; in E. Ó hEoghusa, 'Ionmholta malairt bhisigh', 254

apostrophe, in Matthew of Vendôme, 39; in Gofraidh Fionn Ó Dálaigh's 'Beir eolas dúinn, a Dhomhnuill', 102; in Gofraidh Fionn Ó Dálaigh's 'Madh fiafraidheach budh feasach', 195; in Gofraidh Mac an Bhaird's 'A fhir shealbhas duit an dán', 219

aridity, and bloodlessness, vices of style in John of Garland, 55

arrangement, in Matthew of Vendôme, 35; in Geoffrey of Vinsauf, 40

arrmainte, in an Irish tract, 44

ars dictaminis, in John of Garland, 46

barántas, the eighteenth-century warrant poems and Tadhg Dall's 'A theachtaire théid ar sliabh', by Tadhg Dall Ó hUiginn, 173

bard, as distinct from draoi and file, 141, 371

bathos, and the false climax in 'Mór an feidhm deilbh an dána', by Fear Feasa Ó'n Cháinte, 216

Bittspruch, the petition, 151

cacosynthesis, in Matthew of Vendôme, 30

cáinte, 371

caithréim, the battle roll in 'Geabh do mhúnadh, a mheic bhaoith', by Ádhamh Ó Fialán, 128, 133; in 'Fada an ráitheise romham', by Tadhg Óg Ó hUiginn, 162

cano, 371

canóin, the 'canons' in Gofraidh Fionn Ó Dálaigh's 'Madh fiafraidheach budh feasach', 192

caoiche, rhymes between identical words, listed in Fear Feasa Ó'n Cháinte's 'Créad dá sealbhuinn damh an dán', 242

carmen elegiacum [elegiac poem], in John of Garland, 48

cases, the six cases of the noun in the service of embellishment and in the avoidance of triteness in John of Garland, 51

casus [chance events], in Matthew of Vendôme, 33

cataplexis [menace], in 'Geabh do mhúnadh, a mheic bhaoith', by Ádhamh Ó Fialán, 113

ceard, in 'Mór an feidhm deilbh an dána', by Fear Feasa Ó'n Cháinte, 210

claoinfhighe [a false weave], faulty verse, in Fear Feasa Ó'n Cháinte's 'Créad dá sealbhuinn damh an dán', 242

claon, and faults in Fear Feasa Ó'n Cháinte's 'Créad dá sealbhuinn damh an dán', 386

cli, 371

climax (gradatio), in John of Garland, 49

cóir (.c.) [correct], in Irish preceptive texts, 36

collocations, in Matthew of Vendôme, 35

comedia [comedy], in John of Garland, 48

commoratio [dwelling on the topic], in 'Mór an feidhm deilbh an dána', by Fear Feasa Ó'n Cháinte, 213

comparison, in Gofraidh Fionn Ó Dálaigh's 'Beir eolas dúinn, a Dhomhnuill', 89

conclusio [conclusion], in Matthew of Vendôme, 38; in Gofraidh Fionn Ó Dálaigh's 'Madh fiafraidheach budh feasach', 201

conduplicatio [a variety of repetition], 21; in 'Geabh do mhúnadh, a mheic bhaoith', by Ádhamh Ó Fialán, 132; the mini-climax in 'Fada an ráitheise romham', by Tadhg Óg Ó hUiginn, 161; in Gofraidh Fionn Ó Dálaigh's 'Madh fiafraidheach budh feasach', 186

consignificatione [connotation], in Matthew of Vendôme, 37

consilium [deliberation], in Matthew of Vendôme, 33

contrition, in 'Fada an ráitheise romham', by Tadhg Óg Ó hUiginn, 163

convictus [style of life], in Matthew of Vendôme, 33

corcra, the red/purple hand of Cathal Crobhdhearg, 285

dán díreach, the Irish syllabic poem, 181

deeds, action, the appropriate action in Matthew of Vendôme, 72; and their timing, 33

definitio [statement], in Gofraidh Mac an Bhaird's 'A fhir shealbhas duit an dán', 226

deminutio [subtractive statement], in Fear Feasa Ó'n Cháinte's 'Créad dá sealbhuinn damh an dán', 242

descriptio [description], in 'Mór an feidhm deilbh an dána', by Fear Feasa Ó'n Cháinte, 213

determinatio [appropriate modification of nouns by adjectives, verbs by adverbs], 21

dialogue (sermocinatio), in John of Garland, 49

dicendique color [ornamented expression], in Matthew of Vendôme, 34

dictamen, in John of Garland, 54

dinnsheanchas, as part of the 'topical reserve' and 'textual legacy' in Gofraidh Fionn Ó Dálaigh's 'Beir eolas dúinn, a Dhomhnuill', 103

discovery (inventio), in 'Mór an feidhm deilbh an dána', by Fear Feasa Ó'n Cháinte, 204

divisio [division], in Gofraidh Fionn Ó Dálaigh's 'Madh fiafraidheach budh feasach', 186

dos, 371

draoi, 140

drisiuc, 371

dúnadh [formal closure], in 'A theachtaire théid ar sliabh', by Tadhg Dall Ó hUiginn, 175; in Gofraidh Fionn Ó Dálaigh's 'Madh fiafraidheach budh feasach', 194, 201; in 'Mór an feidhm deilbh an dána', by Fear Feasa Ó'n Cháinte, 217; in E.

Ó hEoghusa, '*Ionmholta malairt bhisigh*', 252

eissídh [a state of unpeace], between the poet and the excuse for a poem, in '*Fada an ráitheise romham*', by Tadhg Óg Ó hUiginn, 161

enarratio poetarum, 25

entreaty, in '*Fada an ráitheise romham*', by Tadhg Óg Ó hUiginn, 163

envoy, in '*Geabh do mhúnadh, a mheic bhaoith*', by Ádhamh Ó Fialán, 136

eochair [(the) key], in Gofraidh Fionn Ó Dálaigh's '*Madh fiafraidheach budh feasach*', 195

epanaphorial repetitio, in Tadhg Dall Ó hUiginn's '*Cóir Dé eadram is Uilliam*', 179

epithalamium (*epytalamicum*), in John of Garland, 54

epithet, in Matthew of Vendôme, 32, 35; in direct address in Gofraidh Fionn Ó Dálaigh's '*Beir eolas dúinn, a Dhomhnuill*', 71

eulogy, in '*Fada an ráitheise romham*', by Tadhg Óg Ó hUiginn, 163

exemplum, 21, in Gofraidh Fionn Ó Dálaigh's '*Beir eolas dúinn, a Dhomhnuill*', 70, 74; in *Rhetorica ad Herennium*, 87; in Geoffrey of Vinsauf, 87

exhortation, in Gofraidh Fionn Ó Dálaigh's '*Beir eolas dúinn, a Dhomhnuill*', 93

explication of proverbs, in '*Geabh do mhúnadh, a mheic bhaoith*', by Ádhamh Ó Fialán, 123

expolitio [refining], in the service of the debate, in '*Mór an feidhm deilbh an dána*', by Fear Feasa Ó'n Cháinte, 214

fable, in John of Garland, 54

facta [deeds], in Matthew of Vendôme, 33

fear, *a fhir*, in '*A fhir shealbhas duit an dán*', and that of '*a fhir do thairg mo thochrádh*', in the Fear Feasa Ó'n Cháinte 'response' '*Créad dá sealbhuinn damh an dán*', 365; in Gofraidh Fionn Ó Dálaigh's '*Madh fiafraidheach budh feasach*', 187

fear leanamhna (a client or member of the household of the lord), in Tadhg Dall Ó hUiginn's '*Cóir Dé eadram is Uilliam*', 176

fer cerda, 371

figura etymologica, in Gofraidh Mac an Bhaird's '*A fhir shealbhas duit an dán*', 377

fluctuation, of words or diction (*fluctuans ex parte uerbi uel uocis*), 55

fochloc, 371

fortuna [fortune], in Matthew of Vendôme, 33

'frankness of speech', 108

fulcrum, the rhetorical fulcrum in '*Geabh do mhúnadh, a mheic bhaoith*', by Ádhamh Ó Fialán, 117; in E. Ó hEoghusa, '*Ionmholta malairt bhisigh*', 254; in '*Geabh do mhúnadh, a mheic bhaoith*', by Ádhamh Ó Fialán, 326

gnás [platitude], in Fear Feasa Ó'n Cháinte's '*Créad dá sealbhuinn damh an dán*', 242 *gradatio* [increment, climax], in Gofraidh Fionn Ó Dálaigh's '*Madh fiafraidheach budh feasach*', 186, 196; in '*Mór an feidhm deilbh an dána*', by Fear Feasa Ó'n Cháinte, 216; in '*Geabh do mhúnadh, a mheic bhaoith*', by Ádhamh Ó Fialán, 131, 132

habitus [quality], in Matthew of Vendôme, 33; in Gofraidh Fionn Ó Dálaigh's '*Beir eolas dúinn, a Dhomhnuill*', 69

historia, in Gofraidh Fionn Ó Dálaigh's '*Beir eolas dúinn, a Dhomhnuill*', 94; in '*Fada an ráitheise romham*', by Tadhg Óg Ó hUiginn, 163; in John of Garland, 48, 54

hyperbole, in '*Mór an feidhm deilbh an dána*', by Fear Feasa Ó'n Cháinte, 215

hypophora [rhetorical question], in Gofraidh Fionn Ó Dálaigh's '*Madh fiafraidheach budh feasach*', 190; in Fear Feasa Ó'n Cháinte's '*Créad dá sealbhuinn damh an dán*', 234

inflation, and bombast (*turgidem et inflatum*), vices of style in John of Garland, 55

inntleacht [intellect, discernment], in Gofraidh Fionn Ó Dálaigh's '*Madh fiafraidheach budh feasach*', 187

interior favus [inner charm], in Matthew of Vendôme, 34

interpretatio, in '*Geabh do mhúnadh, a mheic bhaoith*', by Ádhamh Ó Fialán, 130

interrogatio, in Gofraidh Mac an Bhaird's '*A fhir shealbhas duit an dán*', 225

invective (*inuectiuum*), in John of Garland 54

inventio, the finding of a topic, 12; in Geoffrey of Vinsauf, 41; [*inueniendi*] in John of Garland, 47; in Gofraidh Fionn Ó Dálaigh's 'invention' of Domhnall Mac Carthaigh's journey in '*Beir eolas dúinn, a Dhomhnuill*', 69; in '*Fada an ráitheise romham*', by Tadhg Óg Ó hUiginn, 159; in '*A theachtaire théid ar sliabh*', by Tadhg Dall Ó hUiginn, 173; in Tadhg Dall Ó hUiginn's '*Cóir Dé eadram is Uilliam*', 176; in Gofraidh Fionn Ó Dálaigh's '*Madh fiafraidheach budh feasach*', 186, 193; in '*Mór an feidhm deilbh an dána*', by Fear Feasa Ó'n Cháinte, 205, 213; in Gofraidh Mac an Bhaird's '*A fhir shealbhas duit an dán*', 218–220; in Fear Feasa Ó'n Cháinte's '*Créad dá sealbhuinn damh an dán*', 234, 241; in E. Ó hEoghusa, '*Ionmholta malairt bhisigh*', 251

iomarbhágh, and *ymrysonau*, in '*Mór an feidhm deilbh an dána*', by Fear Feasa Ó'n Cháinte, 369

ionannas [monotony], in Fear Feasa Ó'n Cháinte's '*Créad dá sealbhuinn damh an dán*', 242

joglar (*jogral*), as distinct from *trovador* and *segrel*, 335

laoithe cumainn [love-poems], and *dánta grá*, in Irish literary commentary, 330 *licentia*, in praise and blame, 108; in the pseudo-Ciceronian *Rhetorica ad Herennium*, 108; in '*Geabh do mhúnadh, a mheic bhaoith*', by Ádhamh Ó Fialán, 119; in '*Fada an ráitheise romham*', by Tadhg Óg Ó hUiginn, 160ff.

litotes, in '*Geabh do mhúnadh, a mheic bhaoith*', by Ádhamh Ó Fialán, 131; in Gofraidh Fionn Ó Dálaigh's '*Madh fiafraidheach budh feasach*', 198; in Fear Feasa Ó'n Cháinte's '*Créad dá sealbhuinn damh an dán*', 242

littere curiales [legal letter], in John of Garland, 48

littere scolastice [academic letter], in John of Garland, 48

lochtach (*.l.*) [incorrect/faulty], in Irish preceptive texts, 36

looseness of ideas (*dissolutum ex parte sentenciarum*), vices of style in John of Garland, 55

macfhuirmid, 371

messenger, in '*A theachtaire théid ar sliabh*', by Tadhg Dall Ó hUiginn, 173

metalepsis, in Matthew of Vendôme, 35

metaphor, in Matthew of Vendôme, 35

metaplasm, in Matthew of Vendôme, 35; in Gofraidh Fionn Ó Dálaigh's '*Beir eolas dúinn, a Dhomhnuill*', 73; in '*Geabh do mhúnadh, a mheic bhaoith*', by Ádhamh Ó Fialán, 124

metatheses, in Matthew of Vendôme, 35

metonomy, in Matthew of Vendôme, 30, 35

modus locutionis [manner of speaking], in Matthew of Vendôme, 35

narration (kinds of) (*de speciebus narrationem*), in John of Garland, 54, 295; *narratio*, in Gofraidh Fionn Ó Dálaigh's '*Beir eolas dúinn, a Dhomhnuill*', 94

natura [nature], in Matthew of Vendôme, 33

nomen [name], in Matthew of Vendôme, 33

oblaire, 371

occultatio/paralipsis, in '*Geabh do mhúnadh, a mheic bhaoith*', by Ádhamh Ó Fialán, 130

occupacio/praeteritio, in '*Fada an ráitheise romham*', by Tadhg Óg Ó hUiginn, 162

ollam, in the Irish primers, 371; and *ollamh flatha*, 153

orationes [speech], in Matthew of Vendôme, 33

oxymoron, in E. Ó hEoghusa, '*Ionmholta malairt bhisigh*', 252

paradox, in Fear Feasa Ó'n Cháinte's '*Créad dá sealbhuinn damh an dán*', 243

paralipsis, occultatio [disavowing], to emphasize, in Tadhg Dall Ó hUiginn's '*Cóir Dé eadram is Uilliam*', 179

parallelism, in '*Geabh do mhúnadh, a mheic bhaoith*', by Ádhamh Ó Fialán, 122

paromologia [self-accusation], in '*Fada an ráitheise romham*', by Tadhg Óg Ó hUiginn, 162 paronomasia (*annominatio*), in John of Garland, 49; in '*Geabh do mhúnadh, a mheic bhaoith*', by Ádhamh Ó Fialán, 126; in Fear Feasa Ó'n Cháinte's '*Créad dá sealbhuinn damh an dán*', 244

periphrasis, in Matthew of Vendôme, 35, 37

permissio [concessionary figure to secure advantage], in '*Fada an ráitheise romham*', by Tadhg Óg Ó hUiginn, 161; in Gofraidh Mac an Bhaird's '*A fhir shealbhas duit an dán*', 226

personification (*conformatio*), in Gofraidh Fionn Ó Dálaigh's '*Madh fiafraidheach budh feasach*', 198

petition (*Bittspruch*), in '*Fada an ráitheise romham*', by Tadhg Óg Ó hUiginn , 163

pleonasm, in Matthew of Vendôme, 37

prolepsis (anticipation), in '*Geabh do mhúnadh, a mheic bhaoith*', by Ádhamh Ó Fialán, 113; in Gofraidh Fionn Ó Dálaigh's '*Madh fiafraidheach budh feasach*', 192; in Fear Feasa Ó'n Cháinte's '*Créad dá sealbhuinn damh an dán*', 243

rabhán, and *abhrán*, in Fear Feasa Ó'n Cháinte's '*Créad dá sealbhuinn damh an dán*', 245

razo, 341

recrimination, in '*Fada an ráitheise romham*', by Tadhg Óg Ó hUiginn, 163

repetitio, in '*Geabh do mhúnadh, a mheic bhaoith*', by Ádhamh Ó Fialán, 131

repetition (*repeticio, epanaphora*), in John of Garland, 49; in Gofraidh Fionn Ó Dálaigh's '*Madh fiafraidheach budh feasach*', 186

reprimand (*reprehensio*), in John of Garland, 54

rhapsody, in '*Mór an feidhm deilbh an dána*', by Fear Feasa Ó'n Cháinte, 216

rota Virgilii [Virgil's wheel], and matters of style in John of Garland, 53

satire (*satyra*) (*aor*), in John of Garland, 48, 54; and the satiric javelin, in Fear Feasa Ó'n Cháinte's '*Créad dá sealbhuinn damh an dán*', 384; in '*Geabh do mhúnadh, a mheic bhaoith*', by Ádhamh Ó Fialán, 132; in Tadhg Dall Ó hUiginn's '*Cóir Dé eadram is Uilliam*', 179

scéal (*fabula*), in Gofraidh Fionn Ó Dálaigh's '*Beir eolas dúinn, a Dhomhnuill*', 94; in a fifteenth-century Irish tract, 44

séad suirghe, the love-token poem in '*Fada an ráitheise romham*', by Tadhg Óg Ó hUiginn, 162

searbhrádh [discordant utterance], in Fear Feasa Ó'n Cháinte's '*Créad dá sealbhuinn damh an dán*', 242

segrel, as distinct from *trovador* and *joglar*, 335

sententia [proverb], in Matthew of Vendôme, 38; in Geoffrey of Vinsauf, 69; in Gofraidh Fionn

Ó Dálaigh's 'Beir eolas dúinn, a Dhomhuill', 69; in 'Geabh do mhúnadh, a mheic bhaoith', by Ádhamh Ó Fialán, 110; in Tadhg Dall Ó hUiginn's 'Cóir Dé eadram is Uilliam', 176; in Gofraidh Fionn Ó Dálaigh's 'Madh fiafraidheach budh feasach', 185, 186, 193, 201; in 'Mór an feidhm deilbh an dána', by Fear Feasa Ó'n Cháinte, 205; in Gofraidh Mac an Bhaird's 'A fhir shealbhas duit an dán', 218, 222; in E. Ó hEoghusa, 'Ionmholta malairt bhisigh', 251

significatione cognita [denotation], in Matthew of Vendôme, 37

species, the five species of invention in John of Garland: where, what, what kind, how and why, 48

speculum principis, in 'Geabh do mhúnadh, a mheic bhaoith', by Ádhamh Ó Fialán, 112

stair [revelation of things performed], in a fifteenth-century Irish tract, 44

studium [diligence], in Matthew of Vendôme, 33

style, 'high', 'middle', and 'low', in John of Garland, 52; the use of the metaphor of style as part of a column, as a pen, in John of Garland, 296

summula, Matthew of Vendôme's hypochoristic term for his treatise, 39

synecdoche ('sidonoche'), in Matthew of Vendôme, 35; in 'Geabh do mhúnadh, a mheic bhaoith', by Ádhamh Ó Fialán, 115

synonymy (interpretatio), in John of Garland, 49

taman, 371

tautology, in Matthew of Vendôme, 36

threat, in 'Fada an ráitheise romham', by Tadhg Óg Ó hUiginn, 163

tmesis, in 'Geabh do mhúnadh, a mheic bhaoith', by Ádhamh Ó Fialán, 327

tomhas, in 'Mór an feidhm deilbh an dána', by Fear Feasa Ó'n Cháinte, 209

traductio, in John of Garland, 49; in 'Geabh do mhúnadh, a mheic bhaoith', by Ádhamh Ó Fialán, 129; in Gofraidh Mac an Bhaird's 'A fhir shealbhas duit an dán', 225

tragedia [tragedy], in John of Garland, 48

transitio [recapitulation and summary], in 'Geabh do mhúnadh, a mheic bhaoith', by Ádhamh Ó Fialán, 113; in Gofraidh Fionn Ó Dálaigh's 'Madh fiafraidheach budh feasach', 189, 193

transposition, in Matthew of Vendôme, 35

transsumption, in 'Fada an ráitheise romham', by Tadhg Óg Ó hUiginn, 161, 320

trefhocal, in Irish poetics, 286

trobar clus, 332

troigh, in 'Mór an feidhm deilbh an dána', by Fear Feasa Ó'n Cháinte, 209

uirsgéal, in Gofraidh Fionn Ó Dálaigh's 'Beir eolas dúinn, a Dhomhuill, 70 *verba polita* [polished words], in Matthew of Vendôme, 34

vida, and razo, 341

zeugma, in MS Auct. F. III.15, 10; in Matthew of Vendôme, 30; in '*Geabh do mhúnadh, a mheic bhaoith*', by Ádhamh Ó Fialán, 129

Index of people and places

Aed mac Criomhthainn (*fl.* 1150s), 'lector of the high-king of Leth Moga', 8

Anonymous of Bologna (*fl.* 1130s), and the *ars dictaminis*, 8

Apollinaris, Sidonius (*c.* 430–*c.* 487?), 39

Arnulf (Rufinus) (*fl.* 1170s), in Matthew of Vendôme, 27, 283

Arnulf, of St Evurcius, Arnulf of Orléans, and see, Rufinus, 28; as a figure, 29, 279 (see also, Rufinus)

Augustine, St (*c.* 354–430), works, 181

Bede (*c.* 672–*c.* 735), 9

Bernard of Chartres [Bernard Silvester] (*c.* 1180–1167), 9, 27, 46

Bernard of Clairvaux, St Bernard and St Malachy, 279

Búrc, Uilleog (*r.* 1424–1485), 159

Búrc, Uilliam (*fl.* 1580s), 137

Cambridge, Irish students at, 293

Cashel (Caiseal), 58ff.

Chartres, the school of Chartres, and Irish students, 9, 295

Cicero, 25; Tullius Cicero, in Matthew of Vendôme, 31

Clairvaux, and St Malachy, 279

Conall Corc, and the discovery of Cashel, 65, 302

Dafydd ab Gwilym, and the Provençal poets, 17

Dante Alighieri, and *De vulgari eloquentia*, 332

Demetrius, *On Style*, 109

Donatus (*fl.* 350), 3, 25, 272

Eberhard the German, and the end of the 'preceptive movement', 26

England, and the literate classes, 13; poets of England, 17

Eoghanacht kings and the kingship of Munster, 68; territory, 103

Geoffrey of Vinsauf (*fl.* 1210), 21, 25–27; *Poetria Nova* 39–44ff.

Germany, poets of Germany, 17

Gervase of Melkley, 26

Henry of Avranches (*fl.* 1214–1260), and notable mediaeval writers' quarrels, 220

Horace, 25

Hugh Primas (*fl.* 1140s), 27

Iceland, Icelandic vernacular literature, 270

Innocent III (*r.* 1198–1216), Geoffrey of Vinsauf dedicated his *Poetria Nova* to him, 39, 40

Isidore of Seville, 9, 272, 292

Italy, and the troubadours, 282

John of Garland (*fl.* 1230), 25, 26, 28; *Parisiana Poetria* 45–56ff.

John of London, teacher of John of Garland, 45

John Scottus Eriugena (*c.* 810–*c.* 877), 9, 25

Keating, Geoffrey [Seathrún Céitinn], *Foras Feasa ar Éirinn*, 16; reputedly murdered, 353

Mac an Bhaird, Fearghal Óg, 21; and poems about poetry, 183; '*Fuaras iongnadh, a fhir chumainn*', 21; in

'*Cuimseach sin, a Fhearghail Óig*', 202

Mac an Bhaird, Gofraidh, poems about poetry, 183; '*A fhir shealbhas duit an dán*', 184, 202, 219–229; attrib., '*Cuimhnigh, a Mháire, an cunnradh do cheanglabhar*', 300

Mac Carthaigh, Cormac (d. 1359), 75, 299

Mac Carthaigh, Domhnall, king of Desmond between 1359 and 1392, 67ff., 301; ancestors, 58; and Cashel, 58; poem for him, 65ff.

Mac Craith, Maolmhuire, poet, 57

Mac Fhirbhisigh, Dubhaltach (*c.* 1600–1671, murdered by T. Crofton), 352

Macrobius (*fl.* 399–422), and a fifteenth-century Irish tract possibly linked to his *Saturnalia*, 292

Mág Shamhradháin, family, 111; Tomás (*c.* 1303–1343), and *Leabhar Mhéig Shamhradháin*, 109

Marcabru, and his murder, 166

Martianus Capella, 272

Matthew of Vendôme (*fl. c.* 1175), 25, 27, 30, 279–280; and the definition of verse, 30

Mellifont Abbey, 279

Michael of Cornwall (*fl.* 1250), and notable mediaeval writers' quarrels, 220

Michael, the Archangel, appealed to by Gofraidh Fionn Ó Dálaigh, in his poem for Domhnall Mac Carthaigh, '*Beir eolas dúinn, a Dhomhnuill*', 66, 74

Monasterboice Abbey, 279

Ó Briain, granting of Cashel to the Church in 1101, 58

Ó'n Cháinte, Fear Feasa, and poems about poetry, 181ff; his surname, 203; '*Bean dá chumhadh críoch Eallaá*', 369, 373; '*Créd dá sealbhuinn damh an dán*', 184, 202, 229–245; '*Mór an feidhm deilbh an dána*', 184, 202, 203–218

Ó Cianáin, Ruaidhrí, scribe of parts of *Leabhar Mhéig Shamhradháin*, 325

Ó Conchubhair, Cathal Crobhdhearg (d. 1224), and the attribute of the red hand, 35

Ó Dálaigh, Gofraidh Fionn and '*Madh fiafraidheach budh feasach*', 57ff., 65, 181; '*A Ghearóid déana mo dháil*', for Gerald the third earl of Desmond, 62; '*Beir eolas dúinn, a Dhomhnuill*', 57–105; '*Madh fiafraidheach budh feasach*', 185–201, 203; '*Mór ar bfearg riot a rí Saxan*', 300; '*Iongaibh thú orm a Iarla*', 356

Ó Dálaigh, Muireadhach Albanach, 18; '*Tabhrum an Cháisg ar Chathal*', 285; '*Créd agaibh aoidhigh a gcéin*', 323

Ó Domhnaill, Rudhraighe (Rory O'Donnell, d. 1608), 256

Ó Gnímh, Fear Flatha, and poems about poetry, 183, 298; '*Cuimseach sin, a Fhearghail Óig*', 18, 183, 202, 258–260, 298; '*Mairg do-chuaidh re ceird ndúthchais*', 203

Ó hEoghusa, Eochaidh, and the Maguire lords, 154; and poems about poetry, 182ff., 251, 330;

'*Ionmholta malairt bhisigh*', 203, 251–258; '*Anois molfam Mág Uidhir*', 354; '*Atám i gcás idir dhá chomhairle*', 354; '*Ní mé bhur naithne, a aos gráidh*', 389; '*Bíodh aire ag Ultaibh ar Aodh*', 391

Ó hEoghusa, Giolla Brighde, seventeenth-century grammatical works, 384

Ó Maolchonaire, Flaithrí, 181

Ó hUiginn, Tadhg Dall (d. 1590), 'biography', 164; '*Ag so an chomairce a Chormaic*', 168; '*A theachtaire théid ar sliabh*', 171, 172–176; '*Cóir Dé eadram is Uilliam*', 169, 171, 176–180; '*Lios Gréine is Eamhain d'Ultaibh*', 354; '*Molfaid Connallaigh clann Táil*', 355; '*Déanam cunntus, a Chathail*', 356; '*Fearann cloidhimh críoch Bhanbha*', 356

Ó hUiginn, Tadhg Óg (d. 1448), 18, 138, 160; '*Fada an ráitheise romham*', 159–163; '*Ón aird thuaidh thig an chobhair*', 319

Ovid, 279

Oxford, Geoffrey of Vinsauf at Oxford, 39; Irish students at, 293

Paris, Irish students in Paris, 9; Geoffrey of Vinsauf at Paris, 39, John of Garland teaching in, 45

Peire Vidal, troubadour, and his 'murder', 166

Portugal, and the troubadours, 282

Priscian (*fl.* 450), 3, 25, 272

Quintillian, 25

Robert of Normandy, and the naming of an early Ó hUiginn, 167

Salamanca, the Irish college in, 182

Salmon/Solamh, student named in MS Auct. F. III.15, 8

Scandinavia, vernacular literature of, 270

Scotland, and the literate classes, 13

Sedulius Scottus (*fl.* 850–870), 1

Servius, 25

Southern France, and the troubadours, 282

Spain, and the troubadours, 284

Toulouse, John of Garland at the University of, 45

Tours, 27

Tuilecnad [Tuileagna], scribe of MS Auct. F. III.15, 8, 9

Úa Gormáin, Fionn (Find) (bishop of Kildare 1148), 8, 11

Ua Gormáin, Flann, 7, 11

Victor, the Archangel, with whom the finding of Cashel is associated, 304

Virgil, a source of examples in John of Garland, 52; eclogues, 1, 24

Wales, and the literate classes, 13

William of Conches, and his commentary on Timaeus, 9; and Irish students in Paris, 9

Index of first lines of poems

A fhir shealbhas duit an dán, by Gofraidh Mac an Bhaird, 184, 202, 219–229
A fhir théid go Fiadh bhFuinidh, by Maol Muire Ó hUiginn, 360
A Ghearóid déana mo dháil, by Gofraidh Fionn Ó Dálaigh, for Gerald the
  third earl of Desmond, 62
Ag so an chomairce a Chormaic, by Tadhg Dall Ó hUiginn, 168
Anois molfam Mág Uidhir, by Eochaidh Ó hEoghusa, 355
Atám i gcás idir dhá chomhairle, by Eochaidh Ó hEoghus, 355
A theachtaire théid ar sliabh, by Tadhg Dall Ó hUiginn, 171, 172–176
Bean dá chumhadh crioch Ealla, by Fear Feasa Ó'n Cháinte, 370, 374
Beir eolas dúinn, a Dhomhnuill, by Gofraidh Fionn Ó Dálaigh, 57–105
Bíodh aire ag Ultaibh ar Aodh, by Eochaidh Ó hEoghusa, 391
Briathra cogaidh con chath Laighnech, 357
Cóir Dé eadram is Uilliam, by Tadhg Dall Ó hUiginn, 171, 176–180
Créad dá sealbhuinn damh an dán, by Fear Feasa Ó'n Cháinte, 184, 202,
  229–245
Créd agaibh aoidhigh a gcéin, by Muireadhach Albanach Ó Dálaigh, 323
Cuimhnigh, a Mháire, an cunnradh do cheanglabhar, attrib. to Gofraidh Mac
  an Bhaird, 297–298
Cuimseach sin, a Fhearghail Óig, by Fear Flatha Ó Gnímh: 18, 183, 202,
  258–260, 298
Dá ghabhladh dhéag insan dán, by Donnchadh Óg Albanach (?), 348
Damhnaidh dúind cóir, a chléirche, by Diarmuid Ó Briain (?), 295
Déanam cunntus, a Chathail, by Tadhg Dall Ó hUiginn, 356
Déanum síodh mbunaidh, a Bhriain, unknown, 321, 328
D'fhigh duine éigin roimh an ré so, by Dáibhí Ó Bruadair, 372, 387
Fada an ráitheise romham, by Tadhg Óg Ó hUiginn, 159–163
Feadha an oghaim aithnidh damh, unknown, 240, 385
Fearann cloidhimh crioch Bhanbha, by Tadhg Dall Ó hUiginn, 356
Fuaras iongnadh, a fhir chumainn, by Fearghal Óg Mac an Bhaird, 21
Geabh do mhúnadh, a mheic bhaoith, by Ádhamh Ó Fialán, 110–136
Iongaibh thú orm a Iarla, by Gofraidh Fionn Ó Dálaigh, 356
Ionmholta malairt bhisigh, by Eochaidh Ó hEoghusa, 203, 251–258
Lios Gréine is Eamhain d'Ultaibh, by Tadhg Dall Ó hUiginn, 354
Madh fiafraidheach budh feasach, by Gofraidh Fionn Ó Dálaigh, 185–203
Mairg chaitheas dlús re dhalta, 297
Mairg do-chuaidh re ceird ndúthchais, by Fear Flatha Ó Gnímh, 203
Molfaid Connallaigh clann Táil, by Tadhg Dall Ó hUiginn, 355

Mór an feidhm deilbh an dána, by Fear Feasa Ó'n Cháinte, 184, 202, 203–218

Mór ar bfearg riot a rí Saxan, by Gofraidh Fionn Ó Dálaigh, 300

Ní beag an léansa ar Leath Cuinn, by Maol Pádraig Mac Naimhin, 362

Ní mé bhur n-aithne, a aos gráidh, by Eochaidh Ó hEoghusa, 389

Olc beatha na gcoisidheadh, by Giolla Pádraig Mac Naimhin, 362

Ón aird thuaidh thig an chobhair, by Tadhg Óg Ó hUiginn, 319

Tabhrum an Cháisg ar Chathal, by Muireadhach Albanach Ó Dálaigh, 285

Tairgidh mo sheachna, a shíol mBriain, by Tadhg (mac Dáire) Mac
Bruaideadha, 384

Tánag d'Fhánaid an einigh, by Giolla na Naomh Ó hUiginn, 362